TELECOMMUNICATIONS PLANNING: INNOVATIONS IN PRICING, NETWORK DESIGN AND MANAGEMENT

OPERATIONS RESEARCH/COMPUTER SCIENCE INTERFACES SERIES

Professor Ramesh Sharda
Oklahoma State University

Prof. Dr. Stefan Voß
Universität Hamburg

Other published titles in the series:

TELECOMMUNICATIONS PLANNING: INNOVATIONS IN PRICING, NETWORK DESIGN AND MANAGEMENT

Edited by

S. RAGHAVAN
University of Maryland

G. ANANDALINGAM
University of Maryland

 Springer

S. Raghavan   G. Anandalingam
University of Maryland   University of Maryland
College Park, MD, USA   College Park, MD, USA

Library of Congress Control Number: 2005933050

ISBN-10: 0-387-29222-5   e-ISBN-10: 0-387-29234-9
ISBN-13: 978-0387-29222-9 e-ISBN-13: 978-0387-29234-2

Printed on acid-free paper.

Printed in the United States of America.

9 8 7 6 5 4 3 2 1   SPIN 11055006

springeronline.com

Contents

Preface

This edited book serves as a companion volume to the Seventh INFORMS Telecommunications Conference held in Boca Raton, Florida, March 7-10, 2004. The 18 papers in this book were carefully selected after a thorough review process. The research presented within these articles focuses on the latest methodological developments in three key areas—pricing of telecommunications services, network design, and resource allocation—that are most relevant to current telecommunications planning.

With the global deregulation of the telecommunications industry, effective pricing and revenue management, as well as an understanding of competitive pressures are key factors that will improve revenue in telecommunications companies. Chapters 1-5 address these topics by focusing on pricing of telecommunications services. They present some novel ideas related to pricing (including auction-based pricing of network bandwidth) and modeling competition in the industry.

The successful telecommunications companies of the future will likely be the ones that can minimize their costs while meeting customer expectations. In this context the optimal design/provisioning of telecommunication networks plays an important role. Chapters 6-12 address these topics by focusing on network design for a wide range of technologies including SONET, SDH, WDM, and MPLS. They include the latest research developments related to the modeling and solving of network design problems.

Day-to-day management/control of telecommunications networks is dependent upon the optimal allocation of resources. Chapters 13-18 provide insightful solutions to several intriguing resource allocation problems.

We thank all of the authors for their hard work, and invaluable contributions to this book. We are very pleased with the outcome of this edited volume, and hope these papers will fawn new ideas and research in their respective domains.

S. RAGHAVAN AND G. ANANDALINGAM

Chapter 1

PRICING AND RESOURCE ALLOCATION FOR POINT-TO-POINT TELECOMMUNICATION SERVICES IN A COMPETITIVE MARKET: A BILEVEL OPTIMIZATION APPROACH

Mustapha Bouhtou[1], Guillaume Erbs[1] and Michel Minoux[2]

[1]*France Telecom Research and Development*
38-40, rue du Général Leclerc - 92794 Issy-les-Moulineaux Cedex 9 - France
mustapha.bouhtou@francetelecom.com
guillaume.erbs@francetelecom.com

[2]*University Paris 6*
4, place Jussieu - 75005 Paris - France
michel.minoux@lip6.fr

Abstract   With the deregulation of the telecommunication markets worldwide, network operators have to develop and offer new services to their clients in order to gain market share. In this context, yield management techniques can be used to optimize tariff computation and resource allocation so that an operator's profit can be maximized.

   This paper presents a problem of revenue optimization and resource allocation for point-to-point services in a competitive market. The bilevel programming paradigm is used to model the clients' behavior against the tariffs. Hence, the competition is explicitly taken into account. A mathematical model is introduced. In the process of solving the problem, we focus on exact solution methods using currently available commercial MIP solver. Numerical results are presented illustrating the computational complexity of this approach depending on the data used and the size of the network.

Keywords: telecommunications, revenue management, pricing, resource allocation, bilevel programming, Stackelberg equilibrium

1.   Introduction

Many companies in various industries are today successfully using Revenue Management as a means of optimizing their income in a highly competitive environment. These methods were introduced in the late 70's with the deregulation in the airline industry, and aim at trying to offer the right product to the right customer, at the right price, at the right time. This might consist in solving a joint problem of pricing a scarce resource while allocating it optimally. One of the main aspects of the pricing problem is the definition of a market segmentation: customers have different needs and are willing to pay the price for that. In the airline industry, this translates for example into different perceptions of the length of a flight (one or two legs, etc.), different classes (economic, business, etc.), and seat allocation for each of the defined segments. Another important aspect is to take into account the competition but this makes the problem more difficult to tackle.

As the telecommunications industry has been deregulated, an increasing competition must be accounted for by an operator when setting tariffs for services, in order to keep or gain market share, and the application of Revenue Management is an increasing area of research. The specificities of the telecommunication industry have to be taken into account: an operator can offer different types of services (voice, Internet, mobile, leased lines, interconnection agreements, etc.) and all of these services have specific underlying protocols, network management methods and network topologies.

There is a growing interest on the field of pricing for telecommunication services. An extensive literature review on these subjects is out of the scope of this paper, but the following trends can be observed. There have been numerous papers using game theory in order to achieve an equilibrium between the users' needs and an operator's strategy, for example in the works of Altman and Wynter, 2004 or Basar and Srikant, 2002. Also, many have proposed schemes to price network services in order to avoid congestion and regulate traffic, for example MacKie-Mason and Varian, 1993 or Kelly, 1997, Kelly et al., 1998. Another trend are auctions, which are applied to determine the price users are willing to pay for a service and to allocate resources, for example in the works of Lazar and Semret, 1998.

An interesting case of Revenue Management is to study the strategy of a leader facing competition in a market as the customers choose their services according to the prices and qualities of the offers. This kind of problems was studied for transportation, for example by Labbé et al., 1998 and Brotcorne et al., 2000 on highway tolls. In the paper from Côté et al., 2003, the authors present a new modeling approach to solve the joint problem of capacity allocation and pricing in the airline industry, using the bilevel programming paradigm. In the telecommunications field, the literature is more limited. However, the papers from Bouhtou et al., 2003a, Bouhtou et al., 2003b, Bouhtou et al., 2003c on edge pricing, and also the papers from Keon and Anandalingam, 2003, Keon and Anandalingam, 2004 on multiservice networks are, as far as we know, the only works in which competition is explicitly taken into account. These papers inspired our study.

In general, the interaction between an operator and its customers can be modeled as a Stackelberg equilibrium game between a leader (the operator) and a follower (its customers). In a point-to-point telecommunication network in the context of a competitive environment, an operator wants to know what price to apply to network services, and what capacity to allocate in the network for each of the services. As different customers have different values for these services, a market segmentation can be realized by grouping customers that have a similar utility for these services. By offering different services and different classes of tariffs, the operator can target specific segments. In order to dimension the network accordingly, the operator needs to know how to allocate resources to each of the defined segments. The customers can choose between the operator and the competition by analyzing the offers they propose. Thus, for each class of service, the operator wants to maximize its revenue, while the clients want to minimize their expenses by comparing the tariffs of the competition. From an optimization point of view, the bilevel paradigm has often been used to model this Stackelberg equilibrium.

Bilevel programs have been extensively studied for general cases. Comprehensive bibliographies have been written by Dempe, 2003 and Vicente and Calamai, 1994. The books by Bard, 1998, Migdalas et al., 1998 and Dempe, 2002 also provide a good introduction. These kinds of problems have been shown to be difficult to solve practically, and are generally NP-hard. For example, the problem of network edge pricing is strongly NP-hard (Roch et al., 2003, Labbé et al., 1999). To solve the problem, heuristic methods might be used (many have been proposed for bilevel programs, as stated in Dempe, 2003, and more specifically in the papers from Anandalingam and White, 1990, White and Anandalingam, 1993 or Labbé et al., 1998 or Brotcorne et al., 2001). However, we will be providing an exact algorithm for this study.

This paper is organized as follows. Section 2 presents some specificities of the point-to-point telecommunication services problem which we are considering. In section 3, a generic mathematical formulation of the problem using the bilevel programming paradigm is introduced. Under some realistic hypotheses, the application of this model to telecommunications is then given. For the case of linear pricing, we show that the problem is equivalent to a mixed integer programming (MIP) formulation. This program is solved using the branch-and-bound algorithm from the commercial solver CPLEX. In section 4, computational experiments and numerical results are provided, illustrating the performances and limitations of this approach depending on the data used and the size of the instances.

2.   Point-to-point pricing problem

We consider point-to-point telecommunication services, ie. services that are offered from an origin to a destination, without the need to define the underlying network. Many telecommunication services can be considered as point-to-point, eg. leased lines, Internet service, VPNs, etc. By considering only origin-destination pairs, and not the underlying network directly except for its link capacities, this can be applied to any network topology. Also, one can either dynamically find the routing for each demand on the network or use static routing information for each offer.

The services we consider are characterized by a price and a set of characteristics. The operator can also offer different qualities of service (QoS) for each of the services, and price them differently, for example through the use of Service Level Agreements (SLA). What we call "characteristics" and "QoS" can be interpreted in any other way that fits a given application in order to reflect the preferences of clients for a particular service. For example, characteristics could practically be the "free" services – personal web pages, e-mail addresses, newsgroup access, etc. – of a DSL subscription and QoS the different speeds of the DSL service.

The clients have different perceptions of the services the operator offers: for example, some might prefer high throughputs regardless of the transmission time (file transfer, etc.), while others might need "real time" transmissions (VoIP, video-conferencing, etc.). Using marketing information, the market is thus decomposed into different segments. Some clients might also want to pay more to have additional quality of service: for example, guaranteed high availability of the network and/or quick restoration in case of failure. Using marketing information, groups of customers with similar needs and perceptions of the offers can be identified, and form market segments.

The operator can target the segments with different offers. It wants to allocate network resources (eg. capacity) optimally in order to adapt to the segments that are expected to choose the operator instead of the competition.

3.   Modeling the problem as a bilevel program

3.1   General formulation

The problem can be modeled as a Stackelberg game between an operator and its clients: the operator wants to maximize its revenue under network operation constraints, while the clients will try to minimize their cost by comparing the prices of the services of the operator and the competition, in order to satisfy their demand. From an optimization point of view, this corresponds to a bilevel program, that is a mathematical program where a constraint is the solution to another mathematical program.

Let T denote the tariff set by the operator, y the answer of the clients to T (ie. what quantity of traffic will the clients send on the operator's network?), $P(T, y)$ the perception of the total price the clients pay to the operator and the competition. Let $g(y)$ and $h(y)$ be the set of customers' constraints: for example $h(y)$ can represent demand satisfaction and $g(y)$ variables non negativity. Given T, the clients' problem is:

$$\min_{y} \quad P(T, y)$$
$$\text{s.t.} \quad g(y) \leq 0$$
$$h(y) = 0$$

Let $R(T, y)$ be the revenue generated by tariff T and quantity of traffic y, $g'(T, y)$ and $h'(T, y)$ be for example network operation constraints and non negativity constraints. For the operator, the problem to solve is:

$$\max_{T,y} \quad R(T, y)$$
$$\text{s.t.} \quad y \in \arg\min_{y}\{P(T, y) : g(y) \leq 0, h(y) = 0\}$$
$$g'(T, y) \leq 0$$
$$h'(T, y) = 0$$

Analytical forms of these functions will be presented in subsection 3.3.

In order to model the decision process of the clients, we use disutility functions that represent the loss of value of an offer for a client, according to different criteria. For example, a client that needs a low delay for its transmission will find that an offer with high delay is expensive. This means that the clients want to minimize their total disutility.

To model the perception of an offer by the clients (ie. money value of an offer), the "apparent price" $\Theta(T, U)$ is generally defined as a compromise between the price and some function representing the disutility of a market segment for the QoS offered. Disutility functions can be associated with a group of clients, and this permits to segment the market, and thus adapt the offers to the demands.

3.2   Main assumptions

We assume that the tariffs and characteristics of the offers of the competition are available, and that they are static, ie. the competition does not change its offers when the operator sets its tariffs.

We assume that the operator cannot have a monopolistic position on any market, so competition must be present on all the markets we consider.

We also assume that if there is not enough capacity to meet the total demand, a competitor will want to offer services on this market. This implies that the competition can be assumed to have infinite capacity on its network.

We assume that the clients make their decision according to the apparent price (ie. disutility) of each offer, and choose the lowest one.

We also assume that a client can split its demand on several offers.

3.3   Model

In order to model the problem, we represent the telecommunication network of the operator as a directed graph $N = (V, A)$ with a capacity on each arc. The competitors' networks are represented as a single graph; indeed, the competition can be aggregated to consider only the lowest priced offers, which are the ones the customers would choose.

On these graphs, a market is defined by an origin-destination pair and an offer is defined by the corresponding routing (ie. path on the graph) between the o-d pair. We assume here that the routing is known, even if this is not restrictive. The approach that will be presented can easily be extended to the case where the optimal routing has to be determined.

Before introducing the model, here is the notation we use. We denote by $\mathcal{A}$ the set of indices of the arcs of the operator network, $\mathcal{M}$ the set of indices of the markets, $\mathcal{F}^o$ the set of indices of the offers of the operator, $\mathcal{F}^c$ the set of indices of the offers of the competition, $\mathcal{S}$ the set of indices of the segments and $\mathcal{C}$ the set of indices of the classes.

The decision variables of the problem are:

$T_{f,q}$ operator tariff for class q of offer f;

T_q vector of $T_{f,q}$ variables $T_q = (T_{f,q})_{f \in \mathcal{F}^o}$;

$\phi^o_{f,s,q}$ traffic sent on offer f of the operator by clients of segment s choosing class q;

$\phi^o_{s,q}$ vector of $\phi^o_{f,s,q}$ variables $\phi^o_{s,q} = (\phi^o_{f,s,q})_{f \in \mathcal{F}^o}$;

$\Theta^o_{f,s,q}$ apparent price of the operator tariffs for class q of offer f for clients of segment s;

$\Theta^o_{s,q}$ vector of $\Theta^o_{f,s,q}$ variables $\Theta^o_{s,q} = (\Theta^o_{f,s,q})_{f \in \mathcal{F}^o}$;

$\phi^c_{f,s,q}$ traffic sent on offer f of the competition by clients of segment s choosing class q;

$\phi^c_{s,q}$ vector of $\phi^c_{f,s,q}$ variables $\phi^c_{s,q} = (\phi^c_{f,s,q})_{f \in \mathcal{F}^c}$;

C_f	capacity allocated by the operator to offer f;
C	vector of C_f variables
	$C = (C_f)_{f \in \mathcal{F}^o}$.

Data of the problem is:

$\Theta^c_{f,s,q}$	apparent price of the competition tariffs for class q of offer f for clients of segment s;
$\Theta^c_{s,q}$	vector of $\Theta^c_{f,s,q}$ data
	$\Theta^c_{s,q} = (\Theta^c_{f,s,q})_{f \in \mathcal{F}^c}$;
G	arc-offer incidence matrix
	$G(i,j) = 1$ if offer j contains arc i, $= 0$ otherwise;
c_a	physical capacity of arc a;
c	vector of c_a data
	$c = (c_a)_{a \in \mathcal{A}}$;
H^o	market-offer incidence matrix for operator
	$H^o(i,j) = 1$ if offer j is on market i, $= 0$ otherwise;
H^c	market-offer incidence matrix for competition;
d^k_s	demand of segment s on market k;
d_s	vector of d^k_s data
	$d_s = (d^k_s)_{k \in \mathcal{M}}$.

The model can now be written as follows:

$$\max_{T_q, C, \phi^o_{s,q}} \quad \sum_q R\left(T_q, \sum_s \phi^o_{s,q}\right) \tag{1.1}$$

$$\text{s.t.} \quad GC \leq c \tag{1.2}$$

$$T_q \geq 0 \quad \forall q \tag{1.3}$$

$$\min_{\phi^o_{s,q}, \phi^c_{s,q}} \quad \sum_s \sum_q P(\Theta^o_{s,q}, \phi^o_{s,q}) + P(\Theta^c_{s,q}, \phi^c_{s,q}) \tag{1.4}$$

$$\text{s.t.} \quad \sum_q H^o \phi^o_{s,q} + H^c \phi^c_{s,q} = d_s \quad \forall s \tag{1.5}$$

$$\sum_s \sum_q \phi^o_{s,q} \leq C \tag{1.6}$$

$$\phi^o_{s,q}, \phi^c_{s,q} \geq 0 \tag{1.7}$$

From the operator's point of view, the objective is to maximize its net revenue (equation 1.1) while allocating capacities for each service that do not exceed physical (or already pre-allocated) capacities of each link (constraint 1.2). The tariff is non-negative (constraint 1.3).

From the clients' point of view, the objective is to minimize the price they pay to either the operator or the competition (equation 1.4), considering the quality of service offered through the apparent prices. The clients want all their demand to be satisfied (constraint 1.5), while it can only be met up to the allocated capacity on the operator's network (constraint 1.6). The traffic is non-negative (constraint 1.7).

Remark. If there is no customer segmentation, one might easily solve the problem. Indeed, the operator can set the apparent price of its tariffs to the apparent price of the competition tariffs on each market. Hence, this is equivalent to a resource allocation problem that can be solved by a linear program. This shows that the segmentation is what makes the problem difficult.

3.4   Linear pricing study

In this case, we suppose that the price is a linear function of the traffic, ie. $R(T_q, \sum_s \phi^o_{s,q}) = T_q^\mathsf{T} \sum_s \phi^o_{s,q}$ and $P(\Theta_{s,q}, \phi_{s,q}) = \Theta_{s,q}^\mathsf{T} \phi_{s,q}$. We also use an additive function for the apparent price: $\Theta_{s,q} = T_q + U_s(D) + V_s(Q)$, where U_s and V_s are the disutility functions of segment s for two QoS criteria D and Q.

As hinted for example in Labbé et al., 1999, one can write the Karush-Kuhn-Tucker conditions for the follower which is a linear program if C and $\forall q$, T_q are fixed. This leads to a difficult optimization problem with complementarity constraints. The KKT conditions for the follower are:

$$\sum_q H^o \phi^o_{s,q} + H^c \phi^c_{s,q} = d_s \quad \forall s \tag{1.8}$$

$$\sum_s \sum_q \phi^o_{s,q} \leq C \tag{1.9}$$

$$-\lambda + H^{o^\mathsf{T}} \mu_s \leq \Theta^o_{s,q} \quad \forall s, \forall q \tag{1.10}$$

$$H^{c^\mathsf{T}} \mu_s \leq \Theta^c_{s,q} \quad \forall s, \forall q \tag{1.11}$$

$$\lambda(C - \sum_s \sum_q \phi^o_{s,q}) = 0 \tag{1.12}$$

$$\phi^o_{s,q}(\Theta^o_{s,q} + \lambda - H^{o^\mathsf{T}} \mu_s) = 0 \quad \forall s, \forall q \tag{1.13}$$

$$\phi^c_{s,q}(\Theta^c_{s,q} - H^{c^\mathsf{T}} \mu_s) = 0 \quad \forall s, \forall q \tag{1.14}$$

$$\phi^o_{s,q}, \phi^c_{s,q}, \lambda \geq 0 \tag{1.15}$$

By using the "big M" method, the complementarity constraints (1.12), (1.13), (1.14) can be linearized as follows. These constraints are in the form $uv = 0$, $u \geq 0$, $v \geq 0$. We introduce constants M and N and binary variables α and β and obtain the equivalent linear inequalities:

$$0 \leq u \leq M\alpha$$

$$0 \le v \le N\beta$$
$$\alpha + \beta \le 1$$
$$\alpha, \ \beta \in \{0, 1\}$$

If u is positive, then $\alpha = 1$ and $v = 0$ (and *vice versa*). Thus, we can linearize all the complementarity constraints from the KKT conditions.

The objective can also be rewritten as a linear one with the strong duality condition for the follower. Thus, we obtain a linear MIP, that can then be solved using a branch-and-bound algorithm such as the one from the commercial package CPLEX.

3.5 Model improvements

In order for the linearized MIP to be equivalent to the original problem, the parameters M and N need to be large enough. But M and N must also be small enough if we want to have a good relaxation value at the root of the branch-and-bound tree. This implies that we need a good choice of values for M and N.

Constraint (1.12) results in

$$\lambda \le M\alpha$$
$$C - \sum_s \sum_q \phi^o_{s,q} \le N\beta$$

where N can be bounded by C, itself bounded by c.

Proposition. *One can compute an upper bound of the value of the multiplier λ corresponding to the capacity constraint as a function of the revenue:*

$$\lambda^*_i \le \frac{\sum_s d^T_s \min_q \{\Theta^c_{s,q}\} - R}{c_i} \tag{1.16}$$

where R is any lower bound of the optimal revenue.

Proof. Consider the optimal solution of the problem, R^*. As a result of the linearization of the objective function of the leader by writing the strong duality for the follower,

$$
\begin{aligned}
R^* &= -c^T \lambda^* + \sum_s d^T_s \mu^*_s - \sum_s \sum_q \Theta^{c^T}_{s,q} \phi^{c*}_{s,q} \\
&\quad - \sum_s \sum_q (U_s(D) + V_s(Q))^T \phi^{o*}_{s,q} \\
&\ge R.
\end{aligned}
$$

Then $c_i \lambda^*_i \le \sum_i c_i \lambda^*_i = c^T \lambda^*$. But

$$c^T \lambda^* \le \sum_s d^T_s \mu^*_s - \sum_s \sum_q \Theta^{c^T}_{s,q} \phi^{c*}_{s,q} - \sum_s \sum_q (U_s(D) + V_s(Q))^T \phi^{o*}_{s,q} - R.$$

As $\mu_s \leq \min_q\{\Theta_{s,q}^c\}$, this yields

$$\lambda_i^* \leq \frac{\sum_s d_s^{\mathsf{T}} \min_q\{\Theta_{s,q}^c\} - R}{c_i}$$

□

So, the value of λ at the optimum can be estimated as a function of R and this can be used as a bound for M.

Constraint (1.13) results in

$$\phi_s^o \leq M\alpha$$
$$\Theta_{s,q}^o + \lambda - H^{o\mathsf{T}}\mu_s \leq N\beta$$

where M can be bounded by $\min(C, d_s)$ and N, following the proposition above, can be bounded by $\max_q\{T_q\} + U_s(D) + V_s(Q) + \frac{\sum_s d_s^{\mathsf{T}} \min_q\{\Theta_{s,q}^c\} - R}{c_i}$.

Constraint (1.14) results in

$$\phi_{s,q}^c \leq M\alpha$$
$$\Theta_{s,q}^c - H^{c\mathsf{T}}\mu_s \leq N\beta$$

where M can be bounded by d_s and N by $\min_q\{\Theta_{s,q}^c\}$, as μ_s is positive.

Remark. For a given tariff, one can easily compute the value of the revenue R. For instance one can try to solve the problem using the trivial value $R = 0$; if not successful, take the best feasible revenue value z found by the branch-and-bound, and solve the problem anew for $R = z$.

4.   Computational experiments and numerical results

In this section, we present numerical results from computational experiences on a few typical instances of the problem. These results are not studied from the point of view of cost or revenue economics, nor interpreted economically, but from an algorithmic perspective, using an exact approach. That is, we want to check how efficiently the problem could be solved using the exact branch-and-bound algorithm.

Our experiments aim at investigating the effects of the following criteria:

- Size of the problem: number of nodes/arcs, number of offers per market, number of segments, number of classes

- Arcs capacities

- Sensibility to parameters: customers distribution, competition tariffs, disutility values

Our approach has been tested on many instances. We will present the observations we made on the following two operator networks:

First, a network with 20 nodes and 22 arcs (fig. 1.1), composed of 6 markets: Am->Ld, Ld->Pr, Md->Ld, Mn->Rm, Pr->Am and Pr->Rm.

Second, a network with 15 nodes and 26 arcs (fig. 1.2), composed of 10 markets: 0->4, 1->0, 1->4, 2->1, 2->3, 3->0, 4->2, 4->3, 4->5, 5->0.

For both networks, the operator sells two offers with different characteristics on each market.

For each of the networks, we have the global demand for each market, and a distribution function (which can be uniform, random, or bimodal for example) of this demand that defines the segmentation.

The competition networks in these cases link directly the origin-destination pairs, and values are chosen for the offers characteristics and tariffs.

We denote by $|\mathcal{M}|$ the number of markets, $|\mathcal{S}|$ the number of segments, $|\mathcal{C}|$ the number of classes. "Nodes" are the number of nodes explored in the branch-and-bound tree, and "Time" is the time spent solving the problem. A '*' means that CPLEX ran out of memory before finding the optimal solution (this means the computation lasted several hours); in this case, a rough approximate number of explored nodes was taken.

We used the branch-and-bound algorithm from the solver CPLEX 7.5 on a Sun UltraSparc II 400 MHz workstation.

On small problem instances (ie. with a small network, and few segments and classes), the solver can easily find the optimal solution, as shown on table 1.1 for the example. This is the case on all the small instances we tried.

Table 1.1.   Network 1, one class of service

$|\mathcal{M}|$	$|\mathcal{S}|$	$|\mathcal{C}|$	Nodes	Time
6	3	1	57	1 sec.
6	5	1	368	2 sec.

Table 1.2 shows numerical results from instances on the same network, but with more classes. We can see that CPLEX cannot solve the problem in reasonable time. This observation, which might seem surprising at first sight, illustrates the very important increase in practical difficulty of the problem with the number of segments and classes. It is to be noted that the number of binary variables between table 1.1 and table 1.2 has been multiplied by an order of 5 to 7. For example, the instance on the second row of table 1.1 has 324 binary variables, while the instance on the first row of table 1.2 has 1764 binary variables and the one on the second row has 2436 binary variables. This can explain the result.

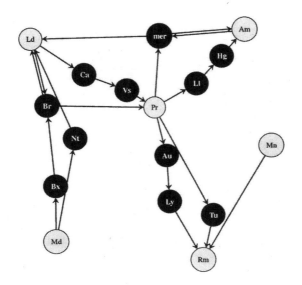

Figure 1.1.   Example network 1: 20 nodes, 22 arcs, 6 markets

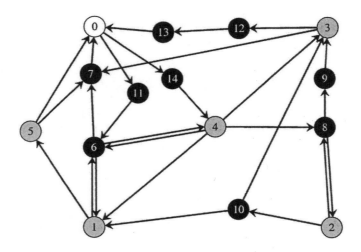

Figure 1.2.   Example network 2: 15 nodes, 26 arcs, 10 markets

By observing figure 1.1, one can observe that the markets and offers are not coupled. Although one could decompose the problem and solve it on each market independently, CPLEX explores the branch-and-bound tree without finding the optimal solution. Solving the problem on one market is not "easy" in the sense that it is still combinatorial (and CPLEX explores a few nodes), but the time spent in solving it is short, so by decomposing the problem we should obtain a solution.

Table 1.2. Network 1, seven classes of service

$|\mathcal{M}|$	$|\mathcal{S}|$	$|\mathcal{C}|$	Nodes	Time
6	5	7	> 100000	* (> 10000 sec.)
6	7	7	> 50000	* (> 12000 sec.)

Table 1.3 shows that the problem is very sensitive to a change in a disutility value; here, we just changed the values (originally taken as the segment number times the value given to the characteristics of the offer) by a factor of 10. Table 1.4 shows sensitivity to a change of demand repartition. Although we can solve the instances in these cases, we can observe big differences between computation times just by changing data value.

Table 1.3. Sensitivity to disutility values

$|\mathcal{M}|$	$|\mathcal{S}|$	$|\mathcal{C}|$	$U_s(D)$	Nodes	Time
10	5	1	sD	23	1 sec.
10	5	1	$10sD$	488	18 sec.

Table 1.4. Sensitivity to demand repartition

$|\mathcal{M}|$	$|\mathcal{S}|$	$|\mathcal{C}|$	Repartition	Nodes	Time
10	5	1	uniform	613	7 sec.
10	5	1	random	3601	30 sec.

Even though it was not expected to solve the problem, much larger instances using a realistic network topology were tried in order to get an idea of the behavior of the model on "real life" examples. This network, based on a real network linking major French cities has 41 nodes and 122 arcs, and is composed of 319 markets. Many instances were tested, but unfortunately CPLEX failed to find a solution for the vast majority of them. However, among the many instances tested, we succeeded in solving two of them thanks to the model improvements given in section 3.

Table 1.5.   Illustration of the big M improvements

$\|\mathcal{M}\|$	$\|\mathcal{S}\|$	$\|\mathcal{C}\|$	M & N	*Nodes*	*Time*
319	5	1	10	infeasible	
319	5	1	1000	> 120000	* (> 6000 sec.)
319	5	1	$M(R = 0)$	47	27 sec.

In table 1.5, the last row corresponds to one of the solved instances, choosing for M and N the values proposed in section 3. On the contrary, the first and second rows show that by using arbitrary values of M and N we could not solve the problem. The first row shows that too small a value of M and N makes the problem infeasible. This is due to the fact that the MIP formulation is not equivalent to the bilevel formulation in this case. On the other hand, too large a value has a negative effect on the computation time, as illustrated by the second row.

These numerical results show that the MIP formulation still needs to be improved in order to solve larger instances.

5.   Conclusion

In this paper, we introduced an application of Revenue Management in the context of the telecommunications industry. This problem consists in optimizing the revenue and resource allocation of point-to-point telecommunication services in a competitive environment. Market segments are introduced in order to take into account the customers' perception of an offer. The competition is taken into account through this perception, as customers can compare prices and qualities of an offer and choose the best one according to their needs.

This Stackelberg game between an operator and its customers has been modeled as a bilevel mathematical program. Focusing only on exact solution approaches, the problem was rewritten as a mixed integer program. Using this approach numerous numerical results were obtained so that practical difficulties could be analyzed.

On small instances (ie. with a small number of arcs and nodes, few markets and classes), the problem could be solved within a few seconds. By increasing the problem size gradually, instances for which the problem could not be solved were reached, and especially with large-scale networks no solution could be found.

Even in the case of small networks, large variations of the computational times could be observed by changing the numerical values of the parameters of the problem (such as the disutility values).

Improvements could be made by adjusting the values of the M parameter in the model, but this was not sufficient to solve larger instances.

In further work, we intend to investigate a new formulation of the problem that addresses some of these difficulties, as well as some extensions to the problem in order to make it more realistic, for example by taking into account a more accurate behavior of the clients (demand elasticity, ...) and/or of the network (QoS based on network load, ...).

Acknowledgments

We would like to thank two anonymous referees for their useful comments and suggestions.

References

Altman, E. and Wynter, L. (2004). Equilibrium, games, and pricing in transportation and telecommunications networks. *Networks and Spatial Economics*, 4:7–21.

Anandalingam, G. and White, D. J. (1990). A solution method for the linear Stackelberg problem using penalty functions. *IEEE Transactions on Automatic Control*, 35(10):1170–1173.

Bard, J. F. (1998). *Practical Bilevel Optimization: Algorithms and Applications*. Kluwer Academic Publishers, Dordrecht.

Basar, T. and Srikant, R. (2002). Revenue-maximizing pricing and capacity expansion in a many-users regime. In *Proceedings of IEEE INFOCOM*.

Bouhtou, M., Diallo, M., and Wynter, L. (2001). Price-directive resource allocation, extensions of utility maximizing and proportional fairness strategies. Technical Report NT/FTR&D/7459, France Telecom R&D.

Bouhtou, M., Diallo, M., and Wynter, L. (2003a). Capacitated network revenue management through shadow pricing. In Stiller, B., Carle, G., Karsten, M., and Reichl, P., editors, *Group Communications and Charges; Technology and Business Models*, Lecture Notes in Computer Science, pages 342–352. Springer Verlag.

Bouhtou, M., Diallo, M., and Wynter, L. (2003b). Fair network ressource allocation and link pricing: a numerical study. In Pardalos, Tsevendorj, and Enkhbat, editors, *Optimization and Optimal control*, pages 37–58. World scientific publishing.

Bouhtou, M., van Hoesel, S., van der Kraaij, A. F., and Lutton, J.-L. (2003c). Tariff optimization in networks. Meteor Research Memorandum RM03011, Maastricht University. Submitted.

Brotcorne, L., Labbé, M., Marcotte, P., and Savard, G. (2000). A bilevel model and solution algorithm for a freight tariff setting problem. *Transportation Science*, 34:289–302.

Brotcorne, L., Labbé, M., Marcotte, P., and Savard, G. (2001). A bilevel model for toll optimization on a multicommodity transportation network. *Transportation Science*, 35:1–14.

Côté, J.-P., Marcotte, P., and Savard, G. (2003). A bilevel modelling approach to pricing and fare optimisation in the airline industry. *Journal of Revenue and Pricing Management*, 2(1):23–36.

Dempe, S. (2002). *Foundations of Bilevel Programming*. Kluwer Academic Publishers, Dordrecht et al.

Dempe, S. (2003). Annotated bibliography on bilevel programming and mathematical programs with equilibrium constraints. *Optimization*, 52:333–359.

Kelly, F. (1997). Charging and rate control for elastic traffic. *European Transactions on Telecommunications*, 8:33–37.

Kelly, F., Maulloo, A., and Tan, D. (1998). Rate control in communication networks: shadow prices, proportional fairness and stability. *Journal of the Operational Research Society*, 49:237–252.

Keon, N. and Anandalingam, G. (2003). Optimal pricing for multiple services in telecommunications networks offering quality-of-service guarantees. *IEEE/ACM Transactions on Networking*, 11(1):66–80.

Keon, N. and Anandalingam, G. (2004). A new pricing model for competitive telecommunications services using congestion discounts. *INFORMS Journal on Computing*. To appear.

Labbé, M., Marcotte, P., and Savard, G. (1998). A bilevel model of taxation and its application to optimal highway pricing. *Management Science*, 44:1608–1622.

Labbé, M., Marcotte, P., and Savard, G. (1999). On a class of bilevel programs. In Pillo, G. Di and Gianessi, F., editors, *Nonlinear Optimization and Related Topics*, pages 183–206. Kluwer Academic Publishers.

Lazar, A. and Semret, N. (1998). The progressive second price auction mechanism for network resource sharing. In *8th Int. Symp. on Dynamic Games and Applications, Maastricht.*

MacKie-Mason, J. K. and Varian, H. R. (1993). Pricing the Internet. In *Public Access to the Internet, JFK School of Government*, page 37.

Migdalas, A., Pardalos, P. M., and Värbrand, P., editors (1998). *Multilevel Optimization: Algorithms and Applications*. Kluwer Academic Publishers, Dordrecht.

Minoux, M. (1986). *Mathematical Programming: Theory and Algorithms*. Wiley.

Nemhauser, G. and Wolsey, L. (1988). *Integer and combinatorial optimization*. Interscience Series In Discrete Mathematics And Optimization. Wiley.

Roch, S., Savard, G., and Marcotte, P. (2003). Design and analysis of an approximation algorithm for Stackelberg network pricing. *Optimization Online.*

Vicente, L. N. and Calamai, P. H. (1994). Bilevel and multilevel programming: a bibliography review. *Journal of Global Optimization*, 5(3):291–306.

White, D. J. and Anandalingam, G. (1993). A penalty function approach for solving bi-level linear programs. *Journal of Global Optimization*, 3:397–419.

Chapter 2

PRICING ANALYSIS IN INTERNATIONAL INTERCONNECTED NETWORKS

Livio Cricelli[1], Francesca Di Pillo[2], Massimo Gastaldi[3] and Nathan Levialdi[4]

[1] *Dipartimento di Meccanica, Strutture, Ambiente e Territorio, Università degli Studi di Cassino, Via G. Di Biasio 43, 03043 Cassino (Fr) Italy;* [2,4]*Dipartimento di Ingegneria dell'Impresa, Università degli Studi di Roma "Tor Vergata", Via del Politecnico 1, 00133 Roma Italy;* [3]*Dipartimento di Ingegneria Elettrica, Università degli Studi di L'Aquila, Monteluco di Roio, 67100 L'Aquila Italy*

Abstract: The international telecommunications market is characterised by the need of operators in different countries to be interconnected. These operators enter into agreements whose principal variables are, firstly the interconnection tariff, and secondly the traffic volumes. The liberalisation of the telecommunications market has affected the dynamics of the bilateral agreements between international operators. This paper examines the interactions between fixed telephone operators in interconnected countries and analyses the effects that various settlement agreements can have in terms of the operators profitability.

Key words: Interconnection tariff, bargaining power, two way network, network competition.

1.   INTRODUCTION

The changes occurring in the telephony industry in many industrialised countries, both on a legislative and technological level, have affected competitive scenarios in various national contexts. This paper examines the international telephony industry where the need of interconnection induces problems for interaction between countries which are characterised by different market contexts, legislative restrictions, and sizes on the catchment areas. These differences have a reciprocal impact in each country: changes to the macroeconomic variables in one country arising out of either the strategic choices of an individual operator or from the implementation of economic policy involve multiplicity of effects for the operators in a country interconnected with it. In particular, the cost supported by the interconnection is established by the interconnection or access tariff, or rather the price that an operator must pay to terminate the call on the network of the operator in the destination country. The Federal Communications Commission in the United States[1], in its directive on international interconnection tariffs, set the interconnection tariff values payable by U.S. operators to foreign operators for outgoing traffic from the USA so as to bar the phenomenon of "whipsawing", that is to say, the practice of applying a relatively high access tariff adopted by foreign monopolies which, consequently, interferes with the competitive dynamics in the American market. In fact, only large operators managed to sustain the interconnection cost, meaning the small operators were excluded from the market. However, this directive was rescinded from the beginning of liberalisation of this industry in the major industrialised countries. As a result, the dynamics of bilateral agreements between international operators changed radically. The analysis carried out in this paper aims to examine the impact of the actual negotiating policies on the profitability of operators characterised by different sizes and possessing various bargaining powers.

The problems relating to the interconnection tariff negotiations have been discussed in the literature. In "two way" networks[2-5], which characterise the international telecommunications market, reciprocal interconnection can distort social welfare. In fact, the interconnection tariff can be exploited as an instrument of collusion in cases where the operators offer services with a degree of differentiation so that it maintains a higher price level for the end user than would be the case in a competitive scenario. In this case, the Authority regulating this industry needs to intervene in order to maximise social welfare. Carter and Wright[6] examined the threat of collusion on two way networks in asymmetric conditions arising out of the fact that the incumbent operators possess the competitive advantage of brand loyalty over other competitors. The asymmetry, besides being relative to the size of operators in the same market, can be considered in terms of the size of interconnected operators belonging to different countries. The analysis of the interactions between different operators without considering the possibility of collusion, but within a competitive scenario characterised by a great deal of competition, was conducted by Madden and Savage[7] who developed an econometric model analysing the interaction between the pricing choices and the structure of the market. The results obtained revealed that a relationship existed between the reduction in market share of large U.S. operators and the decrease in price of international calls from foreign operators. Furthermore, the results obtained revealed the existence of a relationship between increased competition in foreign countries and reduced price levels, not only by foreign operators but also by U.S. operators.

The actual practice of international negotiations on the rate making for the interconnection reflects Accounting Rate System (Ars) regulation based on fixing a common interconnection tariff. In reality, this negotiation practice can lead to several distortions such as the increase of the price to the end user or the reduction of the traffic volume. The Accounting Rate System was efficient when interconnection occurred between two monopolistic operators in which there was a perfect balance in the exchange of volumes of traffic and when the inflation and exchange rates were relatively constant in the two interconnected countries. However, the present international telecommunications scenario no longer reflects any of these conditions. Although liberalisation of the industry has occurred in the last decade, the ex-monopolistic operators continue to hold on to market leadership. The onset of competition has caused an unbalanced relationship between the quantities exchanged so that the larger operators are in a position of considerable bargaining power. In negotiation the larger operators, generating high quantities of outgoing traffic, can impose the tariff conditions which are most favourable to them.

The purpose of the analysis in this paper is therefore to model this negotiation practice and to test its profitability in relation to several variables, such as the gap between level of competition and the difference in the size of the catchment areas in interconnected countries. In order to model this bargaining process we use a game theoretic model[8-9].

The paper is organised as follows. After this introduction, an analysis of the competitive scenario is carried out. In the third part of the paper a model is proposed for the competitive context in which operators belonging to two countries act. In the fourth part the model simulates the impact of principal key variables, and the suitability of the negotiation strategy of the interconnection charges based on the relationship between the quantities of traffic exchanged. Lastly, conclusions are elaborated in the final section.

2. THE COMPETITIVE SCENARIO

In the last ten years the volume of international telephone traffic has increased to an annual average of 15%[10]. In 2001 international telephone calls across the world equalled 144 billions of minutes. The revenues in the international telephony industry amounted to USD 61 billions. In July 2002, worldwide 4,726 operators possessed licenses to operate on the international telephony market. It should be noted that only as long ago as 1997 there were slightly less than 600 operators in the international telephony industry. The technological innovations and the process of liberalization of the telecommunications industry which have occurred in the major industrialized nations have contributed to this growth.

In the decade 1990-2000 the opening up of a competitive regime has involved numerous countries. In 1990 only six countries in the world had been liberalized in the telecommunications industry whereas by 2002 there were 59.

In the United States the level of competition in the industry has grown exponentially in recent years. In 2003 there are over 1,800 international telephony operators in contrast to the 175 present in 1997. Globally the competitive scenario is characterised by a competitive regime in which the ex-monopolists, almost always, retain the leadership, as shown in figure 1. In particular, in Italy where there are 120 international telephony operators in various market segments, the ex monopolist Telecom Italia had about 60% of the total international telephone call minutes.

An important consequence of the wider competition has been a progressive reduction in prices. From the onset of liberalisation, the dominant operators have decreased the cost of international calls by approximately 40%[11]. This decrease in prices has also been made possible by technological improvements which have substantially modified the cost structure for international telephony operators, causing a significant reduction in the costs of call completion.

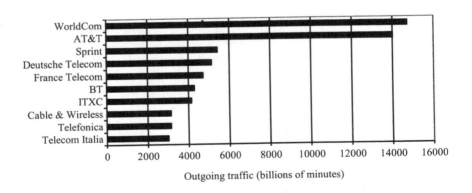

Figure 1. Top ten international carriers (source: Telegeography, 2003)

The liberalization of the industry within the individual countries has increased the strategic importance of the interconnection tariff. In 2003 the determination of the conditions of interconnection and the price for the end user represent a crucial factor in a complex competitive context such as the international telephony. In fact, in this industry the competition is not only based on attracting the national subscribers for international telephone calls, but also on the determination of the interconnection tariff for the termination of calls coming from foreign countries. The determination of the interconnection tariffs assumes greater complexity because they are fixed in a reciprocal manner by the operators of the two countries who want to connect. Therefore, the competition takes place in two stages: firstly, on a national level in order to compete for the subscribers of international telephone services, and secondly on an international level in order to make more favourable agreements with foreign operators for the termination of international calls.

In Europe, European Union legislation protects the possibility of operators negotiating *"transfrontier agreements"* between them for access and interconnection on a *"commercial basis"*, or rather, negotiations not subjected to legislative restrictions. Notwithstanding this freedom of behaviour, until 2003 the negotiating practice used by the international telephony operators had closely followed the regulations of Ars which, as already seen above, contain numerous weaknesses. In practice, Ars provides for the fixing of a common interconnection tariff. Where there is a difference in volumes of traffic exchanged, the operator in the country which generated the greater call volume compensates the operator to which it connects with a sum equal to the difference in the quantity exchanged multiplied by the value of the access tariff. This negotiation practice produces paradoxical results. The operator which generates the larger call volume is disadvantaged, probably applying lower final prices. Vice versa, the operators which fix higher final prices and produce a lower volume of traffic are in an advantageous position, collecting a higher active interconnection tariff than its partner operator.

This method of negotiation, in addition to bringing distortions, is largely bypassed through several alternative methods:
1. call-back. This is a form of re-directing the call. The call from country A to country B is first directed to country C where the call back operator interconnects the operators of the two countries, profiting on the difference in final price imposed in the different countries.
2. Collect calls. This is a service which makes the subscriber receiving the call pay for the call.
3. Refile. This is a form of commercial agreement for the delivery of traffic between two administrations via a third party where the final transit point

appears as the technical, and more importantly the commercial origin of the traffic and declares the traffic as such. In 2002, 25% of international telephone traffic was transported using the refile technique.

Besides the technique of negotiating using Ars regulations, when the quantities exchanged diverge appreciably, for example when an incumbent operator negotiates with a competitor, the method of negotiation is based on the relative contractual power possessed by the operators. In this case, the distortions generated by the traditional type of negotiation are overcome since the operator which sends the most telephone traffic is rewarded. However, it is important to analyse the limits of this negotiation method in that the dominant operator can behave anti-competitively and undermine the competitiveness of the market.

3.   ANALYSIS OF NEGOTIATION FOR INTERCONNECTION

With the purpose of analysing competition in the international telephony industry, two different national markets of fixed telephony are considered, market A and market B, in which two competitors in each market operate, one an incumbent the other a competitor, as shown in figure 2.

Each operator is able to operate in both: in the intermediate market in which international connections take place, and in the final market, offering full service coverage. Competition between carriers therefore takes place on two levels: firstly, in the national market where the decision variable is the price to the end user, and, secondly, in the international market where the decision variable is the interconnection tariff.

The utility of a generic consumer subscribing to the j-th operator is given by[6]:

$$U = w_j^A + \theta_j^A + v_0^A \tag{1}$$

where:

w_j^A is the utility deriving from carried out calls;

θ_j^A represents the additional benefit derived from the connection with operator *j*;

v_0^A is the constant fixed surplus caused by the use of the interconnection service.

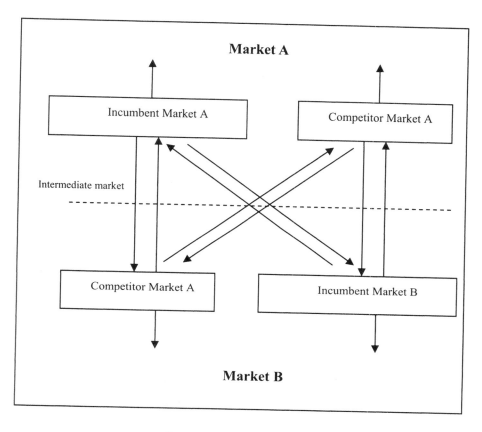

Figure 2. Competitive Scenario

Since the subscribers are assumed uniformly distributed with value x, on the classic Hotelling[12] segment of unitary length and the carriers are localised on the segment of length $1+\beta^A$, where β^A represents the degree of asymmetry in terms of brand loyalty, we obtain:

$$\theta_1^A = \frac{\beta^A}{2\sigma^A} + \frac{1-x}{2\sigma^A} \text{ and } \theta_2^A = \frac{x}{2\sigma^A} \tag{2}$$

the variable β^A can vary between 0 and 1. When it is equal to 0 the operators have the same brand loyalty and the market shares are only influenced by prices. When it is equal to 1, the incumbent operator has a strong competitive advantage since it possesses maximum brand loyalty. The variable σ^A represents the degree of substitutability between operators; when σ^A is moving to 1, the switching cost of the subscriber is annulled. The function of net surplus of the subscriber belonging to the j-th operator is given by:

$$w_j^A = u\left(q_j^A\right) - p_j^A q_j^A\left(p_j^A\right)$$

(3)

A subscriber localised on the Hotelling[12] segment at point x will choose one of the two carriers indifferently if his utility is the same:

$$w_1^A + \frac{\beta^A}{2\sigma^A} + \frac{1-x}{2\sigma^A} = w_2^A + \frac{x}{2\sigma^A}$$

(4)

By solving x, the following shares for market A are obtained:

$$S_1^A = \frac{1+\beta^A}{2} + \sigma^A\left(w_1^A - w_2^A\right)$$

$$S_2^A = \frac{1-\beta^A}{2} + \sigma^A\left(w_2^A - w_1^A\right)$$

(5)

The same considerations are valid for market B.

In order to set up carrier profit functions, the following negotiation hypotheses are assumed:

1. the incumbent in market A draws up an interconnection agreement with the incumbent in market B, while the competitor in market A does the same with the competitor in market B.
2. the incumbent in market A draws up an interconnection agreement with the competitor in market B, while the competitor in market A does the same with the incumbent in market B.

So, the profit function of the j-th operator in the market A interconnected with i-th operator in market B ($i = 1,2$; 1 is referred to market incumbent and 2 to market competitor) is given by:

$$\pi_j^A = \left(p_j^A - c_j^A - t_j^{Ap}\right)q_j^A S_j^A N + \left(t_j^{Aa} - c_j^A\right)q_i^B S_i^B M$$

(6)

Similarly, the profit function of the i-th operator in market B interconnected with j-th operator in market A is given by:

$$\pi_i^B = \left(p_i^B - c_i^B - t_i^{Bp}\right)q_i^B S_i^B M + \left(t_i^{Ba} - c_i^B\right)q_j^A S_j^A N$$

(7)

where:

p_j^A is the price of one minute of a telephone call starting from A and ending in B carried out by the end user in market A subscribing to operator j;

p_i^B is the price of one minute of a telephone call starting from B and ending in A carried out by the end user in market B subscribing to operator i;

c_j^A is both the originating and termination cost of one minute of telephone traffic towards B of operator j in market A;

c_i^B is both the originating and termination cost of one minute of telephone traffic towards A of operator i in market B;

t_j^{Ap} is the interconnection tariff paid by operator j in market A to the operator i in market B to terminate one minute of a telephone call in market B (passive interconnection tariff of operator j);

t_i^{Bp} is the interconnection tariff paid by operator i in market B to the operator j in market A to terminate one minute of a telephone call in market A (passive interconnection tariff of operator i);

t_j^{Aa} is the interconnection tariff received by operator j in market A for one minute of a telephone call coming from market B paid by the operator i (active interconnection tariff of operator j);

t_i^{Ba} is the interconnection tariff received by operator i in market B for one minute of a telephone call coming from market A paid by the operator j (active interconnection tariff of operator i);

q_j^A is the quantity of calls made by a subscriber of the j-th operator and directed to market B ($q_j^A = a - bp_j^A$);

q_i^B is the quantity of calls made by a subscriber of the i-th operator and directed to market A ($q_i^B = r - sp_i^B$);

S_j^A is the market share of operator j in market A in terms of percentage of subscribers;

S_i^B is the market share of operator i in market B in terms of percentage of subscribers;

N and M are the number of subscribers belonging respectively to market A and market B who make international telephone calls.

The focus of this paper is the analysis of competition in international telecommunications industry, showing the importance of operators bargain power. So, we overcome the hypothesis of a common interconnection tariff stated in literature[13] and we consider that the interconnection tariff is negotiated depending on carriers bargaining power. Therefore, we assume that the operators compete on price in the final market (p_j^A and p_i^B are the decision variables of the model), whilst they may negotiate the interconnection tariff using their own bargaining power based on the quantity of the telephone traffic exchanged. In this way, interconnection tariff is fixed as a function of exchanged traffic volumes. Therefore, the passive interconnection tariff of j-th operator in market A is given by:

$$t_j^{Ap} = K \frac{q_i^B MS_i^B}{q_j^A NS_j^A} t_j^{Aa} \tag{8}$$

whereas the passive interconnection tariff of i-th operator in market B is given by:

$$t_i^{Bp} = \frac{1}{K} \frac{q_j^A NS_j^A}{q_i^B MS_i^B} t_i^{Ba} \tag{9}$$

where K represents a multiplication factor of the quantity. Notice that the passive interconnection charge for the operator j in market A is equal to the active interconnection tariff for the operator i in market B, and vice versa ($t_i^{Ba} = t_j^{Ap}$ and $t_i^{Bp} = t_j^{Aa}$).

When the quantity exchanged is equivalent, K=1 and the interconnection tariff is common in that the passive tariff coincides with the active one. When there is considerable asymmetry between the quantity of traffic exchanged, the operator sending the most traffic claims a higher active tariff than the related passive tariff. According to this negotiation methodology, the greater the gap between the volumes of traffic exchanged, the greater the gap between the active and passive tariffs. This negotiating method is, therefore, efficacious when an appreciable difference exists between the volumes of traffic exchanged, but on the other hand when the quantity exchanged does not vary much, applying a contractual method which does not raise the size of the gap is better. In fact, when the gap between the exchanged traffic volumes is low, the observed carrier behavior is to fix asymmetric interconnection tariff only on the imbalance. Since the analysis is based on the hypothesis of asymmetrical conditions for several variables regarding the interconnected countries, the negotiating method based on the relationship between the quantities exchanged proved to be the most efficacious.

On the basis of the above assumptions, the final price is simultaneously fixed by the two operators solving the two systems (one for each market) of first order conditions of the profit functions:

$$
\begin{cases}
\dfrac{\partial \pi_1^A}{\partial p_1^A} = 0 \\[2ex]
\dfrac{\partial \pi_2^A}{\partial p_2^A} = 0
\end{cases}
\text{for market A}
\qquad
\begin{cases}
\dfrac{\partial \pi_1^B}{\partial p_1^B} = 0 \\[2ex]
\dfrac{\partial \pi_2^B}{\partial p_2^B} = 0
\end{cases}
\text{for market B}
\qquad (10)
$$

The maximization process (10) is shown in the appendix. The solutions of previous system are obtained through a software for advanced mathematics (Maple 9).

4.   SIMULATION RESULTS

In order to analyse the impact of a settlement agreement based on the exchanged traffic volumes, for simulation purposes on carrier profitability, we consider the following key variables:
- the level of competition in each country, represented by the degree of asymmetry and of substitutability between operators;
- the size of the catchment area.

The competitive scenario can not only be influenced by the prices applied by individual operators, but also by the brand loyalty possessed by the incumbent compared to that possessed by the competitor which leads to asymmetry in the market share and a greater switching cost for the subscriber.

With regard to the second variable, in the international telephone scenario considerable asymmetry exists between the catchment areas. As shown in figure 3, in 2003 almost 80% of the international telephone traffic is generated in Europe and North America.

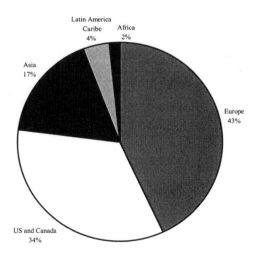

Figure 3. International traffic volume by the country of origin (source: Telegeography, 2003)

The simulations applied to the relative sizes of the operators are reported in tables 1 and 2. In particular, in table 1, the starting situation is characterised by the market B incumbent (1B) having strong market power ($\beta^B = 1$). The existence of a strong brand loyalty induces both the highest price level of the incumbent and the lowest for the competitor; moreover the total traffic volume produced by the incumbent ($Q_1^B = q_1^B S_1^B M$) is greater than the volume produced by the competitor Q_2^B. This is due to the prevalence of the market share effect with respect to price impact. It is interesting to note that the greater the reduction in brand loyalty the greater the total traffic volume produced Q. Such increase is composed by two opposite effects: the first one is related to the reduction in traffic volume produced by the incumbent although the price reduction, whereas the second one is related to an increase in traffic volume produced by the competitor although the price increase, as shown in columns ΔQ_1^B and ΔQ_2^B. This means that the brand loyalty effect is prevalent with respect to price impact. Now it is interesting to analyse the impact of variations in the competitive scenario in term of profits. So, it is necessary to consider the interconnection tariff representing a high share of revenue and cost. The bargaining power gap between incumbent and competitor induces to consider the two different negotiation hypotheses defined above. The obtained results can be summarised in table 2.

Table 1. Optimal values of prices, calls and market shares related to β^B

β^B	P_1^B	P_2^B	S_1^B	Q_1^B	ΔQ_1^B	Q_2^B	ΔQ_2^B	Q
1	2.22	1.02	0.88	4903 (84%)		952 (16%)		5855
0.8	2.19	1.33	0.81	4577 (77%)	-7%	1361 (13%)	+43%	5938
0.6	2.16	1.57	0.74	4219 (70%)	-8%	1770 (30%)	+30%	5989
0.4	2.11	1.75	0.66	3834 (64%)	-9%	2183 (36%)	+23%	6017
0.2	2.06	1.88	0.58	3431 (57%)	-11%	2600 (43%)	+19%	6031
0	1.98	1.98	0.50	3018 (50%)	-12%	3018 (50%)	+16%	6036

(Notice that price are in €/min. and quantities are in millions of minutes)

Table 2. Carriers profits variations with respect to β^B

β^B	Negotiation hypothesis 1				Negotiation hypothesis 2			
	π_1^A	π_2^A	π_1^B	π_2^B	π_1^A	π_2^A	π_1^B	π_2^B
1	54525	56110	102924	462	68675	43030	104512	-2179
0.8	55481	53171	94321	10991	64943	44129	95654	9144
0.6	56459	51453	84801	21617	62842	45251	85992	20197
0.4	57457	50187	74654	32447	60786	46358	75705	31296
0.2	58326	48784	64107	43824	60138	47406	65023	42227

(Notice that profits are €x1000)

The reduction of the brand loyalty β^B has an impact in terms of profits in market B, as shown in figures 4 and 5. Notice that, in both negotiating hypothesis, the profits made by the incumbent is decreasing, since a reduction in the quantity of outgoing traffic occurs, which in turn causes a worsening in the negotiating position of the passive tariff. In particular, the incumbent in market B finds an advantage in negotiating the interconnection with the competitor in market A due to better bargaining power.

On the contrary (figure 5), in both negotiating hypotheses the profits of the competitor in market B increase because of the raise of its market share and the consequent improvement in its bargaining power. Figures 4 and 5 show that for the incumbent it will be better to bargain with the competitor since it increases the strength ratio that defines the passive tariff; the same consideration is true for the competitor. Such effect is greater than that arising from the low traffic volume deriving from the interconnection with the competitor (instead of the incumbent), so involving a high level of profits.

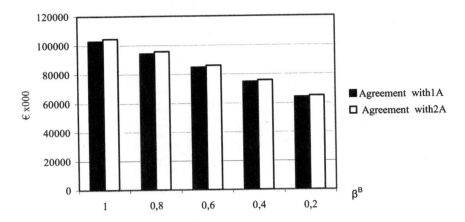

Figure 4. Incumbent profits variations in market B with respect to β^B

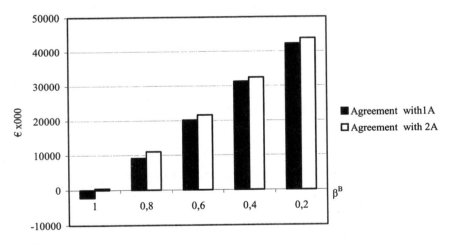

Figure 5. Competitor profits variations in market B with respect to β^B

Now we analyse the impact of a reduction of brand loyalty in market B on carriers profits in market A. With the reduction of β^B, the first hypothesis of negotiation results a progressive growth of profit. Moreover, the second hypothesis of negotiation is always better for both market A carriers, obtaining a high level of profits, as shown in figures 6 and 7. Such advantage is declining with respect of reduction of β^B since the difference in bargaining power between the incumbent and the competitor in market B become negligible.

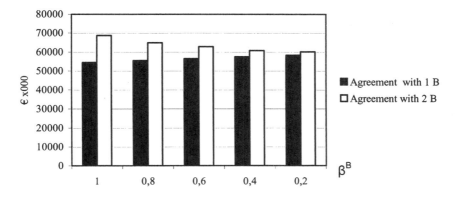

Figure 6. Incumbent profits variations in market A with respect to β^B

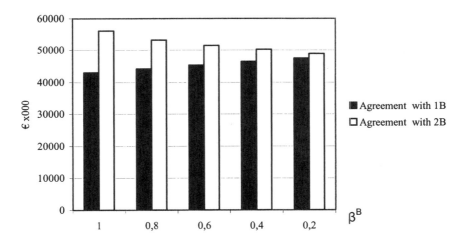

Figure 7. Competitor profits variations in market A with respect to β^B

Table 3. Profits variations with respect to market B catchment area

Market B size	Negotiation hypothesis 1				Negotiation hypothesis 2			
	π_1^A	π_2^A	π_1^B	π_2^B	π_1^A	π_2^A	π_1^B	π_2^B
N=200000 subscribers	58756	48783	58756	48783	59644	47888	59644	47888
1.25*N	56942	47202	75284	62580	58159	45805	76457	61579
1.50*N	54724	45276	92103	76645	56466	43272	93687	75460
1.75*N	52255	43052	96055	79893	54407	40399	97024	78424
2*N	49082	40360	127175	106003	52183	36792	129390	104092

Analysis of the catchment area is carried out by assuming an increase in the size of market B, ceteris paribus, as we can observe in table 3.

The obtained results show how both carriers in market A are not favoured by interconnection with countries having larger catchment areas because of the imbalance in the relationship between the quantity of traffic transmitted. All the same, it is better for both carriers to conclude interconnection agreements with the competitor in the other country. Results show that both carriers in market B obtain an increased profit from the growth of their catchment area. The growth in the number of subscribers increases the quantity of outgoing traffic and improves the negotiating conditions of the interconnection. Furthermore, both carriers prefer to negotiate with the competitor in market A as it allows them to make a greater profit because it improves the ratio between the quantities exchanged.

All the simulations show that for both incumbent and competitor it is always best to negotiate the interconnection conditions with smaller carriers.

To complete the analysis it is worthwhile to compare the impact on profitability caused by difference in the degree of asymmetry of interconnected markets and those differences derived from variation in the market B catchment area.

As table 4 and 5 show, the effects produced by variation in the catchment area on the profits of market A carriers are greater compared to those stemming from the degree of market asymmetry. When market A incumbent negotiates with market B incumbent, it suffers a decrease in profit when the degree of market B asymmetry increases. Moreover, such profit loss of market A incumbent is greater when the market B catchment area increases.

In the case in which the market A incumbent negotiates with the competitor in market B, its profit grows when the degree of market B asymmetry rises, because it obtains the better contractual conditions. On the contrary, it obtains a profit decrease with an increase in the market B catchment area because of the worsening of the ratio between the exchanged traffic. The situation of the market A competitor is analogous.

Table 4. Incumbent profits variations in market A

Negotiation with market B incumbent		Negotiation with market B competitor	
β	N	β	N
-1.5%	-3.0%	+1.1%	-2.4%
-3.2%	-6.9%	+4.5%	-5.3%
-4.9%	-11.1%	+8.0%	-8.8%
-6.5%	-16.5%	+14.2%	-12.5%

Table 5. Competitor profits variations in market A

Negotiation with market B incumbent		Negotiation with market B competitor	
β	N	β	N
+2.9%	-3.2%	-2.2%	-4.3%
+5.5%	-7.2%	-4.5%	-9.6%
+9.0%	-11.7%	-6.9%	-15.6%
+15.0%	-17.3%	-9.2%	-23.2%

The variations in terms of profitability compared to the carriers in market B are shown in table 6, in which the second negotiating hypothesis has been omitted since it does not present any relevant differences compared to the first.

The market B incumbent obtains increased profits in both cases and by negotiating with all carriers in market A. Moreover, its profit increases most in the case in which its catchment area increases. The competitor in market B, negotiating with either carrier, experiences a reduction in profit when the competitive scenario changes, since its passive interconnection tariff increases on the reduction in its size. Vice versa, its profits rise when its catchment area increases since the bargaining power with the market A partner carriers grows.

The results of the simulation demonstrate the relative sizes of the catchment areas produce more incisive effects on profitability of all interconnected carriers compared to those generated by changes in the competitive scenario caused by changes in the degree of asymmetry between carriers. In particular, for the carriers with the smallest catchment area, the increase in the size of the catchment area in the country with which they are interconnected, produces a considerable deterioration in their negotiating position through the imbalance in the bargaining power between partner carriers.

Table 6. Carriers profits variations in market B

Negotiation between market B incumbent and market A incumbent		Negotiation between market B competitor and market A competitor	
β	N	β	N
+16.4%	+28.1%	-25.9%	+28.1%
+32.3%	+56.8%	-50.7%	+57.1%
+47.1%	+63.5%	-74.9%	+63.7%
+60.6%	+116.4%	-98.9%	+117.3%

5.   CONCLUSIONS

In recent years the increased competitive pressure developed in the major industrialised countries has impacted on the international telephone traffic agreements. When, internationally, a monopolistic regime operated, the common interconnection tariff was determined according to bilateral agreements between carriers in different countries. From the beginning of liberalisation, the interconnection tariff experienced a radical decrease and, at the same time, became an important strategic leverage in the choice of foreign carrier.

Furthermore, the liberalisation has allowed interaction between carriers of different dimensions, consequently resulting in changes in the bargaining power. Large carriers in the negotiating situation hold considerable contractual power because of the greater telephone traffic generated. The aim of the analysis in this paper is to determine the advantages of adopting the negotiating typology based on the quantities of traffic exchanged compared to the level of competition and in relation to the relative sizes of the carriers. The advantage of adopting such a contractual typology can, therefore, depend on the composition and the dimension of the market with which interconnection is desired. The analysis carried out revealed how the size of the catchment area of the interconnected country's market causes a more incisive effect on the carrier's profitability. In particular, the increased size of the market in one country causes an improvement in its negotiating conditions and so on the profitability of the carriers in that country, while it has a negative effect on the interconnected carriers having a small catchment area, that suffer a worsening of their negotiating strength and of their profits as a result.

In addition, the results obtained from the simulation concerning the level of competition and the size of catchment area converge towards a particular contractual solution. All the simulations show how size (that is, both the number of subscribers and the volume of traffic transmitted) gives carriers greater negotiating power so that large carriers benefit from negotiating with small carriers since the bargaining power is greater. On the contrary, for small carriers it is advantageous to negotiate with carriers of the same size. When a contractual methodology based on telephone traffic exchanged is applied, a strategy of polarisation is only advantageous for small sized carriers. Since both the carriers of the market prefer to make interconnection agreements with a competitor carrier in the other country, it triggers a process of negotiation which is inevitably unsatisfactory to someone.

A possible solution is that the larger carriers offer the smaller carriers some form of compensation for the profit loss, a solution already proposed by Wright[13] for multilateral negotiations.

The contractual typology based on the relationship between the quantities of exchanged telephone traffic, even though it eliminates the distortion of social welfare caused by traditional negotiating methodologies, only brings about improved efficiency if the smaller carriers are offered some form of incentive.

References

1. FCC, *IB Docket 96/261 In the Matter of International Settlement Rates* (1997).
2. M. Armstrong, Network interconnection in telecommunications, *Economic Journal*, **108**, 545-564 (1998).
3. J-J. Laffont, P. Rey and J. Tirole, Network competition: I Overview and nondiscriminatory pricing, *Rand Journal of Economics*, **29** (1), 1-37 (1998).
4. J-J. Laffont, P. Rey and J. Tirole, Network competition: II Discriminatory pricing, *Rand Journal of Economics*, **29** (1), 38-56 (1998).
5. L. Cricelli, M. Gastaldi and N. Levialdi, Vertical Integration in International Telecommunication System, *Review of Industrial Organization*, **14** (3), 337-353 (1999).
6. M. Carter and J. Wright, Interconnection in network industries, *Review of Industrial Organization*, **14**, 1-25 (1999).
7. G. Madden and S.J. Savage, Market structure, competition and pricing in United States international telephone markets, *Review of Economics and Statistics*, **82** (2), 291-296 (2000).
8. J. Tirole, *The Theory of Industrial Organization*, (MIT Press, Cambridge- Massachusetts, 1988).
9. R. Gibbons, *Game Theory of Applied Economists*, (Princeton University press, Princeton- New Jersey, 1992).
10. Telegeography, *Country Traffic Statistic*, (2003).
11. Agcom, *Relazione Annuale sull'Attività Svolta e sui Programmi di Lavoro-2003*, (2003).
12. H. Hotelling, Stability in Competition, *Economic Journal* **39**, 41-57 (1929).
13. J. Wright, International Telecommunications, Settlement Rates, and the FCC, *Journal of Regulatory Economics*, **15** (3), 267-292 (1999).

Appendix

Proof of proposition (10)

Substituting the demand function and the tariff expression (8) in the profit function (6), we obtain:

$$\pi_1^A = \left(p_1^A - c_1^A - \frac{K\left(r - sp_1^B\right)MS_1^B t_1^{Aa}}{\left(a - bp_1^A\right)NS_1^A} \right)\left(a - bp_1^A\right)S_1^A N + \left(t_1^{Aa} - c_1^A\right)\left(r - sp_1^B\right)S_1^B M$$

$$\pi_2^A = \left(p_2^A - c_2^A - \frac{K\left(r - sp_2^B\right)MS_2^B t_2^{Aa}}{\left(a - bp_2^A\right)NS_2^A} \right)\left(a - bp_2^A\right)S_2^A N + \left(t_2^{Aa} - c_2^A\right)\left(r - sp_2^B\right)S_2^B M$$

the maximization process is given by:

$$\frac{\partial \pi_1^A}{\partial p_1^A} = \left\{ 1 - \frac{b\left(r - sp_1^B\right)MKS_1^B t_1^{Aa}}{\left(a - bp_1^A\right)^2 NS_1^A} + \frac{\sigma\left(-a + 2bp_1^A\right)\left(r - sp_1^B\right)MKS_1^B t_1^{Aa}}{\left(a - bp_1^A\right)NS_1^{A^2}} \right\}\left(a - bp_1^A\right)NS_1^A +$$

$$\left\{ p_1^A - c_1^A - \frac{\left(r - sp_1^B\right)MKS_1^B t_1^{Aa}}{\left(a - bp_1^A\right)NS_1^A} \right\}\left\{ N\sigma\left(a - bp_1^A\right)\left(-a + 2bp_1^A\right) - bNS_1^A \right\} = 0$$

$$\frac{\partial \pi_2^A}{\partial p_2^A} = \left\{ 1 - \frac{b\left(r - sp_2^B\right)MKS_2^B t_2^{Aa}}{\left(a - bp_2^A\right)^2 NS_2^A} + \frac{\sigma\left(-a + 2bp_2^A\right)\left(r - sp_2^B\right)MKS_2^B t_2^{Aa}}{\left(a - bp_2^A\right)NS_2^{A^2}} \right\}\left(a - bp_2^A\right)NS_2^A +$$

$$\left\{ p_2^A - c_2^A - \frac{\left(r - sp_2^B\right)MKS_2^B t_2^{Aa}}{\left(a - bp_2^A\right)NS_2^A} \right\}\left\{ N\sigma\left(a - bp_2^A\right)\left(-a + 2bp_2^A\right) - bNS_2^B \right\} = 0$$

Analogous solutions can be derived for market B.

The solution of the system (available from authors on request) is obtained using a software for advanced mathematics (Maple 9).

Chapter 3

MODELING COMPETITION AMONG WIRELESS SERVICE PROVIDERS

Alexander Zemlianov[1], Gustavo de Veciana[1] *

[1]*Department of Electrical and Computer Engineering*
The University of Texas at Austin
zemliano,gustavo@ece.utexas.edu

Abstract   We consider a scenario where a population of customers is spatially distributed in a region which is served by two wireless service providers that offer Internet Access via two noninterfering technologies: one having a uniform coverage over the region (e.g. WAN), and the other, a limited coverage (e.g. WiFi "hotspots"). We assume that customers are equipped with "dual mode" wireless communication devices that have the capability to select which among the available providers to use. We introduce a stochastic geometric model for the locations of customers and providers' access points and a utility-based mechanism modeling how devices select among providers. In particular, we assume that each device makes greedy decisions at random times, i.e., selects the available provider offering the highest utility at that time. We demonstrate that this process may have multiple equilibria, and prove that the system will almost surely evolve to one of the equilibrium configurations, starting from any initial configuration for users' choices. We also provide conditions under which the set of equilibria is relatively "tight" – in this case the equilibrium configuration of agents' choices is "maxmin fair" and thus is desirable if providers wish to cooperate in providing users with worst case performance guarantees. As an application of our framework we analyze the WAN and WiFi competition in an asymptotic scenario where the service zones of WAN provider are much larger than those of WiFi access providers.

Keywords: 3G, WiFi, multi-mode devices, decision making, heterogeneous wireless networks, multi-provider wireless networks, competition, equilibria, performance, scalability

*The authors' research has been supported in part by National Science Foundation under grant ECS-0225448.

Introduction

Moving decision-making from access points to communication devices provides a path to achieving scalability in future complex and diverse networking landscapes [1]. Thus, we believe that increasingly, end-nodes will have the capability to use multiple communication modes to transfer data among themselves and/or connect to the wired network. For example, a "dual-mode" phone may be able to connect to a wide area cellular network or to an IEEE 802.11 LAN access point [2]. Users of such devices are able to decide which mode of communication they will use. In fact, such decision-making would likely be carried out by a software "agent" driven by users' preferences or engineering design goals. For example, decisions could be based on proximity, amount of interference, quality of service, or, more abstractly, based on a utility function capturing a user's valuation for the available services and their respective costs. Furthermore, decisions might be based on "local" estimates and/or "global" signaling from providers, e.g., a "price" signal. Through such signals, the providers can guide agent's local decisions towards ones that are system or socially optimal.

Giving such freedom of choice to end-nodes is likely to affect system performance, and will result in competition among devices for the best resource (e.g. access point) as well as competition among providers to get a larger share of subscribers. This paper is a first step towards understanding such competition. We consider a scenario where a spatially distributed population of customers are equipped with dual mode devices and are served (on the downlink) by two wireless service providers. We assume that one of the providers utilizes a wide area network (WAN) technology, e.g. IS95, whereas the other provider uses a set of non-interfering wireless local area network access points (APs) e.g. IEEE 802.11 (WiFi "hotspots"). Our objective is to develop a framework to analyze the interplay among the agents' decision rules, technological aspects, such as coverage and aggregate bandwidth available at the access points, and the densities of agents and access points, will affect the ability of providers to compete for a share of subscribers.

In Section 1 we formulate the stochastic geometric model for providers' service zones and define utility-based decision rules. In Section 2 we prove convergence to equilibrium configurations for agents' decisions, and then investigate the properties of the equilibrium in Section 3. Lastly, in Section 4 we will demonstrate how our results can be used to estimate the regimes where the hotspots and WAN APs are competitive, i.e. the majority of agents exert nontrivial choices.

1. Model for the network geometry and agents' decisions

To model the geometry of the network we use the stochastic-geometric framework introduced in [4]. The basic idea is to represent the locations of subscribers and access points as realizations of spatial point processes (e.g. Poisson) and the service zones associated with the access points as functionals of the realizations of these processes. The main advantage of such models is that they allow one to analytically capture the effect of spatial variations in the system based on a reduced set of salient parameters.

We will use three point processes Π^a, Π^h and Π^w, to represent the locations of agents, hotspots and WAN APs respectively. At this point we do not restrict ourselves by considering particular distributions those processes might have. Instead, we require all three of them be simple processes (see, e.g. [5]) so that the location of each WAN or hotspot AP is not shared by any other AP. Below we define some notation that will be used throughout the paper.

- $\pi^a = \{a_i\}_{i=1}^{\infty}$, $\pi^h = \{h_k\}_{k=1}^{\infty}$ and $\pi^w = \{w_m\}_{m=1}^{\infty}$ – represent realizations of Π^a, Π^h and Π^w on the plane. For brevity, we use a_i to denote both the agent and its location (similarly for hotspots and WAN APs).

- $\pi(A)$ – all points of the realization π of a point process Π that fall within the set A.

- $|\pi(A)|$ – the number of points of the realization π that fall within the set A.

- $|x|$ – the length of vector $x \in \mathbb{R}^2$.

- $B(x, r)$ – the disc of radius r centered at point $x \in \mathbb{R}^2$.

- V_m^w – the Voronoi cell of WAN AP $w_m \in \pi^w$. (The Voronoi cell associated with the point y_i of realization π is defined as the set of points on the plane that are closer to y_i than to any other point $y_j \in \pi \setminus \{y_i\}$.)

- V_k^h – the Voronoi cell of hotspot AP $h_k \in \pi^h$.

- $\mathcal{K}_m = \{k : h_k \in \pi^h(V_m^w)\}$ – the indices of hotspots located within the Voronoi cell V_m^w.

- S_k^h – the service zone (see below) of hotspot AP h_k.

- S_m^w – the service zone of WAN AP w_m.

We will refer to the "service zone" of WAN or hotspot AP as the set of locations on the plane, that the AP can serve. We assume that agents which fall within the service zones of several APs are able to choose which AP to connect to. In the next few paragraphs we describe our models for the service zones associated with each AP as well as the criterion each agent uses to connect to a particular access point.

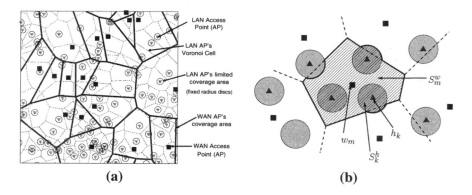

Figure 3.1. (**a**): Boxes represent APs of the WAN provider, whereas triangles represent the APs of the hotspots. The coverage area of each box is modeled by its Voronoi cell, while that of the triangles is modeled by discs of radius d centered at the triangles. (**b**): Voronoi cell of WAN AP "augmented" with hotspots' service zones as the service zone for this WAN AP.

Service zones for hotspots.   Note that the coverage of a hotspot is usually limited due to constraints on transmit power of devices operating in unlicensed spectrum. Thus with each hotspot AP $h_k \in \pi^h$ we associate a disc $B(h_k, d)$ of some radius $d > 0$ and assume that the service from h_k is feasible only within this disc (see Figure 3.1 (a)). In addition, we assume that agents desiring to connect to a hotspot will connect only to the closest feasible hotspot, which yields a service zone S_k^h for hotspot AP h_k given by:

$$S_k^h \triangleq V_k^h \cap B(h_k, d).$$

Service zones for the WAN.   By contrast with hotspots, WAN service covers all spatial locations. Still, the definition of service zones depends on the underlying technology. For instance, in CDMA-based technologies the association of mobiles with APs is different for the up- and down-links [6]. Moreover, the service zones corresponding to two different WAN APs are in general not disjoint and, in fact, overlap to permit soft handoffs.

Appropriate models for CDMA service zones have been recently considered in [7], [8]. In particular the authors have shown that under some conditions (large enough power at APs, large attenuation) the service zone associated with any AP converges to its associated Voronoi cell. This suggests that Voronoi cells might be a reasonable model for service zones.

Note, however, that if we represent the service zones as Voronoi cells, agents that belong to hotspots that are crossed by the boundary of a Voronoi cell associated with some WAN AP might be choosing between this hotspot and one of two WAN APs. This poses certain problems in the analysis of the model, because agents' decisions interact across WAN AP service zones. To overcome this difficulty we shall impose a constraint that each agent $a_i \in \pi^a$ selects between the closest hotspot AP h_k (if it is covered by its service zone) and the WAN AP w_m *which contains h_k in its service zone* (see Figure 3.1 (b)). Whenever the hotspots' service range d is much smaller than the average size of a WAN cell, this assumption will not significantly affect our results. We will define the service zone of WAN AP w_m as the "augmented" Voronoi cell V_m^w:

$$S_m^w = V_m^w \bigcup \left(\bigcup_{k \in \mathcal{K}_m} S_k^h \right) \setminus \left(\bigcup_{l \in \cup_{n \neq m} \mathcal{K}_n} S_l^h \right) .$$

Assumption 1.1. *The service zones S_m^w, $\forall m \in \mathbb{N}$, contain an a.s. finite number of agents and hotspots.*

Agents' selection criterion.   Let C_m be the subset of S_m^w that includes only the area where agents have the option to choose among a hotspot and WAN AP w_m:

$$C_m \triangleq \bigcup_{k \in \mathcal{K}_m} S_k^h ,$$

and let $\bar{C}_m = S_m^w \setminus C_m$. We assume that any agents whose location is in $\bar{C}_m$ can not make a choice and thus connect to the WAN AP w_m. By contrast, an agent $a_i \in C_m$ is also covered by some hotspot h_k's service zone and can choose between *either* connecting to h_k or the WAN AP w_m.

Consider an agent a_i that is connected to a WAN AP at time t. We model her level of satisfaction with the service via a the utility function $U^w(N^w(a_i,t))$ of the total number of agents $N^w(a_i,t)$ that at time t are connected to the same WAN AP as agent a_i. Similarly, we assign a utility function $U^h(N^h(a_j,t))$ to an agent a_j to model her level of satisfaction if she is connected to a hotspot, where $N^h(a_j,t)$ denotes the total number of agents that are connected at time t to the same hotspot as the agent a_j. Thus, in this framework, utility functions are only "congestion" dependent and independent of positions of agents relative to the access points[1]. In the sequel we will use the following assumption for the utility functions:

Assumption 1.2. $U^w(\cdot) : \mathbb{R}^+ \mapsto \mathbb{R}$ *and* $U^h(\cdot) : \mathbb{R}^+ \mapsto \mathbb{R}$ *are continuous, monotonically decreasing functions.*

Now we describe how we model the decision process in this system. We postulate that an agent $a_i \in C_m$ switches at time t to the WAN AP w_m from its hotspot if and only if she was connected to this hotspot AP at time t^- and

$$U^w \left(N^w(a_i,t^-) + 1 \right) > U^h \left(N^h(a_i,t^-) \right),$$

where t^- refers to the time immediately prior to t. Similarly, the agent a_i switches to a hotspot AP at time t if and only if she was connected to a WAN AP at t^- and

$$U^h\left(N^h(a_i,t^-)+1\right) \geq U^w\left(N^w(a_i,t^-)\right).$$

Note that we break ties in favor of hotspots.

Assumption 1.3. *Agents' decision times within C_m are given by a simple point process Φ_m with realizations ϕ_m which obey the following:*

- ϕ_m *almost surely contains infinitely many points in $\mathbb{R}^+$, i.e. $\phi_m = \{s_k\}_{k=1}^{\infty}$, where $s_k \in \mathbb{R}^+$ for $k = 1,2,\ldots$*

- *each point of ϕ_m is associated with a decision time for a unique agent within C_m*

- *a point $s_k \in \phi_m$ is a decision time of the agent $a_i \in C_m$ with some **positive** probability p_i, which possibly depends on realization ϕ_m up to time s_k and the history of agents choices up to time s_k.*

Assumption 1.3 postulates that only one agent within C_m can make decision at a time, each agent has unlimited opportunities for decision making, and any decision time with some positive probability is associated with a particular agent.

2.   Convergence to equilibrium.

We call a particular configuration of agent's choices an equilibrium configuration, if and only if the system remains in this configuration indefinitely provided it starts in this configuration.

Proposition 2.1. *(**Convergence to equilibrium.**) Consider the service zone S_m^w for a particular fixed realization π^a, π^h and π^w. Then under Assumptions 1.1-1.3, given any initial configuration of connections at time $t = 0$, the system converges a.s. to an equilibrium configuration as $t \to \infty$.*

Here we will give the essential idea of the proof whereas the rest of the details we placed in Appendix 3.A.1. Note that the dynamics of the configuration of agents' decisions in S_m^w follow a continuous-time Markov chain with state $X(t) := \{X(a_i,t)|\ a_i \in \pi^a(C_m)\}$, where $X(a_i,t) \in \{0,1\}$ denotes the "connection state" of the agent a_i at time t. It takes the value 0 if the agent is connected to a hotspot, and 1 if she is connected to a WAN AP. We shall classify decision times for this chain as "up", "down" and "stay", corresponding to an agent switching from a hotspot to the WAN AP, vice versa, or staying with her current choice. For simplicity we uniformize the continuous time chain, and focus on a discrete-time Markov chain capturing the state at decision times.

Initialization:
  $s = 1$ and $X(s) = X(0)$
  go to Up-transition phase

Up-transition phase:
  repeat:
    { choose $a_j = \arg\max_{a_i \in A^u(s)} N^h(a_i, s)$
    $K(s) := N^h(a_j, s)$
    let a_j make an "up" transition
    update the state $X(s)$
    $s := s + 1$ }
  until $A^u(s) = \emptyset$
  go to Down-transition phase

Down-transition phase:
  if $A^d(s) \neq \emptyset$:
    { choose any $a_j \in A^d(s)$
    let a_j make a "down" transition
    update the state $X(s)$
    $K(s) := K(s-1)$
    $s := s + 1$
    go to Up-transition phase }
  otherwise: done

Table 3.1. Pseudo-code for constructing the path $\mathcal{P}$ converging to equilibrium.

We shall denote these times via $s = 1, 2, \ldots$. The transition probabilities for the discrete-time Markov chain are comprised of two factors: the probability that a particular agent reconsiders her decision at that time and whether, given the current configuration, the agent would change providers.

By Assumption 1.1, each service zone contains an a.s. finite number of agents, thus there is an a.s. finite number of possible configurations for agents' choices. It follows that some of the states must be revisited by the chain infinitely often. To show the convergence of the process to an equilibrium, it suffices to construct a feasible path for the chain evolution which starting from any initial configuration hits an equilibrium state, and has a positive probability of occurring. Since the state space is a.s. finite, and at least one state is visited infinitely often, this guarantees that the chain is transient, i.e. reaches an equilibrium state with probability 1.

Below we describe the steps of an algorithm to construct a path $\mathcal{P}$ consisting of a sequence of transitions for the state $X(s)$, which, starting from any arbitrary configuration of agents' choices $X(0)$, ends up in an equilibrium configuration after a finite number of steps. Let $A^u(s)$ denote the set of agents that, given the configuration at time s, could make "up" transitions and $A^d(s)$ the set of agents that can make "down" transitions. We describe our algorithm in terms of the pseudo-code shown in Table 3.1. Note that the algorithm assumes that an agent making her decision at time slot $s \geq 1$ is basing this decision by observing the state of the system prior to that time, i.e. at time $s - 1$.

In short, after initialization, the algorithm alternates between phases where "up" and "down" transitions occur. During the Up-transition phase only the "up"-switches occur, and agents performing these transitions are selected from the most "congested" hotspots. This phase ends once the set of agents able to perform the "up" switches is empty. At that time the algorithm switches to the Down-transition phase, where at most one agent performs a "down" switch. If an agent performs an "up" switch at time s, we track the number of agents, $K(s)$, that shared the hotspot with this agent prior to her switching at time s.

To show that this algorithm finishes in finite time in Appendix 3.A.1 we prove that $K(s), s = 1, 2, \ldots$ is a non-increasing sequence that at each time bounds above the number of agents within each hotspot in S_m^w. Thus since $K(\cdot)$ is integer valued and non-negative, it must converge to some value K_m^* in an a.s. finite time. Once $K(\cdot)$ converges, we prove that only down transitions can occur, and since there is an a.s. finite number of agents in each WAN APs service location, an equilibrium must be reached in finite time.

In summary, we have shown that from any starting configuration there exists a path, $\mathcal{P}$, that reaches an equilibrium state. Moreover, by Assumption 1.3 the overall probability of the path $\mathcal{P}$ is strictly positive. Since the state space is finite, there must be a state which is visited infinitely often. Whence the Markov chain will necessarily eventually hit an equilibrium state.

3.   Structure of equilibrium.

In this section we will give a characterization of the system state, i.e., configuration of agents' decisions, define a notion of uniqueness, and analyze under what conditions the system equilibrium is unique. We first introduce some additional notation[2]

- $M_m^w = \left| \pi^a(S_m^w) \right|$ – the number of agents located within the service zone of WAN AP w_m.

- $M_k^h = \left| \pi^a(S_k^h) \right|$ – the number of agents located within the service zone of hotspot h_k.

- $M_{C_m}^w = \left| \pi^a(C_m) \right|$ – the number of agents located within C_m, i.e. agents that can make choices.

- $M_{\bar{C}_m}^w = M_m^w - M_{C_m}^w$ – the number of agents located within $\bar{C}_m$, i.e. the agents that can *not* make choices.

- $H_m = \left|\pi^h(S_m^w)\right|$ – the number of hotspots located within the service zone of WAN AP w_m.

- $X_m^{\pi^a,\pi^h,\pi^w} \triangleq \{X(a_i)| \; a_i \in \pi^a(C_m)\}$ – denotes the system configuration in service zone S_m^w associated with a fixed realization π^a, π^h and π^w. Here $X(a_i) \in \{0,1\}$ takes the value 0 if agent a_i is connected to a hotspot, and 1 if she is connected to a WAN AP.

- $\mathcal{T}_m = \mathcal{T}_m(\pi^a,\pi^h,\pi^w)$ – the a.s. finite set of possible system configurations (states) in S_m^w for a given realization π^a, π^h and π^w.

- $\mathcal{E}_m$ – the set of all system configurations $c \in \mathcal{T}_m$ that correspond to equilibria in S_m^w.

- $\mathcal{F}_m = \mathcal{F}_m(\pi^a,\pi^h,\pi^w)$ – subset of $\mathcal{E}_m$ which consists of only "fair" equilibria (see below).

- $N_m^w(c)$ – the number of agents that connect to WAN AP w_m in configuration $c \in \mathcal{T}_m$.

- $N_k^h(c)$ – the number of agents that connect to hotspot AP h_k in configuration $c \in \mathcal{T}_m$.

- $(U^w)^{-1}(\cdot)$ – unique and decreasing, by Assumption 1.2 inverse of $U^w(\cdot)$.

- $(U^h)^{-1}(\cdot)$ – unique and decreasing inverse of $U^h(\cdot)$.

- $G(\cdot) \triangleq (U^h)^{-1} \circ U^w(\cdot)$ – nondecreasing composition of $(U^h)^{-1}$ and $U^w(\cdot)$

- $J(\cdot) \triangleq (U^w)^{-1} \circ U^h(\cdot)$ – nondecreasing composition of $(U^w)^{-1}$ and $U^h(\cdot)$

Characterization of a configuration. For any fixed realization π^a, π^h and π^w consider only WAN APs w_m that have at least one hotspot in their service areas, i.e. $\mathcal{K}_m \neq \emptyset$. For such m we characterize the system configuration $c \in \mathcal{T}_m$ for the service zone S_m^w by a vector $\mathbf{N}_m(c) \triangleq \{N_k^h(c)| \; k \in \mathcal{K}_m\}$. The vector $\mathbf{N}_m(c)$ determines how many agents are connected to each hotspot h_k for $k \in \mathcal{K}_m$ in configuration $c \in \mathcal{T}_m$.

Definition 3.1. *We say that two configurations for agents' choices characterized by $\mathbf{N}_m(c)$ and $\mathbf{N}_m(c')$ are equivalent, and write $\mathbf{N}_m(c) \sim \mathbf{N}_m(c')$, if the components of the vector $\mathbf{N}_m(c)$ are a permutation of those of $\mathbf{N}_m(c')$.*

Fair equilibria.

Definition 3.2. *We say that a configuration $c \in \mathcal{T}_m$ is "fair" if its characterization $\mathbf{N}_m(c) = \{N_k^h(c)|k \in \mathcal{K}_m\}$ satisfies, for some $K \in \mathbb{Z}^+$:*

$$\forall k \in \mathcal{K}_m : \begin{cases} K-1 \leq N_k^h(c) \leq K, & \text{if } M_k^h \geq K, \\ N_k^h(c) = M_k^h, & \text{otherwise}. \end{cases}$$

If c is also an equilibrium configuration we say that c is a "fair" equilibrium.

We shall interpret this definition via Figure 3.2. The hexagonal region is a schematic representation of the service zone S_m^w, while the positions of the cylinders represent the locations of hotspots. The height of each cylinder represents the overall number of agents that fall within the service zone of a particular hotspot.

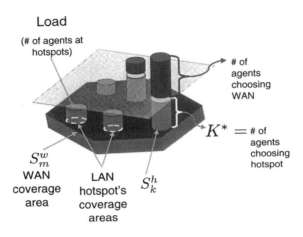

Figure 3.2. Structure of a "fair" configuration.

Assume that the slicing plane in Figure 3.2 is one unit thick and its upper surface is placed at integer-valued heights K above the surface of S_m^w. Any "fair" configuration has the following assignment of agents to APs:

- All agents in $S_m^w \setminus C_m$ connect to WAN AP w_m.

- A number of agents corresponding to the parts of cylinders that fall under the lower surface of the slicing plane connect to their respective hotspots.

- A number of agents corresponding to the parts of cylinders above the upper surface of the plane connect to the WAN AP w_m.

- Finally, a number of agents corresponding to the parts of cylinders within the slice connect to either their associated hotspots or WAN AP w_m.

In what follows, to avoid ambiguity we will always associate a fair configuration f with the "cutoff" plane at level[3] $K_m(f) = \max_{k \in \mathcal{K}_m} N_k^h(f)$. Note, that in fair configuration f the hotspots having more than $K_m(f)$ agents in their service zones yield the "overload" to the WAN AP w_m. As a result the number of agents connected to those hotspots is nearly the same, i.e. either $K_m(f)$ or $K_m(f) - 1$.

By the construction used to prove Proposition 2.1 we can always find a position of the slicing plane, $K = K_m^*$, and an assignment of agents corresponding to the parts of cylinders at the slice, so that the connection configuration in S_m^w is a fair equilibrium. This results in statement **(i)** of Proposition 3.1.

Proposition 3.1. *For any realization π^a, π^h and π^w we have that:*
(i) The set of all fair equilibria, $\mathcal{F}_m$, is not empty.
(ii) All fair equilibria have equivalent characterizations, i.e. for all $f, f' \in \mathcal{F}_m$, $\mathbf{N}_m(f) \sim \mathbf{N}_m(f')$.

For the proof of statement (ii) of Proposition 3.1, see Appendix 3.A.2.

Non-uniqueness of equilibrium.

Definition 3.3. *For a particular realization π^a, π^h and π^w we say that the equilibrium in S_m^w is unique if for any $e, e' \in \mathcal{E}_m$ we have $\mathbf{N}_m(e) \sim \mathbf{N}_m(e')$.*

Note that agents' decisions are discrete in nature, and unfortunately, this can lead to multiple equilibria in the system, even when we understand uniqueness in the weak sense of Definition 3.3. Below we show this via a simple example. Observe that for all equilibrium configurations $e \in \mathcal{E}_m$ we must have that:

$$U^h\left(N_k^h(e)+1\right) < U^w\left(N_m^w(e)\right) \text{ and } U^h\left(N_k^h(e)\right) \geq U^w\left(N_m^w(e)+1\right) \quad (3.1)$$

for all $k \in \mathcal{K}_m$ such that the service zone S_k^h has an agent connected to the WAN AP w_m and an agent connected to h_k. Also we must have that:

$$U^h\left(N_l^h(e)\right) \geq U^w\left(N_m^w(e)+1\right),$$

for all $l \in \mathcal{K}_m$ such that the service zone S_l^h has *all* of its agents connected to h_l. Lastly,

$$U^h(1) < U^w\left(N_m^w(e)\right), \quad (3.2)$$

must be satisfied for all $p \in \mathcal{K}_m$ such that all agents within S_p^h are connected to w_m in equilibrium. It follows from (3.1) that:

$$G\left(N_m^w(e)\right) - 1 < N_k^h(e) \leq G\left(N_m^w(e)+1\right), \quad (3.3)$$

for hotspots $h_k \in \pi^h(S_m^w)$ with at least one agent connected to the WAN AP w_k. Note that, depending on the utility functions there can be more than one integer solution to the inequalities (3.3). Consider, for example:

$$U^h(N) = N^{-\beta}, \quad U^w(N) = N^{-\alpha}, \quad (3.4)$$

where $\alpha > \beta > 0$. In this case $G(N) = N^{\alpha/\beta}$, and the gap between the right and left hand side in (3.3) increases with $N_m^w(e)$. In other words, when the number of agents, not covered by hotspots is large enough, there can be many integer solutions to the inequalities (3.3). Hence, "unfair" equilibria can be constructed easily from the fair one. For example we could switch some number L of agents from WAN AP w_m to a particular hotspot h_k and the same number L of agents from some other hotspot h_l within the same WAN AP w_m. Note that this procedure would not change the number of agents connected to the WAN AP. If L is selected so that the $N_k^h(e) - L$ and $N_l^h(e) + L$ are still within the bounds (3.3), this procedure would result in a feasible equilibrium which is not equivalent to the fair one.

Conditions guaranteeing uniqueness and fairness.   One might ask under what conditions the equilibrium in S_m^w is unique. The following result assumes that the utilities have a particular property, and that the cells of the WAN provider are large enough to guarantee that a sufficiently large number of agents connects to the WAN AP in equilibrium.

Proposition 3.2. *Suppose that there exists $\overline{N}$ such that for all $N \geq \overline{N}$*

$$G(N+1) - G(N) < 1, \tag{3.5}$$

and assume that the number of agents that can not make choices in service zone S_m^w satisfies:

$$M_{\tilde{C}_m}^w \geq \overline{N}. \tag{3.6}$$

Then, the equilibrium in S_m^w is unique and fair.

We prove this proposition in Appendix 3.A.3. In general, if the property (3.5) holds then it must be the case that the utility function associated with connections to hotspots decrements faster in the number of connected agents than the utility associated with connections to the WAN AP[4]. One such example is given by (3.4) with $\beta > \alpha > 0$.

System performance in equilibrium.   Let us define $U_m^{min}(c)$ to be the minimum over the utilities of agents within S_m^w that choose according to configuration $c \in \mathcal{T}_m$. We refer to $U_m^{min}(c)$ as the utility of the bottleneck agent for the configuration c.

Proposition 3.3. *If the equilibrium in S_m^w is unique, then $U_m^{min}(c) \leq U_m^{min}(f)$, for all $f \in \mathcal{F}_m$ and $c \in \mathcal{T}_m$.*

We prove this proposition in Appendix 3.A.4. Thus, when equilibrium configuration of agents' choices is unique, it would maximize the utility of the bottleneck agents over all possible configurations of agents' choices. When agents' utilities are associated with a congestion-only-dependent performance metric, utility based choice mechanism would realize equilibria that are favorable from the point of view of worst case performance. We further explore the performance aspect of a multi-provider scenario in [11].

4. Estimation of competitiveness of WAN vs WiFi hotspots.

In this section we discuss how to compute the fractions of agents that are connected to WAN APs and hotspots in equilibrium. We choose these fractions to be our metric to assess the competitiveness of one provider versus another. For simplicity of exposition we assume[5] that $\Pi^{w,\alpha}$ is a deterministic process such that the Voronoi cells associated with each WAN AP are geometrically similar and have the same area α. We further assume that the processes Π^h and Π^a are stationary Poisson processes with densities λ^h and λ^a respectively.

The non-uniqueness of equilibria poses certain difficulties in analyzing the model for arbitrary utilities, densities and cell sizes. Note that in practice, the sizes of WAN service zones typically would exceed that of hotspots[6]. Thus, to simplify our analysis we will study the system where the size of WAN service zones, α is large enough to contain a large number of agents and hotspots. Intuitively, one might expect that when the WAN service zones grow in area, the set of different equilibria becomes tighter, i.e., a type of the Law of Large Numbers making the system more amenable to analysis. In the next paragraph we demonstrate that this intuition is indeed correct.

Setup for asymptotic analysis.. We consider a collection of deterministic point processes $\{\Pi^{w,\alpha}\}$ indexed by $\alpha \in \mathbb{R}^+$ where each represents the spatial locations of WAN APs that are increasingly spread out. In particular, we suppose that the area of the Voronoi cell associated with any point $w_m^\alpha \in \pi_\alpha^w$ is equal to α, and let α grow. Let us also assume that for each $\alpha > 0$, $\pi^{w,\alpha}$ contains a point w_0^α at the origin.

In what follows we will consider the service zones of WAN AP w_0^α and we will use the same notation as before to refer to the number of agents and hotspots falling within the service zone of the WAN AP $w_0^\alpha \in \pi^{w,\alpha}$, but indicate the dependence on the area α via the corresponding superscript. Thus, for example we will write H_0^α to indicate the number of hotspots that fall within the service zone $S_0^{w,\alpha}$ of the WAN AP w_0^α. In addition, we use $\mathbb{E}_0^h[A_0]$ to denote the expectation of the quantity A_k associated with a typical hotspot h_k (see, e.g. [10]).

For fixed λ^h and λ^a the service area of each WAN AP will have to support a larger (roughly linear in α) number of users as α grows. Therefore, we will assume that the WAN resources also scale with α. This leads to a scaling requirement on the utility function associated with connecting to the WAN. Let $U^{w,\alpha}(\cdot)$ denote the utility function associated with connecting to the WAN when the area of a Voronoi cell of any WAN AP is α, and assume that $U^{w,\alpha}(\cdot)$ satisfies Assumption 1.2 for utility functions. Define $J^\alpha(N) = (U^{w,\alpha})^{-1} \circ U^h(\cdot)$ (where $U^h(\cdot)$ is independent of α) and assume the following:

Assumption 4.1. *The scaling of $J^\alpha(N)$ with α is such that:*

1. $J^\alpha(N) = \alpha j(N)$ *for any* $N \in \mathbb{N}$,

2. $\lim_{N\to\infty} j(N) = \infty$,

3. *There exists $\bar{N}$, such that $j^{-1}\left((N+1)/\alpha\right) - j^{-1}\left(N/\alpha\right) < 1$, for all $N \geq \bar{N}$ and each $\alpha > 0$.*

4. *For any integer $K \geq 2$, $u(K) \neq j(K), j(K-1)$, where*

$$u(K) = \lambda^a e^{-\lambda^h \pi d^2} + \lambda^h \mathbb{E}_0^h \left[(M_0^h - K + 1)\mathbf{1}_{\{M_0^h \geq K\}} \right]. \qquad (3.7)$$

The interpretation of these assumptions are as follows. Condition 1 means that the resources of WAN APs scale linearly in the area α of their service zones. For example, we might have $U^h(N) = \frac{B^h}{N}$ and $U^{w,\alpha}(N) = \frac{\alpha B^w}{N}$, in which case $J^\alpha(N) = \frac{\alpha B^w}{B^h} N$. The second condition follows if, as more agents connect to a resource, the utility of those agents is strictly decreasing to zero. The third condition will allow us to use Proposition 3.2 to argue that the equilibrium in $S_m^{w,\alpha}$ is unique with probability approaching 1 as $\alpha \to \infty$. Finally, the last condition is technical (see Appendix 3.A.5), and satisfied for the cases of interest.

We study the asymptotics of this system in Appendix 3.A.5. The results of our study are summarized in Theorem 4.1. Here when we say that an event E^α happens with high probability (w.h.p.) we mean that $\lim_{\alpha\to\infty} \mathbb{P}(E^\alpha) = 1$.

Theorem 4.1. *Consider any realization of the Poisson point processes Π^a and Π^h and the sequence of deterministic processes $\{\Pi^{w,\alpha}\}$ with Voronoi cells of area α and each with a typical cell centered at the origin. Under the scaling Assumption 4.1 we have:*

1. *The equilibrium f_0^α in $S_0^{w,\alpha}$ is unique and fair w.h.p.*

2. *The largest number of agents connected to each hotspot in this equilibrium, $N_{\max}^{h,\alpha}(f_0^\alpha) = \max_{k \in \mathcal{K}_0^\alpha} N_k^h(f_0^\alpha)$ has a limit:*

$$\lim_{\alpha\to\infty} N_{\max}^{h,\alpha}(f_0^\alpha) = N_{max}^{h,\infty},$$

for some integer $N_{max}^{h,\infty} \geq 0$.

3. *We have that $N_{\max}^{h,\infty} > 0$ if and only if $j(1) \leq \lambda^a$ in which case it is given by the largest integer solution for $K \geq 1$ of the inequality*

$$u(K) \geq j(K), \qquad (3.8)$$

where u(K) is given by (3.7).

The basic idea of the proof is to leverage the analogs of the Law of Large Numbers for functionals on random sets, e.g. Voronoi cells, which have distributions dependent on realizations of point processes. We also show that fluctuations from averages for the quantities of interest do not grow "too fast" as the area of the WAN service zones grows. This allows us to express the position of the asymptotic "cutoff" $N_{max}^{h,\infty}$, in terms of averages of functionals of the realizations of Π^h and Π^a.

Based on Theorem 4.1 the analysis of competition when the WAN cell sizes are "large" reduces to comparing the number $N_{max}^{h,\infty} = K^*$ to the average number of agents falling within the service zone of a typical hotspot. In particular, if

$$K^* \gg \mathbb{E}_0^h \left[M_0^h \right] = \frac{\lambda^a (1 - e^{-\lambda^h \pi d^2})}{\lambda^h}, \tag{3.9}$$

then hotspots retain most of the agents that fall within their service zones in equilibrium. We classify this case as hotspots effectively competing with the WAN. On the other hand if

$$K^* \ll \frac{\lambda^a (1 - e^{-\lambda^h \pi d^2})}{\lambda^h}, \tag{3.10}$$

the hotspots yield most of their agents to the WAN APs in equilibrium. In this case we say that hotspots are not competitive with respect to the WAN. Using Theorem 4.1, we can suggest the following heuristic approach to estimate the value of N_{max}^h. In general one has to solve for $K \geq 0$ the equation:

$$U^w \left(\lambda^a |V| e^{-\lambda^h \pi |d|^2} + \lambda^h \mathbb{E}_0^h [P_0(K)] \right) = U^h(K), \tag{3.11}$$

where $P_0(K) = (M_0^h - K + 1)\mathbf{1}_{\{M_0^h \geq K\}}$. Note that since the left side of (3.11) is monotonically increasing in K and the right – monotonically decreasing, the solution either does not exist ($K^* = 0$) or is unique, when it exists. Unfortunately, there is no closed form expression for the term $\mathbb{E}_0^h [P_0(K)]$ and hence simulation has to be used to estimate it. However, to test if hotspots are not competitive with respect to the WAN one could use the following simple criterion. Clearly, (3.10) holds if the solution to:

$$U^w(\lambda^a |V| - \lambda^h K |V|) = U^h(K), \tag{3.12}$$

falls much below the value $\lambda^a / \lambda^h (1 - e^{-\lambda^h \pi d^2})$. Note that this allows for a simple intuitive interpretation. The number of agents and hotspots occupying WAN service zone tends to $\lambda^a |V|$ and $\lambda^h |V|$ respectively when $|V|$ is large. The number of agents connected in equilibrium to hotspots tends to $\lambda^h |V| K$, whenever $K \ll \lambda^a \mathbb{E}|S_k^h|$, since then we can assume that each hotspot has exactly K agents connected to its AP in equilibrium. Thus the number of agents connected to the WAN AP must tend to:

$$\lambda^a |V| - \lambda^h K |V|,$$

once the size of the WAN service zone gets large enough. Thus, (3.12) follows by equating the utility of agents that are connected to the WAN AP and utility of the ones that are connected to hotspots.

5.   Conclusion

To summarize, we have developed a stochastic geometric model for a system where subscribers with dual mode devices select among two noninterfering wireless service providers – a WAN provider and a second provider (or aggregator) of LAN hotspots. Our model is of interest in that, on the one hand, it captures wireless providers using technologies that might have different capacity and coverage, and on the other hand it captures the role of subscribers decision-making mechanisms in determining the eventual equilibrium. Assuming each subscriber's decision-making agent makes greedy decisions, based on comparing two "congestion" dependent utilities, at random times, we show that an equilibrium configuration would eventually be reached. Further we have characterized such equilibria and shown that they are likely to be close to the fair equilibrium, which corresponds to slicing the excess loads on hotspots, and shifting these to the WAN. In an effort to get numerical estimates for the level at which this slicing occurs, we developed an asymptotic result for the case where WAN service areas are large, which would permit an evaluation of this setting.

The results in this paper can be viewed from different perspectives. On the one hand they permit an evaluation of the competitiveness of the two providers to attract subscribers in their service areas. On the other, they permit a study of how to design decision making mechanisms, i.e., appropriate utility functions, to realize equilibria that may be desirable equilibrium for the overall system. The highlight of this paper is a characterization of such equilibria, that would permit further consideration of the performance and network design implications of wireless systems where users are capable to switch among multiple providers, depending on the key parameters of the system.

Appendix

1.   Details of proof of Proposition 2.1

Proof. Here we show that $K(s)$ is a non-increasing sequence. Indeed, during the execution of an Up-transition Phase, $K(s)$ may change, but can only be reduced, since only agents in $A^u(s)$, and which belong to the most congested hotspots, are selected to make a transition. Now suppose that an Up-transition phase finished at time τ, then $K(\tau-1)$ is the number of agents that shared the hotspot with the last eligible agent prior to her "up" transition. Consider $a_j \in A^d(\tau)$, an eligible agent for a down transition. Note that for any such agent it must be the case that

$$N^h(a_j,\tau) \leq K(\tau-1)-2 \qquad (3.A.1)$$

otherwise the agent that switched up at time $\tau-1$ could not have improved her utility. Indeed, suppose at time $\tau-1$, the agent a_i switched "up", then the following inequality must have been true:

$$U^w\left(N^w(a_i,\tau-1)+1\right) > U^h\left(N^h(a_i,\tau-1)\right). \qquad (3.A.2)$$

Note that $N^w(a_j,\tau) = N^w(a_i,\tau-1)+1$, since both a_j and a_i belong to the same WAN service zone and no other transitions have occurred in the interim. Thus if

$$U^w\left(N^w(a_j,\tau)\right) \leq U^h\left(N^h(a_j,\tau)+1\right)$$

this would contradict to (3.A.2) unless $N^h(a_j,\tau) \leq N^h(a_i,\tau-1)-2 = K(\tau-1)-2$. Thus an agent that makes a "down" transition right after an Up-transition phase can not increase the number of agents on her hotspot beyond $K(\tau-1)-1$. Whence upon reentering the Up-transition phase, if up switches occur they can again only decrease the value of $K(\cdot)$.

Note, that if one or more "down" switches occur in sequence without any intermediate "up" transitions, it still remains the case that $K(s)$ must be an upper bound on the number of agents sharing a hotspot, of an agent that chooses to make an "up" transition at time s. Indeed, assume that the last Up-transition phase, that had an "up" switch, has finished at time $\tau-1 < s$ and the agent a_i has switched "down" at time τ. The agent's a_i's switch has occurred due to the fact that:

$$U^w\left(N^w(a_i,\tau)\right) \leq U^h\left(N^h(a_i,\tau)+1\right)$$

Note that for an agent a_j switching "down" at time $\tau+1$, we have $N^h(a_j,\tau+1) \geq N^h(a_j,\tau)$ and $N^w(a_j,\tau+1) = N^w(a_i,\tau)-1$. Hence,

$$U^w\left(N^w(a_j,\tau+1)\right) \leq U^h\left(N^h(a_j,\tau+1)+1\right)$$

could only be feasible if $N^h(a_j,\tau+1) \leq N^h(a_i,\tau)$, by monotonicity of utilities. But then, in view of (3.A.1):

$$N^h(a_j,\tau+1)+1 \leq K(\tau)-1.$$

By induction, we can show that if $m+1$ such "down" transitions took place without any intermediate "up" transitions, then:

$$N^h(a_k,\tau+m)+1 \leq K(\tau)-1,$$

where a_k is the agent that has performed the last "down"-transition.

Thus $K(s)$ is a non-increasing sequence which bounds the number of agents connected to any hotspot at time s. Also since $K(\cdot)$ is integer valued sequence, it must converge to some value K_m^* in a finite time. Once $K(\cdot)$ converges, only down transitions can occur, and since there is an a.s. finite number of agents in each WAN APs service location, an equilibrium must be reached in finite time. $\qquad \square$

2.   Proof of Proposition 3.1

Proof. Consider any fair equilibrium configuration $f \in \mathcal{F}_m$ and let $K_m(f) = \max_{k \in \mathcal{K}} N_k^h(f)$ give the level of the corresponding slicing plane (see Figure 3.2). We will first show that for any two fair equilibria f and f' we have that $K_m(f) = K_m(f')$.

We show this by contradiction, suppose, in fact that there exist $f, f' \in \mathcal{F}_m$ such that $K_m(f) \neq K_m(f')$. Without loss of generality assume that $K_m(f) > K_m(f')$. Note that in this case for some $l \in \mathcal{K}_m$ we have $N_l^h(f) = K_m(f) \geq 1$. Considering the hotspot h_l, we get

$$U^h\left(K_m(f)\right) \geq U^w(N_m^w(f)+1) \qquad (3.A.3)$$

since otherwise an agent connected to this hotspot would choose to switch to WAN AP w_m which would contradict the fact that f is an equilibrium. Now, for equilibrium f' all hotspots have fewer than or equal to $K_m(f') \leq K_m(f) - 1$ agents, so in particular $N_l^h(f') \leq K_m(f) - 1$. It follows by adding 1 to both sides and the fact that $U^h()$ is monotonically decreasing that:

$$U^h(N_l^h(f')+1) \geq U^h\left(K_m(f)\right). \qquad (3.A.4)$$

At the same time, since $K_m(f') < K_m(f)$ it follows that $N_m^w(f') \geq N_m^w(f) + 1$. Using the fact that $U^w()$ is monotonically decreasing we have that

$$U^w(N_m^w(f)+1) \geq U^w(N_m^w(f')). \qquad (3.A.5)$$

Now putting (3.A.3),(3.A.4) and (3.A.5) together we have that

$$U^h(N_l^h(f')+1) \geq U^w(N_m^w(f'))$$

which implies that under f' an agent on WAN AP w_m would choose to switch to hotspot h_l. This contradicts the fact that f' is an equilibrium. Thus we conclude that for any $f \in \mathcal{F}_m$ we have $K_m(f) = K_m^*$ for some integer K_m^*.

In order to show that all fair equilibria are equivalent, we first argue that for two fair equilibria $f' \neq f$ we must have $N_m^w(f) = N_m^w(f')$. Without loss of generality suppose $N_m^w(f') \geq N_m^w(f) + 1$. Then, for at least one hotspot, say h_l, $N_l^h(f') \leq N_l^h(f) - 1$ which also implies that $N_l^h(f) \geq 1$. For f to be an equilibrium we must have that:

$$U^h\left(N_l^h(f)\right) \geq U^w(N_m^w(f)+1) \geq U^w(N_m^w(f')), \qquad (3.A.6)$$

which follows from the fact that no agent in hotspot h_l wishes to switch to the WAN AP and our assumption. Considering the hotspot h_l under the equilibrium configuration f' we obtain:

$$U^w(N_m^w(f')) > U^h\left(N_l^h(f')+1\right) > U^h(N_l^h(f)), \qquad (3.A.7)$$

which is the consequence of the fact that an agent in h_l connected to the WAN AP w_m has no desire to switch to the hotspot h_l. Clearly, by monotonicity of utilities we have that (3.A.6) is in contradiction to (3.A.7).

Thus we know that if $f, f' \in \mathcal{F}_m$, then we have $N_m^w(f) = N_m^w(f')$ and $K_m(f) = K_m(f') = K_m^*$, for some integer K_m^*. Next we show that all fair equilibria must have equivalent characterizations. Let R denote the number of hotspots in S_m^w that have at least $K_m^* - 1$ agents in their service zones. The equilibrium number of agents connected to such hotspots is between $K_m^* - 1$ and K_m^*. Now assume that $r < R$ of the R hotspots have $K_m^* - 1$ agents and the remaining $R - r$ hotspots have K_m^* agents, connected to their APs under the equilibrium configuration f. Similarly, we assume that $r' < R$ hotspots have $K_m^* - 1$ agents in the equilibrium configuration f'. Equating the total number of agents in the service zone S_m^w in equilibria f and f', we have that:

$$(K-1)r + K(R-r) + \sum_{k \in \mathcal{K}_m,\ M_k^h < K_m^* - 1} M_k^h + N_m^w(f)$$

$$= (K-1)r' + K(R-r') + \sum_{k \in \mathcal{K}_m,\ M_k^h < K_m^* - 1} M_k^h + N_m^w(f').$$

Since $N_m^w(f) = N_m^w(f')$ this leads to $r = r'$, showing that $\mathbf{N}_m(f) \sim \mathbf{N}_m(f')$. □

3. Proof of Proposition 3.2

Proof. By part (i) of Proposition 3.1 there exists a fair equilibrium in S_m^w. Let $f \in \mathcal{F}_m$ be one such equilibrium and let $K_m(f) = \max_{k \in \mathcal{K}_m} N_k^h(f)$. We will consider three cases based on the value of $K_m(f)$ and show that under the assumptions of the proposition, any other equilibrium, $e \in \mathcal{E}_m$ has the same characterization.

Case 1: $K_m(f) = 0$. In this case there is no agent in S_m^w which connects to a hotspot. If there are no agents within any of the hotspots' service zones, then it is nothing to prove, since no agents make any choices. Otherwise, considering the equilibrium conditions for agents that fall within some hotspot we have:

$$U^w(M_m^w) > U^h(1). \tag{3.A.8}$$

It follows that no other equilibrium configuration can exist. Indeed, if $e \neq f$ is some other equilibrium configuration, we must have $N_l^h(e) \neq N_l^h(f)$, and thus $N_l^h(e) \geq 1$ yielding $N_m^w(e) \leq M_m^w - 1$. By Assumption 1.2 on utilities, we obtain:

$$U^w\left(M_m^w\right) \leq U^w\left(N_m^w(e) + 1\right) \text{ and } U^h\left(N_l^h(e)\right) \leq U^h(1). \tag{3.A.9}$$

Since e is an equilibrium, we should have:

$$U^w\left(N_m^w(e) + 1\right) \leq U^h\left(N_l^h(e)\right), \tag{3.A.10}$$

since no agent in S_l^h wishes to switch to WAN AP w_m. Combining inequalities (3.A.9) and (3.A.10) we obtain:

$$U^w\left(M_m^w\right) \leq U^h(1),$$

which contradicts inequality (3.A.8).

Case 2: $0 < K_m(f) = \max_{k \in \mathcal{K}_m} M_k^h$. In this case we have that there are no agents in C_m connected to the WAN AP w_m in configuration e and thus we have $\mathbf{N}_m(f) = \{M_k^h | k \in \mathcal{K}_m\}$. This can only be feasible if:

$$U^w\left(M_{C_m}^w\right) \leq U^h(M_k^h),$$

for $k \in \mathcal{K}_m$. Using this inequality instead of (3.A.8) and following the steps similar to the Case 1 one can prove that no equilibrium e exists, such that $N_k^h(e) < M_k^h$ for some $k \in \mathcal{K}_m$.

Case 3: $0 < K_m(f) < \max_{k \in \mathcal{K}_m} M_k^h$.   Consider any other equilibrium $e \neq f$ and note that $N_m^w(e) \geq M_{\bar{C}_m}^w$. Hence the inequalities (3.3) admit at most two integer solutions. It follows that, for some $K \geq 1$ we have that:

$$K - 1 \leq N_k^h(e) \leq K,$$

for $k \in \mathcal{K}_m$ such that $M_k^h \geq K$ and

$$N_k^h(f) = M_k^h,$$

otherwise. Hence e must be a fair equilibrium, characterized by the slicing plane at level $K_m(e) = K$. Since by part **(ii)** of Proposition 3.1, all fair equilibria are equivalent, we have, that $\mathbf{N}(e) \sim \mathbf{N}(f)$. $\square$

4.   Proof of Proposition 3.3

For any configuration $c \in \mathcal{T}_m$ we will refer to agents that have utility equal $U_m^{min}(c)$ as the "bottleneck" agents. Let $c \in \mathcal{T}_m$ be a configuration that maximizes utility of a bottleneck agent and $c \notin \mathcal{F}_m$. We will show that $U_m^{min}(c) \leq U_m^{min}(f)$, for all $f \in \mathcal{K}_m$. Since, by assumption of the proposition, all fair equilibria in S_m^w are equivalent, we have that $N_m^w(f) = N_m^w(f')$, for all $f, f' \in \mathcal{F}_m$. Thus to prove the proposition it suffices to consider the following three cases.

Case 1: $N_m^w(c) > N_m^w(f)$, **for all** $f \in \mathcal{F}_m$.   In this case we have that $N_l^h(c) \leq N_l^h(f) - 1$ for at least one $l \in \mathcal{K}_m$. First we prove, that without loss of generality, one can assume that the bottleneck agents for configuration c are connected to a hotspot. Indeed, we have:

$$U^h\left(N_l^h(c) + 1\right) \geq U^h\left(N_l^h(f)\right),$$

and

$$U^w\left(N_m^w(c)\right) \leq U^w\left(N_m^w(f) + 1\right),$$

by Assumption 1.2 on utilities. Since in equilibrium f we must have $U^h(N_l^h(f)) \geq U^w(N_m^w(f) + 1)$ we arrive at:

$$U^h\left(N_l^h(c) + 1\right) \geq U^h\left(N_l^h(f)\right) \geq U^w(N_m^w(f) + 1) \geq U^w\left(N_m^w(c)\right).$$

Hence, $U^h\left(N_l^h(c) + 1\right) \geq U^w\left(N_m^w(c)\right)$ and thus the utility of the bottleneck agent stays the same or improves when an agent is switched from the WAN AP w_m to hotspot h_l.

Thus if c is maximizing the bottleneck among all configurations of agents choices, the bottleneck agents could be assumed to be connected to a hotspot. However, consider $l = \arg\max_{k \in \mathcal{K}_m} N_k^h(c)$. Then any agent connected to the hotspot h_l is the bottleneck for configuration c. Thus, since no agent connected to the WAN is the bottleneck for c, we have $U^h(N_l^h(c)) < U^w(N_m^w(c))$. Then we have the following chain of inequalities:

$$U^h(N_l^h(c)) \quad < \quad \underset{(a)}{U^w(N_m^w(c))} \leq \underset{(b)}{U^w(N_m^w(f) + 1)} \leq \quad U^h(N_l^h(f)),$$

where inequality (a) follows from the assumption of Case 1, and inequality (b) – from the fact that f is an equilibrium. Thus $U^h(N_l^h(c)) < U^h(N_l^h(f))$ which means that $N_l^h(c) \geq N_l^h(f) + 1$. Since f is a fair configuration, we have $\max_{k \in \mathcal{K}_m} N_k^h(f) \leq N_l^h(f) + 1$. But then, $N_l^h(c) \geq \max_{k \in \mathcal{K}_m} N_k^h(f)$, and hence $U_m^{min}(c) \leq U_m^{min}(f)$.

Case 2: $N_m^w(c) < N_m^w(f)$, **for all** $f \in \mathcal{F}_m$.   We first prove that no agents connected to the WAN can be the bottleneck for configuration c. Indeed, by assumption of this paragraph, we have that there exists at least one $l \in \mathcal{K}_m$ such that $N_l^h(c) \geq N_l^h(f) + 1$. Now assume that the agents connected to the WAN are the bottleneck for configuration c, hence $U^w(N_m^w(c)) \leq U^h(N_k^h(c))$, for all $k \in \mathcal{K}_m$. Then we have the following chain of inequalities:

$$U^w(N_m^w(f)) \quad < \quad U^w(N_m^w(c)) \quad \leq \quad U^w(N_l^h(c)) \quad \leq \quad U^h(N_l^h(f)+1).$$

Hence $U^w(N_m^w(f)) < U^h(N_l^h(f) + 1)$ which contradicts the fact that the agents connected to h_l in configuration f are in equilibrium. This shows that no agent connected to the WAN could be the bottleneck for the configuration c.

It follows that the agents within the hotspot h_n, such that $n = \arg\max_{k \in \mathcal{K}_m} N_k^h(c)$ are the bottleneck. Since there exists l such that $N_l^h(c) \geq N_l^h(f) + 1$, we have that $N_n^h(c) \geq \max_{k \in \mathcal{K}_m} N_n^h(f)$, by the fair structure of f. This yields that $U_m^{min}(c) \leq U_m^{min}(f)$, which we claimed to show.

Case 3: $N_m^w(c) = N_m^w(f)$, **for all** $f \in \mathcal{F}_m$.   First, we show again that no agent connected to the WAN could be the bottleneck for configuration c. Indeed, since $\mathbf{N}_m(f) \not\succ \mathbf{N}(c)$ we have that, by fair structure of f, there exists at least one $l \in \mathcal{K}_m$ such that $N_l^h(c) \geq N_l^h(f) + 1$. Assuming that the agents connected to the WAN are the bottleneck in configuration c, we have the following chain:

$$U^w(N_m^w(f)) = U^w(N_m^w(c)) \leq U^h(N_l^h(c)) \leq U^h(N_l^h(f)+1).$$

Thus, $U^w(N_m^w(f)) \leq U^h(N_l^h(f) + 1)$ indicating that f could not be an equilibrium configuration. This contradiction shows that the bottleneck agents for configuration c must be connected to hotspots. It is easy to see that $\max_{k \in \mathcal{K}_m} N_k^h(c) \geq \max_{k \in \mathcal{K}_m} N_k^h(f)$ which yields $U_m^{min}(c) \leq U_m^{min}(f)$.

5.   Proof of Proposition 4.1

Prior to giving a proof of Proposition 4.1 we provide several technical lemmas.

Lemma 5.1. *For any realization of the Poisson processes Π^a and Π^h consider a service zone associated with the WAN AP $w_0^\alpha \in \pi^{w,\alpha}$. Let*

$$L_k(K) = (M_k^h - K)\mathbf{1}_{\{M_k^h \geq K\}}, \quad P_k(K) = (M_k^h - K + 1)\mathbf{1}_{\{M_k^h \geq K\}}. \quad (3.A.11)$$

For any $m \in \mathbb{N}$ we have the following a.s. limits:

$$\lim_{\alpha \to \infty} \frac{H_0^\alpha}{\alpha} = \lambda^h, \quad \lim_{\alpha \to \infty} \frac{M_0^{w,\alpha}}{\alpha} = \lambda^a, \quad (3.A.12)$$

$$\lim_{\alpha \to \infty} \frac{\sum_{k \in \mathcal{K}_0^\alpha} L_k(K)}{H_0^\alpha} = \mathbb{E}_0^h[L_0(K)], \quad \lim_{\alpha \to \infty} \frac{\sum_{k \in \mathcal{K}_0^\alpha} P_k(K)}{H_0^\alpha} = \mathbb{E}_0^h[P_0(K)], \quad (3.A.13)$$

$$\lim_{\alpha \to \infty} \frac{M_{C_0}^{w,\alpha}}{\alpha} = \lambda^a(1 - e^{-\lambda^h \pi |d|^2}), \quad \lim_{\alpha \to \infty} \frac{M_{\check{C}_0}^{w,\alpha}}{\alpha} = \lambda^a e^{-\lambda^h \pi |d|^2}, \quad (3.A.14)$$

$$\lim_{\alpha \to \infty} \mathbb{P}\left(\exists h_k \in S_0^{w,\alpha} : M_k^h \geq K\right) = 1, \forall K \geq 0. \quad (3.A.15)$$

Proof. The limits (3.A.12) follow by ergodicity [5] of the process π^a and π^h. One needs only to note that the ratio $\alpha/|S_0^{w,\alpha}|$ converges to 1 as $\alpha \to \infty$ since d (the radius of hotspot coverage) is bounded.

Consider now the limits (3.A.13). Note that for each k, and any fixed K, both $L_k(K)$ and $P_k(K)$ are functionals of the realization of processes Π^h and Π^a within some a.s. bounded region (Voronoi "flower" [12] associated with the Voronoi cell V_k^h). Thus $L_k(K)$ and $P_k(K)$ are "local statistics" as defined in [12], and thus one can use Theorem 3.1 therein to obtain these limits.

Now consider the limits (3.A.14). By (3.A.12) and (3.A.13) and noting that:

$$\sum_{k \in \mathcal{K}_0^\alpha} M_k^h = \sum_{k \in \mathcal{K}_0^\alpha} L_k(K)|_{K=0},$$

we have:

$$\lim_{\alpha \to \infty} \frac{\sum_{k \in \mathcal{K}_0^\alpha} M_k^h}{\alpha} = \lambda^h \mathbb{E}_0^h \left[M_0^h \right].$$

Evaluating this expectation, we get:

$$\mathbb{E}_0^h \left[M_0^h \right] = \mathbb{E}_0^h \left[\sum_{a_i \in \Pi^a(V_0^h)} \mathbf{1}_{\{a_i \in V_0^h\}} \mathbf{1}_{\{|a_i| \le d\}} \right] = \mathbb{E}_0^h \left[\sum_{a_i \in \Pi^a} \mathbf{1}_{\{\Pi^h(B(a_i,|a_i|))=\emptyset\}} \mathbf{1}_{\{|a_i| \le d\}} \right],$$

where the second equality uses the fact that if $a_i \in V_0^h$ then there can be no other point of Π^h within the ball of radius $|a_i|$ centered at a_i. Now by independence of Π^h and Π^a and also using Campbell's formula and Slyvnyak's theorem (see e.g. [13]) we get:

$$\mathbb{E}_0^h \left[M_0^h \right] = \mathbb{E}_0^h \left[\int_{x \in B(0,d)} \mathbf{1}_{\{\Pi^h(B(x,|x|))=\emptyset\}} \lambda^a dx \right] = \int_{x \in B(0,d)} e^{-\lambda^h \pi |x|^2} \lambda^a dx$$

$$= \frac{\lambda^a}{\lambda^h} (1 - e^{-\lambda^h \pi |d|^2}),$$

from which the first limit in (3.A.14) follows. The second limit in (3.A.14) follows by taking into account the limit (3.A.13) and the first limit in (3.A.14).

Finally, to obtain the limit (3.A.15), we apply the Strong Law of Large Numbers to the sum of random variables $Z_k \triangleq \mathbf{1}_{\{M_k^h > K\}}$ to obtain:

$$\lim_{\alpha \to \infty} \frac{1}{H_0^\alpha} \sum_{k \in \mathcal{K}_0^\alpha} \mathbf{1}_{\{M_k^h > K\}} = \lim_{\alpha \to \infty} \frac{1}{H_0^\alpha} \sum_{k \in \mathcal{K}_0^\alpha} Z_k = \mathbb{P}(M_k^h > K) > 0 \quad a.s.. \tag{3.A.16}$$

Here we used the fact that the variables Z_k are i.i.d., since they depend on the number of points of homogeneous Poisson process sampled on disjoint sets S_k^h. Thus, at least one term in the sum in (3.A.16) is nonzero, for sufficiently large α, which proves the limit (3.A.15). $\square$

Lemma 5.2. *Let Δ_i^α where $i = 1,2,3,4$ be defined as follows:*

$$\Delta_1^\alpha = M_0^{w,\alpha}, \quad \Delta_2^\alpha(K) = \sum_{k \in \mathcal{K}_0^\alpha} L_k(K), \quad \Delta_3^\alpha(K) = \sum_{k \in \mathcal{K}_0^\alpha} P_k(K), \quad \Delta_4^\alpha = M_{\bar{C}_0}^{w,\alpha}.$$

Then for each i, $1 \le i \le 4$ and any $C > 0$ we have:

$$\lim_{\alpha \to \infty} \mathbb{P} \left[|\Delta_i^\alpha - \mathbb{E}[\Delta_i^\alpha]| > C\sqrt{\alpha \log \alpha} \right] = 0. \tag{3.A.17}$$

Proof. To prove the lemma we will use Chebyshev's inequality:

$$\mathbb{P}\left[|\Delta_i^\alpha - \mathbb{E}[\Delta_i^\alpha]| > C\sqrt{\alpha \log \alpha}\right] \le \frac{\mathbf{var}[\Delta_i^\alpha]}{C^2 \alpha \log \alpha}.$$

First we show that for $1 \le i \le 4$:

$$\mathbf{var}[\Delta_i^\alpha] = O(\alpha). \tag{3.A.18}$$

Indeed, $\Delta_1^\alpha = M_0^{w,\alpha}$ is just a Poisson random variable with average that scales linearly in α. Hence (3.A.18) is satisfied for $i = 1$. To obtain the bound on the variances of Δ_2^α and Δ_3^α we use Lemma 1 in [12], which yields:

$$\mathbf{var}[\Delta_2^\alpha(K)] = O(\alpha), \quad \mathbf{var}[\Delta_3^\alpha(K)] = O(\alpha).$$

Finally for the variance of $M_{\bar{C}_0}^{w,\alpha}$ observe that

$$M_{\bar{C}_0}^{w,\alpha} = M_0^{w,\alpha} - \Delta_2^\alpha(0).$$

Since the variances of both terms on the right are $O(\alpha)$ we get:

$$\mathbf{var}[\Delta_4^\alpha] = O(\alpha).$$

Now using Chebychev's inequality and (3.A.18) we obtain, for any $C > 0$,

$$\mathbb{P}\left(|\Delta_i^\alpha - \mathbb{E}[\Delta_i^\alpha]| > C\sqrt{\alpha \log \alpha}\right) = \frac{O(\alpha)}{\Theta(\alpha \log \alpha)} \to 0, \text{ when } \alpha \to \infty.$$

$\square$

Lemma 5.3. *Under the scaling Assumption 4.1, the equilibrium f_0^α in $S_0^{w,\alpha}$ is unique and fair w.h.p..*

Proof. Using Lemma 5.2 we have that, eventually, $M_{\bar{C}_0}^{w,\alpha} \ge \bar{N}$ a.s. as $\alpha \to \infty$. Taking into account Assumption 4.1, the conditions of Proposition 3.2 hold w.h.p. Using Proposition 3.2 yields the statement of the lemma. $\square$

Lemma 5.4. *For any equilibrium configuration f_0^α in $S_0^{w,\alpha}$ we have that:*

$$\max_{k \in \mathcal{K}_0^\alpha} N_k^h(f_0^\alpha) < \max_{k \in \mathcal{K}_0^\alpha} M_k^h, \text{ w.h.p.} \tag{3.A.19}$$

Proof. Note that (3.A.19) has a strict inequality. Thus (3.A.19) implies that the largest number of agents connected to any hotspot within S_0^w in equilibrium f_0^α is strictly less than the maximum number of agents in any one of the hotspots – at least asymptotically. We prove the lemma by contradiction. Suppose that there exists a sequence $\xi^\varepsilon = \{\alpha_n > 0 | \lim_{n \to \infty} \alpha_n = \infty\}$ with the following property. For any $\alpha \in \xi^\varepsilon$, f_0^α is such that for some $l^\alpha \in \mathcal{K}_0^\alpha$ we have $N_{l^\alpha}^h(f_0^\alpha) = \max_{k \in \mathcal{K}_0^\alpha} M_k^h$ with probability greater than ε. Then, for any $\alpha \in \xi^\varepsilon$:

$$J^\alpha(M_{l^\alpha}^h) \le N_0^{w,\alpha}(f_0^\alpha), \tag{3.A.20}$$

since no agent desires to switch to the WAN AP w_0 from the hotspot h_{l^α}. Now, note that f_0^α is fair w.h.p. by Lemma 5.3 and thus:

$$M_k^h - 1 \le N_k^h(f_0^\alpha) \le M_k^h,$$

where we took into account that there are no $k \in \mathcal{K}_0^\alpha$ such that $M_k^h > M_{l\alpha}^h$. This yields, that at most one agent within each hotspot h_k, for $k \in \mathcal{K}_0^\alpha$ selects the WAN, thus

$$N_0^{w,\alpha}(f_0^\alpha) \leq M_{\bar{C}_0}^{w,\alpha} + H^m, \qquad (3.A.21)$$

Now, using Assumption 4.1 and Lemma 5.1, the inequalities (3.A.20) and (3.A.21) imply:

$$j\left(M_{l\alpha}^h\right) \leq \lambda^a e^{-\lambda^h \pi d^2} + \lambda^h. \qquad (3.A.22)$$

Taking into account that by Lemma 5.1 and Assumption 4.1:

$$\liminf_{\alpha \to \infty} \max_{k \in \mathcal{K}_0^\alpha} M_k^h = \infty, \qquad \lim_{N \to \infty} j(N) = \infty, \; a.s.$$

we find that the inequality (3.A.22) is violated with probability tending to 1 as $\alpha \to \infty$. Thus, ξ^ε can not exist for any $\varepsilon > 0$, which proves the lemma. $\square$

Lemma 5.5. *Consider a configuration f_0^α for service zone $S_0^{w,\alpha}$ and let $N_{max}^{h,\alpha}(f_0^\alpha) = \max_{k \in \mathcal{K}_m} N_k^h(f_0^\alpha)$. For any $\alpha > 0$, a necessary and sufficient condition for f_0^α to be an equilibrium w.h.p. is that f_0^α is a fair configuration that obeys either of the following:*

$$N_{max}^{h,\alpha}(f_0^\alpha) = 0, \quad J^\alpha(1) > M_0^{w,\alpha}, \qquad (3.A.23)$$

$$N_{max}^{h,\alpha}(f_0^\alpha) \geq 1, \quad J^\alpha\left(N_{max}^{h,\alpha}(f_0^\alpha)\right) - 1 \leq N_0^{w,\alpha}(f_0^\alpha) < J^\alpha\left(N_{max}^{h,\alpha}(f_0^\alpha) + 1\right) \qquad (3.A.24)$$

where $N_k^h(f_0^\alpha) = N_{max}^{h,\alpha}(f_0^\alpha)$ for all $k \in \mathcal{K}_0^\alpha$, such that $M_k^h \geq N_{max}^{h,\alpha}(f_0^\alpha)$, or:

$$N_{max}^{h,\alpha}(f_0^\alpha) \geq 1, \quad J^\alpha\left(N_{max}^{h,\alpha}(f_0^\alpha)\right) - 1 \leq N_0^{w,\alpha}(f_0^\alpha) < J^\alpha\left(N_{max}^{h,\alpha}(f_0^\alpha)\right), \qquad (3.A.25)$$

where $\exists k,l \in \mathcal{K}_0^\alpha$, such that $M_k^h, M_l^h \geq N_{max}^{h,\alpha}(f_0^\alpha)$, and $M_k^h = N_{max}^{h,\alpha}(f_0^\alpha)$, $M_l^h = N_{max}^{h,\alpha}(f_0^\alpha) - 1$.

Proof. We already proved in Lemma 5.3 that all equilibria in $S_0^{w,\alpha}$ have the same fair characterizations w.h.p. In case $N_{max}^{h,\alpha}(f_0^\alpha) = 0$ there are no agents connected to any hotspots in S_0^w. The necessary and sufficient condition for that, as follows from the inequality (3.2), is given by (3.A.23).

Consider the case $N_{max}^{h,\alpha}(f_0^\alpha) \geq 1$. First assume that for all $k \in \mathcal{K}_0^\alpha$, such that $N_{max}^{h,\alpha}(f_0^\alpha)$ we have that $N_k^h(f_0^\alpha) = N_{max}^{h,\alpha}(f_0^\alpha)$. By Lemma 5.4 we have $N_{max}^{h,\alpha}(f_0^\alpha) < \max_{k \in \mathcal{K}_0} M_k^h$, and thus we can use the equilibrium conditions (3.1) to obtain (3.A.24).

Now assume, instead, that there exist such $k,l \in \mathcal{K}_0^\alpha$, so that $M_k^h, M_l^h \geq N_{max}^{h,\alpha}(f_0^\alpha)$, and $M_k^h = N_{max}^{h,\alpha}(f_0^\alpha)$, $M_l^h = N_{max}^{h,\alpha}(f_0^\alpha) - 1$. For the hotspots having $N_{max}^{h,\alpha}(f_0^\alpha) - 1$ agents connected to them in configuration f_0^α, via equilibrium conditions (3.1) we get:

$$J^\alpha\left(N_{max}^{h,\alpha}(f_0^\alpha) - 1\right) - 1 \leq N_0^{w,\alpha}(f_0^\alpha) < J^\alpha\left(N_{max}^{h,\alpha}(f_0^\alpha)\right), \qquad (3.A.26)$$

while for the hotspots having $N_{max}^{h,\alpha}(f_0^\alpha)$ agents connected to them:

$$J^\alpha\left(N_{max}^{h,\alpha}(f_0^\alpha)\right) - 1 \leq N_0^{w,\alpha}(f_0^\alpha) < J^\alpha\left(N_{max}^{h,\alpha}(f_0^\alpha) + 1\right), \qquad (3.A.27)$$

Now, using monotonicity of $J^\alpha(\cdot)$, by combining (3.A.26) and (3.A.27) we get (3.A.25). $\square$

Proof of Theorem 4.1. Let f_0^α denote an equilibrium configuration in the service zone $S_0^{w,\alpha}$ of the WAN AP $w_0^\alpha \in \pi_\alpha^w$. By Lemma 5.3 such configurations have equivalent and fair characterizations w.h.p, which gives Part 1 of the theorem. Let $N_{max}^{h,\alpha} = \max_{k \in \mathcal{K}_0^\alpha} N_k^h(f)$ where $f \in \mathcal{F}_0^\alpha$ is any fair equilibrium configuration. In what follows we will consider two cases that depend on whether the density of agents λ^a is less than the value $j(1)$. Our goal is to show that the $\lim_{\alpha \to \infty} N_{max}^{h,\alpha}(f_0^\alpha)$ exists.

Case 1: $\lambda^a < j(1)$. We will show that $\lambda^a < j(1)$ if and only if:

$$\lim_{\alpha \to \infty} N_{max}^{h,\alpha} = 0.$$

Indeed, the "only if" part follows from the condition (3.A.23) by dividing both sides by α and taking limits as $\alpha \to \infty$. Now using the limit (3.A.12) we obtain that $N_{max}^{h,\alpha} = 0$ w.h.p. implies $\lambda^a < j(1)$.

Next we prove that if $\lambda^a < j(1)$ then $N_{max}^{h,\alpha} = 0$ w.h.p. Indeed, by Lemma 5.1 we know that:

$$M_0^{w,\alpha} = \lambda^a \alpha + \varepsilon(\alpha),$$

where $|\varepsilon(\alpha)| = O\left(\sqrt{\alpha \log \alpha}\right)$. But then, for sufficiently large α we have:

$$M_0^{w,\alpha} < J^\alpha(1),$$

which, by Lemma 5.5 implies $N_{max}^{h,\alpha} = 0$ w.h.p.

Case 2: $\lambda^a \geq j(1)$. We first prove that $N_{max}^{h,\alpha}$ has a limit once $\alpha \to \infty$. Consider any sequence $\xi := \{\alpha_n | n \in \mathbb{N}\}$, where $\lim_{n \to \infty} \alpha_n = \infty$. We define the following disjoint subsequences of ξ:

$$\xi_1 = \left\{ \alpha | \alpha \in \xi, \ 1 \leq N_{max}^{h,\alpha} < \max_{k \in \mathcal{K}_0^\alpha} M_k^h \text{ and } \forall k \in \mathcal{K}_0^\alpha, \text{ s.t. } M_k^h \geq N_{max}^{h,\alpha}, \ N_k^h(f^\alpha) = N_{max}^{h,\alpha} \right\}$$

$$\xi_2 = \left\{ \alpha | \alpha \in \xi, \ 1 \leq N_{max}^{h,\alpha} < \max_{k \in \mathcal{K}_0^\alpha} M_k^h, \text{ and } \right.$$

$$\left. \exists k, l \in \mathcal{K}_0^\alpha, \text{ s.t. } M_k^h, M_l^h \geq N_{max}^{h,\alpha}, \text{ and } N_k^h(f^\alpha) = N_{max}^{h,\alpha}, \ N_l^h(f^\alpha) = N_{max}^{h,\alpha} - 1 \right\}$$

$$\xi_3 = \left\{ \alpha | \alpha \in \xi, \ 1 \leq N_{max}^{h,\alpha} = \max_{k \in \mathcal{K}_0^\alpha} M_k^h \right\}$$

$$\xi_4 = \left\{ \alpha | \alpha \in \xi, \ N_{max}^{h,\alpha} = 0 \right\}$$

Clearly, $\xi = \bigcup_{i=1}^4 \xi_i$. However, by Lemma 5.4, the sequence ξ_3 is finite. Moreover, we have proved above that when $\lambda^a \geq j(1)$ the sequence ξ_4 is finite too. Thus, asymptotically, ξ consists only of the members of the sequences ξ_1 and ξ_2. Note that either ξ_1 or ξ_2 or both ξ_1 and ξ_2 have to be infinite, since ξ is infinite.

By definition of ξ_1 and ξ_2, we have, that $\max_{k \in \mathcal{K}_0^\alpha} M_k^h > N_{max}^{h,\alpha}$ when $\alpha \in \xi_1 \cup \xi_2$. Thus, if any of ξ_1 or ξ_2 is finite, to prove the statement of the theorem we have to show that $N_{max}^{h,\alpha}$ converges along the other infinite sequence. If both ξ_1 and ξ_2 are infinite, then we need to show that $N_{max}^{h,\alpha}$ is asymptotically the same along each subsequence, and in addition that:

$$\lim_{\alpha \in \xi_1, \ \alpha \to \infty} N_{max}^{h,\alpha} = \lim_{\alpha \in \xi_2, \ \alpha \to \infty} N_{max}^{h,\alpha}.$$

We will consider first the sequence ξ_1 and assume that it is infinite. We will show that:

$$\lim_{\alpha \in \xi_1, \, \alpha \to \infty} N_{max}^{h,\alpha} = K_1 \,, \tag{3.A.28}$$

where K_1 is independent of α. We argue by contradiction. In particular, assume that there exist arbitrary large $\gamma, \delta \in \xi_1$ such that $N_{max}^{h,\gamma} \neq N_{max}^{h,\delta}$. Without loss of generality let $\gamma < \delta$, and consider the equilibrium conditions in $S_0^{w,\delta}$. By Lemma 5.5 we have that:

$$J^{\delta}\left(N_{max}^{h,\delta}\right) - 1 \le N_0^w(f_0^{\delta}) < J^{\delta}\left(N_{max}^{h,\delta} + 1\right) \,,$$

Now multiplying these inequalities by γ/δ, and using Assumption 4.1, we obtain:

$$J^{\gamma}\left(N_{max}^{h,\delta}\right) - \gamma/\delta \le \gamma/\delta N_0^{w,\delta}(f_0^{\delta}) < J^{\gamma}\left(N_{max}^{h,\delta} + 1\right) \,.$$

Note that by Lemma 5.1 we have:

$$\gamma/\delta N_0^{w,\delta}(f_0^{\delta}) = \gamma\left(\lambda^a e^{-\lambda^h \pi d^2} + \lambda^h \mathbb{E}_0^h\left[P_0^{\delta}(N_{max}^{h,\delta})\right]\right) + \varepsilon_1(\gamma,\delta) \,,$$

where, by Lemma 5.2, $|\varepsilon_1(\gamma,\delta)| = O\left(\gamma\sqrt{\log \delta/\delta}\right) = O\left(\sqrt{\gamma \log \gamma}\right)$. This yields:

$$J^{\gamma}\left(N_{max}^{h,\delta}\right) - 1 \le \gamma\left(\lambda^a e^{-\lambda^h \pi d^2} + \lambda^h \mathbb{E}_0^h\left[P_0^{\delta}(N_{max}^{h,\delta})\right]\right) + \varepsilon_1(\gamma,\delta) < J^{\gamma}\left(N_{max}^{h,\delta} + 1\right) \,. \tag{3.A.29}$$

Now consider a fair configuration $\tilde{f}_0^{\gamma}$ for service zone $S_0^{w,\gamma}$, such that $\max_{k \in \mathcal{K}_0^{\alpha}} N_k^h(\tilde{f}_0^{\gamma}) = N_{max}^{h,\delta}$ and such that for all $k \in \mathcal{K}_0^{\gamma}$ for which $M_k^h \ge N_{max}^{h,\gamma}$ we have $N_k^h(\tilde{f}_0^{\gamma}) = N_{max}^{h,\delta}$. Clearly, in this case Lemma 5.1 and Lemma 5.2 yield:

$$N_0^w(\tilde{f}_0^{\gamma}) = \gamma\left(\lambda^a e^{-\lambda^h \pi d^2} + \lambda^h \mathbb{E}_0^h P_0^{\delta}\left(N_{max}^{h,\delta}\right)\right) + \varepsilon_2(\gamma) \,,$$

where $|\varepsilon_2(\gamma)| = O\left(\sqrt{\gamma \log \gamma}\right)$. By Assumption 4.1 (item 4) we have, for all integer K:

$$\lambda^a e^{-\lambda^h \pi d^2} + \lambda^h \mathbb{E}_0^h P_0^{\delta}(K) \neq j(K) \,,$$

which then translates the inequalities (3.A.29) into:

$$j\left(N_{max}^{h,\delta}\right) < \lambda^a e^{-\lambda^h \pi d^2} + \lambda^h \mathbb{E}_0^h P_0^{\delta}\left(N_{max}^{h,\delta}\right) < j\left(N_{max}^{h,\delta} + 1\right) \,. \tag{3.A.30}$$

Now note that $|\varepsilon_1(\gamma,\delta) + \varepsilon_2(\gamma)| = O\left(\sqrt{\gamma \log \gamma}\right) = o(\gamma)$. Hence, using (3.A.29), one gets

$$J^{\gamma}\left(N_{max}^{h,\delta}\right) - \gamma/\delta \le N_0^{w,\gamma}(\tilde{f}_0^{\gamma}) < J^{\gamma}\left(N_{max}^{h,\delta} + 1\right) \,,$$

once $\gamma < \delta$ are selected large enough. By Lemma 5.5 we have that $\tilde{f}_0^{\gamma}$ is a fair equilibrium that is different from f_0^{γ}. By Lemma 5.3 this can not happen w.h.p. Thus we obtain that

$$\lim_{\alpha \in \xi_1, \alpha \to \infty} N_{max}^{h,\delta} = K_1$$

for some positive integer K_1.

Now, if ξ_2 is finite, we are done, since asymptotically ξ consists only of ξ_1 and we have already shown that along ξ_1 the value of $N_{max}^{h,\alpha}$ has a limit. Now we will prove that if ξ_2 is infinite, then the value of $N_{max}^{h,\alpha}$ along ξ_2 also converges to a limit. Take any $\gamma \in \xi_2$ then, by Lemma 5.5 we have, that

$$J^\alpha(N_{max}^{h,\gamma}) - 1 \le N_0^{w,\gamma}(f^\gamma) < J^\alpha(N_{max}^{h,\gamma}).$$

Dividing these inequalities by γ, by Assumption 4.1, we have:

$$j(N_{max}^{h,\gamma}) - 1/\gamma \le \frac{N_0^w(f^\gamma)}{\gamma} < j(N_{max}^{h,\gamma}). \tag{3.A.31}$$

We now show that $N_{max}^{h,\gamma} < K_0$ for some K_0 independent of γ. Indeed, otherwise, there exists a subsequence $\xi_5 \subset \xi_2$, with $\lim_{\gamma \to \infty, \gamma \in \xi_5} N_{max}^{h,\gamma} = \infty$. Now using Lemma 5.1, we have that

$$\limsup_{\gamma \to \infty, \gamma \in \xi_5} \frac{N_0^w(f^\gamma)}{\gamma} < \lambda^a e^{-\lambda^h \pi d^2} + \lambda^h \lim_{\gamma \to \infty, \gamma \in \xi_5} \mathbb{E}_0^h\left[P_0^\gamma\left(N_{max}^{h,\gamma}\right)\right] = \lambda^a e^{-\lambda^h \pi d^2}.$$

At the same time we have that

$$\lim_{\gamma \to \infty, \gamma \in \xi_5} j(N_{max}^{h,\gamma}) = \infty,$$

which means that the inequalities (3.A.31) could not be satisfied along the subsequence ξ_5. Thus we have a contradiction, and $\exists K_0$, such that $N_{max}^{h,\gamma} < K_0$.

Thus the set $\{N_{max}^{h,\gamma} | \gamma \in \xi_2\}$ is finite, hence if ξ_2 is infinite, at least some values from this set must realize infinitely often along ξ_2. Consider any value K which is achieved infinitely often along ξ_2, i.e. there exists a subsequence $\xi_6 \subset \xi_2$, with $\sup\{\gamma | \gamma \in \xi_6\} = \infty$ and for any $\gamma \in \xi_6$, $N_{max}^{h,\gamma} = K$. Note that $N_0^{w,\gamma}(f_0^\gamma)$ must satisfy:

$$M_{\tilde{C}_0}^{w,\gamma} + \sum_{k \in \mathcal{K}_0^\gamma} (M_k^h - K)\mathbf{1}_{\{M_k^h \ge K\}} < N_0^w(f_0^\gamma) < M_{\tilde{C}_0}^{w,\gamma} + \sum_{k \in \mathcal{K}_0^\gamma} (M_k^h - K + 1)\mathbf{1}_{\{M_k^h \ge K\}} \; w.h.p.,$$

since f_0^γ is asymptotically fair w.h.p. Dividing these inequalities by γ, and comparing to inequalities (3.A.31), one finds that K must satisfy:

$$l(K) \triangleq \lambda^a e^{\lambda^h \pi d^2} + \lambda^h \mathbb{E}_0^h[L_0(K)] < j(K) \le \lambda^a e^{\lambda^h \pi d^2} + \lambda^h \mathbb{E}_0^h[P_0(K)] \triangleq u(K), \tag{3.A.32}$$

where we used Lemma 5.1. Note that $u(K) = l(K+1)$ and thus the intervals $(l(K), u(K)]$ are disjoint for different integer K. Moreover $\bigcup_{K=1}^{\infty}(l(K), u(K)] = (0, u(1)]$. Since $j(K)$ is increasing in K and $\lim_{K \to \infty} j(K) = \infty$, there exists exactly one integer solution to the inequalities (3.A.32), since we assumed

$$j(1) \le \lambda^a,$$

and $u(1) = \lambda^a$. But then the value of $N_{max}^{h,\gamma}$ is asymptotically unique w.h.p., when $\gamma \in \xi_2$ and $\gamma \to \infty$.

We are left to show that if both ξ_1 and ξ_2 are infinite, then the asymptotic values K_1 and K_2 along ξ_1 and ξ_2 respectively satisfy $K_1 = K_2$. Observe that the condition (3.A.30) implies for K_1:

$$j(K_1) < u(K_1) < j(K_1 + 1).$$

Now, since K_2 is a unique integer solution to (3.A.32) we obtain that $K_2 = K_1$. Since $N_{max}^{h,\alpha}(f_0^\alpha) = K_1$ w.h.p. when $\alpha \in \xi_1$ and $N_{max}^{h,\alpha}(f_0^\alpha) = K_2 = K_1$ w.h.p when $\alpha \in \xi_2$, we obtain Part 2 of the theorem. Lastly, Part 3 of the theorem follows from the above analysis.

Notes

1. A more general case with utilities dependent on congestion and distance from a serving AP is treated in [11].

2. Note that we use letter M with different sub- and super- scripts to refer to the actual number of agents that fall within different sets, while we use the letter N to refer to the number of agents within different sets to refer to the agents *actually connected* to particular APs.

3. The ambiguity arises in the case when for a particular fair configuration $f \in \mathcal{F}_m$ we have $0 < N_k^h = K_m < \max_k M_k^h$, for all $k \in \mathcal{K}_m$ and for some $K_m \geq 0$. Then the upper surface of the "slicing plane", associated with this configuration can be drawn at either the levels K_m or $K_m + 1$.

4. Since, as we alluded above, the WAN service might be degrading slower with the number of connections than that of hotspots, the assumption that (3.5) holds may be reasonable.

5. This is, perhaps, not a bad assumption since WAN network would be carefully designed and optimized.

6. See e.g. [9] for a nice comparison of WiFi vs. 3G technologies.

References

[1] G. Rittenhouse, "Next generation wireless networks," in *Proc. INFORMS*, March 2004.

[2] GTRAN, "GTRAN dual-mode 802.11/CDMA wireless modem," http://www.gtranwireless.com.

[3] T.S. Rappaport, "Wireless Communications: Principles and Practice," Prentice Hall, 2002

[4] F. Baccelli, M. Klein, M. Lebourges, and S. Zuyev, "Stochastic geometry and architecture of communication networks," *J. Telecommunication Systems*, vol. 7, pp. 209–227, 1997.

[5] D. Vere-Jones D. Daley, *An Introduction to the Theory of Point Processes*, Springer Verlag, 2 edition, 2002.

[6] V. V. Veeravalli and A. Sendonaris, "The coverage-capacity tradeoff in cellular CDMA systems," *IEEE Trans. on Vehicular Technology*, vol. 48, no. 5, pp. 1443–1450, September 1999.

[7] B. Blaszczyszyn F. Baccelli and F. Tournois, "Spatial averages of coverage characteristics in large cdma networks," Tech. Rep. 4196, INRIA (France), 2001.

[8] F. Baccelli and B. Blaszczyszyn, "On a coverage process ranging from the boolean model to the Poisson Voronoi tessellation, with applications to wireless communications," *Adv. Appl. Prob.*, vol. 33, no. 2.

[9] CDMA Development Group, "CDMA2000 and WiFi: Making a business case for interoperability", September 2003, available at http://www.cdg.org

[10] P. Bremaud F. Baccelli, *Elements of Queueing Theory: Palm Martingale Calculus and Stochastic Recurrences*, Springer-Verlag (New York), December 1999.

[11] A. Zemlianov and G. de Veciana "Cooperation and decision-making in a wireless multi-provider setting (extended version)", Tech. Rep. UT-Austin, Dept. of Electrical and Computer Engineering, August 2004, available at http://www.ece.utexas.edu/ ˜zemliano/infocomext.pdf

[12] S. Zuyev, P. Desnogues, and H. Rakotoarisoa, "Simulations of large telecommunication networks based on probabilistic modeling," *J. Electronic Imaging*, vol. 6, no. 1, pp. 68–77, 1997.

[13] J.F.C. Kingman, *Poisson Processes*, Clarendon Press, 1997.

Chapter 4

A SUPPLY NETWORK OF OLIGOPOLY FOR THE ADVANCED INTELLIGENT NETWORK

Vinh Quan[1] and Scott Rogers[2]

[1] *Mechanical & Industrial Engineering, Ryerson University, vquan@ryerson.ca;*
[2] *Mechanical & Industrial Engineering, University of Toronto, rogers@mie.utoronto.ca*

Abstract: This paper develops mathematical models to conduct analysis of the production and pricing of Advanced Intelligent Network (AIN) software products where an incumbent vendor sells applications and tools to a telephone company (telco) to deploy on its network to deliver AIN services to end-users. This basic supply network is then modified to consider the case in which a new entrant competes with the incumbent in selling applications to the telco. Profit maximizing models for each firm are formulated and solved to obtain a Nash equilibrium for the firms. The results show that the telco does not necessarily earn higher profits when it gives the vendor a smaller share of the revenue generated by an application purchased from the vendor. The results also show that the new entrant has no effect on the tool price charged by the incumbent vendor.

Key words: Supply Network; Oligopoly; Advanced Intelligent Network.

1. INTRODUCTION

After the introduction of the Intelligent Network (IN) in the 1980's and the popular 800 Services, the telephony industry extended the concept and began deploying the Advanced Intelligent Network (AIN). With AIN, network elements perform several generic functionalities and are not application specific. This has enabled vendors to not only develop and sell applications to telephone companies (telcos) but also develop and sell service-creation tools to telcos to use to develop their own applications. The telco then deploys all the applications, purchased and/or made, on its network to deliver AIN services to residential and business users. The supply of AIN software applications and tools by vendors to telcos to deliver

AIN services to residential and business end-users form the AIN supply network of this study. A more simplified problem was examined in Quan & Rogers [10]. However, in that study, the authors considered a supply network with only one vendor. Furthermore, the problem was solved via a Complementarity Problem procedure using the mathematical software GAMS[1]. In this paper, we shall examine supply networks with two vendors and the problems will be solved analytically. The model examined in this paper is part of a larger model given in Quan's dissertation[2], which has two competing telcos, three competing vendors and two different types of AIN markets.

The creation of each AIN service requires a software program to be developed. These programs are called AIN applications. Telcos can purchase AIN applications from vendors. Telcos also have the option of purchasing service creation tools from the vendor, allowing them to create their own applications. Service creation tools (also known as Service Independent Building Blocks) are basically small program modules or subroutines that can be used to develop applications (Steffen et al. [3] and Wennerber et al. [19]). For additional information about AIN, see Farnham [6], Feldman [7] and Tweddell [15]. Roltsch et al. [12] discussed the steps that a telco needed to take to migrate from its existing network infrastructure to an AIN infrastructure. The economics associated with locating Service Control Points is discussed in Axelsson et al. [2]. The cost of a distributed architecture is compared with a centralized architecture for metropolitan areas and rural areas. The International Engineering Consortium's website http://www.iec.org offers several tutorials on AIN (see tutorials "Access Mediation", "Access Gateway", "Intelligent Network" and "Intelligent Network Service Creation"). The book by Anderson [1] provides technical details about AIN. There are also numerous business & market research reports that provide estimates of the market for AIN services as well as equipment sales. These include reports by The Pelorus Group[3], Venture Development Corporation[4] and the Business Research Group[5].

Unterstein [17] studied the potential penetration of different AIN services for the residential market, which can be used to estimate the potential revenue each of these services can generate. The various business research reports noted above also provide such estimates. Subtracting the operating, maintenance and integration costs for each service would yield the potential

[1] See http://www.gams.com
[2] Vinh Quan's Ph.D. dissertation, March 2004, University of Toronto, Canada
[3] The Perolus Group, *The Future of The Advanced Intelligent Network*, 1994
[4] Venture Development Corporation, *High Availability And Enhanced Services Platforms in The Advanced Intelligent Network*, 1995
[5] Business Research Group, *Market Demand For Advanced Intelligent Network Services*, 1994

net revenue a telco could earn from each AIN service. As in Quan and Rogers [10], by ranking the (different) AIN services from highest to lowest net revenue, a value-in-use curve can be constructed, as shown in Figure 1.

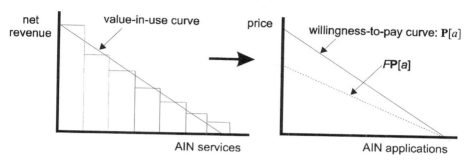

Figure -1. Value-in-use curve and willingness-to-pay curve

Offering each AIN service in Figure 1 requires that the telco purchase the corresponding AIN application (software program) from the vendor. Hence, the value-in-use curve also represents the maximum amount the telco is willing to pay for each AIN application purchased from the vendor. For the models in this paper, it is assumed that the willingness-to-pay curve is linear and given by $P[a] = M - S \cdot a$ where M is the height and S is the slope of the curve. The case of nonlinear willingness-to-pay curve is left for future investigation. The mathematical expression for the willingness-to-pay curve is similar to that for a typical linear inverse demand curve in the economics literature (Hirshleifer and Glazer [9]). However, because the telco pays a different price for each application on the X-axis, this situation is equivalent to what is called perfect price discrimination[6].

The production of AIN applications and service creation tools can be described as follows. When the telco purchases service creation tools to make applications, the incremental cost of making each application, not including the cost of purchasing tools, is denoted by CT. For vendors that produce applications and tools, the production process involves developing a set of "basic tools" and then using them to create applications or repackaging them for sale to the telco. The cost of making basic tools is denoted by CB, the repackaging cost is denoted by CR, and the cost of producing an application using the basic tools is denoted by CV. The basic tools are essentially software objects that are created for internal use, so selling them would require additional "repackaging", including source code documentation and customization. For vendors that produce AIN applications only and no tools, the production process consists of creating

---

[6] see Hirshleifer and Glazer [9], pp227-231

applications without producing basic tools. The incremental cost of creating applications directly is denoted by *CBV*, which signifies that it is a combination of tool and application costs.   Constant production costs are used in this study, other cost functions can be investigated in future research. Each AIN application produces one AIN service. Each increment in the number of AIN applications requires an increment of n tools.   For the models developed in this study, it is assumed $n = 1$. Sherali and Leneno [13] also made a one-to-one assumption, in which producing one incremental unit of finished copper required one incremental unit of ore. It was also used in Tyagi [16] and Corbett and Karmarkar [4]. The general case where $n \neq 1$ is left for future investigation.

When the telco buys tools from a vendor, it will pay the vendor *pt* dollars for each tool. The tool price *pt* is a decision variable for the vendor. Since the vendor does not know whether the telco will use the tool to make a high value application or a low value application, the vendor charges the telco the same amount for each tool. When the telco buys applications from a vendor, it will pay the vendor a fraction *F* of the net revenue it receives from deploying the application. If application number "*a*" generates $\mathbf{P}[a]$ dollars of net revenue for the telco, then the telco pays the vendor a total of $F \cdot \mathbf{P}[a]$ dollars as shown in Figure 1.   In essence, the telco pays the vendor a percentage of the revenue it receives, which constitutes a revenue sharing scheme between the two firms. The idea of a revenue sharing scheme was discussed by Paul Vlasek[7]. Since each application generates a different amount of revenue, the telco pays the vendor a different amount or "price" for each application. This is in contrast to the telco paying the same price *pt* for each tool.   For the models in this study, it is assumed there is a prespecified fraction *F*, so *F* is a parameter of the model.   Sensitivity analysis will be conducted in Section 6 for different values of *F*.

2.   STRUCTURE OF THE PAPER

A survey of the literature is given in Section 3. In Section 4, we study a basic AIN supply network in which an incumbent vendor (vendor 1) sells applications and tools to a telco to deliver AIN services to end-users. The basic supply network is then modified to consider the case where a new entrant (vendor 2) competes to sell applications to the telco in Section 5. These supply networks are illustrated in Figure 2. Vendor 2 is assumed to be a vendor that specializes in producing applications only and does not produce any tools.   It is assumed that the incumbent vendor 1 is the

---

[7] Presentation entitled "Pricing Options" delivered at the IN World Forum, February 14, 2000, Miami Florida.

"preferred vendor" in the sense that the telco will choose to buy applications from vendor 1 first and then from vendor 2. This will result in vendor 1 selling the high value applications to the telco and vendor 2 selling the low value applications.

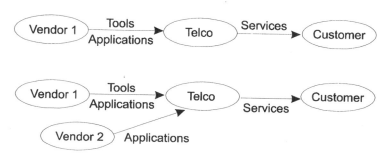

Figure -2. Supply networks studied in this paper

This practice is not uncommon since a telco often considers the maker of its switches to be the preferred supplier due to historical or other reasons. The results for the two supply networks will be compared to examine the effects of the new entrant on the incumbent's profits. Nonlinear profit maximizing models are formulated for each vendor and telco and solved analytically to obtain a Nash equilibrium set of outputs and prices for each firm.

Definition. A Nash equilibrium solution for a supply network of oligopoly is a point at which the values of the decision variables simultaneously maximize profits for each of the firms, given the beliefs and knowledge that each firm has about the behaviour of the others.

The models are solved analytically as well as numerically with a sample data set in Section 6. Insights gained from the analysis in this paper include the following:

- Results from the literature (Sherali and Leneno [13], Corbett and Karmarkar [4]) shows that when a new semi-finished good firm enters, the semi-finished good price will decrease. However, in the case of AIN, the price of tools is unchanged when vendor 2 enters.
- Results from the literature also show that when a new semi-finished good firm enters, the incumbent semi-finished good firm's output will drop. However, the results obtained here show that the entry of vendor 2 results in fewer tools, but *more* applications, produced by the incumbent vendor.

3.   LITERATURE REVIEW

Although the problem addressed in this study lies in the area of AIN, it can be viewed as a problem that involves

- the supply of two products (applications and tools) by one or two firms (vendor 1, vendor 2) to another firm (telco);
- a substitution effect between two products (the telco can buy applications or buy tools to make applications);
- a different pricing scheme for the two products sold by vendors (the vendor receives a fraction F for each application sold to the telco but receives a price pt for each tool);
- an oligopoly market structure;
- a supply network structure (vendors sell products to the telco which are used to make services to sell to residential/business end-users);
- different capabilities among the firms (vendor 1 can produce tools and applications but vendors 2 can produce applications only).

From this perspective, the literature on oligopoly supply networks is examined. The articles of Sherali and Leneno [13], Corbett and Karmarkar [4], Choi [3], and Tyagi [16] are discussed. In Sherali and Leneno, the authors studied a supply network for the copper industry in an oligopoly setting. There is a set of firms competing to supply a semi-finished good to another set of firms which use the semi-finished good to produce a final good to sell to customers.   Sherali and Leneno dealt with homogeneous goods. In this paper, the applications under the willingness-to-pay curve represent different applications. Choi studied price competition in a channel structure with a common retailer.   He examined two manufacturers competing to sell a single product to one retailer which then put this product on its shelves to sell to customers.   Choi assumed that the products are slightly differentiated (e.g., two different brands of soap), so each manufacturer can charge a slightly different price even though the product is essentially the same. The model presented here differs from Choi's model in that each AIN application is viewed as a different product, so there is perfect price discrimination for the product. Tyagi studied a supply network in which retailers buy a single product from one manufacturer. He gives conditions under which the entry of a new retailer will cause profits for each retailer to (i) remain unchanged, (ii) decrease, or (iii) increase, for different demand curves (e.g. linear, constant elasticity). Whereas Tyagi dealt with a single product in his model, the AIN model considers two products, applications and tools. Corbett and Karmarkar examined a basic supply network in which a set of firms supply a semi-finished product to another set of firms that use the semi-finished product to make the final product. They investigated how changes in each firm's production costs affect prices and outputs of all the firms in the supply network. They also described what happened when additional firms entered the industry to compete with existing firms. How will output of each firm change? What will be the new equilibrium price for the semi-finished good? Final good? Similar analysis will be conducted in this study for the case of AIN.

4.   THE BASIC SUPPLY NETWORK

In this section, we will study a basic AIN supply network in which an incumbent vendor (vendor 1) sells applications and tools to one telco, as illustrated in Figure 2.

NOTATION

Number of applications made by telco = xt
Number of tools made by vendor 1 = xvt_1,
Number of applications made by vendor 1 = xv_1
Tool price = pt
Fraction of revenue telco pays vendor 1 to purchase applications = F
Willingness-to-pay curve for applications = $\mathbf{P}[a] = M - S \cdot a$
Incremental cost of telco making applications = CT
Incremental cost of vendor 1 making applications, basic tools = CV, CB
Incremental cost of vendor 1 repackaging tools = CR
Telco profits = zt, Vendor 1 profits = zv_1

The problem is illustrated graphically in Figure 3 where the telco pays the vendor a tool price of pt for each tool purchased.

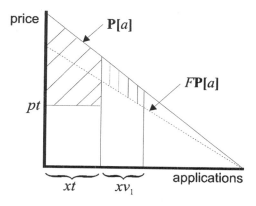

Figure -3. Graphical illustration of the problem

The number of applications made by the telco is given by xt, and the number of applications purchased from vendor 1 is xv_1. The diagonally shaded area is the telco's revenue from deploying its self-made applications. The vertically shaded area is the telco's profits from deploying applications purchased from the vendor. It is assumed that the telco will make high value applications, if it makes applications at all, and purchase lower value applications from the vendor. Hence, along the X-axis, xt appears to the left of xv_1.

4.1   Telco's Profit Maximizing Problem

Given a tool price pt and number of applications xv_1 supplied by vendor 1, the telco wishes to determine the number of applications xt it should make to maximize profits. The telco believes that vendor 1 will not change the tool price pt or output xv_1 when the telco changes output xt. This is similar to the assumptions made for the Cournot oligopoly model (Henderson and Quandt [8]; Varian [18]). Note that xv_1 represents, for example, 10 general applications that vendor 1 is willing to supply, but it does not indicate which specific 10 applications they are. The number of tools that the telco will need to purchase from vendor 1 is equal to xt since it is assumed that an increment of one application requires an increment of one tool as discussed in Section 1. Referring to Figure 3, the telco's profit maximizing problem can be constructed as follows:

Telco profits = revenue from deploying applications it makes − cost of making applications − cost of purchasing tools to make applications + profits from buying and deploying vendor 1 applications

$$zt = \int_0^{xt} \mathbf{P}[a] \cdot da - CT \cdot xt - pt \cdot xt + (1 - F) \int_{xt}^{xt+xv_1} \mathbf{P}[a] \cdot da$$

Substituting out $\mathbf{P}[a]$ by $\mathbf{P}[a] = M - S \cdot a$ and performing the integration, the telco's profit maximizing problem is

Max
$$zt = (M - CT - pt)xt - S \cdot xt^2 / 2 + (1 - F)(M \cdot xv_1 - S \cdot xt \cdot xv_1 - S \cdot xv_1^2 / 2)$$
s.t. $xt \geq 0$

The telco's profit function is quadratic with second order derivative $\partial zt / \partial xt \partial xt = -S$. Since the slope S is a positive quantity, zt is a concave function (Edwards and Penny [5]). Taking the derivative of zt w.r.t. the telco's decision variable xt and assuming an interior solution (i.e., $xt^* > 0$) gives $\partial zt / \partial xt = M - CT - pt - S \cdot xt - S(1-F)xv_1 = 0$ and so

$$xt = (M - CT - pt - (1-F) \cdot S \cdot xv_1)/S \qquad (1)$$

Equation (1) provides the number of applications xt that the telco will want to make given a tool price pt and xv_1 applications supplied by vendor 1. For this reason, Eq. (1) is referred to as the telco's reaction function, analogous to the reaction functions derived for the Cournot oligopoly model in the literature (Henderson and Quandt [8]; Varian [18]).

4.2   Vendor 1's Profit Maximizing Problem

Vendor 1 wishes to determine the number of applications xv_1 and the tool price pt to charge to maximize profits. It is assumed that vendor 1 has knowledge of the telco's reaction function Eq. (1) and uses this knowledge in its profit maximizing behaviour. A similar assumption was made in Sherali and Leneno [13] and Corbett and Karmarkar [4] where the semi-finished good firm knows the reaction function of the finished good firm. Referring to Figure 3, vendor 1's profit maximizing problem can be constructed as follows:

Vendor 1's profits = revenue from selling tools – cost of making tools + revenue from selling applications – cost of making applications

$$zv_1 = pt \cdot xvt_1 - (CR + CB) \cdot xvt_1 + \int_{xt}^{xt+xv_1} F \cdot \mathbf{P}[a] \cdot da - (CV + CB)xv_1$$

Substituting out $\mathbf{P}[a]$ by $\mathbf{P}[a] = M - S \cdot a$ and performing the integration

$$zv_1 = (pt - CB - CR)xvt_1 + (F \cdot M - CV - CB)xv_1 - F \cdot S(xt \cdot xv_1 + xv_1^2 / 2)$$

Since an increment of one tool corresponds to an increment of one application made by the telco, xvt_1 can be replaced by xt:

$$zv_1 = (pt - CB - CR)xt + (F \cdot M - CV - CB)xv_1 - F \cdot S(xt \cdot xv_1 + xv_1^2 / 2)$$

Since vendor 1 knows the telco's reaction function, it is possible to substitute for xt using Eq. (1). Vendor 1's profit maximizing problem is

$$\text{Max}\quad zv_1 = (pt - CB + CR)(M - CT - pt - (1 - F)S \cdot xv_1)/S$$
$$+ (F \cdot M - CV - CB)xv_1 - F(M - CT - pt - (1 - F)S \cdot xv_1)xv_1 - F \cdot S \cdot xv_1^2/2$$
$$\text{s.t.}\quad pt, xv_1 \geq 0$$

LEMMA 1
   Vendor 1's profit function zv_1 is concave for $F > 0.5$ and is not concave or convex for $F < 0.5$.

PROOF
Vendor 1's profit function is quadratic with Hessian matrix

$$\mathbf{H} = \begin{bmatrix} -2/S & (2F-1) \\ (2F-1) & -F \cdot S(2F-1) \end{bmatrix}.$$

   According to Winston [20][8], zv_1 is concave if all nonzero principal minors have the same sign as $(-1)^k$ and is convex if all principal minors are nonnegative. The first (k=1) principal minors are $-2/S$ and $-F \cdot S(2F-1)$; the second principal minor is $(2F-1)$. Hence, zv_1 will be concave if $-2S < 0$, $-F \cdot S(2F-1) < 0$ and $(2F-1) > 0$. This is true for $F > 0.5$. For $F < 0.5$, the first principal minors have opposite signs, i.e., $-2S < 0$, $-F \cdot S(2F-1) > 0$. Hence, zv_1 is not convex or concave for $F < 0.5$. ◆

   This study focuses on solving profit functions using data values such that the profit function for each firm is concave. This enables one to easily verify that solutions generated indeed maximize the profits for each firm (and hence forms an equilibrium). For example, if (xv_1^*, pt^*) is a critical point for vendor 1's problem, since zv_1 is a concave function, the critical point is a maxima. This implies vendor 1's profits are maximized at (xv_1^*, pt^*). Sherali and Leneno [13] also made the assumption that the profit function of each firm in their supply network is a concave function.

4.3   Solution Procedure

   We are interested in determining the quantities xt^*, xvt_1^*, xv_1^* and pt^*, which simultaneously solve the telco and vendor 1's profit maximizing problems given above. Assuming an interior solution $(xt^*, xvt_1^*, xv_1^*, pt^* > 0)$, this can be accomplished by solving the following system of two equations with two unknowns.

---

[8] See pp657 in Winston [20]

$$\partial z v_1 / \partial pt = (M - CT + CB + CR - 2pt + (2F - 1) \cdot S \cdot xv_1) / S = 0$$
$$\partial z v_1 / \partial xv_1 = F \cdot (CT - CB - CR) + CR - CV + (2F - 1)pt - F(2F - 1)S \cdot xv_1 = 0$$

The equilibrium solution is:

$$pt^* = F \cdot M - CV + CR \tag{2}$$

$$xv_1^* = ((2F - 1)M + CT - 2CV - CB + CR) / ((2F - 1)S) \tag{3}$$

Substituting pt^* and xv_1^* into the telco's reaction function Eq. (1) gives

$$xt^* = (CV + CB - F(CT + CR + CB) / ((2F - 1)S) \tag{4}$$

Since an increment of one tool corresponds to an increment of one application made by the telco, $xvt_1^* = xt^*$. The total output for applications is

$$xt^* + xv_1^* = \frac{(2F - 1)M + (1 - F)(CT + CR) - CV - F \cdot CB}{(2F - 1)S} \tag{5}$$

LEMMA 2

As the revenue sharing fraction F increases, the number of applications made by the telco will decrease; the number of applications made by vendor 1 will increase; and the tool price will increase.

PROOF

From Eq. (4) we have $xt^* = (CV + CB - F(CT + CR + CB) / ((2F - 1)S)$; as F increases the numerator decreases and the denominator increases, therefore xt^* will decrease. From Eq. (3) we have $xv_1^* = ((2F - 1)M + CT - 2CV - CB + CR) / ((2F - 1)S)$; as F increases, the numerator increases at a rate of $2M$ while the denominator increases at a rate of only $2S$. Since the height of the willingness-to-pay curve (M) is much larger than the slope (S), therefore xv_1^* will increase as F increases. From Eq. (2) we have $pt^* = F \cdot M - CV + CR$; clearly as F increases, pt^* will increase. ◆

An explanation of *Lemma 2* is that as F increases, the vendor can earn more profits from making applications, therefore xv_1^* increases. At the same time, the vendor will increase the tool price in an attempt to get the telco to switch from making applications to buying applications from the vendor, therefore, pt^* increases and xt^* decreases. Will the total output of applications be such that the revenue from the last application made by vendor 1 is equal to the cost of making that application? That is, given an output K where $F\,\mathbf{P}[K] = CB + CV$, will $xt^* + xv_1^* = K$ as shown in Figure 4? This question is addressed in *Lemma 3*.

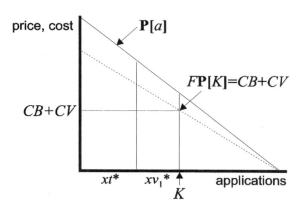

Figure -4. Illustration of Lemma 3

LEMMA 3

Total output of applications will be such that the revenue from the last application made by vendor 1 is equal to the cost of making that application, provided $F = (CV + CB)/(CB + CR + CT)$. Furthermore,
if $F > (CV + CB)/(CB + CR + CT)$, then $xt^* + xv_1^* > K$
if $F < (CV + CB)/(CB + CR + CT)$, then $xt^* + xv_1^* < K$
where $F \cdot \mathbf{P}[K] = CB + CV$

PROOF

$F \cdot \mathbf{P}[K] = CB + CV$ in   Figure   4   expands   to
$F \cdot (M \cdot K - S \cdot K) = CB + CV$ and   so $K = (F \cdot M - CB - CV)/(F \cdot S)$.
$K - (xt^* + xv_1^*)$ gives $(CV + CB - F(CB + CT + CR))/(2F^2 - F) = \Delta$.
Therefore:
xt^* + $xv_1^* = $ K if $\Delta = 0$. It is equal to zero for
$F = (CV + CB)/(CB + CR + CT)$.
xt^* + $xv_1^* <$ K if $\Delta > 0$. It is greater than zero for
$F < (CV + CB)/(CB + CR + CT)$.
xt^* + $xv_1^* >$ K if $\Delta < 0$.   It is less than zero for
$F > (CV + CB)/(CB + CR + CT)$. ◆

$xt^* + xv_1^* < K$ implies that even though the vendor can earn additional revenue from producing an additional application, it should not produce the application. This is because producing that additional application may cause the vendor to lose more profits from tools than profits gained from selling the application. This situation will occur if the vendor's cost of making an application CV is less than the cost of the telco making an application CT.

5. COMPETITION FROM A NEW APPLICATIONS SUPPLIER

This section extends the basic supply network of Section 4 to the case where a new entrant, vendor 2, competes with the incumbent vendor 1 to sell applications to the telco. Vendor 2 is assumed to be a vendor who specializes in producing applications only and does not produce any tools. The following additional notation is required for this model:

Number of applications made by vendor 2 = xv_2
Incremental cost of vendor 2 making applications = CBV
Vendor 2 profits = zv_2

5.1 Telco's Profit Maximizing Problem

Given a tool price pt and numbers of applications xv_1 and xv_2 vendors 1 and 2 are willing to sell, the telco wishes to determine the number of applications xt it should make to maximize profits. The telco believes that vendor 1 and 2 will not change the values of their decision variables when it changes its output xt. With the addition of vendor 2, the telco's profit function from Section 4.1 changes to

$$zt = \int_0^{xt} \mathbf{P}[a] \cdot da - CT \cdot xt - pt \cdot xt + (1-F) \int_{xt}^{xt+xv_1+xv_2} \mathbf{P}[a] \cdot da$$

As described in Section 2, vendor 1 is a "preferred vendor" i.e., the telco will buy high value applications from vendor 1 and buy low value applications from vendor 2. This is incorporated by integrating from xt to $(xt+xv_1+xv_2)$ in the fourth term of zt. If vendor 2 is the preferred vendor, the integration will be from xt to $(xt+xv_2+xv_1)$, i.e., the order of xv_1 and xv_2 will be reversed. Note that telco does not sacrifice any profits by purchasing applications from the preferred vendor 1 since both vendors sell applications at the same revenue sharing fraction F. Substituting out $\mathbf{P}[a]$ by $\mathbf{P}[a] = M - S \cdot a$ and performing the integration, the telco's profit maximizing problem is

$$\text{Max} \quad zt = (M - CT - pt) \cdot xt - S \cdot xt^2 / 2$$
$$+ (1 - F) \cdot (M \cdot (xv_1 + xv_2) - S \cdot (xv_1 + xv_2)) \cdot xt - S(xv_1 + xv_2)^2 / 2)$$
$$\text{s.t.} \quad xt \geq 0$$

The telco's profit function is quadratic with second order derivative also equal to $\partial zt / \partial xt \partial xt = -S$. Hence, following Section 4.1, zt is concave. Taking the derivative w.r.t. xt and assuming an interior solution (i.e., $xt^* > 0$), the telco's reaction function is obtained analogous to Section 4.1: $\partial zt / \partial xt = M - CT - pt - S \cdot xt - (1 - F) \cdot S \cdot (xv_1 + xv_2) = 0$ giving

$$xt = (M - CT - pt - (1 - F) \cdot S \cdot (xv_1 + xv_2)) / S \qquad (6)$$

5.2   Vendor 1's Profit Maximizing Problem

Vendor 1 wishes to determine the number of applications xv_1 and tool price pt it should charge to maximize profits. Similar to Section 4.2, it is assumed that vendor 1 knows the telco's reaction function Eq. (6). It is assumed that vendor 1 believes vendor 2 will not change its output xv_2 when vendor 1 changes tool price pt or output xv_1. With the addition of vendor 2, vendor 1's profit maximizing problem from Section 4.2 changes to

$$\text{Max} \quad zv_1 = (pt - CB - CR)(M - CT - pt - (1 - F)S \cdot xv_1) / S$$
$$+ (F \cdot M - CV - CB) \cdot xv_1 - F(M - CT - pt - (1 - F)S \cdot xv_1) \cdot xv_1$$
$$- F \cdot S \cdot xv_1^2 / 2 - (1 - F)S((pt - CB - CR) / S - F \cdot xv_1) \cdot xv_2$$
$$\text{s.t.} \quad pt, xv_1 \geq 0$$

This is identical to vendor 1's problem given in Section 4.2 except for the addition of the last term. Vendor 1's profit function is quadratic with Hessian matrix also equal to the one given in Section 4.2, i.e.,

$$\mathbf{H} = \begin{bmatrix} -2/S & (2F-1) \\ (2F-1) & -F \cdot S(2F-1) \end{bmatrix}.$$

Hence following *Lemma 1*, zv_1 is concave for $F > 0.5$.

5.3　Vendor 2's Profit Maximizing Problem

Given that the telco produces xt number of applications and vendor 1 produces xv_1 applications and charges tool price pt, vendor 2 wishes to determine the number of applications xv_2 it should make so as to maximize profits. Vendor 2 believes the telco and vendor 1 will not change the values of their decision variables when vendor 2 changes its output xv_2. Vendor 2's profit maximizing problem can be constructed as follows:

Vendor 2's profits = revenue from selling applications – cost of make applications

$$zv_2 = \int_{xt+xv_1}^{xt+xv_1+xv_2} F \cdot \mathbf{P}[a] \cdot da - CBV \cdot xv_2$$

Substituting out $\mathbf{P}[a]$ by $\mathbf{P}[a] = M - S \cdot a$ and performing the integration, vendor 2's profit maximizing problem is:

Max $zv_2 = (F \cdot M - CBV) \cdot xv_2 - F \cdot S \cdot (xt + xv_1) \cdot xv_2 - F \cdot S \cdot xv_2{}^2 / 2$

s.t. $xv_2 \geq 0$

Vendor 2's profit function is quadratic with second order derivative $\partial zt / \partial xt \partial xt = -F \cdot S$. Hence, zv_2 is concave since the slope S and revenue sharing fraction F are positive values.

5.4　Solution Procedure

We are interested in determining the quantities $xvt_1{}^*$, xt^*, $xv_1{}^*$, $xv_2{}^*$ and pt^*, which simultaneously solve the telco's, vendor 1's and vendor 2's profit maximizing problems given above. Assuming an interior solution ($xvt_1{}^*$, xt^*, $xv_1{}^*$, $xv_2{}^*$, $pt^* > 0$), this can be accomplished by solving the following system of four equations and four unknowns.

$\partial zt / \partial xt = (M - CT - pt - S \cdot xt - (1-F) \cdot S \cdot (xv_1 + xv_2)) / S = 0$
$\partial zv_1 / \partial pt = M - CT + CB + CR - 2pt + (2F-1)S \cdot xv_1 - (1-F) \cdot S \cdot xv_2 = 0$
$\partial zv_1 / \partial xv_1 = F(CT - CB) + (1-F)(CR + F \cdot S \cdot xv_2) - CV + (2F-1)(pt - F \cdot S \cdot xv_1) = 0$
$\partial zv_2 / \partial xv_2 = F \cdot M - CBV - F \cdot S \cdot (xt + xv_1) - F \cdot S \cdot xv_2 = 0$

The equilibrium quantities are:

$$xt^* = ((1 - F)CBV + F \cdot (CV - CT - CR))/(F^2 S) = xvt_1^* \tag{7}$$

$$xv_2^* = (F^2 CB + F \cdot CV - (2F - 1)CBV - F(1 - F)(CT + CR))/(F^3 S) \tag{8}$$

$$xv_1^* = \frac{F^3 M - (F^2 + F)CV - F^2 CB - (1 - F)CBV + F(CT + CR)}{F^3 S} \tag{9}$$

$$pt^* = F \cdot M - CV + CR \tag{10}$$

It is interesting to note that the optimal tool price formula pt^* given by Eq. (10) is the same as the one given by Eq. (2). That is, the introduction of a new entrant, vendor 2, does not change the tool price at all. This result is different from the models from the literature (shown in Sections 6.1). This is because $\partial zv_1 / \partial pt$ in both supply networks can be expressed as $\partial zv_1 / \partial pt = xt - (pt - CB - CR)/S + F \cdot xv_1$. Hence, from vendor 1's perspective, the change in profits when it changes its tool price pt is the same with or without vendor 2.

The total output of applications can be obtained by adding xt^*, xv_1^* and xv_2^* which simplifies to $xt^* + xv_1^* + xv_2^* = (F \cdot M - CBV)/(F \cdot S)$. The following lemma shows that this total output of applications will always be such that the revenue from the last application made by vendor 2 equals the incremental cost of vendor 2 making that application. It also shows that as the revenue sharing fraction increases, total output increases.

LEMMA 4

The total output of applications will always be such that the revenue from the last application made by vendor 2 equals the incremental cost of making that application, that is, $F \cdot \mathbf{P}[xt^* + xv_1^* + xv_2^*] = CBV$ as illustrated in Figure 5. Furthermore, as F increases, total output will increase.

PROOF

$xt^* + xv_1^* + xv_2^* = (F \cdot M - CBV)/(F \cdot S)$ can be written as $F \cdot (M - S(xt^* + xv_1^* + xv_2^*)) = CBV$. But $M - S(xt^* + xv_1^* + xv_2^*)$ is simply $\mathbf{P}[xt^* + xv_1^* + xv_2^*]$ and so $F \cdot \mathbf{P}[xt^* + xv_1^* + xv_2^*] = CBV$. As the revenue sharing fraction F increases, total output always increases since $\partial(xt^* + xv_1^* + xv_2^*)/\partial F = CBV/(F^2 S)$ is always positive. ♦

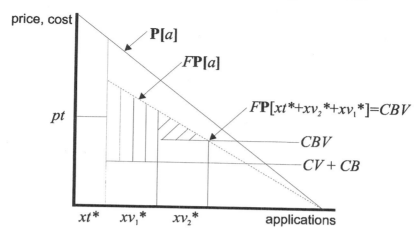

Figure -5. Illustration of Lemma 4

6.   NUMERICAL INSIGHTS

In addition to the above analytical results, this section will provide some additional insights by solving each of the two supply networks numerically. Two supply networks from the literature (Sherali and Leneno [13] and Corbett and Karmarkar [4]) will also be solved with a similar data set so that the results can be compared. Finally, sensitivity analysis will be performed by varying the revenue sharing fraction F.

To illustrate the use of the models, numerical solutions for the supply networks developed in Sections 4 and 5 will be computed using the sample data set shown in Table 1.

Table -1. Data set for AIN supply networks

Data Set	Section 4	Section 5
M	2600	2600
S	26	26
CT	200	200
CV	300	300
CB	200	200
CR	30	30
CBV	-	575
F	0.65	0.65

In the data set, a revenue sharing fraction between the vendor and telco of $F = 0.65$ is used. That is, for every \$1 of net revenue that an application generates, the telco will give the vendor $0.65. The willingness-to-pay curve is constructed to have approximately 100 plausible applications which is approximately the numbers estimated by the Perolus Group[9]. Once basic tools are produced, the cost of repackaging them into retail tools is deemed to be about 15% of the basic tool cost, hence CB = $200/tool and CR = $30/tool. The data set was chosen to have a higher cost new entrant competitor. The cost of vendor 1 to produce an application (basic tool cost + application cost) is $500. The cost of vendor 2 to produce an application is $575, which is 15% higher than the incumbent vendor 1's cost. The cost of vendor 1 producing tools (basic tool cost + repackaging cost) is $230.

6.1   Base Case Solution For Models Adapted From Literature

To compare the results in this paper with those from the literature, the model given in Sherali and Leneno [13] and Corbett and Karmarkar [4] are solved using a similar data set. A supply network in which there is one semi-finished good firm is solved (Figure 6 - left). The semi-finished good firm sells a semi-finished good x to the finished good firm that uses x to make the finished good y. This supply network is extended to the case where there are two semi-finished good firms (Figure 6 - right). Comparing these two networks will show the effects of semi-finished good firm 2 on "incumbent" semi-finished good firm 1 as well as the finished good firm. This is analogous to the effect of the new vendor 2 on incumbent vendor 1 and telco for the case of AIN. The results are summarized in Table 2.

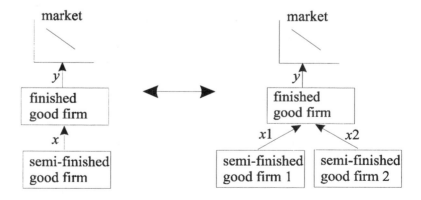

Figure -6. Models from the literature

[9] The Perolus Group, *The Future of The Advanced Intelligent Network*, 1994

Table -2. Data set and solution for models from literature

Data Set	Figure 6 left	Figure 6 right
Height of demand curve for finished good	2600	2600
Slope of demand curve for finished good	26	26
Finished good firm production cost	200	200
Semi-finished good firm 1 production cost	230	230
Semi-finished good firm 2 production cost	-	264.5
Solution		
Number of finished good	20.8	27.5
Number of semi-finished good: firm 1	20.8	14.1
Number of semi-finished good: firm 2	-	13.4
Semi-finished good price	1315	964.8
Finished good firm profit	11319	19804
Semi-finished good firm 1 profit	22638	10384
Semi-finished good firm 2 profit	-	9432

The following observations are made and will be used to compare with our AIN models.

a) Comparing the outputs for the semi-finished good firm 1 before and after the entry of a second semi-finished good firm shows that when a new semi-finished good firm enters to compete with the incumbent firm, the output of the incumbent firm will drop.

b) The equilibrium semi-finished good price drops when a new semi-finished good firm enters the market to compete with the incumbent firm. In the AIN model, the tool price is unchanged when vendor 2 enters. This was discussed in Section 5 where it was noted that the tool price equations (2) and (10) are the same.

In the following sections, a sensitivity analysis will be conducted to show how changes in the revenue sharing fraction F affect the incumbent vendor 1's product mix, as well as vendor 1 and the telco's profits. The results are shown in Figures 7 through 9. In each case, results are plotted for the supply network of Section 4 with just one vendor (labeled as "v1" on the graphs) as well as for supply network in Section 5 with vendors 1 and 2 (label as "v1v2" on the graphs).

6.2   Effect of New Entrant on Applications & Tools Produced

Figure 7 shows that the number of applications produced by vendor 1 increases when vendor 2 enters. This is different from the results obtained from models in the literature as given by point (a) in Section 6.1 which indicates that output *should decrease* and not increase.   Comparing plots "v1 (vendor 1)" and "v1v2 (vendor 1)" show that for a small value of F, vendor 2 has a large effect on vendor 1's output. Vendor 2's effect on vendor 1 decreases as F increases. Finally, the plot shows that vendor 2 will produced zero applications (does not enter the market) if $F > 0.76$ for our data set. The value of $F = 0.67$ represents the point where equation (8) equals zero. As the revenue sharing fraction F increases, the profit margin for each application made by the incumbent vendor 1 increases. Hence, vendor 1 will produce and sell more applications to the telco, leaving fewer applications for vendor 2 to produce and sell to the telco.

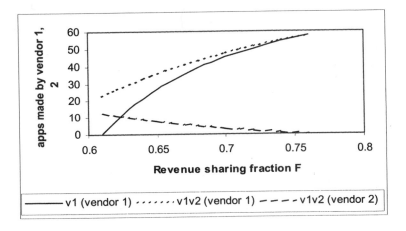

Figure -7. Number of applications produced by vendor 1 and 2

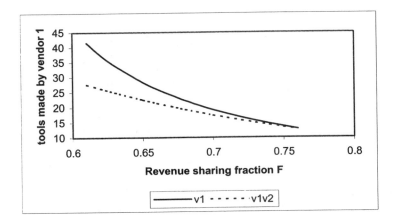

Figure -8. Effect o new entrant on number of tools produced by incumbent vendor

Figure 8 shows that the number of tools produced by vendor 1 decreases when vendor 2 enters. This result concurs with those in the literature as noted in point (a) in Section 6.1. Again, whether the effect of vendor 2 on vendor 1's output of tools is small or large depends on the value of F.

6.3 Effect of New Entrant on Telco Profits

Figure 9 shows that the telco's profits increase when vendor 2 enters. This result is the same as that given by in Figure 6 where the finished good firm's profits increases when a new semi-finished good firm enters. As F increases, the effect of vendor 2 on the telco's profits is less pronounced. Looking at the plot "v1", it is interesting to note that the telco makes the most profits when it gives vendor 1 a fraction of about $F = 0.67$. This is contrast to the thinking that the telco will make more money if it gives the vendor a smaller share, i.e., lower revenue sharing fraction for applications purchased from the vendor.

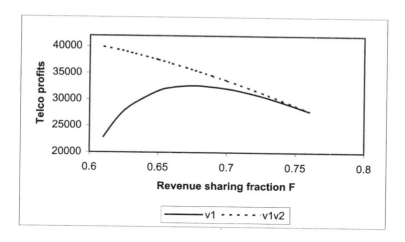

Figure -9. Effect of new entrant on telco profits

The explanation for this is that at a low F, the vendor will want to sell mainly tools and very few applications, and so the profits that the telco will earn comes mainly from applications that it makes using vendor's tools. As F increases, vendor 1 will sell more and more applications xv_1 (*Lemma 2*), and so the telco will earn profits from both applications that it makes (xt) as well as from applications that it buys from the vendor (xv_1), and so total profits for the telco increases as F increases. However, as F continues to increase, the telco's profit margin from buying and selling applications drops (since it has to pay the vendor more for applications), therefore, overall profits for the telco will begin to decline.

7.   FURTHER RESEARCH & CONCLUSIONS

The focus of this paper is to study the AIN supply network in which vendors sell applications and tools to a telco to deliver AIN services to its customers. Of interest is the impact of a new vendor entering the industry and competing with the incumbent vendor. Some ideas for extension of the analysis would be to examine the case where the revenue sharing fraction F is a decision variable of the model as opposed to being a parameter of the model. Constant production costs functions are assumed throughout this paper. Other cost functions maybe be investigated in future work. A linear willingness-to-pay curve is employed in this paper, perhaps nonlinear curves with different elastics can be examined in future work. Another extension would be to examine the case where the telco and the vendor are vertically integrated. Finally, supply networks studied in this paper has multiple vendors but just one telco. Hence, a natural extension would be to consider the case where there are multiple vendors and telcos.

REFERENCES

[1] Anderson, John, *Intelligent Networks: Principles and Applications*, Institution of Electrical Engineers, ISBN0852969775, (2002).
[2] Axlesson M. et al., "Intelligent Networks. Architectural Principles And an Economical Analysis", in *Network Planning in the 1990's*, Elsevier Science Publishers B.V. (North-Holland), pp351-358, (1989).
[3] Choi, S.C., "Price Competition in A Channel Structure With A Common Retailer", *Marketing Science* Vol 10, No. 4, pp271-291, (1991).
[4] Corbett, CJ, Karmarkar US, "Competition and structure in serial supply chains with deterministic demand", *Management Science* Vol 47, pp966-978, (2001).
[5] Edwards Jr., C.H. and Penny, D.E., *Calculus and Analytic Geometry*, Prentice-Hall Englewood Cliff, N.J., (1985).
[6] Farnham T., "Basics of AIN" in *Annual Review of Communications*, Vol 48, pp443-446, (1995).
[7] Feldman, M. Samuel, "Intelligent Network System Architecture" in *Annual Review of Communications*, Vol 49, pp879-886, (1996).
[8] Henderson, J.M. and R.E. Quandt, *Microeconomic Theory*, McGraw Hill, New York, (1971).
[9] Hirshleifer, Jack and Glazer, Amihai, *Price Theory and Applications, 5th Edition*, Prentice Hall, New Jersey, (1992).
[10] Quan V. and J.S. Rogers. Modelling A Vendor-Telco Supply Network To Deliver Two Types of Telephony Services. In: *Computers & Industrial Engineering,* Vol 46, pp893-903 (2004)

[11] Ratnatunga, Janek, "Pricing in Intelligent Routing Networks", In *Intelligent Networks, The Path to Global Networking*, Proceedings of the International Council For Computer Communication Intelligent Networks Conference, Tampa, Florida, May 4-6, (1992).

[12] Roltsch S.A., et al., "Modeling The Economics of Transition Towards an intelligent Network" in *Network Planning in The 1990's*, Elsevier Science Publishers B.V. (North-Holland), pp347-349, (1989).

[13] Sherali H.D. and Leneno J.M., "A Mathematical Programming Approach to a Nash-Corunot Equilibrium Analysis for a Two-Stage Network of Oligopolies", *Operations Research* Vol 36, No.5, pp682-702, (1988).

[14] Steffen, Bernhard; Margaria, Tiziana; Classen, Andreas; Braun, Volker, "An Environment for the Creation of Intelligent Network Services" in *Annual Review of Communications*, Vol 49, pp919-930, (1996).

[15] Tweddell, Gordon, "Advanced Intelligent Network Services: A Canadian Perspective" in *Annual Review of Communications*, Vol 49, pp937-944, (1996).

[16] Tyagi, RK, "On the Effects of Downstream Entry", *Management Science* Vol 45, pp59-73, (1999).

[17] Unterstein, Richard, "Intelligent Network Services Is The Residential Market Willing to Pay?" in *Intelligent Networks, The Path to Global Networking*, Proceedings of the International Council For Computer Communication Intelligent Networks Conference, Tampa, Florida, May 4-6, (1992).

[18] Varian, Hal R. *Microeconomic Analysis 3ed*, W.W. Norton & Company, (1992).

[19] Wennerber, M., Van Hal, P. and Wegner D.C., "An Advanced Service Creation Environment Using SIBs" in *Annual Review of Communications*, Vol 47, pp454-459, (1994).

[20] Winston W.L, *Operations Research: Applications and Alogrithms 3ED*, Wadsworth Publishing Company, Belmont California USA, (1994).

Chapter 5

A NETWORK PROVISIONING SCHEME BASED ON DECENTRALIZED BANDWIDTH AUCTIONS

Sandford Bessler

Telecommunications Research Center Vienna, FTW

bessler@ftw.at

Peter Reichl

Telecommunications Research Center Vienna, FTW

reichl@ftw.at

Keywords: Network pricing, Internet Economics, bandwidth auctions, MPLS provisioning, flow optimization

1.   Introduction and Related Work

With the rapidly increasing interest in providing QoS in the Internet, Internet pricing has now been recognized to be a cornerstone of the Internet of the future. Over the last couple of years, this has led to establishing "Internet Economics" as a new research area of its own, which investigates packet-switched networks from an economical rather than an engineering perspective. In this context, pricing Internet services has always been the central focus of this research, leading to a huge variety of proposed mechanisms (as surveyed e.g. in [2] or [11]). Starting with the seminal "smart market" approach due to MacKie-Mason [8], the usage of auctions has gained some popularity in this context. Whereas the original smart market proposal dealt with second-price auctions on a packet level, subsequent proposals like the "Progressive Second-Price" (PSP) mechanism due to Lazar and Semret [6] are able to deal with flows over arbitrary divisible capacities. More recently, some efforts have been directed towards the case of auctions for multi-link paths [1] and/or multi-period sessions [10].

In this paper, we describe a mechanism combining optimal provisioning of QoS-enabled MPLS networks and auction-based pricing of network bandwidth. The basic idea is to solve the provisioning problem on a slow time-scale by an appropriate multi-commodity flow problem and a utility function which is aggregated from the ordered linear user requests. Once provisioned, the bandwidth is allocated on a fast time-scale to the winners of a second-price auction taking place at the edge nodes between all users competing for the respective commodity. Simulation examples for time-varying traffic of hundreds of users in small networks demonstrate the validity and efficiency of this approach.

Certain aspects of network dynamic pricing (especially congestion pricing) and efficient resource allocation have been extensively studied using primal or dual formulation of a flow optimization problem with capacity and routing constraints. With the goal to maximize the total welfare, Kelly [5] finds a decomposition into independent user problems and a network problem and in this way, firstly, avoids the not scalable central approach and secondly, replaces the user utility function (which is not known to the network) with costs obtained from the duality theory. Many of the pricing control schemes like Smart Market [8] or Proportional Fair Pricing [4] act on packet/message level, i.e. on a very short time scale. In [9] the authors conclude that a static pricing that does not depend on instantaneous congestion and corresponds to a time-of-day pricing closely matches the optimal pricing strategy. To our knowledge, there are very few works that use network auctions in a provisioning time-scale of minutes to hours. Yuksel and Kalyanaraman [14] also consider larger time scales in their Distributed Dynamic Capacity Contracting scheme. Wang and Schulzrinne [12] use multiple bid (M-bid) auctions for congestion pricing at session duration time scale, however they report on the difficulty in splitting the available budget on the required network resources. Our approach also considers time-of-day time scales, abstracts the auctioned resource to commodity bandwidth instead of link bandwidth and exploits the interdependence between bandwidth provisioning, pricing and admission control to maximize welfare.

The rest of the paper is organized as follows: in section 2 we formulate the provisioning problem with welfare maximization as the objective. The aggregated utility function and its approximation is presented in section 3, and the proposed distributed system architecture is shown is section 4. Computation results on a small network in section 5 are followed by concluding remarks and further research in section 6.

2.   Model and Provisioning Problem

Consider an MPLS network with N nodes and L directed links, where each of the links has capacity C_l. There is a total of K commodities, each defined by the triple (source node, destination node, traffic class). Based on the QoS parameters associated with the traffic class of a path (delay bound, maximum link disjointness, etc.), we assume there is a number $p(k)$ of path variants for each commodity k that are used for load sharing the user sessions. For any link

l, let $P_j^k(l) = 1$ if l is contained in the j-th path variant for commodity k and $P_j^k(l) = 0$ otherwise (link path matrix).

Assume user m competes for capacity on commodity k and has a utility function $U_m^k(y_m^k)$, where y_m^k describes the capacity allocated to user m. If we want to maximize the social welfare of the system, i.e. the sum of satisfied user utilities, two issues arise: (a) which capacity $c(k)$ should be assigned to commodity k ("provisioning problem"), and (b) which user requests for commodity k should be fulfilled, given the capacity restriction $c(k)$ ("admission problem")? Of course, these questions can be answered by a joint optimization problem where all users report their utility functions to a central planner which subsequently provisions and allocates optimally the available capacity. In practice, however, this scheme is not scalable: all users would have to report their respective utility functions in the same time to the central planner which has to solve a highly complex non-linear optimization problem to answer the questions (a) and (b) above. Moreover obtaining correct utility functions from the users is a task of huge difficulty on its own.

In order to avoid these complications, in a first simplification step we follow [5], [8] in aggregating all M^k users competing for commodity k to a single user k with aggregated utility $U^k(y^k)$ and total capacity demand D^k. Assuming that these aggregated utility functions are concave, the question of optimal provisioning may be formulated as the following multi-commodity flow problem:

SYSTEM:

$$\max_{x_j^k} \sum_{k=1}^{K} U^k\left(\sum_{j=1}^{p(k)} x_j^k\right) \tag{5.1}$$

subject to :

$$\sum_{k=1}^{K} \sum_{j=1}^{p(k)} P_j^k(l) x_j^k \leq C_l, l = 1, ..., L \tag{5.2}$$

$$\sum_{j=1}^{p(k)} x_j^k \leq D^k, k = 1, ...K \tag{5.3}$$

$$x_j^k \geq 0, j = 1, ..., p(k), k = 1, ..., K \tag{5.4}$$

In 5.1, the commodity flows y^k have been replaced with the sum of contributing flows x_j^k for each path j. The inequalities 5.2 state that the flow on each link should not exceed the reserved link capacity C_l. The inequalities 5.3 express the multiple path routing constraints: the total sum of calculated flows cannot exceed the traffic demand D^k. The slack represents the lost traffic, i.e. the part of the demand traffic that is rejected. Therefore, we obtain always a feasible solution, even if some traffic demands D^k exceed the network capacity. Solving the SYSTEM problem results in a set of capacities $y^k = \sum_{j=1}^{p(k)} x_j^k$ which optimizes the provisioning problem, provided the utility functions U^k of the aggregated users $k = 1, ..., K$ are given.

3.   Admission Problem and Aggregated Utility Function

Assume y^k describes the total capacity available for fulfilling requests for commodity k. Then, Generalized Vickrey Auctions (GVA) are the standard mechanism to distribute this capacity efficiently among the competing users. This edge-to-edge pricing scheme requires to perform auctions at each source node. Under GVA, each user submits a two-dimensional bid (ξ_m^k, β_m^k), where ξ_m^k corresponds to the amount of bandwidth requested and β_m^k is the bid price which the user is willing to pay per time and bandwidth unit. Whereas in general, user are assumed to have an individual concave utility function [5], the assumption of a per-unit bid leads directly to linear user utility functions which differ only by the respective slopes. Note that the mentioned bid is the only information we can expect in practice from a user, and moreover that the GVA mechanism charges the winning bidders uniformly the highest losing bid and thus guarantees incentive compatibility, i.e., for any user, truthful revelation of the willingness-to-pay is the optimal strategy. More details on the auctioning procedure and the extensions proposed for repeated auctions due to long sessions have been presented in [10].

It is very important to see that, whereas the individual users are assumed to have linear utility functions, the aggregated utility function per commodity is again strictly concave: assuming the requests are ordered with decreasing price β_m^k, i.e. $\beta_1^k \geq \beta_2^k \geq ... \geq \beta_M^k$, the aggregation process for each commodity yields a piecewise linear aggregated utility function as depicted in Figure 5.1, whose concavity is guaranteed by the falling order of bids. Without loss of generality we assume that the $(M+1)$-th bidder is the network provider, offering the lowest bid and buying the remaining available capacity. Putting this idea more formally, define $s \in 1, ..., M+1$ such that $\sum_{m=1}^{s} \xi_m^k \leq y^k < \sum_{m=1}^{s+1} \xi_m^k$. Then, the s highest bidding users get their requested bandwidth for commodity k, user $s+1$ gets part of his request, and all lower bidding users are denied their requests, whereas the market price charged uniformly to all winners is derived essentially from β_{s+1}^k.

Whereas the aggregation process already decreases the signalling overhead significantly, in fact we can go even further. To simplify the analytical result, we assume that all the users request the same bandwidth. We will see in simulation results in Section 5 that this assumption has a negligible impact on the solution accuracy. As before, we assume also that the willingness-to-pay of users is uniformly distributed between a minimum p_{min} and a maximum price value

p_{max}. In this case, using standard order statistics [13] for the random variables $\beta_1^k \geq \ldots \geq \beta_s^k \geq \ldots \geq \beta_n^k$ we know that the estimated value of the s-th variable is $E(\beta_s^k) = p_{max} - s(p_{max} - p_{min})/(n+1)$. Therefore, the expected values for different s are on a line with negative slope. As this line essentially describes the unit bid price for increasing capacity provisioned to the respective commodity, its integration leads to the total willingness-to-pay of the aggregated competitors with respect to total allocated capacity. As integrating a linear function straightforwardly yields a quadratic function, we may conclude that the expectation of the cumulative function U(y) is quadratic $U^k(y) = ay^2 + by$. In order to obtain the coefficients a, b, we impose $U(y_s^k) = \sum_{m=1}^{s} \beta_m^k \xi_m^k = ay_s^2 + by_s$ and $U'(y_s) = 2ay_s + b = \pi^k$, (where y_s^k is the current bandwidth of the commodity k, and π^k is the resulted auction price). This approximation allows to reduce the information that has to be reported by each edge auction agent to the provisioning system to only two coefficients. Note in this context that a high auction frequency corresponds to a high number of samples of the aggregated utility function. Thus, the law of large numbers leads to an increasing accuracy of the averaged aggregated utility function as an additional benefit from separating the fast auction time-scale from the slow provisioning time-scale.

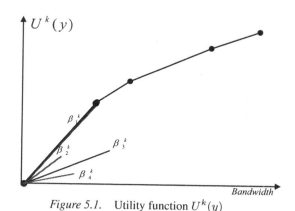

Figure 5.1. Utility function $U^k(y)$

4. System architecture

Returning to the problem SYSTEM, we notice that in case of a congested commodity k, the solution provides both the optimal bandwidth x_i^k and determines which requests fill this bandwidth, corresponding to the outcome of a second price auction. This implies however that all the auctions are performed simultaneously and are synchronized with the run of the problem SYSTEM - a condition that cannot be fulfilled in practice.

The major novelty of our approach consists in decoupling the auctions on each commodity k from the provisioning step. (see Figure 5.2 for a sketch of this architecture). This allows to perform the auctions at a fast time scale and average the results, while the provisioning is done in a much slower cycle. The interval between the auctions should be a function of the average session length, such that the auction represents an efficient mean for admission control in congestion case. Long sessions are handled with the second chance scheme [10]. The provisioning step represents a much slower adaption of the whole network bandwidth to eventual traffic shifts.

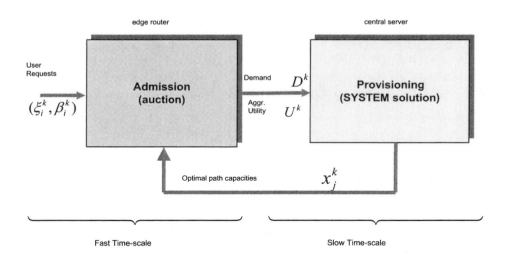

The data collection of the provisioning system will request from the edge routers the utility function coefficients for each commodity participating to the system. This can be any subset of edge nodes and corresponding paths. Also the offered demand D^k is used for the calculation. Depending on the technology used, the path capacities can be enforced in MPLS network by using the RSVP-TE protocol.

The scenarios are not restricted to private customers: the network seen as connectivity infrastructure provider could offer QoS services to service providers and enterprises in a much more flexible manner as today's subscription models.

5. Numerical Results

The optimization and auction algorithms have been implemented in AMPL-CPLEX [3] and tested on a network with 10 nodes, 17 links and 8 commodities (see Figure 5.3 and Table 1). The distributed auctions at the edges are simulated: the sessions created with Poisson arrival rate have uniformly distributed duration, bid and bandwidth demand. In a first experiment, congestion is created by raising suddenly the demand of commodity 2→7. Figure 5.4 shows the dynamic provisioning effect during 100 auction periods: the allocated bandwidth follows the demand change (with a delay because, after every n (n=4) auctions, a provisioning step is performed). The first periods are not relevant since the system starts from some given initial solution flow. In Figure 5.5 we depict the market price evolution of commodity 2→7 and the commodity 2→8 (that shares links with 2→7, but has a constant demand): 2→7, which is highly congested at the beginning (period 50), is provisioned in such a way that it gets more bandwidth allocated, leading to a price decrease. Due to the capacity constraints, the bandwidth of commodity 2→8 has to decrease until the prices on both commodities become equal in steady state. The average and variance values of the market prices in the whole network in Figure 5.6 show that, through bandwidth adaptations the system reacts quickly to demand changes, after which the prices stabilize again.

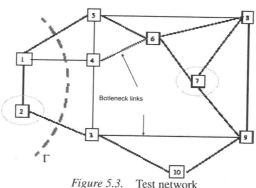

Figure 5.3. Test network

Another interesting question to investigate is, how does the performance worsen by a) decoupling the auctions from provisioning and by b) approxi-

Table 5.1.   Test network commodities and paths

Commodity	Path 1	Path 2	Arrival rate
1→7	1-4-6-7	1-5-8-7	20
1→8	1-5-6-8	1-4-6-8	20
1→10	1-2-3-10	1-5-8-9-10	20
2→7	2-3-9-7	2-1-4-6-7	10 to 50
2→9	2-3-9	2-3-10-9	20
2→10	2-3-10	2-3-9-10	20
1→9	1-5-8-9	1-2-3-9	20
2→8	2-3-9-8	2-1-4-6-8	40

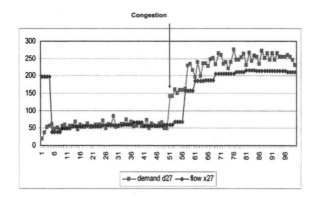

Figure 5.4.   Congestion impact on commodity flow during 100 auction periods

mating the utility function. We use as criterion the total user payoff, that is the difference between the offered valuation and the actual price paid (summed up over the winning users): $P_U = \sum_{i \in I_+^k, k \in K} (\beta_i^k - \pi^k) q_i^k$ where we denote by I_+^k the set of winning users. Figure 5.7 compares P_U for three cases: the ideal joint optimization with exact (piece linear) objective function (JE), the joint optimization with approximated utility (JA) and the decoupled auctions with approximated utility (DA). The effect of the quadratic approximation of the utility is negligible. Together with the simplifying assumption that all the requests have the same bandwidth, the difference in the average user payoff in the JE versus the JA case is 1,85% when the demands are uniformly distributed between 1 to 5 units. If this distribution narrows down from 2 to 4 bandwidth units, the payoff difference is only 1%. Note that the bottleneck link bandwidth is 200 units, that is much larger than the individual requests.

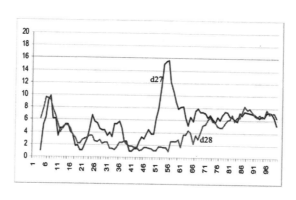

Figure 5.5. Price equalization on competing congested commodities

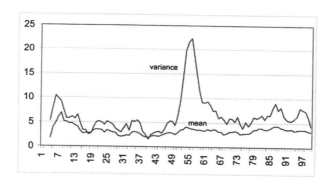

Figure 5.6. Market price average and variance during 100 auction periods

As expected, the performance degradation is mainly due to decoupling the auctions from the provisioning step (reaching a total of 13%), the market prices in DA case are in general higher because of a sub-optimal resource allocation, resulting in a lower payoff. As an additional performance indication, we count the total number of completed sessions. Thus, we observe in the DA case that higher market prices cause to an increase in the number of dropped sessions which have exhausted their budget too early.

In general, the DA architecture behaves like any control system: the signal coming from the auctions is filtered (average building), while the feedback signal is represented by the bandwidth update calculated in the provisioning step. Oscillation can occur theoretically if a demand increase is in phase with a decrease of the provisioned bandwidth. Aggregation of commodities and average building of demands over many periods drastically reduce however the oscillation probability. The auctioning period itself does not affect the performance of the system, it just has to be defined in relation to the average session length to optimally capture the change in the traffic load of the commodities. The performance of the decoupled system depends more on the provisioning time scale: a large provisioning period will better smoothen traffic variations, but increase the reaction delay to a net load shift on the network paths.

Performance. avg. over 100 periods	Joint exact **JE**	Joint approx. **JA**	Decoupled Approx. **DA**
User profit	3528	3463	3086
Sessions completed	15488 (95%)	14934 (95%)	13559 (93%)

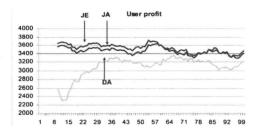

Figure 5.7.   Total user payoff as performance index for JE, JA, and DA schemes during 100 auctions

6.   Summary

The work presented in this paper deals with practical aspects of auctioning and provisioning in packet networks. For our study we have chosen an MPLS environment, but our results pertain to much more general cases where a set of customers compete for divisible end-to-end commodities, which are combined from several links, whereas the network provider needs to allocate link capacity to the various end-to-end commodities. The complexity of combinatorial auctions on links has lead us to consider a higher abstraction level of pricing the commodity (source, destination class of service) that also fits better the user terminology, but that has a global effect on routing and capacity assignment in the network. We have shown that the solution could consist of auctions at the edge nodes combined with global capacity provisioning. Since synchronous operation between the auction and the provisioning cycles is not feasible in practice, we proposed to decouple these steps in time. However, for such interfaces between systems we have to pay with penalties in the system efficiency: in this case the auction prices are higher and the user profits lower then in the ideal, joint optimization case.

Finally, for the goal of welfare maximization we derive a piece-wise linear aggregated utility function for which we have shown a quadratic function to be a natural approximation candidate. While the accuracy of the approximation increases with the auction frequency, the number of parameters per commodity to be transmitted from the edge to the central provisioning engine reduces to merely two coefficients describing the best quadratic approximation which is a truly drastic reduction of signalling overhead.

Further simulations on larger networks will be performed to measure the performance and the quality of the decoupled auctions solution (DA) in comparison to the ideal exact case (JE).

Acknowledgments

This work has been performed partially in the framework of the Austrian Kplus Competence Center programme.

References

[1] C. Courcoubetis, M. P. Dramitinos, G. D. Stamoulis, An Auction Mechanism for Bandwidth Allocation over Paths, International Teletraffic Congress ITC-17, Salvador da Bahia, Brazil, Dec 2001, pp 1163-1174.

[2] M. Falkner, M. Devetsikiotis, I. Lamdadaris, An Overview of Pricing Concepts for Broadband IP Networks, IEEE Communications Surveys, 2nd Quarter 2000, pp 2-13.

[3] R. Fourer, D.M.Gay, B.W. Kernighan: AMPL. A modelling language for mathematical programming. Boyd and Fraser, 1993.

[4] F.P. Kelly, A. K. Maulloo, D. K. Tan, Rate control in communication networks: shadow prices, proportional fairness and stability, Journal of Operations Research Society 49 (1998) 237-252.

[5] Frank Kelly, Charging and rate control for elastic traffic, 1997

[6] A. A. Lazar, N. Semret, Design and Analysis of the Progressive Second Price Auction for Network Bandwidth Sharing, Telecommunications Systems, Special Issue on Network Economics, 2000.

[7] S.H. Low, D.E. Lapsley, Optimization flow control, I: Basic algorithm and convergence, IEEE/ACM Transactions on Networking 7(6) (1999) p.861-875.

[8] J. K. MacKie-Mason, A smart market for resource reservation in a multiple quality of service information network, 1995

[9] I.C. Paschalidis, J.N. Tsitsiklis, Congestion dependent pricing of network services, IEEE/ACM Transactions of Networkin 8 (2) (2000) 171-184.

[10] P. Reichl, S. Bessler, B. Stiller: Second-chance auctions for multimedia session pricing, Proc. MIPS'03, Naples, Italy, Nov. 2003.

[11] B. Stiller, P. Reichl, S. Leinen, Pricing and Cost Recovery for Internet Services: Practical Review, Classification and Application of Relevant Models, NETNOMICS - Economic Research and Electronic Networking, vol. 3 no. 1, March 2001.

[12] X. Wang, H. Schulzrinne, Auction and Tatônnment, Finding Congestion pricing for adaptive applications, Proceedings 10th International Conference on Network Protocols (INCP'02).

[13] Elmar Wolfstetter, Topics in Microeconomics, Cambridge Press, 1999.

[14] M. Yuksel, S. Kalyanaraman, Distributed dynamic capacity contracting: an overlay congestion pricing framework, Computer Communications, 26(2003)1484-1503.

Chapter 6

AN OPTIMIZATION-BASED APPROACH TO MODELING INTERNET TOPOLOGY

David Alderson
California Institute of Technology
alderd@cds.caltech.edu

Walter Willinger
AT&T Labs–Research
walter@research.att.com

Lun Li
California Institute of Technology
lun@cds.caltech.edu

John Doyle
California Institute of Technology
doyle@cds.caltech.edu

Abstract   Over the last decade there has been significant interest and attention devoted towards understanding the complex structure of the Internet, particularly its topology and the large-scale properties that can be derived from it. While recent work by empiricists and theoreticians has emphasized certain statistical and mathematical properties of network structure, this article presents an optimization-based perspective that focuses on the objectives, constraints, and other drivers of engineering design. We argue that Internet topology at the router-level can be understood in terms of the tradeoffs between network performance and the technological and economic factors constraining design. Furthermore, we suggest that the formulation of corresponding optimization problems serves as a reasonable starting point for generating "realistic, yet fictitious" network topologies.

Finally, we describe how this optimization-based perspective is being used in the development of a still-nascent theory for the Internet as a whole.

Keywords: Internet topology, network optimization, router constraints, protocol stack, highly optimized tolerance, topology generator.

1.   The Importance of Internet Topology

Understanding the large-scale structural properties of the Internet is critical for network managers, software and hardware engineers, and telecommunications policy makers alike. On a practical level, models of network topology factor prominently in the design and evaluation of network protocols, since it is understood that although topology should not affect the *correctness* of a protocol, it can have a dramatic impact on its *performance* [94]. Accordingly, the ability to shape network traffic for the purposes of improved application performance often depends on the location and interconnection of network resources. In addition, a detailed understanding of network topology is fundamental for developing improved resource provisioning, as most network design problems assume a detailed description of existing/available network components.

More broadly, models of network topology may also play an important role in gaining a basic understanding of certain aspects of current large-scale network behavior. For example, the ability to understand, detect, react to, and deal with network attacks such as denial of service (DoS) attacks or network worms/viruses can depend critically on the topology over which those attacks propagate [80]. As the Internet and related communication networks become an increasingly important component of the national economic and social fabric, national security experts and government policy makers seek to understand the reliability and robustness features of this now critical infrastructure [84, 98], and the topological aspects of the Internet are primary to this purpose.

However, understanding the large-scale structural properties of the Internet has proved to be a challenging problem. For a host of technological and economic reasons, the current Internet does not lend itself to direct inspection. Since the Internet is a collection of thousands of smaller networks, each under its own administrative control, there is no single place from which one can obtain a complete picture of its topology. Whereas coordination among the administrative organizations of these separate networks was relatively easy during the Internet's initial days as a research project, the diversity of technologies and organizational entities in the current landscape make this prohibitive. Today, the sheer number of the network components (e.g. nodes, links) in the Internet preclude even the ability to visualize the network in a simple manner [27]. Also, since the decommissioning of the NSFNet in 1995, when administrative control of the Internet was given over to commercial entities, the fear of losing competitive advantage has provided a strong disincentive for network owners and operators to share topology information.

Since the Internet does not lend itself naturally to direct inspection, the task of "discovering" the network has been left to experimentalists who develop more or less sophisticated methods to infer this topology from appropriate network measurements [19, 89, 40, 44, 87, 90]. Because of the elaborate nature of the network protocol suite, there are a multitude of possible measurements that can be made, each having its own strengths, weaknesses, and idiosyncrasies, and each resulting in a distinct, yet fundamentally incomplete, view of the network as a whole.

These factors suggest the need for a theoretical framework that facilitates the modeling of network topology on a large scale and which also provides an understanding of the relationship between network topology and network behavior. This article describes the importance of *an optimization-based perspective* in the development of an explanatory model for Internet topology. Essentially, we argue that Internet topology can be understood in terms of the tradeoffs between network performance and the technological and economic factors constraining design. Furthermore, we suggest that appropriate optimization-based formulations can be used to generate "realistic, yet fictitious" Internet topologies. Finally, we describe how this view of topology is really just a small piece of a much larger picture, where the ultimate goal is to use this optimization-based framework to obtain a fundamental understanding of *the entire Internet protocol stack*. In this manner, recent successes in the use of optimization to capture essential features of network topology and behavior [62] can be viewed as part of an ongoing effort to develop a more comprehensive *mathematical theory for the Internet* [56, 99] and perhaps even a starting point for understanding the "robust, yet fragile" structure of complex engineering systems [33].

2.   Previous Work on Internet Topology

Due to the multilayered nature of the Internet protocol stack, there is no one single topology that reflects the structure of the Internet as a whole. Rather, because any two network components (e.g. routers, end hosts) that run the same protocol at the same layer of the architecture can communicate, each protocol induces its own natural graph on the network, representing in turn the connectivity among all such components. For example, the *router-level graph* of the Internet reflects one-hop connectivity between routing devices running the *Internet Protocol (IP)*. Because the router-level graph has received significant attention by the computer networking community, it is sometimes misinterpreted as *the only* Internet graph, but there are many other graphs having very different structural properties and features. For example, the *AS-graph* reflects the "peering relationships" between independent subnetworks, known as *au-*

tonomous systems (ASes). That is, when two independent network providers (e.g. AT&T and Sprint) enter into a business relationship by which they agree to exchange traffic, they connect their router-level infrastructure together at various peering points. Currently, there are over 10,000 ASes in the Internet, and their aggregate peering structure induces an alternate graph in which each AS (composed of hundreds or thousands of router-level components) can be represented as a single node and each peering relationship (again, possibly reflecting many physical peering points) can be represented as a single link between two ASes. At an entirely different level of abstraction, recent interest in the World Wide Web (WWW) has brought attention to the large-scale graph structure among web documents (represented as nodes) that are connected by hyperlinks (represented as links). Thus, the router-level graph reflects a type of physical connectivity, the AS-level graph represents a type of organizational connectivity, and the WWW-graph represents a type of virtual overlay connectivity. However, there is no direct relationship between each of these "Internet graphs", and in general the features of each graph are quite different.

The development of abstract, yet informed, models for network topology generation has followed the work of empiricists. The first popular topology generator to be used for networking simulation was the Waxman model [97], which is a variation of the classical Erdos-Renyi random graph [35]. In this model, nodes are placed at random in a two-dimensional space, and links are added probabilistically between each pair of nodes in a manner that is inversely proportional to their distance. As a representation of the router-level graph, this model was meant to capture the general observation that long-range links are expensive. The use of this type of random graph model was later abandoned in favor of models that explicitly introduce non-random structure, particularly hierarchy and locality, as part of the network design [30, 21, 107]. The argument for this type of approach was based on the fact that an inspection of real router-level networks shows that they are clearly not random but do exhibit certain obvious hierarchical features. This approach further argued that a topology generator should reflect the design principles in common use. For example, in order to achieve desired performance objectives, the network must have certain connectivity and redundancy requirements, properties which are not guaranteed in random network topologies. These principles were integrated into the Georgia Technology Internetwork Topology Models (GT-ITM) simulator.

These *structural topology generators* were the standard models in use until the discovery of scaling or "power law" relationships in the connectivity of both the AS-graph and the router-level graph of the Internet [38, 88] and in the WWW-graph [55, 5, 2]. More specifically, these findings suggest that the distribution of *degree* (i.e. number of connections, denoted here as x) for each node is appropriately represented in the tail by a function $d(x) \propto k_1 x^{-\beta}$, where $0 < \beta < 2$ and k_1 is a positive finite constant. This conjecture/observation has been highly influential in spawning a line of research focused on the identification and explanation of power law distributions in network topology [102, 26, 70, 100, 74], and it has also influenced research on the development of network topology generators. As a result, state-of-the-art generators have recently been evaluated on the basis of whether or not they can reproduce the same types of power law relationships [20]. Since the Transit-Stub and Tiers structural generators in GT-ITM fail to produce power laws in node degree, they have been largely abandoned in favor of new *degree-based* models that explicitly replicate these observed statistics [94]. Examples of these generators include the INET AS-level topology generator [52], BRITE [69], the Power Law Random Graph (PLRG) method [4], the Carnegie Mellon power-law generator [83], as well as general preferential attachment methods [102].

Our belief is that it is possible to capture and represent realistic drivers of Internet deployment and operation in order to create a topology generation framework that is inherently *explanatory* and will perforce be *descriptive* as well, in the sense of [100]. Instead of explicitly fitting certain characteristics of measured Internet topologies, any such agreements between our models and empirical observations would instead be evidence of a successful explanatory modeling effort. For the purposes of router-level topology, this approach naturally focuses on the perspective of the Internet Service Provider (ISP), who acts as the owner and operator of this network infrastructure. As discussed in [9], we believe that an understanding of the key issues facing ISPs will naturally lead to the ability to generate "realistic, but fictitious" ISP topologies and that this understanding in turn will yield insight into the broader Internet. Our starting premise is that the design and deployment decisions of the ISP are to a large degree the result of an (explicit or implicit) optimization that balances the functionality of the network with the inherent *technological* and *economic* constraints resulting from available networking equipment and the need for the ISP to operate as a successful business. The power of this approach to contrast optimization-based models with their degree-based counterparts was recently shown in [62]. It is the purpose of this paper to put this work in a broader context that highlights the role of optimization-based models as a starting point for synthetic topology generators and also suggests the potential for an optimization-based perspective to be a unifying concept for understanding the Internet as a whole. At the same time, we also identify aspects of this story in need of additional work by researchers in optimization and network design.

3.   Optimization-Based Topology Models

The use of combinatorial optimization in network design has a long history for applications in telecommunication and computer systems, as well as transportation, scheduling, and logistics planning [67, 73, 3]. In particular, the rapid buildout of telephone infrastructure since the early 1960s led to massive interest in network design problems from the operations research community in capacitated network design problems (see [42] for a comprehensive survey of models and algorithms). Most recently, the prevalence of optical networks have brought significant attention to network design problems at the physical and link layer of the Internet. Recent emphasis has been on problems related to routing and wavelength assignment in wave division multiplexing (WDM) networks [104, 103, 59]; the relationship between equipment at the physical layer and the link layer topology for the purposes of minimizing communication equipment costs [71, 72, 47]; and network survivability in the face of component losses [46, 50, 85, 86, 31, 76, 109, 60].

While an optimization-based framework is natural when faced with important network design decisions having complicated combinatorics, it is not immediately clear how this approach is helpful as a tool for modeling Internet structure. On the one hand, because the Internet was designed and built using a *layered architecture* (more on this in the sequel), there are distinctly different network design problems at different layers of the network. In addition, there can be tremendous differences in model details—such as the arc costs (both installation costs and variable use costs), budget constraints, constraints on traffic patterns, constraints on network configuration, and redundancy/survivability constraints—at each level of network design, and these can have significant effect on the network topologies that result. Finally, while the traditional focus of network optimization has been on obtaining quantifiably "good" problem solutions, there has been little work to explain any possible relationship between good design and empirically observed large-scale network features such as power-laws.

The general power of an optimization-based approach to understanding power-laws in complex systems has been documented as part of the so-called *HOT* concept, for *Highly Optimized Tolerance* [23] or *Heuristically Optimized Tradeoffs* [37]. By emphasizing the importance of design, structure, and optimization, the HOT concept provides a framework in which the commonly-observed highly variable event sizes (i.e., scaling) in systems optimized by engineering design are the results of tradeoffs between yield, cost of resources, and tolerance to risk. *Tolerance* emphasizes that robustness (i.e., the maintenance of some desired system characteristics despite uncertainties in the behavior of its component parts or its environment) in complex systems is a constrained and limited quantity that must be diligently managed; *Highly Optimized* alludes to the fact that this goal is achieved by highly structured, rare, non-generic configurations which—for highly engineered systems—are the result of deliberate design. In turn, the characteristics of HOT systems are high performance, highly structured internal complexity, apparently simple and robust external behavior, with the risk of hopefully rare but potentially catastrophic cascading failures initiated by possibly quite small perturbations [23].

The first explicit attempt to cast topology design, modeling, and generation as a HOT problem was by Fabrikant et al. [37]. They proposed a toy model of incremental access network design that optimizes a tradeoff between connectivity distance and node centrality. More specifically, when adding a new node i, connect it in order to

$$\min_{j < i} \; \alpha \cdot dist(i, j) + h_j,$$

where $dist(i, j)$ is the distance between nodes i and j, and where h_j is some measure of "centrality" (e.g. number of hops). They showed that changes in the relative weights of these two terms in the overall objective function leads to a range of hierarchical structures in resulting topology, from simple star-networks to trees. More specifically, by tuning the relative importance of the two factors, the authors provided analytical proof that the resulting node degree distributions can be either exponential (non-heavy tailed) or of the scaling (heavy-tailed) type. That is, if $d(x)$ equals the number of nodes with degree $\geq x$, then for $\alpha < 1/\sqrt{2}$, resulting topology is a star; for $\alpha = \Omega(\sqrt{n})$, $E[d(x)] < n^2 e^{-k_2 x}$; and for $\alpha \geq 4$ and $\alpha = O(\sqrt{n})$, $E[d(x)] = k_3 (\frac{x}{n})^{-\beta}$. Subsequent work on this model has suggested that the resulting degree distribution follows a power law only up to a cutoff [15]. While this work successfully illustrated the power of HOT to generate heavy-tailed distributions in topology generation, their construction was not intended to be a realistic model of router level topology.

3.1   An Engineering-Based Approach

Our approach to modeling the structural topology of the Internet is rooted in two beliefs. First, as key decision makers in the design and operation of their own network topologies, Internet Service Providers (ISPs) play a fundamental role in the ongoing evolution of Internet structure as a whole. Second, an understanding of the layered architecture of the Internet is critical to the appropriate interpretation of key drivers affecting the decisions made by ISPs.

The robustness and user-perceived simplicity of the Internet is the result of a modular architecture that builds complex functionality from a succession of simpler components [29]. These components are organized into vertical *layers* whereby each component relies on the functionality of the layer below it and provides in turn a new set of functionality to the layer above. Each layer can be implemented more or less independently, provided that it adheres to specified rules for interacting with its adjacent layers. In this manner, layering provides modularity and gives rise to the "hourglass" metaphor—a 5-layer suite of protocols (the "TCP/IP protocol stack") where the Internet protocol (IP) constitutes the waist-layer of the hourglass and provides a simple abstraction of a generic but unreliable data delivery service [78] (see Figure 3.1). The physical layer and link layer below the waist deal with the wide variety of existing transmission and link technologies and provide the protocols for running IP over whatever bit-carrying network infrastructure is in place. Above the waist is where the transport layer and application layer provide the protocols that enhance IP (e.g., at the transport layer, TCP ensures reliable transmission) and greatly simplify the process of writing applications (e.g., WWW) through which users actually interact with the Internet. By including multiple layers of feedback control, this architecture provides much more than mere modularization, being largely responsible for the legendary ability of the Internet to perform robustly even in the presence of component losses [99].

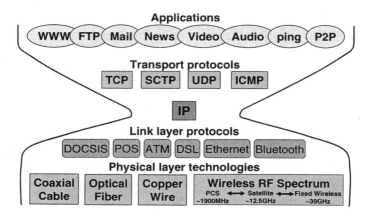

Figure 6.1. The Internet "hourglass". The physical layer and link layer below the waist deal with the wide variety of existing transmission and link technologies and provide the protocols for running IP over whatever bit-carrying network infrastructure is in place ("IP over everything"). Above the waist is where the transport layer and application layer provide the protocols that enhance IP (e.g., at the transport layer, TCP ensures reliable transmission) and greatly simplify the process of Writing applications (e.g., WWW) through which users actually interact with the Internet ("everything over IP").

Internet Service Providers (ISPs) are the owners and operators of the public Internet infrastructure, and as such, the decisions they make in designing and building their networks largely determine the overall structure of the Internet. Modern ISPs face significant challenges in their ongoing operations [49], and network design problems can factor prominently in their ultimate success as a business. Over the last decade, IP-based networking has emerged as the dominant technology in use within the Internet, and IP now functions as a type of "common currency" within the Internet—nearly all applications are designed to run on it, and most physical network infrastructures are designed to support it. Typically, ISPs do not specify which technologies are used at the upper layers, leaving them open instead to the needs of customers (e.g. end users) and their applications. However, an ISP must provide transmission and link technologies as well as the protocols for running IP over whatever physical infrastructure is in place.

3.2   Network Drivers

Our starting premise is that any explanatory framework for router-level Internet topology modeling should incorporate both the *economic* and *technological* factors faced by ISPs. For example, because of the costly nature of procuring, installing, and maintaining the required facilities and equipment, the ISP is economically constrained in the amount of network that it can support. At the same time, ISPs must configure their limited network resources in a manner that satisfies the service requirement of their customers. In designing the topology that best supports its business, the ISP is further constrained by the technologies currently available to it. While a complete review of these issues is beyond the scope of this paper, we argue that these drivers in their simplest form can be understood in terms of *link costs*, *router technology*, *customer requirements* and *service requirements*.

3.2.1   Link Costs.   Operation of an ISP at a national scale requires the installation, operation, and maintenance of communication links that span great distances. For the purposes here, we use the term "link" to mean both the physical network cable and the link layer equipment used to send traffic along that cable. At the national level, the cables are usually fiber optic and the equipment consists of transmitter/receivers at the end points and signal repeaters along the way. In addition, we assume in the remainder of this section that there are no significant differences between the connectivity observed at the IP layer and the underlying link connectivity. While this simplifying assumption holds true for some real networks (such as Abilene described below), we describe in Section 5 how higher fidelity optimization models could treats these layers in isolation. While a significant portion of the link cost is often associated with obtaining the "right of way" to install the network cables, there is generally an even greater cost associated with the installation and maintenance of the equipment used to send the traffic across these cables. Both the installation and maintenance costs tend to increase with link distance. Thus, one of the biggest infrastructure costs facing a network provider is the cost associated with the deployment and maintenance of its links.

National ISPs are one type of network provider for which link costs are significant. However, their challenge in providing network connectivity to millions of users spread over large geographic distances is made somewhat easier by the fact that most users tend to be concentrated in metropolitan areas. Thus, there is a natural separation of the connectivity problem into providing connectivity within a metropolitan region and providing connectivity between these regions[1]. In considering the costs associated with providing connectivity between metropolitan regions, the ISP has strong economic incentive to spread the cost of an intercity link over as many customers as possible. This is the basic motivation for *multiplexing*—a fundamental concept in networking by which a link is shared by many individual traffic streams. Multiplexing one of the most basic design principles in networking and has tremendous impact on the types of topologies chosen by network architects. In it simplest form, it states that the only type of design that makes sense from an economic perspective is one that aggregates as much traffic on the fewest number of long distance links. This principle applies at all levels of network design, including the local and regional levels, and not just the national backbone[2].

3.2.2   Router Technology.   Another major constraint affecting the types of topologies available to network designers is related to the routing equipment used to control the flow of traffic on the network. Based on the technology used in the cross-connection fabric of the router itself, a router has a maximum number of packets that can processed in any unit of time. This constrains the number of link connections (i.e., node *degree*) and connection speeds (i.e., bandwidth) at each model type, thereby creating an "efficient frontier" of possible bandwidth-degree combinations available for each router. That is, a router can have a few high bandwidth connections or many low bandwidth connections (or some combination in between). In essence, this means that the router must obey a form of *flow conservation* in the traffic that it can handle. While it is always possible to configure the router so that it falls below the efficient frontier (thereby underutilizing the router capacity), it is not possible to exceed this frontier (for example, by having an ever increasing number of high bandwidth connections). For any particular router model, there will be a frontier representing the possible combinations that are available. Router models with greater capacity are generally more expensive.

Consider as an example the Cisco Gigabit Switch Routers (GSRs), which are one of the most widely deployed routers within the Internet backbone[3]. In Figure 6.2(a), we show an example of the technology constraint of the Cisco 12416 GSR. This router has a total of 15 available "slots" for line cards each of which may have one more ports (i.e. physical connections). When the total number of

---

[1]Within the ISP industry, this distinction often separates service offerings into two lines of business known as "metro service" and "long-haul service" respectively.

[2]The telephone network is subject to the same economics associated with link costs and also exhibits the same type of network design in which local traffic is aggregated along "trunks" which interconnect local regions. Given a history in which the modern data networks grew out of traditional phone networks, the reuse of commonly accepted and successful design principles is not surprising.

[3]As reported in [34], Cisco's share of the worldwide market for service provider edge and core routers was approximately 70% during 2002.

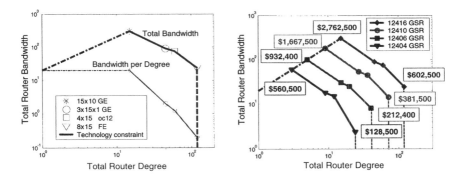

Figure 6.2. *(a) Technology constraint for Cisco 12416 Gigabit Switch Router (GSR): Degree vs. maximum throughput.* Each point on the plot corresponds to a different combination of ports on each line card. The router can achieve any combination of maximum throughput and degree below the technology constraint line. *(b) Technology constraints for GSR Models 12404, 12406, 12410, 12416.* Each line represents one type of router, and each point on the plot corresponds to routers with different interfaces, with the corresponding price shown in the enclosed inbox.

connections is less than 15, each line card need only support a single port, the throughput of each port is limited by the maximum speed of supported line cards (10 GE), and the router's maximum throughput increases with the number of connections. When the number of connections is greater than 15, the maximum router throughput *decreases* as the total number of ports increases. The reason for this decrease is related to an increased routing overhead for handling traffic over a greater number of ports. Figure 6.2(b) illustrates the efficient frontiers and corresponding prices (associated with different line card configurations) of several Cisco GSR routers taken from a recent product catalog [28]. Although engineers are constantly increasing the frontier with the development of new routing technologies, network architects are faced with tradeoffs between capacity and cost in selecting a router and then must also decide on the quantity and speed of connections in selecting a router configuration.

As noted in Figure 6.2(b), these high capacity core routers can have node degree on the order of only 100 direct connections. As a result, observed IP measurements for nodes having thousands of connections cannot correspond to physical connections between these routers. Until new technology shifts the frontier, the only way to create throughput beyond the frontier is to build networks of routers. In making this claim, we are not arguing that limits in technology fundamentally preclude the possibility of high-degree, high-bandwidth routers, but simply that the product offerings recently available to the marketplace have not supported such configurations[4]. While we expect that companies will continue to innovate and extend the feasible region for router configuration, it remains to be seen whether or not the economics of these products will enable their wide deployment within the Internet.

The current Internet is populated with many different router models, each using potentially different technologies and each having their own technology constraint. However, these technologies are still limited in their overall ability to tradeoff total bandwidth and number of connections. Thus, networking products tend to be specialized to take advantage of one area of an aggregate feasible region, depending on their intended role within the network hierarchy. Figure 6.2 presents an aggregate picture of many different technologies used both in the network core and at the network edge.

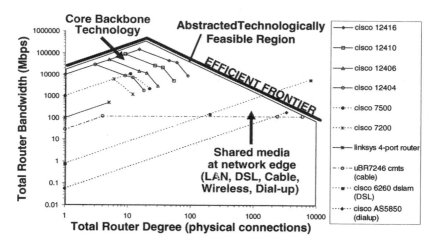

Figure 6.3.   Aggregate picture of router technology constraints. In addition to the Cisco 12000 GSR Series, the constraints on the somewhat older Cisco 7000 Series is also shown. The shared access technology for broadband cable provides service comparable to DSL when the total number of users is about 100, but can only provide service equivalent to dialup when the number of users is about 2000. Included also is the Linksys 4-port router, which is a popular LAN technology supporting up to 5 100MB Ethernet connections. Observe that the limits of this less expensive technology are well within the interior of the feasible region for core network routers.

Economic drivers to minimize wiring costs have spawned extreme hetero-geneity in the types of technologies that connect at the network edge; for example, dial-up and digital subscriber line (DSL) leverage existing copper telephone lines, broadband cable leverages existing coaxial cable lines, and wireless technology removes the need for wires altogether. These technologies are somewhat

---

[4]A few companies such as Avici Systems (www.avici.com) have started to offer scalable routing devices built from "stacks" of routers, with some recent success in the marketplace [93].

different from core routers in their underlying design, since their intention is to be able to support large numbers of end users at fixed (DSL, dialup) or variable (cable) speeds. They can support a much greater number of connections (upwards of 10,000 for DSL or dialup) but at significantly lower speeds. Collectively, these individual constraints form an overall aggregate feasible region on available topology design.

3.2.3   Customer Constraints.   Since the business of the ISP is to provide network service to its customers, there are certain features of ISP network structure that will be driven by the customers it supports. For example, in the current environment there is tremendous variability in the connection speeds used by customers to connect to the Internet. As shown in Table 6.1, an estimated half of all users of the Internet in North America during 2003 still had dial-up connections (generally 56kbps), only about 20% had broadband access (256kbps-6Mbps), and there was only a small number of end users with large (10Gbps) bandwidth requirements [8]. While some of the disparity in consumer choices may be attributed to incomplete deployment of broadband services, it is reasonable to believe that much of this disparity is due to a wide variability in the willingness to pay for network bandwidths.

Table 6.1.   Estimated distribution of end host connection types in the United States for 2003. It is important to note that the bandwidth performance seen by an individual user may be less than the total connection speed if the user's network interface card (NIC) is relatively slow. For example, a user on a university campus with a Fast Ethernet (100Mb) card will never achieve more than 100Mbps even if the university has a 10Gbps connection to the Internet.

Type of *Edge Connection*	*Typical Connection* *Speed*	*Approx.* *Connections*	*Relative* *Frequency*
Campus Users	1.544Mbps(T-1) – 10Gbps(OC-192)	38.1 M	33.6%
Broadband DSL	512kbps – 6Mbps	7.6 M	6.7%
Broadband Cable	300kbps – 30Mbps	13.4 M	11.8%
Dial-Up	56kbps	54.4 M	47.9%
	Total	113.4 M	100%

Another factor facing ISP topology design at the edge is the *location* of its customers. Due to the increased cost of longer links, customers that are located farther away from an ISP's network will be more expensive to service (at least when providing an initial connection). Conversely, regions where potential customers are concentrated over small distances will be more attractive to ISPs. Because population densities themselves range widely by geography (see for example U.S. Census data in Figure 6.4), ISPs that want broad coverage of even the most populated metropolitan regions will need to support wide variability in customer density.

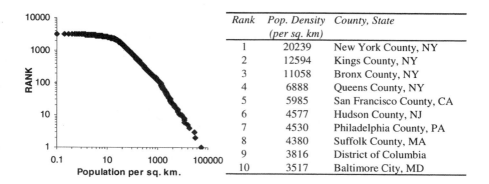

Rank	Pop. Density (per sq. km)	County, State
1	20239	New York County, NY
2	12594	Kings County, NY
3	11058	Bronx County, NY
4	6888	Queens County, NY
5	5985	San Francisco County, CA
6	4577	Hudson County, NJ
7	4530	Philadelphia County, PA
8	4380	Suffolk County, MA
9	3816	District of Columbia
10	3517	Baltimore City, MD

Figure 6.4.   Population density of the United States by county in 1990. (a) Most counties are sparsely populated, but a few counties have extremely high densities. (b) Top ten most densely populated counties. *Source: United States Census Bureau (Released: March 12, 1996. Revised: June 26, 2000.)*

3.2.4   Service Requirements.

In addition to the constraints imposed by link costs, router technology limitations, and customer connectivity, it is reasonable to expect that ISPs are driven to satisfy certain service requirements imposed by their customers or the industry at large. For example, most ISPs utilize *service level agreements (SLAs)*, which serve as business contracts with their major customers and their peers. SLAs typically specify terms such as delivered bandwidth and limits on service interruptions, and they often include financial penalties for failure to comply with their terms. While SLAs are often negotiated on an individual basis, competition among ISPs often creates industry norms that lead to standard SLA terms. Conversely, some ISPs use special terms in SLAs as a mechanism for differentiating their services and creating competitive advantage over rival companies.

From the provider's perspective, one simple metric for assessing whether or not a given network topology is "good" is its ability to handle the bandwidth requirements of its edge routers. For the purposes of this paper, we define *network performance* as the maximum proportional throughput on a network under heavy traffic conditions based on a gravity model [108]. That is, starting at the network edge we consider the demand for traffic by an access router to be the aggregate connectivity bandwidth of its end hosts. Then, to determine the flow of traffic across the network core, we consider flows on all source-destination pairs of access routers, such that the amount of flow X_{ij} between source i and destination j is proportional to the product of the traffic demand x_i, x_j at end points i, j,

$$X_{ij} = \alpha x_i x_j,$$

where α is a constant representing the proportional level among all flows. We compute the maximum proportional throughput on the network under the router degree bandwidth constraint,

$$\max_{\alpha} \quad \sum_{ij} X_{ij}$$

$$s.t \quad RX \leq B,$$

where R is the routing matrix (defined such that $R_{kl} = \{0, 1\}$ depending on whether or not flow l passes through router k). We use shortest path routing to get the routing matrix. X is a vector obtained by stacking all the flows X_{ij} and B is a vector consisting of all router bandwidths according to the degree bandwidth constraint (Figure 6.2). Due to lack of publicly available information on traffic demand for each end point, we assume the aggregation of end point traffic demand is proportional to the bandwidth of the higher level router. In this manner, we allow for good bandwidth utilization of the higher level routers[5]. While other performance metrics may be worth considering, we claim that maximum proportional throughput achieved using the gravity model provides a reasonable measure of the network to provide a *fair* allocation of bandwidth.

Another important issue in the design of ISP topologies is related to their reliability in the presence of equipment failure, sometimes known as *survivability*. Generally, network survivability is quantified in terms of the ability of the network to maintain end-to-end paths in the presence of node or link losses. Although survivable network design is not a focus of this article, comprehensive surveys of optimization-based formulations for this type of service requirement are available [46, 50].

3.3 HOT: Heuristically Optimal Topology

Our objective is to develop a simple and minimal, yet plausible model for router-level topology that reflects link costs, conforms to the technology constraints of routers, appropriately addresses the aforementioned issues for high variability in end-user connectivity, and achieves reasonably "good" performance. As noted above, the economic drive to minimize link costs promotes a topology that aggregates traffic as close to the network edge as possible. The use of multiplexing in a variety of routing technologies at the network edge supports this aggregation, and the wide variability in the bandwidth demands and geographies of end user connections suggests that one should expect wide variability in the measured connectivity of nodes at the network edge. Since it is generally accepted that most of the computers in the network are at its edge, it is reasonable to expect that the overall connectivity statistics of the network

---

[5]We also tried choosing the traffic demand proportional to the product of end points degree as in [43], and a similar result still holds but has different router utilization.

are dominated by those at the edge. Collectively, these constraints suggest that a "good" design is one in which individual links at the edge of the network have are aggregated in a manner such that the link capacities increase as one moves to the network core. In particular, edge routers may connect to a large number of low bandwidth users or a smaller number of high bandwidth users. In contrast, one can expect that backbone links within the network run at high-speeds and that core routers have necessarily fewer links, making the connectivity of the core much more uniform. As can be seen in the example below and in [62], an inspection of real networks reveals a common theme, namely that the topology at the network edge is designed to aggregate traffic within a local region, while the topology within the core of the network is designed to transport aggregated traffic between geographically disparate regions.

3.3.1   Case Study: The Abilene Network.   To this point, we have argued that the perspective of an ISP in building a national scale network topology is driven by three factors. First, the need to minimize the long distance link costs means that it is driven to aggregate traffic from its edges to its core. Second, the design of its topology, particularly in the core, must conform to the technology constraints inherent in routers. Third, the network should have good performance, measured in terms of its ability to carry large volumes of traffic in a fair manner. While these are certainly not the only factors affecting design, we claim that these three drivers are a sensible starting point for understanding the relationship between ISP network design and resulting router-level topology. As a preliminary validation of whether or not these factors are reasonable, we seek to compare them to the topology of a national ISP. Given that commercial ISPs are reluctant to share information, we consider the national educational network.

The Abilene Network is the Internet backbone network for higher education, and it is part of the Internet2 initiative [1] (see Figure 6.5). It is comprised of high-speed connections between core routers located in 11 U.S. cities and carries approximately 1% of all traffic in North America[6]. The Abilene backbone is a sparsely connected mesh, with connectivity to regional and local customers provided by some minimal amount of redundancy. Abilene maintains peering connections with other higher educational networks (both domestic and international) but does not connect directly to the commercial Internet. Within Abilene, connectivity from core routers to academic institutions is provided

---

[6]Of the approximate 80,000 - 140,000 terabytes per month of traffic in 2002 [81], Abilene carried approximately 11,000 terabytes of total traffic for the year [51]. Here, "carried" traffic refers to traffic that traversed an Abilene router. Since Abilene does not peer with commercial ISPs, packets that traverse an Abilene router are unlikely to have traversed any portion of the commercial Internet.

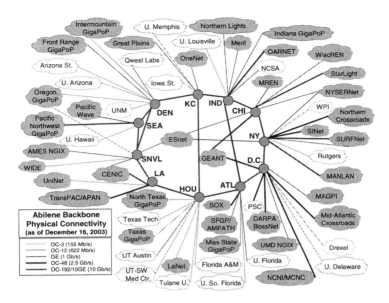

Figure 6.5. Complete physical connectivity for Abilene. Each node represents a router, and each link represents a physical connection between Abilene and another network. End user networks are represented in white, while peer networks (other backbones and exchange points) are represented in blue. ESnet is another national backbone network. Each router has only a few high bandwidth connections, however each physical connection can support many virtual connections that give the appearance of greater connectivity to higher levels of the Internet protocol stack.

through local GigaPoPs[7]. The core router in Los Angeles, for example, is connected to core routers in Sunnyvale and Houston, and is also connected to regional networks such as CENIC (the educational backbone for the State of California) and peering networks such as UniNet. In places where no GigaPoP is available, university campuses may be allowed to connect to Abilene directly. For example, the University of Florida is directly connected to an Abilene core router in Atlanta. Within Abilene, there is no difference between the network at the IP layer and the link layer, and the physical connectivity of central core nodes is low (ranging from five to twelve).

We claim that the Abilene backbone is heuristically optimal in its ability to tradeoff performance and link cost, subject to router technology constraints, so we use it as a starting point to construct a toy model of a heuristically optimal topology. Specifically, we replace each of the edge network clouds with a single gateway router whose role is to aggregate the traffic of a certain number of end

---

[7]The term "PoP" is an abbreviation for "Point of Presence". A GigaPoP is a point of presence that interconnects many different networks at very high bandwidths.

hosts. Thus, most of the nodes in the network are at its edge, and the high degree nodes are located exclusively at the edge of the network. This flexibility makes it trivial to assign just about any node degree distribution to the network as a whole, and here we assign end hosts to gateway routers in a manner that yields an approximate power law for the overall node degree distribution. Figure 6.6(a) shows the resulting network topology, while Figure 6.6(b) shows the degree distribution for the entire network. This network has total 865 nodes (68 internal routers and 797 end hosts) and 874 links. In approximating Abilene, peering networks ESnet and GEANT are represented as direct connections between Chicago and Sunnyvale, New York and Sunnyvale, and Chicago and Washington D.C. To evaluate the performance of this construction, we assume

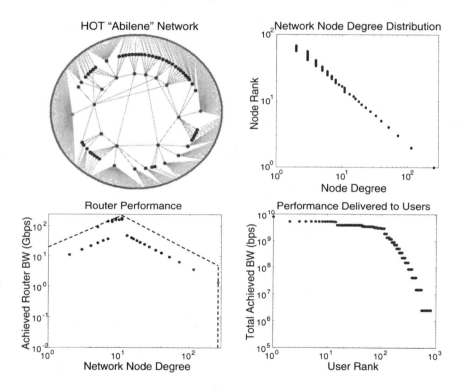

Figure 6.6.   Abilene-inspired HOT model of router-level topology. (a) Topology for toy version of Abilene. (b) Network degree distribution. (c) Achieved router performance under maximum flow. (d) Achieved end user bandwidths under maximum flow.

that the network is built using a single router model having an abstracted feasible region, shown in Figure 6.6(c). Then, this network achieves a total performance of 576 Gbps and its routers are used with high efficiency, i.e. they are close to the efficient frontier of the router feasible region. It also provides wide variability in the ultimate bandwidths delivered to its end users, shown in Figure 6.6(d).

This simple toy model is obviously a severe abstraction, and we do not claim that it is an accurate representation of Abilene. However, this toy model illustrates a few important points. First, it is relatively straightforward to use engineering design to construct a network topology that conforms to the constraints of available router technology, has high variability (or even power laws) in overall node degree distribution, and supports a wide variability in end user bandwidths. Second, a network that has low degree, high bandwidth connections in the core and high degree, low bandwidth connections at the edge results in high performance and achieves efficient router utilization (Figure 6.6(c)). From an engineering perspective that explicitly considers the tradeoffs of network design, these points may seem so obvious that it is hard to imagine modeling router-level graphs in any other way. However, there exists a popular alternate approach that considers only the mathematical and graph theoretic aspects of network connectivity.

3.4   Equivalent Degree-Based Models

The starting point for many models of network topology has been to try to replicate the mathematical or statistical properties observed in real networks. With this approach, one usually starts with a sequence of well-understood metrics or observed features of interest—such as hierarchy [107], node-degree distributions [52, 69, 4, 13], clustering coefficients [20], expansion, resilience [94], etc.—and then develops a method that matches these metrics. The result is predictably successful, in the sense that it is always possible to develop models of increasing fidelity in order to tune specific statistics to desired values. Indeed, the common themes of this work are empirical findings that suggest degree based generators provide topologies that are more statistically representative of real networks which are reported to exhibit power law degree distributions [94]. However, this approach suffers from several drawbacks. First, it is hard to choose the "right" metric, since what is right is apt to vary, depending on the intended use of the topology. Second, any generative method that does a good job of matching the chosen metric often does not fit other metrics well. Finally, this approach tends to have little, if any, predictive power, since resulting models tend to be descriptive but not explanatory, in the sense of [100]. Nonetheless, recent attention on power laws in network connectivity has made degree distributions a popular metric for evaluating topology, and degree-based models of Internet topology remain prevalent.

The drawbacks of using the degree-based approach become clear with a closer look at the methods by which these networks are generated. In general, there are many network generation mechanisms that can yield networks having highly variable (or power-law) degree distributions. However, the aforementioned degree-based topology generators all use one of two methods. The first is *preferential attachment* [13] which says (1) the growth of the network is realized by the sequential addition of new nodes, and (2) each newly added node connects to an existing node preferentially, such that it is more likely to connect with a node that already has many connections. As a consequence, high-degree nodes are likely to get more and more connections resulting in a power law in the distribution of node degree. While, preferential attachment has been a popular mechanism within the complex network literature, its utility as a general network modeling tool is limited to particular power law degree distributions. The second, and more general, generation mechanism is based on graph theoretic methods that yield topologies whose expected degree distribution matches any chosen distribution. An example is the Power-law Random Graph (PLRG) model which constructs a graph by first assigning each node its degree and the randomly inserting edges between the nodes according to a probability that is proportional to the product of the given degrees of two endpoints [4]. If the assigned degree distribution for all nodes follows the power-law, the generated network is expected to reproduce the same power law.

One of the most important features of networks having power law degree distributions that are generated by these two mechanisms is that there are a few centrally located and highly connected "hubs" through which essentially most traffic must flow. For the networks generated by preferential attachment, the central hubs are the earliest nodes, and application of the preferential attachment model to the Internet has suggested that these hubs represent the "Achilles' heel of the Internet" because they make the network highly vulnerable to attacks that target these high-degree hubs [6]. The nodes with high expected degree in PLRG have higher probability to attach to other high degree nodes and these highly connected nodes form a central cluster.

Consider as an example a degree-based model for a network having the degree distribution shown in Figure 6.6. Starting with the PLRG approach and using some additional heuristic tuning, it is possible to obtain a network that matches the degree distribution exactly. The resulting network also has 865 nodes (68 internal routers and 797 end hosts) and 874 links, and it is shown in Figure 6.7(a). While it matches the degree distribution of the HOT model, it achieves an inferior performance of only 4.89 Gbps, more than two orders of magnitude worse. A look at the router performance (Figure 6.7(c)) and the distribution of bandwidths to end users (Figure 6.7(d)) also reveals the functional inferiority of this network. The reason for the poor performance of this degree-based model is exactly the presence of the highly connected "hubs" that create low-bandwidth bottlenecks. In contrast, the HOT model's mesh-like core, like the real Internet, aggregates traffic and disperses it across multiple high-bandwidth routers.

While the graph shown in Figure 6.7(a) is not the only network that could have resulted from a probabilistic degree-based construction, its structure is representative of the features of this genre of graph models. Furthermore, its

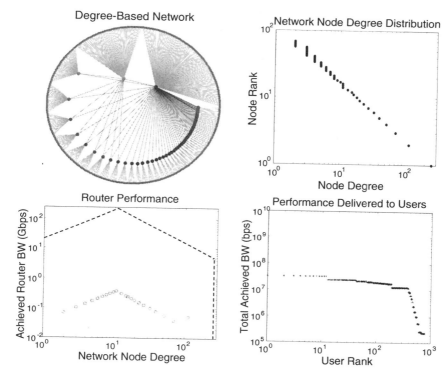

Figure 6.7. *Result of degree-based generation for network having the same degree distribution as in Figure 6.6.* (a) Network topology. (b) Network degree distribution. (c) Achieved router performance under maximum flow. (d) Achieved end user bandwidths under maximum flow.

comparison with the Abilene-inspired network is fair, in the sense that two different graphs constructed from the same respective processes would compare in a qualitatively similar manner. There are a number of graph theoretic arguments that suggest why probabilistic degree-based networks result in this type of structure (some of which are presented in [62]), but they are beyond the scope of this article.

3.5   Discussion

The objective here has been to uncover "significant" drivers of topology evolution so that we understand the structure of the real Internet and gain insight for generating synthetic topologies. The Abilene-inspired example and degree-based example were selected to highlight how graphs that share certain macroscopic statistical characteristics can appear very different from a perspective that considers issues such as performance, technology constraints, and economic considerations. The HOT framework tries to emphasize optimization, tradeoffs, and robustness. The Abilene-inspired network is the simplest nontrivial example. There may be additional constraints, such as link costs and redundancy, that would be important and needed in the model. However, since HOT views performance and constraints and tradeoffs, we can generalize the HOT model to include any additional objectives and constraints. In this manner, HOT design is an example of a process, whereby additional constraints and tradeoffs can be added in a systematic manner. Degree-based methods are representative of a process too, but the process is a search for macroscopic statistical characterizations to constrain an otherwise random network construction. Although both approaches could be extended, the HOT approach makes engineering sense while the degree-based approach does not. Even so, the results here are really only a "proof of concept" in the development of "fictitious, yet realistic" models of Internet topology.

4.   Towards Generative Models

In considering how we might use the aforementioned optimization-based framework to generate synthetic network topologies, we return to the perspective of the national ISP that is looking to build its infrastructure from scratch. While there are many distinct network design problems of concern to ISPs, we distinguish here between the problem of *access* design and *backbone* design. *Network access design* typically occurs at the metropolitan area, where the challenge is to provide connectivity to local customers who are dispersed over some regional geographic area. This connectivity is rooted at the ISP's *point of presence (PoP)*, which serves as the focal point for local traffic aggregation and dissemination between the ISP and its customers. In contrast, *network backbone design* is the problem of providing internal connectivity within the ISP between its different PoPs, which are typically separated by larger geographic distances. The separation of the network design problem into access and backbone design problems and also into different functional layers is important because the resulting optimization formulations often have different objectives and constraints operating at each level of abstraction. In addition, access design problems are inherently local, in the sense that changes to the inputs or incremental growth in the access network have only local affects on the resulting topology or its traffic. In contrast, changes to inputs of the backbone design problem or backbone incremental growth often have global implications on the structure and/or behavior of the network as a whole.

We present here a heuristic "recipe" for generating an annotated router-level graph for a national ISP using this optimization-based approach. The intent here is to provide a minimal level of detail sufficient to illustrate how the various objectives, constraints, and tradeoffs can be synthesized into a reasonable model.

STEP 1: Choose the metropolitan areas to serve (i.e. the PoPs). This decision might be based on the population size of each metropolitan area, or it might be driven by market competition (e.g. the need to have a presence in specific cities).

STEP 2: For each metropolitan area, design an access network, as follows.

- Select the location of the access points (there may be more than one). In modeling specific metropolitan regions, the location of access points may be driven by the presence of *Internet Exchange Points (IXPs)* or *co-location facilities* that serve as central facilities for ISPs to peer with one another.

- Choose an underlying aggregation technology for each access point (e.g. fiber, DSL, broadband cable) or a mixture of them.

- Choose (probabilistic) distributions for customer geography and also for customer bandwidth demands. A reasonable approach would be to choose a mixture of technologies and customer demands that are consistent with market statistics, such as those listed in Table 6.1.

- Formulate an optimization problem (using corresponding technology constraints, link costs, and user demands) in the spirit of [10], and solve to obtain a heuristically optimal local topology.

STEP 3: Design a backbone topology to support traffic between the PoPs.

- Choose a model for traffic demand (e.g a traffic matrix) consistent with the model of local access design (i.e. aggregate PoP demands are derived from the access networks that they serve).

- Decide on the link bandwidths (e.g. OC-48, OC-192) and router models (e.g. Cisco GSR) available for use.

- Select appropriate resource budgets (a simple budget could be the total number of links, or more sophisticated models could use real costs of links and routers) as well as any additional service requirements (e.g. redundancy).

- Formulate the backbone design problem as a constrained optimization problem (in the spirit of [42, 46]). The solution need only be heuristically optimal, but it preferably also has some robustness properties (such as insensitivity to small changes in the inputs or the loss of any single node or link).

STEP 4: Compute theoretical performance of the network as a whole (e.g. throughput, utilization) under initial traffic assumptions.

STEP 5: Consider reverse engineering of real measured ISP topologies (in the spirit of [91]) as a form of heuristic validation, assessment of input assumptions, and examination of engineering details included in the model.

STEP 6: Consider traffic engineering on the generated topology to improve performance, and use improved traffic assumptions as feedback into model and return to STEP 3.

As noted by the final step, this procedure is intended to be a process by which the insights from the resulting topology are used as feedback into the process in order to improve the self-consistency and realism of the model. In the end, the inputs to the model include: distribution of customer demands, distribution of edge technologies, distribution of customer geography (population density), a list of PoPs, a backbone budget constraint, redundancy requirements, and a model of traffic demands. The outputs of the generation process include: an annotated topology with router capacities, link bandwidths, router/link utilization under assumed traffic demand, network performance, and perhaps a measure of robustness to loss of router/links. There are many additional details that could be added, and it's likely that we will need to iterate between modeling, measurement, and analysis to get it right, but this level of modeling is entirely feasible given current understanding of the Internet's most salient features.

There are several advantages of a topology generator that includes this level of detail. First and foremost, the resulting graph models should be consistent with the reality of the engineering systems that they are intended to represent. This alone would represent significant progress in moving beyond the degree-based generators in use today. However, there are a number of additional benefits that would follow. For example, a model at this level of detail provides a natural framework for the study of traffic engineering problems, and moreover it enables one to study of the co-evolving relationship between network design and traffic engineering. In addition, the conceptual framework presented here will enable the exploration of the way in which individual constraints and objectives affect the large-scale features of generated topologies. For example, in comparing the qualitative and quantitative features of real ISP topologies, are the dissimilarities the result of differences in their inputs (customer distributions, geographies) or the result of design decisions (different technologies, different redundancy requirements, budgets)? A better understanding of this "design space" also creates the ability to consider what-if scenarios, for example the potential to predict the consequences of introducing a new technology or the ability to study whether or not there are fundamental limitations in the ability of a network to scale with current technology. Finally, reasonably detailed models of real ISP topologies creates the ability to construct models for the Internet as a whole by interconnecting individual ISPs (similar to what has been suggested for measured ISP topologies [63]). It also enables the systematic investigation of the economics and dynamics of peering relationships (e.g. hot potato routing [95]) which have recently received significant attention by operators and researchers alike.

5. Optimization: A Broader Framework

In this article, we have used optimization primarily as a tool for the *analysis* of Internet topology. That is, we have assumed that the structural features observed in the router-level Internet are the result of some (implicit) optimization problem faced by network architects, and we have tried to identify the way in which fundamental technological and economic forces shape both the current structure and its ongoing development. Furthermore, we have suggested optimization-based formulations as a means for generating representative models of the router-level Internet. This framework contrasts with the traditional use of optimization for solving difficult decision problems related to network *synthesis*—that is, the design of new or incremental network infrastructure. Unlike the problem here, network synthesis problems typically start with precise mathematical formulations where the variables, objectives, and constraints are clearly defined, and the challenge in solving them typically comes from difficult combinatorics or uncertainty in the decision making. The purpose of this section is to illustrate how these two complimentary perspectives are being used to develop a broader theory of the Internet, and we also identify research areas where additional work is needed.

The modularity resulting from a layered network architecture (see Figure 3.1) provides an appropriate *separation theorem* for the engineering of individual network components. That is, it is often possible to investigate the features, behavior, and performance of an individual layer either in isolation or assuming that the lower-layer functionalities are all specified. It is within each individual layer where one observes a horizontal decomposition of functionality into decentralized components. This horizontal decomposition provides robustness to the loss of individual components, supports scalability of the network, and facilitates fully distributed provisioning, control, and management mechanisms, usually implemented through multiple layers of feedback regulation between different end systems.

This collective picture presents a framework for the analysis, evaluation, and design of network components. For the most part, the aforementioned modularity allows network engineers to focus exclusively on a specific portion of the overall architecture when addressing issues related to performance. However, changes to individual components/protocols have often unanticipated and undesirable consequences on the network as a whole or on the entire TCP/IP protocol stack, and it is for those situations when a comprehensive theory of the Internet is most needed. What follows is a brief summary of some of the progress to date in developing this theory for parts of the overall architecture.

Since each of these areas is a deep research area in its own right, the examples here are meant to be representative and not necessarily comprehensive.

5.1   Link Layer: Connectivity

Most of the discussion in this paper has assumed that the network topology defined by the physical/link layer technologies is the same as the topology at the IP (routing) layer, but this is not true for many real networks. Despite its name, the router-level graph (as inferred from measurement studies based on the *traceroute* program) does not necessarily reflect the structure of its underlying physical layer. Depending on the technologies in use, two routers that are "connected" by a single hop at the IP layer may or may not be physically connected to one another. The use of different link layer technologies, such as Ethernet at the network edge or Asynchronous Transfer Mode (ATM) technology in the network core, can give the illusion of direct connectivity from the perspective of IP, even though the routers in question may be separated at the physical level by many intermediate networking devices or even an entire network potentially spanning hundreds of miles. In some cases, network provisioning at these different layers is handled by different companies, and it's possible that an ISP who sells IP networking services actually subcontracts the provisioning of its optical network to another provider.

The separation of the link layer technologies from IP routing leads to a number of interesting and important network design problems, each of which have their own optimization-based formulation. For example, when designing optical network topologies, the question is which fiber pathways to "light up" to form the basic circuit connectivity and what to do in the event that a particular pathway is interrupted either from accident (e.g. a fiber cut) or failure (equipment malfunction). For example, recent work on the design of WDM networks has focused on cost-based solutions to the placement of optical networking equipment within a mesh-like backbone structure [17, 72]. Other work has focused on the ability to protect and restore fiber circuits at the link layer, thereby hiding such failures from the layers above [85, 86, 103, 71]. Current efforts are focusing on optimization-based approaches to the multi-layer design of both link layer structure and routing policies [47, 59, 60, 104].

5.2   IP Layer: Routing

Given the physical infrastructure, the Internet relies on IP to switch any packet anywhere in the Internet to the "correct" next hop. Addressing and routing are crucial aspects that enable IP to achieve this impressive task. Maintaining sufficient and consistent information within the network for associating the identity of the intended recipient with its location inside the network is achieved by means of *routing protocols*; that is, a set of distributed algorithms that are part of IP and that the routers run among themselves to make appropriate routing decisions. Robustness considerations that play a role in this context include randomly occurring router or link failures and restoration of failed network components or adding new components to the network.

The routing protocols in use in today's Internet are robust to these uncertainties in the network's components, and the detection of and routing around failed components remains largely invisible to the end-to-end application—the Internet sees damage and "works" (i.e., routes) around it. The complexity in protocol design that ensures this remarkable resilience to failures in the physical infrastructure of the Internet is somewhat reduced by a division of the problem into two more manageable pieces, where the division is in accordance with separation of the Internet into *Autonomous Systems (AS)* or *autonomous routing domains*: each AS runs a local internal routing protocol (or *Interior Gateway Protocol (IGP)*; e.g., Open Shortest Path First or OSPF), and between the different ASs, an inter-network routing protocol (or *Exterior Gateway Protocol (EGP)*; e.g., Border Gateway Protocol or BGP) maintains connectivity and is the glue that ties all the ASs together and ensures communication across AS boundaries. However, the de-facto standard hybrid BGP/OSPF routing protocol deployed in today's Internet is largely an engineering "solution" and little (if anything) is known about its optimality, fundamental limits, or inherent tradeoffs with respect to, changing or uncertain traffic demands [11], the design of more sophisticated algorithms for tuning OSPF weights [39], the development of semantically richer BGP routing policies [45], or the gradual deployment of new protocols such as *Multi Protocol Label Switching (MPLS)* [18] or *Multiprotocol Lambda Switching (MPIS)* [105]. Furthermore, recent work has provided a systematic investigation into how routing policies are used in real operational networks and has reported that the traditional view of interior and exterior routing policies is insufficient to capture the intention of traffic engineers [68]. Despite an incomplete understanding of routing-level behavior, current research is proposing changes to the routing infrastructure in order to facilitate the routing, switching, and forwarding of packets through next-generation networks as well as support the demands of novel applications.

5.3   Transport Layer: TCP-AQM

By assuming a given physical network infrastructure and a fixed routing matrix, recent investigation into the network transport layer has brought new understanding to the behavior of both the Transmission Control Protocol (TCP) and Active Queue Management (AQM) schemes for providing optimal allocation of network resources. The main insight from this work [57, 64, 75] is to view the TCP-AQM protocol as a distributed *primal-dual algorithm*, in which TCP source rates are viewed as primary variables, while link congestion measures are viewed as dual variables. Collectively, these two protocols solve an implicit, global utility maximization problem across the Internet. Furthermore, it has been shown that different protocol variants solve the same basic resource allocation problem, but use different utility functions [65]. This theoretical framework suggests that by studying the underlying optimization problem, it is possible to understand the equilibrium properties of a large network under TCP/AQM control. These properties include network throughput, transmission delay, queue lengths, loss probabilities, and fairness. Here, insight from this optimization-based perspective comes despite the fact that TCP and AQM were designed and implemented without regard to utility maximization. These results have subsequently been combined with models from control theory to provide additional insight into the dynamics and stability of these networking protocols, and they have even led to new proposals for transport protocols to replace TCP itself [54, 82, 58, 53].

5.4   Application Layer: Mice and Elephants

At the top of the protocol stack, applications are designed to meet particular performance objectives, and their design typically relies on all of the network resources available from the lower layers of the protocol stack. The technology supporting the Wold Wide Web (WWW) is a prime example. The behavior of the WWW is defined by the interaction of web servers and web browsers that run the HyperText Transfer Protocol (HTTP), web documents that are encoded using the HyperText Markup Language (HTML), and users who navigate via feedback through those interconnected documents. Within this scheme, HTTP relies on TCP to provide reliable packet delivery and robust flow control when transferring files. Sometimes, however, the interaction between layers results in unintended and unexpected poor performance that may be hard to identify and resolve. For example, as discussed in [99], version 1.0 of HTTP interacted badly with TCP, causing problems with the latency perceived by web users as well as problems with web server scalability. These problems were ultimately fixed in HTTP 1.1, when the protocol was tuned to provide better performance.

There has been relatively little theoretical work to formalize the relationship between application behavior and the dynamics of the underlying protocol stack. A noticeable exception is [110] that pursues a HOT-based approach to develop a toy model for Web layout design. This model suggests that the organization and layout of web pages is optimized to minimize the latency experienced by users who search for items of interest. Minimizing user-perceived latency is roughly equivalent to minimizing the average size of downloaded files and is motivated by the limitation on the bandwidth available to both the network and the user. In particular, it is highly desirable for the frequently accessed files that are used for navigational purposes to be small and download quickly ("mice"), as the user's next action awaits this information. At the same time, the large files ("elephants") that tend to represent the endpoints of the search process require in general large average bandwidth for timely delivery, but per packet latency is typically less of an issue.

This type of Web layout design problem has features similar to conventional source coding, but with substantial differences in the constraints and design degrees of freedom (e.g., grouping of objects into files, location of hyperlinks). The toy model produces distributions of file sizes and file accesses that are both heavy-tailed in nature and are in remarkable agreement with measurements of real Web traffic. That these heavy-tailed or highly variable characteristics of Web traffic are likely to be an invariant of much of the future network traffic, regardless of the applications, is one important insight to be gained from this new research direction. The current split of most traffic into mice and elephants is likely to persist. Most files will be mice, which generate little aggregate bandwidth demand, but need low latency. Most of the packets will come from elephants, which demand high average bandwidth, but can tolerate varying per packet latency. After all, much of the human-oriented communication process that involves both active navigation and ultimately the transfer of large objects can naturally be "coded" this way, with important implications for proper protocol design at the transport layer.

5.5   Discussion

These successes in the use of an optimization-based framework to gain deeper understanding of individual components within the overall architecture (either from first principles or via "reverse engineering") suggest a potential benefit for extending this perspective to deal with issues that span multiple layers. In its ultimate form, one hopes for a coherent theory in which the various protocol layers can be viewed as part of one giant optimization problem that the network solves in a completely decentralized manner, and where each protocol can be interpreted as a local algorithm that works to achieve some part of the global objective. Yet, much remains to be done before such a theory is in hand. While recent work at the transport layer suggests that the behavior of TCP-AQM is nearly optimal, is it known that the collective behavior of TCP-AQM and IP is not optimal. One recent attempt to understand the ability of IP and TCP-AQM to simultaneously solve the optimal routing problem in conjunction with the resource allocation problem has shown that utility maximization over both source rates and their routes is NP-hard and hence cannot be solved in general by shortest-path routing within IP [96].

Despite the inherent challenges for developing such a theory, the ongoing development and deployment of Internet technologies and our increasing reliance upon them demand that we obtain a deeper understanding of the relationship between the underlying architecture and design objectives such as performance, scalability, robustness, and evolvability. More broadly, whenever considering the deployment of new technologies, it would be useful to know where the current architecture stands with regard to optimality. For example, are there other routing protocols that might perform better than IP? What happens if fundamental changes are made at the routing level, such as would be seen with the deployment of new provisioning and routing technologies such as MPLS or lambda switching? What happens when new applications change fundamentally the traffic patterns that the underlying protocol stack needs to manage? What if new technologies fundamentally change the constraints or economics of network provisioning and management? And finally, the envisioned theory should be able to provide insight into the circumstances under which circuit-switching versus packet switching is the optimal thing to do.

6.   Conclusion

In this paper, we have described several factors that we suggest are key drivers of the router-level Internet as it is designed, built, and operated by ISPs. While this list of key factors is far from exhaustive, what is striking is how the need to annotate network topologies with even simple domain-specific features shows how graphs that may be sensible from a connectivity-only perspective are no longer viable (e.g., non-realizable or non-sensical) in the real world because of constraints that are imposed by their application domains. In this sense, the models for the router-level Internet that result from optimization-based formulations and degree-based formulations could not be more different. Although degree-based models hold a certain appeal from a macroscopic viewpoint, they are entirely inconsistent with the perspective of network engineering. Networks constructed from degree-based models would be costly to build and would yield poor performance. Optimization-based approaches to modeling router-level topology (and the Internet more generally) hold tremendous promise, but significant work remains before we have the level of clarity that is needed by network operators, corporate managers, and telecommunications policy makers.

Acknowledgments

The ideas presented in this article have benefitted tremendously from conversations with many colleagues, including Steven Low, Ramesh Govindan, Matt Roughan, and Reiko Tanaka. The authors would like to express special thanks to Stanislav Shalunov for help in understanding the physical design of the Abilene backbone. This research was sponsored in part by the Institute for Pure and Applied Mathematics (IPAM) at UCLA, as part of their program on Large-Scale Communication Networks.

References

[1] Abilene Network. Detailed information about the objectives, organization, and development of the Abilene network are available from http://www.internet2.edu/abilene.

[2] L.A. Adamic and B.A. Huberman. Power-Law Distribution of the World Wide Web. *Science* 2000; 287(5461):2115.

[3] R.K. Ahuja, T.L. Magnanti, and J.B. Orlin. *Network Flows: Theory, Algorithms, and Applications.* Upper Saddle River, NJ: Prentice-Hall. 1993.

[4] W. Aiello, F. Chung, and L. Lu. A Random Graph Model for Massive Graphs. *Proceedings of the 32nd Annual Symposium in Theory of Computing*, 2000.

[5] R. Albert, H. Jeong, and A.-L. Barabási. Diameter of the World Wide Web. *Nature* 1999; 401:130–131.

[6] R. Albert, H. Jeong, and A.-L. Barabási. Attack and error tolerance of complex networks. *Nature* 2000; 406: 378–382.

[7] R. Albert, and A.-L. Barabási. Statistical Mechanics of Complex Networks. *Reviews of Modern Physics* 2002; 74:47–97.

[8] D. Alderson. Technological and Economic Drivers and Constraints in the Internet's "Last Mile". Technical Report CIT-CDS-04-004, Engineering Division, California Institute of Technology, 2004.

[9] D. Alderson, J. Doyle, R. Govindan, and W. Willinger. Toward an Optimization-Driven Framework for Designing and Generating Realistic Internet Topologies. In *ACM SIGCOMM Computer Communications Review* 2003; 33(1): 41–46.

[10] M. Andrews and L. Zhang. The access network design problem. *Proceedings of the 39th Foundations of Computer Science*, 1998.

[11] D. Applegate and E. Cohen. Making Intra-Domain Routing Robust to Changing and Uncertain Traffic Demands: Understanding Fundamental Tradeoffs. *Proceedings of ACM SIGCOMM* 2003.

[12] A. Balakrishnan, T.L. Magnanti, A. Shulman, and R.T. Wong. Models for planning capacity expansion in local access telecommunication networks. *Annals of Operations Research* 1991; 33: 239–284.

[13] A.-L. Barabási and R. Albert. Emergence of scaling in random networks. *Science* 1999; 286: 509-512.

[14] E. Bender and R. Canfield. The asymptotic number of labeled graphs with given degree sequences. *J. Combinatorial Theory Ser. A* 1978; 24: 296–307.

[15] N. Berger, B. Bollobás, C. Borgs, J. T. Chayes, and O. Riordan. Degree Distribution of the FKP Network Model. *Proceedings of ICALP* 2003; 725–738.

[16] N. Berger, C. Borgs, J.T. Chayes, R.M. D'Souza, and R.D. Kleinberg. Competition-Induced Preferential Attachment. *Proceedings of ICALP* 2004.

[17] G. Birkan, J. Kennington, E. Olinick, A. Ortynski, G. Spiride. Optimization-Based Design Strategies for DWDM Networks: Opaque versus All-Optical Networks. Tech Report 03-EMIS-01, SMU, Dallas, TX; 2001.

[18] U. Black. *MPLS and Label Switching Networks*, 2nd Edition. Prentice Hall PTR, 2002.

[19] A. Broido and K. Claffy. Internet Topology: Connectivity of IP Graphs. *Proceedings of SPIE ITCom WWW Conference* 2001.

[20] T. Bu and D. Towsley. On distinguishing Between Internet Power Law Topology Generators. *Proceedings of IEEE Infocom* 2002.

[21] K.L. Calvert, M. Doar, and E. Zegura. Modeling Internet topology. *IEEE Communications Magazine*, June 1997.

[22] J. M. Carlson and J. C. Doyle. Highly Optimized Tolerance: a mechanism for power laws in designed systems. *Physics Review E* 1999; 60:1412–1428.

[23] J.M. Carlson and J.Doyle. Complexity and Robustness. *Proceedings of the National Academy of Science* 2002; 99(Suppl. 1): 2539-2545.

[24] H. Chang, R. Govindan, S. Jamin, S. Shenker, and W. Willinger. Towards Capturing Representative AS-Level Internet Topologies. *Proceedings of ACM SIGMETRICS* 2002.

[25] H. Chang, S. Jamin, and W. Willinger. Internet Connectivity at the AS-level: An Optimization-Driven Modeling Approach *Proceedings of MoMeTools* 2003 (Extended version, Tech Report UM-CSE-475-03).

[26] Q. Chen, H. Chang, R. Govindan, S. Jamin, S. Shenker, and W. Willinger. The Origin of Power Laws in Internet Topologies Revisited. *Proceedings of IEEE INFOCOM* 2002.

[27] B. Cheswick, H. Burch, and S. Branigan. Mapping and Visualizing the Internet. *Proceedings of Usenix* 2000.

[28] Cisco Catalog. Master Contract for the State of Washington. http://techmall. dis.wa.gov/master_contracts/intranet/routers_switches.asp

[29] D. D. Clark. The design philosophy of the DARPA Internet protocols. *Proceedings of the ACM SIGCOMM'88*, in: *ACM Computer Communication Reviews* 1988; 18(4):106–114.

[30] M. B. Doar. A Better Model for Generating Test Networks. *Proceedings of Globecom '96*, Nov. 1996.

[31] J. Doucette and W.D. Grover. Comparison of mesh protection and restoration schemes and the dependency on graph connectivity. *3rd International Workshop on Design of Reliable Communication Networks (DRCN)* 2001; 121–128.

[32] J. C. Doyle and J. M. Carlson. Power laws, Highly Optimized Tolerance and generalized source coding. *Physics Review Letters* 2000; 84(24):5656–5659.

[33] J. Doyle, J. Carlson, S. Low, F. Paganini, G. Vinnicombe, W. Willinger, J. Hickey, P. Parilo, L. Vandenberghe. Robustness and the Internet: Theoretical Foundations, In *Robust design: A repertoire from biology, ecology, and engineering*, E. Jen, Editor, Oxford University Press (to appear).

[34] J. Duffy. "Cisco's loss is Juniper's gain." *Network World Fusion* February 18, 2003. http://www.nwfusion.com/edge/news/2003/0218mktshare.html.

[35] P. Erdos and A. Renyi. On random graphs I *Publ. Math. (Debrecen) 9* (1959), 290-297.

[36] P. Erdos and A. Renyi. On the evolution of random graphs. *In Publications of the Mathematical Institute of the Hungarian Academy of Sciences* 1960; 5:17–61.

[37] A. Fabrikant, E. Koutsoupias, and C. Papadimitriou. Heuristically Optimized Trade-offs: A new paradigm for Power- laws in the Internet, *Proceedings of ICALP* 2002; 110–122.

[38] M. Faloutsos, P. Faloutsos, and C. Faloutsos. On Power-Law Relationships of the Internet Topology. *Proceedings of ACM SIGCOMM* 1999.

[39] B. Fortz and M. Thorup. Internet Traffic Engineering by Optimizing OSPF Weights. *Proceedings of IEEE INFOCOM* 2000.

[40] L. Gao. On inferring autonomous system relationships in the Internet. in *Proceedings of IEEE Global Internet Symposium* 2000.

[41] B. Gavish. Topological design of telecommunication networks—local access design methods. *Annals of Operations Research* 1991; 33:17–71.

[42] B. Gendron, T.G. Crainic and A. Frangioni. Multicommodity Capacitated Network Design. In B. Sansó and P. Soriano (eds), Telecommunications Network Planning, pp. 1–29. Kluwer, Norwell, MA. 1998.

[43] C. Gkantsidis, M. Mihail, A. Saberi. Conductance and congestion in power law graphs *Proceedings of ACM Sigmetrics* 2003.

[44] R. Govindan and H. Tangmunarunkit. Heuristics for Internet Map Discovery, *Proceedings of IEEE INFOCOM* 2000.

[45] T.G. Griffin, A.D. Jaggard, and V. Ramachandran. Design Principles of Policy Languages for Path Vector Protocols. *Proceedings of ACM SIGCOMM* 2003.

[46] M. Grötschel, C. Monma, and M. Stoer. Design of Survivable Networks, in *Handbook in Operations Research and Management Science*, Volume on "Networks", 1993.

[47] H. Höller and S. Vo. A Mixed Integer Linear Programming Model for Multi-Layer SDH/WDM Networks. Presented at *Seventh Annual INFORMS Conference on Telecommunications* 2004. Boca Raton, Florida.

[48] H. Höller and S. Vo. Software Tools for a Multilayer Network Design. *Proceedings of the Fourth International Conference on Decision Support for Telecommunications and Information Society (DSITS)*, 2004. Warsaw, Poland.

[49] G. Huston. *ISP Survival Guide: Strategies for Running a Competitive ISP.* New York: John Wiley & Sons, 2000.

[50] *IEEE Communications Magazine, Survivability Issue*, August 1999.

[51] Internet2 Consortium. Internet2 NetFlow: Weekly Reports. http://netflow.internet2.edu/weekly/.

[52] C. Jin, Q. Chen, and S. Jamin. Inet: Internet Topology Generator. Technical Report CSE-TR443-00, Department of EECS, University of Michigan, 2000.

[53] C. Jin, D.X. Wei and S.H. Low. FAST TCP: motivation, architecture, algorithms, performance. *Proceedings of IEEE Infocom* 2004.

[54] D. Katabi, M. Handley, and C. Rohrs. Congestion Control for High Bandwidth-Delay Product Networks. *Proceedings of ACM Sigcomm* 2002.

[55] J. Kleinberg, S. R. Kumar, P. Raghavan, S. Rajagopalan and A. Tomkins. The web as a graph: Measurements, models and methods. *Proceedings of the International Conference on Combinatorics and Computing* July 1999.

[56] F.P. Kelly. Mathematical modelling of the Internet. In *Mathematics Unlimited - 2001 and Beyond*, B. Engquist and W. Schmid (eds). Berlin: Springer-Verlag 2001; 685–702.

[57] F.P. Kelly, A. Maulloo and D. Tan. Rate control in communication networks: shadow prices, proportional fairness and stability. *Journal of the Operational Research Society* 1998; 49: 237–252.

[58] T. Kelly. Scalable TCP: Improving Performance in Highspeed Wide Area Networks. *Computer Communication Review* 2003; 32(2).

[59] Kennington, J., E. Olinick, K. Lewis, A. Ortynski, G. Spiride. Robust solutions for the DWDM routing and provisioning problem: models and algorithms. *Optical Networks Magazine* 2003; 4:74–84.

[60] Kennington, J., E. Olinick, A. Ortynski, G. Spiride. Wavelength routing and assignment in a survivable WDM mesh network. *Operations Research* 2003; 51: 67–79.

[61] A. Lakhina, J.W. Byers, M. Crovella, and P. Xie. Sampling Biases in IP topology Measurements, *Proceedings of IEEE INFOCOM* 2003.

[62] L. Li, D. Alderson, W. Willinger, and J. Doyle. A First Principles Approach to Understanding Router-Level Topology. *Proceedings of ACM SIGCOMM* 2004.

[63] M. Liljenstam, J. Liu, and D.M. Nicol. Development of an Internet Backbone Topology for Large-Scale Network Simulations. *Proceedings of the 2003 Winter Simulation Conference*, S. Chick, P. J. Sánchez, D. Ferrin, and D. J. Morrice (eds).

[64] S. H. Low and D. E. Lapsley. Optimization Flow Control, I: Basic Algorithm and Convergence. *IEEE/ACM Transactions on Networking* 1999; 7(6):861–75.

[65] S. H. Low. A duality model of TCP and queue management algorithms. *IEEE/ACM Transactions on Networking* 2003.

[66] T. Luczak. Sparse random graphs with a given degree sequence. *Random Graphs, vol 2* Poznan, 1989.

[67] T.L. Magnanti and R.T. Wong. Network Design and Transportation Planning: Models and Algorithms. *Transportation Science* 1984; 18(1): 1–55.

[68] D. Maltz, G. Xie, J. Zhan, H. Zhang, G. Hjalmtysson, and A. Greenberg. Routing Design in Operational Networks: A Look from the Inside. *Proceedings of ACM SIGCOMM* 2004.

[69] A. Medina, A. Lakhina, I. Matta, and J. Byers. BRITE: An Approach to Universal Topology Generation. in *Proceedings of MASCOTS*, August 2001.

[70] A. Medina, I. Matta, and J. Byers. On the Origin of Power Laws in Internet Topologies. *ACM SIGCOMM Computer Communications Review* 2000; 30(2).

[71] B. Melián, M. Laguna and J. A. Moreno-Pérez. Capacity Expansion of Fiber Optic Networks with WDM Systems: Problem Formulation and Comparative Analysis. *Computers and Operations Research* 2003; 31(3): 461–472.

[72] B. Melián, M. Laguna and J. A. Moreno-Pérez. Minimizing the Cost of Placing and Sizing Wavelength Division Multiplexing and Optical Cross-Connect Equipment in a Telecommunications Network. July 2004. Submitted for publication. Available from http://leeds.colorado.edu/faculty/laguna/publications.htm

[73] M. Minoux. Network Synthesis and Optimum Network Design Problems: Models, Solution Methods and Applications. *Networks* 1989; 19: 313-360.

[74] M. Mitzenmacher. A Brief History of Generative Models for Power Law and Lognormal Distributions. *Internet Mathematics* 2004; 1(2).

[75] J. Mo and J. Walrand. Fair end-to-end window-based congestion control. *IEEE/ACM Transactions on Networking* 2000.

[76] G. Mohan and C.S.R. Murthy. Light-path restoration in WDM optical networks. *IEEE Network*, pp.24-32, November/December 2000.

[77] M. Molloy and B. Reed. A Critical Point For Random Graphs With A Given Degree Sequence, *Random Structures and Algorithms* 1995; 6:161-180.

[78] Computer Science and Telecommunications Board (CSTB), National Research Council. *The Internet's Coming of Age*. National Academy Press, Washington, D.C., 2001.

[79] M.E.J. Newman. Assortative Mixing in Networks. *Phys. Rev. Lett.* 2002; 89(208701).

[80] D. Moore, C. Shannon, G. Voelker, and S. Savage. Internet Quarantine: Requirements for Containing Self-Propagating Code. *Proceedings of IEEE Infocom* 2003.

[81] A.M. Odlyzko. Internet traffic growth: Sources and implications, in *Optical Transmission Systems and Equipment for WDM Networking II*, B. B. Dingel, W. Weiershausen, A. K. Dutta, and K.-I. Sato, eds., Proc. SPIE, 5247:1-15, 2003.

[82] F. Paganini, Z. Wang, S. H. Low and J. C. Doyle. A new TCP/AQM for stable operation in fast networks. *Proceedings of IEEE Infocom* 2003.

[83] C. R. Palmer and J. G. Steffan. Generating network topologies that obey power laws. *Proceedings of GLOBECOM* 2000.

[84] President's Commission on Critical Infrastructure Protection. *Critical Foundations.* Technical report, The White House, 1997.

[85] S. Ramamurthy and B. Mukherjee. Survivable WDM mesh networks, Part I - Protection. *Proceedings of IEEE Infocom* 1999; 744-751.

[86] S. Ramamurthy and B. Mukherjee. Survivable WDM mesh networks, Part II - Restoration. *Proceedings of IEEE International Conference on Communications (ICC)* 1999; 2023–2030.

[87] Route Views. *University of Oregon Route Views Project*, Available at http://www.antc.uoregon.edu/route-views/.

[88] G. Siganos, M. Faloutsos, P. Faloutsos, C. Faloutsos. Power laws and the AS-level internet topology. *IEEE/ACM Transactions on Networking* 2003; 11(4): 514–524.

[89] Cooperative Association for Internet Data Analysis (CAIDA). Skitter. Available at http://www.caida.org/tools/measurement/skitter/.

[90] N. Spring, R. Mahajan, and D. Wetherall. Measuring ISP Topologies with Rocketfuel. *Proceedings of ACM SIGCOMM* 2002.

[91] N. Spring, D. Wetherall, and T. Anderson. Reverse-Engineering the Internet. *Proceedings of ACM Workshop on Hot Topics in Networking (HotNets-II)*. November 2003.

[92] L. Subramanian, S. Agarwal, J. Rexford, and R. Katz. Characterizing the Internet Hierarchy from Multiple Vantage Points. *Proceedings of IEEE INFOCOM* 2002.

[93] SURFnet Press Release. "SURFnet Builds Advanced Research Network Based on Solutions, Services from Nortel Networks, Avici Systems, Telindus". Utrecht, 24 March 2004. Available at http://www.gigaport.nl/publicaties/pers/en_pers240304.html.

[94] H. Tangmunarunkit, R. Govindan, S. Jamin, S. Shenker, and W. Willinger. Network Topology Generators: Degree-Based vs. Structural. *Proceedings of ACM SIGCOMM* 2002.

[95] R. Teixeira, A. Shaikh, T. Griffin, and G.M. Voelker. Network Sensitivity to Hot-Potato Disruptions. *Proceedings of ACM SIGCOMM* 2004.

[96] J. Wang and L. Li and S. H. Low and J. C. Doyle. Can TCP and shortest-path routing maximize utility? *Proceedings of IEEE Infocom* 2003.

[97] B.M. Waxman. Routing of multipoint connections. *IEEE Journal of Selected Areas in Communication*, 1988; 6(9).

[98] The White House. *The National Strategy to Secure Cyberspace.* February 2003.

[99] W. Willinger and J. C. Doyle. Robustness and the Internet: Design and Evolution. In *Robust design: A Repertoire of Biological, Ecological, and Engineering Case Studies*, E. Jen, Editor, Oxford University Press (to appear).

[100] W. Willinger, R. Govindan, S. Jamin, V. Paxson and S. Shenker. Scaling Phenomena in the Internet: Critically examining Criticality *Proceedings of the National Academy of Science* 2002; 99(1):2573–2580.

[101] K.Wu and A. Liu. The Rearrangement Inequality. `http://matholymp.com/TUTORIALS/Rear.pdf`

[102] S.-H. Yook, H. Jeong, and A.-L. Barabási. Modeling the Internet's large-scale topology, *PNAS Proceedings of the National Academy of Science* 2002; 99:13382-13386.

[103] H. Zang. WDM Mesh Networks: Management and Survivability. Kluwer Publishing, December 2002.

[104] H. Zang, J. Jue, and B. Mukherjee. A review of routing and wavelength assignment approaches for wavelength-routed optical WDM networks. *Optical Networks Magazine* 2000; 1:47-60.

[105] H. Zang, J.P. Jue, L. Sahasrabuddhe, R. Ramamurthy, and B. Mukherjee. Dynamic light-path establishment in wavelength routed networks. *IEEE Communications Magazine* 2001; 39(9):100–108.

[106] E. W. Zegura, K. L. Calvert, and S. Bhattacharjee. How to model an internetwork. *Proceedings of INFOCOM* 1996.

[107] E. Zegura, K.L. Calvert, and M.J. Donahoo, A quantitative comparison of graph-based models for Internet topology. *IEEE/ACM Transactions on Networking* 1997; 5(6).

[108] Y. Zhang, M. Roughan, C. Lund and D. Donoho. An information-theoretic approach to traffic matrix estimation, Proc. of ACM Sigcomm, Karlsruhe, Germany, 2003. In *Computer Communication Review* 2003; 33(4).

[109] D. Zhou and S. Subramaniam. Survivability in Optical Networks. *IEEE Network*, pp.16-23, November/December 2000.

[110] X. Zhu, J. Yu and J.C. Doyle. Heavy Tails, Generalized Coding, and Optimal Web Layout. *Proceedings of IEEE Infocom* 2001.

Chapter 7

COMPARING SURVIVABLE MULTI-RING CONFIGURATIONS

Steven Cosares[1], Ondria J. Wasem[2], and Richard Cardwell[3]

[1]Hofstra University, Hempstead NY, USA; [2]Wasem Consulting LLC, West Windsor, NJ, USA; [3]Church Hill Road, Greeneville, TN, USA

Abstract: Self-healing rings continue to be integral components of telecommunications networks that must be designed to provide protection for demands against accidental link and/or node failures. For planning situations in which the distribution of the demands has some predictable patterns, e.g., hub-centers or demand clusters, a ring-based configuration that utilizes multiple interconnected rings may be most economical. This chapter describes a number of strategies for thus interconnecting rings, like stacking rings or creating a ring hierarchy. These are compared to some baseline strategy that utilizes a single centralized ring. In some of the proposed configurations, a reduction in the required total ring equipment capacity is accompanied by an increase in the need for cross-connection devices that switch traffic between rings. We compare the equipment costs associated with these alternatives over a variety of demand patterns. The sizing decisions are based on results from Monte-Carlo simulations to guarantee that planning solutions are relatively insensitive to demand uncertainty and fluctuation. The results of our experiments show that each strategy is most appropriate under some set of assumptions regarding equipment costs and the pattern of the demand. We use these results to formulate a set of guidelines that a network planner can apply when selecting ring-based designs in a network. These also include suggestions about where to install uni-directional and bi-directional rings in a particular design.

Key words: Self-Healing Rings, Network Design, Survivability

1.   INTRODUCTION

Self-healing rings, as provided for in the SONET, SDH, and WDM standards, are commonly used to support telecommunications services that we wish to remain viable, even in the event of some single-point failure in a network. They are an economical alternative for providing such network survivability that are relatively easy to configure, deploy and maintain. In the event of a network link failure, ring equipment automatically switches traffic to route over links that are not impacted. During a node failure, only those demands terminating there cannot be restored by this switching function.

Network planners who wish to maximize the benefits of using self-healing rings face a number of challenges. They must determine where to place such rings. To assure path diversity, each ring must be located over some simple cycle in the network. Planners may assign a point-to-point demand to a single ring or to a sequence of rings, in which case they must assure that (node and link) diversity is maintained throughout the route. For each ring location identified, planners must determine which type of equipment to install, e.g., uni-directional or bi-directional add-drop multiplexers (ADMs), and the total capacity requirement, based on the number and locations of the demands being served and the cost of the fiber and equipment.

The above tasks are confounded by the requirement that the ADMs placed at every node in a self-healing ring must have the same capacity – sufficient to satisfy and protect all of the demands assigned to the ring. This capacity requirement may best be met by either a single ring or by a set of multiple rings, over the same links and nodes, having sufficient total capacity.

To solve these difficult, interrelated problems, network planners often rely on a mix of decision support systems solutions and planning guidelines that have been established through prior experience, research activity, and/or experimentation. Consistent with a "divide and conquer" approach to complex problem solving, each of these tools tends to focus on particular problem components, e.g., "Ring Location", or "Ring Loading and Slotting", or "Ring Sizing".[1] In this chapter, we focus on the task of determining the best way to use self-healing rings to provide end-to-end survivable connectivity. The goal is to find designs that are economical, but also provide sufficient flexibility due to demand uncertainty and potential demand fluctuations over the planning horizon.

There are a number of basic options available. For example, by building rather long rings containing many nodes it is likely that each demand would have both its endpoints on some single ring. In such cases, there would be little need to plan for demands that must cross between rings. At the extreme, if a single ring were to have ADM equipment at every node, then it can be used to satisfy every network demand, as long as there were sufficient total capacity. However, we believe this would not be a cost-effective design because every node in the ring would need to have the same large ADM equipment capacity.

An alternative is to create a "stack" of multiple rings sharing the same links, wherein, each ring in the stack would have a different set of nodes that are equipped with an ADM. Since each ring would serve a different community of nodes and the demands will be split among these rings, the total ADM equipment capacity required for this option is likely to be smaller.[2,3] We point out, however, that this may or may not result in a total cost savings because each ring in the stack would require its own set of fibers and, since the stacked rings would each have smaller capacity, some of the economy of scale of the ADM equipment may be lost.

Another possibility is to interconnect multiple rings that each contain a smaller set of ADM nodes. Some demands would have to cross a path of multiple rings in order to traverse from their origins to their destinations. The switching capability of each ring in the path would ensure that the demands remain viable during any link failures. To prevent a service outage from the failure of an interconnection node between rings, the rings can be interconnected at two locations. This approach would also tend to reduce the total ADM capacity requirement, but would incur the costs associated with ring dual-interconnection.

The next section briefly describes the types of self-healing rings available, (i.e., uni-directional and bi-directional), and how they would contribute to the configuration strategies under study. Section 3 describes a set of Monte-Carlo simulation experiments that have been performed to compare and evaluate these strategies, under a variety of assumptions regarding the pattern of demand. Section 4 provides interpretations of the results of the experiments and suggests some planning guidelines for the appropriate application of each configuration. The section also provides some concluding remarks, including some suggestions for potential further study.

2. SINGLE AND MULTIPLE RING OPERATION

2.1 Uni-directional and Bi-directional Rings

The terms "uni-directional" and "bi-directional" refer to the options available when selecting a self-healing ring architecture to accommodate some set of demands. The two types differ in both the way they route demands under normal operating conditions and how they react when some node or link fails. These differences mean that, for a given set of demands, the amount of capacity required for each type may be vastly different. Furthermore, as we shall see, each type may be the more economical, depending on the demands assigned.

The capacity of a self-healing ring is expressed as a number of "slots" over which units of demand may traverse. In a uni-directional ring, each unit of demand is assigned to a dedicated slot in the ring. Under normal operating conditions, the demand between a pair of nodes would traverse its slots in the clockwise direction, (which we call the "working" route). If some link in the working route were to fail, then the demand can be accommodated by switching to the counter-clockwise direction instead (the "protection" route). Thus the capacity required for a uni-directional ring will always be equal to the total of the demands assigned to it.

In a bi-directional ring, the slots are partitioned so that half are reserved for working traffic and half serve for protection. Working routes that do not overlap are allowed to share the same slot. Thus the amount of working capacity required depends of the level of slot sharing possible with the demands. It is equal to the maximum of number of working slots needed by any link. When a failure occurs, all of the affected traffic will be switched the protection slots around the ring in the unhindered direction, providing complete back-up for the failure. Thus the number of slots of protection capacity needed is equal to the number of working slots needed. Bi-directional rings can be quite cost-effective when many demands are capable of sharing time slots. An objective when installing these rings is to determine a set of working route assignments for the demand that maximizes the sharing of slots[4,5] and thus minimizes the number of slots needed. If it turns out that the slot requirement is less than half of the total demand, (which is very likely for random demands but less so when the demand has certain patterns), then the bi-directional ring will likely be more efficient.

We point out that the required capacity level determined for a particular set of demands may be in excess of the ADM equipment capacity actually available to the planner. In that case, it will be necessary to place multiple rings over the same set of locations whose total capacity is sufficient. For ease of future exposition, however, we will still refer to this as a "single ring" solution and reserve the term "multiple rings" for configurations involving rings that cover different sets of nodes.

2.2   Functional Model for Equipment and Interconnection

Dual interconnection refers to the use of a sequence of self-healing rings to provide for a pair of (node) diverse paths over which to route a demand. This configuration requires that adjacent rings be connected at two node locations, as is illustrated in Figure 1.

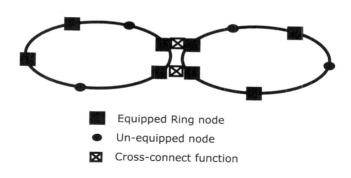

Equipped Ring node
Un-equipped node
Cross-connect function

Figure 1. Equipment Model for Dual Interconnection

Equipped nodes equipped, e.g., having an ADM on the ring, are likely to be endpoints of some demand. Un-equipped nodes do not contribute demand to the ring; they are through points used to assure ring diversity. Interconnect nodes contain equipment providing some cross-connection functionality. At the interconnect nodes, there may be three separate pieces of equipment to provide the needed functionality, such as two ADMs (Add-Drop Multiplexers) and a DCS (Digital Cross-connect System), or two WADMs (Wavelength Add-Drop Multiplexers) and an OXC (Optical Cross-Connect). Alternatively, there might be a single piece of equipment such as an MSPP (Multi-Service Provisioning Platform), which contains a common cross-connect, with plug-ins that provide either SONET or DWDM (Dense Wavelength Division Multiplexing) add-drop functionality.

One can derive a factor F, which is defined to be the approximate ratio of the unit cost of cross-connecting a demand relative to the unit cost of terminating a demand on a ring, e.g., on a multiplexer. When multiplied by the number of cross-connections needed in a configuration, this factor allows for direct economic comparisons between ring-based configuration strategies that require the interconnection function with those strategies that do not. The value of F is based on the specific equipment planned for the network. For instance, when the configuration uses an MSPP, there is no cost associated with the cross-connection, so $F=0$. However, if for instance one has to purchase ports on a DCS or OXC, then F will be some positive factor. For the purposes of our present discussion, we can assume that the value of F will rarely exceed 10.

2.3   Demand Routing Over Multiple Ring Configurations

Multiple rings are said to be "stacked" if they are routed over the same links, but have different equipped nodes and they are not interconnected. A demand is satisfied if it assigned to a ring having equipment at both of its endpoints. We assume that each ring operates independently of the others, so, based on the relative costs of equipment and the pattern of the demands assigned to each ring, (i.e., which pairs of nodes wish to communicate), the planner may decide that some rings in the stack be uni-directional while others be bi-directional.

Multiple ring strategies that apply dual interconnection place a special requirement on how certain demands are routed. If a demand must cross between rings, it places special requirements on each of the rings in order to guarantee that it will survive any failure. This is illustrated in Figure 2.

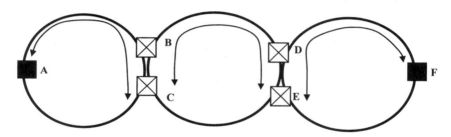

Figure -2. Routing over Multiple Interconnected Rings

Suppose the demand between nodes A and F must traverse three rings to be satisfied. Even if a direct path were used, the rings would provide the usual protection against the failure of any link or non-connecting node. We refer to the ring containing node A and the ring containing node F as "outer" rings. In order to further protect against the failure of one of the interconnect nodes, however, the working route from A in the outer ring must pass through both B and C. With the routing given, if node C fails, then no switching action would be required since the slots associated for this demand are still available at node B. If node B fails, then ring protection would be used to restore the demand. This route provides similar outer ring protection against failures of nodes D or E. To provide protection to the demand in the "inner" ring which   contains multiple pairs of interconnection nodes, the working route must traverse all four nodes, as illustrated.

If uni-directional equipment is used for the inner ring or the outer rings then no additional routing considerations are necessary because the demand is assigned to the entire slot. However, in a bi-directional ring, one must chose between routing counterclockwise from A through C and then to B, or clockwise from A through B to C in the outer ring. This requires a modification to traditional models for the ring loading and slotting problem.[5] Similarly, the could have chosen the counter-clockwise route from B through C and E to D if that would contribute to a final solution with smaller ring capacity.

For the purposes of our experiments, we developed new heuristics to solve the modified sizing problem that arises because of these routing requirements. We have found that either routing choice for the demand leaves little room on the slots for additional demands to share, especially if the other demands similarly require paths containing these interconnection locations. If, as we assume, the cost of a ring, as a function of the required capacity, is the same for both the uni-directional and bi-directional types, then it is unlikely that a bi-directional ring would be selected for an inner ring, especially since each working slot must be accompanied by a protection slot.

3.   EXPERIMENTAL DESIGN

In order to determine which ring configuration is best, in terms of cost and flexibility, we ran a Monte-Carlo simulation-based experiment in which many random instances of a set of point-to-point demands are generated. Network designs that represent each of three basic configuration strategies – a "Single Complete Ring" covering every node, a "Stack" of independent rings covering different sets of nodes, and a set of "Interconnected Rings" which provide a (node) diverse path for any pair of nodes – were applied to the demand sets generated. In our experiments we calculated and compared the total required capacity for the ring(s) and number of ring interconnections required, (if any). These values depend on the types of rings used in the configurations and the heuristic applied for routing and slotting demands in the bi-directional case. Each strategy was compared based on a number of different patterns of demand that might arise in actual network planning contexts.

3.1   Demand Patterns

For consistency in our experiments, we assumed a network with fifteen nodes to fifteen, numbered 1...15. This value corresponds to a common limit applied to longer rings. The total number of demand units among the node-pairs was set to 500. Thus our simulation represents a network planning situation in which the total demand within an area is known, but the specific point-to-point demands would have to be estimated, based on the information available.[6] Experiments were run for four different demand patterns, representing some prior knowledge about where in the network demands are likely to arise. For each pattern, we randomly generated 500 instances of a demand set. The patterns are denoted as follows:

- **Random:** This represents situations where the pattern of demands cannot be anticipated before some network design must be put into place. In each demand set, 35 node-pairs, (out of the possible 105), are randomly selected (with replacement). Then each of the 500 demand units is randomly assigned to one of these pairs. Such a sparse subset of node pairs is necessary to insure adequate variability among the demand set instances.[7]

- **Centralized:** This represents when most of the demands are expected to either originate or terminate at some specific location in the network, e.g., a central office hub. In each demand set, 250 demand units are assigned among all of the nodes as in the Random pattern. The remaining 250 units are randomly assigned among node pairs $(8,i)$, for $i \neq 8$.

- **Two Communities:** This represents when most of the demand is expected to be localized within two disjoint communities, as occurs when the network serves adjacent central office areas in a metropolitan area. In each demand set, 100 demand units are assigned as in Random. 200 units are randomly assigned among 10 node-pairs in 1..8, (of the possible 28 pairs). The remaining 200 are assigned among 10 node-pairs in 9..15.

- **Three Communities:** This represents when the network is expected to consist of three disjoint communities having most of its communication localized. In each demand set, 125 demand units are assigned as in Random. 125 units are assigned randomly among 6 node-pairs in 1..5, (out of a possible 10). 125 units are assigned randomly among 6 node-pairs in 6..10, and 125 units are assigned randomly among 6 pairs in 10..15.

3.2   Configurations

The **Single Complete Ring** configuration, representing the baseline strategy, refers to a design in which the ring has add-drop equipment at every node. The implication in this design is that the ring can accommodate the demands between any pair of the fifteen nodes. For uni-directional rings, the capacity needed to accommodate this strategy for any of the demand sets described is 500, the total number of demand units, (giving a total equipment capacity requirement of 500*15 or 7500). Depending on the demand pattern, a bi-directional ring may be more economical. The available ring equipment, having specific capacities, may dictate that the capacity requirement be met by a set of rings as opposed to a single ring. We will assume, in this baseline configuration, that all such rings are equipped at every node. Hence this strategy has the advantage of being able to accommodate any demand that may arise, but comes at the cost of requiring the high capacity at every node.

Configurations with stacked rings tests whether it would be economical to have rings which are only equipped at some subset of nodes. Such rings would accommodate the demands between the specified nodes, (e.g., among a community of interest), leaving the complete ring to satisfy the remaining demands. To be consistent with the "Two Communities" demand pattern represented in the experiment, the stack would include a complete ring, a ring only visiting only nodes 1..8 and a ring visiting only node 9..15. We call this strategy **Stack Two Plus Complete**. Similarly, for addressing the "Three Communities" demand pattern we developed the strategy, **Stack Three Plus Complete**. This refers to a configuration with a complete ring and one for nodes 1..5, one for nodes 6..10, and one for nodes 11..15. Local demands within a community would be served by these shorter rings; a demand between two communities would be served by the complete ring.

For the sake of comparison, we developed two interconnected ring strategies that are consistent, respectively, with the "Two Communities" and "Three Communities" demand patterns. As with the stacked configurations, smaller rings are to serve each community. However, demands between communities will be routed across interconnected rings, rather than some complete ring. The **Two Interconnected Rings** strategy assumes that one ring serves nodes 1..9, while the other serves 8..15. The rings intersect at two locations (8 and 9) which are selected as the interconnection points containing cross-connection capability. To serve three distinct communities we employ a "ring hierarchy" where local rings are connected by way of a central "hub" ring containing all of the interconnection points.[8,9] This **Three Rings Interconnected by a Hub Ring** strategy is illustrated in Figure 3.

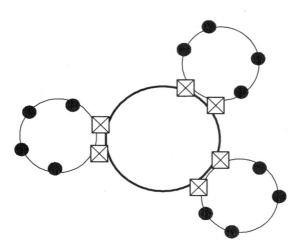

Figure 3. Three Rings Interconnected by a Hub Ring

A second interconnection node is added to every community, so that each community, nodes 1..5, nodes 6..10, and nodes 11..15, is served by a local ring with six nodes, two of which interconnect with some central hub ring having six nodes. Traffic between communities would have to traverse from an outer ring, through an inner ring, to another outer ring.

3.3   Routing Demands and Sizing Rings

Each demand set that was generated in the experiment was routed over each configuration. For both the stacked and interconnected strategies, any demand arising between a pair of nodes in the same community would be assigned to the local ring for that community. Demands between communities are assigned to the complete ring, or in the case of the interconnected strategies, to the appropriate sequence of rings. Once the demands were assigned to the rings, the required size of the uni-directional ring type was determined to be the sum of the demands. For the bi-directional ring type, we applied our adaptation of a "dual weight-based" method to determine the working routes of the demands and the "straddler" method to find the required number of working slots.[5] This number is then doubled to account for the required protection capacity.

The heuristics were applied to all 500 demand sets associated with each of the four demand patterns. From the set of capacity values for the ring(s) and the required number of ring interconnections, (if any), in a particular configuration, we selected the 99th percentile. This would insure that the sizes of the rings were sufficient to accommodate unexpected or fluctuating demand. The sizing decisions associated with the "Three Rings Interconnected by a Hub Ring" configuration for the "Three Communities" demand pattern are demonstrated in Figure 4.

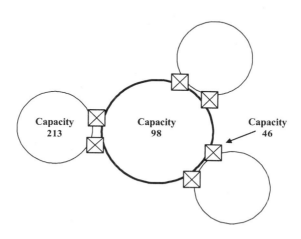

Figure 4. Illustration of Sizing Decisions

For this configuration, it turns out that uni-directional rings are more economical than bi-directional rings. This should comes as no surprise since the demands that traverse multiple rings need to be routed past both interconnection points, so leave little room for sharing slots with the local demands. Because there is symmetry among the communities in our experiments, all three of the outer rings should be given the same capacity, which is 213 for this demand pattern. All six of the interconnection locations between rings need to be capable of supporting 46 cross-connections. At its peak, the inner ring is not expected to support more than 98 demand units.

Our study focuses on the cost of terminating and switching equipment in each configuration and, for the moment, ignores the costs associated with transporting signals between locations, e.g., fiber and regeneration equipment. The total ring capacity requirement, which would determine the total cost of the configuration, is: (6*98)=588 for the 6 ADMs in the inner ring plus (18*213)=3834 for the 18 ADMs in the outer rings, for a total of 4422. In addition, there is a total of (6*46)=276 cross-connections between the inner and outer rings. This gives a "total cost index" of $4422+276*F$. This value can be used to compare this interconnected configurations with the single ring and stacked configurations over the same set of demands.

3.4   Experimental Results

For each demand pattern and for each configuration, the component equipment capacity requirements are calculated as described above. In addition, a total cost index is calculated. The values are determined for every reasonable configuration option and are presented in Table 1.

		Demand Pattern			
		Random	*Centralized*	*Two Communities*	*Three Communities*
Configuration Strategy	**Complete Ring**				
	Ring ADMs	498	492	434	340
	Cost Index	**7472**	**7381**	**6511**	**5100**
	Two Interconnected Rings				
	Ring ADMs	530	406	314	
	Interconnect Devices	289	151	62	
	Cost Index	**9008 + 578*F**	**6909 + 302*F**	**5334+ 124*F**	
	Stack Two plus a Complete Ring				
	Local Ring ADMs	211	177	321	
	Complete Ring ADMs	343	311	75	
	Cost Index	**8309**	**7315**	**5935**	
	Three Rings plus a Hub Ring				
	Outer Ring ADMs	334	260		213
	Hub Ring ADMs	368	264		98
	Interconnect Devices	174	116		46
	Cost Index	**8227 + 1044*F**	**6264 + 696*F**		**4428 + 276*F**
	Stack Three plus a Complete Ring				
	Local Ring ADMs	123	93		224
	Complete Ring ADMs	431	404		110
	Cost Index	**8306**	**7451**		**5011**

Table 1. Equipment Capacity Requirements and Total Cost Index

4.   DISCUSSION AND CONCLUSIONS

For the baseline single complete ring configuration, bi-directional rings appear to be preferable to uni-directional rings, (which would have a total cost index of 7500). This is because the demands generated in each of the patterns are fairly capable of sharing slots with one another. As we have seen, this does not occur with the more "slot greedy" demand routings necessitated by the interconnected ring strategies, which are consequently comprised solely of uni-directional rings. In the stacked strategies, it turns out that the local rings can benefit from the slot sharing of bi-directional rings, while the complete ring, which must now serve longer demands between communities, is appropriately uni-directional.

When the demand pattern cannot be anticipated, as in the Random cases, it may be most appropriate to consider configurations with longer, larger rings, as represented by the Single Complete Ring strategy. With such little information, it is necessary to set fairly high capacities to accommodate the 99th percentile solution from the demand sets and guarantee demand-flexible solutions. Fragmented configurations using multiple rings in a stack require each individual ring to have this relatively high capacity, so the total capacity requirement would tend to be larger than that of the unified solution. Interconnected solutions suffer in this case from the high volume of demands that must pass between rings, which results in higher ring capacity requirements, (from the slot hungry routings necessitated), as well as the need for more cross-connection capacity.

When network demands are expected to arise in some discernable patterns, e.g., when there are well defined demand centers or localized communities of interest, the baseline strategy of placing long rings is less appealing. Hub rings can be placed over demand centers and local rings can be placed in the communities of interest to provide for these demands, leaving very little traffic that would require ring interconnection or longer rings. It appears that thee decision of whether to apply the stacked or the interconnected configurations is dependent on the value assumed for F, the cost of cross-connection, relative to the cost of ring equipment capacity.

In our comparisons of the various strategies, we accounted for the trade off between multiplexing and interconnection costs only. We conjecture if we were to account for fiber costs as well, it would tip the scale further toward the use of an interconnected configuration. A stack would require fiber for each ring, possibly passing through many non-equipped nodes. Fiber routes in the interconnected configurations would be selected to take advantage of cheaper links, shorter distances and or savings on amplification and regeneration. This would tend to create configurations having shorter rings that would not cover all demand pairs. Then interconnection would be the more economical than placing longer rings to satisfy the demands between communities.

In sum, each of the configuration strategies is most appropriate in some reasonable network planning scenario. The complete ring is the most flexible since it can potentially route any demand and is operationally the least expensive, (the presence of all nodes on all rings would simplify provisioning). When anticipated demand patterns can be exploited then deploying a stack of independent rings is more economical. Finally, if cross-connection costs are relatively low then interconnected ring configurations are an appealing option.

ACKNOWLEDGEMENTS

This research was partially supported by a research grant from the Frank G. Zarb School of Business at Hofstra University. Thanks are due to Anil Panicker of RSoft Design Group and Haim Kobrinski of Telcordia Technologies for offering insights on the equipment model.

REFERENCES

1. Cosares, Deutsch, Saniee, and Wasem, "SONET Toolkit: A Decision Support System for the Design of Robust and Cost-Effective Fiber-Optic Networks", *Interfaces* **25**, pp. 20-40, (1995).
2. Gawande and Klincewicz, "Designing a family of bi-directional self-healing rings", *Proc. SPIE Conference on Performance and Control of Network Systems III*, Boston MA, Sept. 1999.
3. Armony, Klicewicz, Luss, and Rosenwein, "Design of Stacked Self-Healing Rings Using a Genetic Algorithm", *Journal of Heuristics* **6** pp. 85-105, (2000).
4. S. Cosares and I. Saniee, "An Optimization Problem Related to Balancing Loads on SONET Rings", *Telecommunications Systems* **3**, pp. 165-181 (1994).
5. T. Carpenter and S. Cosares, "Comparing Heuristics for Routing and Slot Assignment on Ring Networks", *Telecommunication Systems* **21**, pp. 319-337 (2002).
6. Wasem, Gross, and Tlapa, "Forecasting Broadband Demand Between Geographic Areas," *IEEE Communications Magazine*, Vol.33, No. 2, February, 1995, pp. 50-57.
7. S. Cosares, "Planning Self-Healing Ring Capacity under Demand Uncertainty", Telecommunications Network Design and Management, Operations Research/Computer Science Interfaces Series, Volume 23, Kluwer Academic Publishers, pp. 83-98 (2002).
8. Gawande, Klincewicz, and Luss, "Design of SONET Ring Networks for Local Access", *Advances in Performance Analysis* **4**, pp. 159-173, (1999).
9. Thomadsen and Stidsen, "Optimal Design of Hierarchical Ring Networks", *Seventh INFORMS Telecom Conference*, Boca Raton, FL, March 2004.

Chapter 8

THE EFFECT OF HOP LIMITS ON OPTIMAL COST IN SURVIVABLE NETWORK DESIGN

Sebastian Orlowski

Konrad-Zuse-Zentrum für Informationstechnik Berlin
Takustr. 7, 14195 Berlin, Germany
orlowski@zib.de

Roland Wessäly

Konrad-Zuse-Zentrum für Informationstechnik Berlin
Takustr. 7, 14195 Berlin, Germany
wessaely@zib.de

Abstract   We investigate the impact of hop-limited routing paths on the total cost of a telecommunication network. For different survivability settings (dedicated path protection, link and path restoration), the optimal network cost without restrictions on the admissible path set is compared to the results obtained with two strategies to impose hop limits on routing paths. Using optimal solutions for nine real-world based problem instances, we evaluate how much the restriction to short paths can increase network cost.

Keywords: survivable network design, hop limits, restoration, protection, branch-and-cut, mixed-integer programming

1.   Introduction

In telecommunication network design, it is well-established to use short paths for routing communication demands. This approach is in some cases motivated by the underlying routing protocol, such as OSPF, IS-IS, or BGP in IP-networks, or by technological restrictions, such as degradation of signal quality in WDM networks or transmission delay in ATM networks. In other cases, the purpose of a restriction to short routing paths is to reduce the planning complexity.

Each individual demand consumes the least bandwidth in the network if it is routed on a shortest path. However, a shortest path routing is not necessarily cost minimal as soon as modular link capacities are taken into account. Furthermore, the reduction of the solution space caused by a restricted path set potentially increases network cost. The question is: *how much* additional cost is incurred by a restriction to short paths? It is often assumed that a small, well-chosen set of short routing paths is sufficient to reliably obtain near-optimal solutions. However, no published computational study evaluates the necessary additional investment based on provably optimal solutions for different survivability mechanisms. This is the gap we fill with this paper.

On nine real-world based problem instances, we compare the optimal network cost with different classes of admissible path sets: without any restrictions, with demand-independent hop limits, and with demand-dependent hop limits. Different hop limit values are tested with each of these classes and with different survivability settings (dedicated protection, link restoration and path restoration). The main conclusions drawn from our experiments are the following:

- A restriction to short paths can easily induce infeasibility of the planning problem or very high network cost on practical instances. It is worth noticing that the sensitivity to hop limits is much more pronounced for small values.

- With demand-independent hop limits, paths with at least 6 links are needed for networks with 10–20 nodes to reliably obtain a solution which is at most 10% more expensive than an optimal solution with respect to all routing paths.

- With demand-dependent hop limits, at least 4 hops should be allowed in addition to the shortest hop count between the end nodes of a demand. With smaller hop limits, it is not possible to reliably obtain solutions with at most 10% additional cost compared to an optimal solution with respect to all routing paths. In particular, a shortest path routing caused 161% additional cost in one of our problem instances.

- By using a column generation approach, it is possible to deal with any kind of hop restrictions, or even with unconstrained routing paths. In combination with a branch-and-cut algorithm, this approach can be used to prove optimality of solutions. Thus, it is preferable to other methods such as using a small set of predefined routing paths.

Literature.   Many publications on survivable network design present a mathematical model for the arising multicommodity flow subproblems. There are two principal approaches: using an edge-flow (also called node-arc) formulation or a path-flow (also called arc-path) formulation. The latter has the advantage that restrictions on the admissible path set can more easily be modeled, at the expense of a possibly exponential number of path variables.

To cope with the large number of variables in a path-flow formulation and to reduce calculation times, some authors apply column generation techniques [Murakami, 1995; Dahl and Stoer, 1998; Poppe and Demeester, 1998; Wessäly, 2000], while other authors either use an edge-flow formulation [Balakrishnan and Altinkemer, 1992] or feed a fixed, precalculated set of routing paths into an LP or MIP solver. For the latter approach, several ways of defining the admissible path set have been proposed. In [Herzberg and Bye, 1994; Xiong and Mason, 1997], a fixed global hop limit is imposed on all routing paths. In [Iraschko et al., 1998], a demand-dependent hop limit is considered, defined by the length of a shortest hop path for a given demand plus some fixed additional number of hops. Eventually, a demand-dependent hop limit is employed in [Doucette and Grover, 2001], which is iteratively raised until a specified number of paths has been found for each demand. We now briefly present the problems investigated in these papers, together with the solution approach. More general surveys on survivable network design can be found in [Demeester et al., 1999; Soni et al., 1999], among others.

In [Murakami, 1995], a path-flow formulation is used to compare the cost of path restoration with stub release and link restoration under a single link failure scenario. The author considers minimization of continuous spare capacities with respect to a given shortest working path routing as well as joint optimization of working and spare capacities. Column generation is applied to generate working and restoration paths only when needed, using a (quadratic) shortest path algorithm.

In [Stoer and Dahl, 1994; Dahl and Stoer, 1998], the problem of installing discrete link capacities is formulated for the survivability models reservation and diversification with so-called metric inequalities [Iri, 1971]. These inequalities are generated at runtime using a path-flow formulation with routing paths in all operating states, which is solved using column generation.

In [Poppe and Demeester, 1998], a similar model is used to formulate the problem of installing continuous spare capacities for link and path restoration based on a given shortest working path routing. Column generation is used to identify missing restoration paths.

In [Wessäly, 2000], discrete working and spare capacities are determined using a path-flow formulation for the survivability models reservation, diversification, and path restoration. This path-flow LP is solved by generating working and restoration paths only when needed.

In [Balakrishnan and Altinkemer, 1992], an uncapacitated edge-flow formulation with hop limits is presented for determining the topology of a network and a single-path routing of all demands in the failureless state. The objective is to minimize the sum of topology and flow cost. The model is solved using Lagrangian relaxation together with primal heuristics. Besides other computational studies, the authors evaluate the cost effect of a demand-independent hop limit between 1 and 7. On a complete network with 25 nodes, the best solution values (optimality gap $< 5\%$) for hop limits 3 to 7 are almost identical. As expected on a complete network, hop limit 1 is very expensive (412% of the cost with hop limit 7) since all links have to be included in the topology.

In [Herzberg and Bye, 1994], the spare capacity assignment problem with respect to a given working path routing is considered. The network is designed for a single link failure scenario with link restoration. A path-flow formulation with integer capacities is presented. Computational results are presented on one small but well connected test instance (11 nodes, 23 links) with integer capacities. The effect of hop limits is tested by enumerating all restoration paths up to a given number of hops, which varies between 3 and 7. On the investigated test instance, the optimal solution values for hop limits 5, 6 and 7 were identical.

In [Xiong and Mason, 1997], a path-flow formulation for path restoration without stub release and for link restoration under a single link failure scenario is used. A set of working and restoration paths is precalculated, which contains at most 40 paths per demand. A path length restriction of 6 and 10 hops is imposed for the two small and the two larger test instances, respectively.

In [Iraschko et al., 1998], the cost of link and path restoration (with or without stub release) is compared for single link failures both with a predefined shortest path routing and with joint working and spare capacity optimization. The path-flow model contains integer capacities and flow variables. For each demand, the authors enumerate all paths up to a given hop limit, which is the length of a shortest hop path for this demand plus a fixed number of additional hops. This path set is complemented by a small set of link disjoint paths to guarantee a solution. The authors report on very long calculation times due to the resulting large path set even on small test instances, as soon as working and spare capacities are optimized together (9 hours for link restoration, 2.7 days for path restoration without stub release on an instance with 10 nodes, 22 links, and 45 demands).

In [Doucette and Grover, 2001], several protection and restoration mechanisms are compared for networks of varying density. The authors use a path-flow formulation with integer capacities and a predetermined path set. All paths up to an iteratively adapted hop limit are enumerated until at least 5, 10, or 20 paths have been found for each demand (the exact number depends on the considered problem).

Discussion of the different approaches. The main advantage of a pre-defined path set is the fact that "wild" path restrictions can be incorporated in the model. In practice, however, a restricted path set often consists simply of all paths up to a given number of hops (which may be demand-dependent or not), sometimes complemented by a small set of paths which guarantees a solution. The drawback of a predefined path set is that this approach only leads to heuristic solutions without a lower bound.

In contrast, a column generation approach combined with a branch-and-cut algorithm provides a lower bound and thus a quality guarantee for solutions if the pricing problem (i.e., the problem of identifying missing path variables) is exactly solvable. For instance, this is the case if the admissible path set is not restricted at all or by hop limits only.

This paper is structured as follows: after a description of our mathematical model and a brief sketch of our algorithmic approach in Section 2, we report on our computational tests in Section 3. Eventually, we conclude with Section 4.

2. Model and Algorithm

We are investigating network design problems dealing with an integrated planning of

- a topology,
- modular link capacities,
- a routing during normal operation, and
- a protection/restoration routing for single link and node failures.

The mathematical model is derived from the mixed-integer linear programming formulation described in [Orlowski and Wessäly, 2004], which also covers hardware requirements imposed by network elements and interface cards. These and other extensions (e.g., the possibility to respect existing parts of a network) are implemented in our network planning tool DISCNET [Discnet, 2004].

Sections 2.1 and 2.2 describe the parts of our model covering topology and link capacity decisions, and routing planning, respectively.

2.1 Topology and link capacities

The planning network consists of a set V of nodes and a set E of potential (undirected) links between these nodes. For each link $e \in E$, a set $\mathcal{D}_e$ of *link designs* (e.g., STM-N capacities or a certain number of WDM wavelengths) is specified, out of which at most one has to be chosen. Every link design d installable on a given link e has a capacity C_e^d and a cost value K_e^d assigned to it. For every link $e \in E$ and every link design $d \in \mathcal{D}_e$, a binary variable $x_e^d \in \{0, 1\}$ determines whether link design d is installed on link e or not. The inequalities

$$\sum_{d \in \mathcal{D}_e} x_e^d \leq 1 \qquad e \in E \tag{8.1}$$

state that at most one link design has to be chosen on each link. The final topology consists exactly of those links for which a link design is chosen. For notational convenience, the auxiliary variable

$$y_e := \sum_{d \in \mathcal{D}_e} C_e^d x_e^d \tag{8.2}$$

denotes the capacity of the installed link design on link $e \in E$. In particular, choosing no link design implies $y_e = 0$. The objective

$$\min \sum_{e \in E} \sum_{d \in \mathcal{D}_e} K_e^d x_e^d \tag{8.3}$$

minimizes the total cost of all installed link designs.

2.2   Routing

In addition to a topology and link capacities, a survivable routing has to be determined. This section presents an integrated path-flow formulation for the failureless state and the survivability concepts *diversification* (as a relaxation of 1+1 protection), *link* and *path restoration*. In addition to the *normal operating state* (NOS) where the whole network is operational, we consider a set S of *failure states* where at least one link or node fails. In this paper, the set S consists of all single link and node failures, i.e., $S = V \cup E$. For any failure state $s \in S$, let $V^s \subset V$ and $E^s \subset E$ be the sets of surviving nodes and links, respectively. Furthermore, let $D^s := \{uv \in \mathcal{D} \mid u, v \in V^s\}$ be the set of demands whose end nodes are both operational in s.

NOS routing.   Let $\mathcal{D}$ denote the set of all point-to-point demands. For each demand $uv \in \mathcal{D}$, a demand value d_{uv} must be routed between the end nodes u and v. We assume a bifurcated routing, i.e., several paths may be used for each demand.

Let $\mathcal{P}_{uv}$ be the set of *admissible* paths to route the demand $uv \in \mathcal{D}$ in the normal operating state. These are all loopless paths between u and v satisfying a given hop limit. Using non-negative continuous flow variables $f_{uv}(P) \in \mathbb{R}_+$ for all demands $uv \in \mathcal{D}$ and all paths $P \in \mathcal{P}_{uv}$, the following constraints formulate a multicommodity flow problem with hop limits for the normal operating state:

$$\sum_{P \in \mathcal{P}_{uv}} f_{uv}(P) \;=\; d_{uv} \qquad uv \in \mathcal{D}, \tag{8.4}$$

$$\sum_{uv \in \mathcal{D}} \sum_{\substack{P \in \mathcal{P}_{uv}: \\ e \in P}} f_{uv}(P) \;\leq\; y_e \qquad e \in E. \tag{8.5}$$

The demand constraints (8.4) state that all demands have to be satisfied, whereas the capacity constraints (8.5) ensure that the total flow on any link $e \in E$ does not exceed its capacity y_e.

1+1 protection and diversification. With 1+1 protection, each demand is doubled at one node and routed on two link- or node-disjoint paths to some target node, which chooses the signal of better quality. In particular, if a single link (or node, respectively) fails, at least one of the two paths remains operational since the two paths are disjoint. We approximate this mechanism by *diversification*, a formulation introduced in [Dahl and Stoer, 1998].

For every demand $uv \in \mathcal{D}$, the *diversification parameter* $\delta_{uv} \in (0, 1]$ specifies the fraction of demand uv which is allowed to fail in any considered failure state. This is expressed by the diversification constraints

$$\sum_{\substack{P \in \mathcal{P}: \\ P \text{ fails in } s}} f_{uv}(P) \leq \delta_{uv} d_{uv} \qquad s \in S, \; uv \in \mathcal{D}^s, \tag{8.6}$$

which state that in any failure state $s \in S$, at most $\delta_{uv} d_{uv}$ should fail in total for every demand uv whose end nodes are still operational. In other words, at least $(1 - \delta_{uv}) d_{uv}$ should survive. In particular, this implies that the demand is routed on at least $\lceil 1/\delta_{uv} \rceil$ paths. By setting the diversification value δ_{uv} to 0.5 and doubling the demand value, Constraints (8.6) ensure that at least the original demand value d_{uv} survives in any considered failure state. Since every solution of 1+1 protection fulfills these constraints but not vice versa, this formulation is a relaxation of 1+1 protection. It can be used to formulate 1+1 protection exactly by splitting every demand with value d into d demands with value 1, doubling these unit-demands and routing them with diversification value $\delta_{uv} = 0.5$ and integer flow variables. However, since this leads to a very large set of demands and thus to a large integer program, we only use the relaxation here.

Link and path restoration. In contrast to 1+1 protection where backup capacity is preconfigured and dedicated to a particular demand, link and path restoration share backup capacity between the demands. With *link restoration*, each path affected by a failure is locally patched between the two nodes on the path which are adjacent to the failing link or node, as illustrated in Figure 8.1, With *path restoration*, illustrated in Figure 8.2, each affected demand is rerouted between its two end nodes, independent of the kind of failure. In this paper, we consider only path restoration without stub release, i.e., working capacity on operational links of a failing path is *not* released and cannot be used for backup paths.

Figure 8.1: Link restoration   Figure 8.2: Path restoration

With each failure state $s \in S$, a set C^s of *failure commodities* is associated. These are point-to-point demands to be satisfied in failure state s; their exact definition depends on the type of failure and the restoration mechanism.

For instance, applying link restoration to the failure of link $e \in E$ induces one failure commodity between the two end nodes of e, whose demand value is the total NOS flow on e. The failure of a node v induces a failure commodity between every pair u, w of nodes adjacent to v, with a demand value equal to the NOS flow on the three-node-path $u \rightarrow v \rightarrow w$. Path restoration in failure state $s \in S$ leads to a failure commodity for each non-failing demand $uv \in D^s$, whose demand value is the failing part of d_{uv}.

For any failure state $s \in S$ and any failure commodity $c \in C^s$, let $\mathcal{P}_c^s$ be the set of admissible paths to route c. These are all paths between the end nodes of c which do not contain failing nodes or links and which satisfy given hop limits. Furthermore, let $\mathcal{IP}_c^s$ be the set of all *interrupted paths* which are restored by c. The exact definition of this set again depends on the restoration mechanism and the type of failure.

Using non-negative continuous path-flow variables $f_c^s(P) \in \mathbb{R}_+$ for all failure states $s \in S$, all failure commodities $c \in C^s$ and all admissible restoration paths $P \in \mathcal{P}_c^s$, the following constraints formulate both the link and path restoration problem, according to the choice of parameters:

$$\sum_{c \in C^s} \sum_{\substack{P \in \mathcal{P}_c^s: \\ e \in P}} f_c^s(P) + \sum_{uv \in D} \sum_{\substack{P \in \mathcal{P}_{uv}: \\ e \in P}} f_{uv}(P) \leq y_e \quad \begin{matrix} s \in S, \\ e \in E^s \end{matrix} \qquad (8.7)$$

$$- \sum_{P \in \mathcal{P}_c^s} f_c^s(P) + \sum_{uv \in D} \sum_{P \in \mathcal{P}_{uv} \cap \mathcal{IP}_c^s} f_{uv}(P) \leq 0 \quad \begin{matrix} s \in S, \\ c \in C^s \end{matrix} \qquad (8.8)$$

The capacity constraints (8.7) state that in any failure state, the sum of the total NOS flow and the total restoration flow on a given link must not exceed its capacity. The failure demand constraints (8.8) formulate that all failing flow must be restored.

2.3   Algorithm

This section describes the used algorithm and explains how optimality is ensured. The planning problem is solved with our network planning tool DISCNET [Discnet, 2004] using Benders decomposition [Benders, 1962], as illustrated in Figure 8.3. The approach is based on a branch-and-cut algorithm with an LP relaxation containing only link design variables and Constraints (8.1) and (8.2), but no routing conditions. This leads to a valid lower bound on the network cost and thus to a quality guarantee for solutions. In particular, the lower bound can be used to prove optimality of a solution.

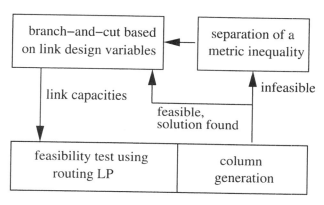

Figure 8.3: Algorithmic approach

Every time an integer capacity vector $\bar{y}$ is identified, it is tested for feasibility with respect to the missing routing conditions. In other words, the path-flow formulation consisting of Constraints (8.4), (8.5), together with (8.6) or (8.7), (8.8), is solved to test whether a feasible routing exists within the capacities $\bar{y}$. If such a routing can be found, an overall feasible solution has been identified. Otherwise, a violated metric inequality [Iri, 1971; Wessäly, 2000; Orlowski, 2003] cutting off $\bar{y}$ can be generated from the dual of the routing LP.

To solve the routing LP, column generation is employed for working and restoration paths. The LP is solved with some initial set of path variables. If no routing can be found within the given link capacities, the question is whether a feasible routing exists using additional path variables not yet included in the routing LP. If this is the case, missing paths can be generated by solving a shortest path problem; in particular, the question can be answered in polynomial time for the presented formulations.

Summarizing, optimality is guaranteed by the branch-and-cut algorithm which considers all relevant capacity vectors, and by the column generation procedure which can be used to exactly test feasibility of each of these capacity vectors. A more detailed description of this approach, further employed cutting planes, and the methods used to identify missing paths can be found in [Wessäly, 2000; Orlowski, 2003].

3.   Computational Results

In this section, we describe our computational tests to evaluate the effect of two kinds of hop limits on the overall network cost. After a short presentation of our nine test instances, we show and discuss our results.

We present two test series, each of them for diversification, link and path restoration. In the first series, a fixed global hop limit between 3 and 7 is imposed. In the second series, demand-dependent hop limits are given by the shortest hop distance for a particular demand plus some fixed number k of hops which varies between 0 and 5. The hop limits are imposed on to both working and backup paths. For diversification and path restoration, the end-to-end backup paths are hop-limited, whereas for the local survivability mechanism link restoration, the hop limits are applied to the local patching paths.

An alternative approach could have been to impose stronger hop restrictions on working paths than on backup paths. However, there is no distinction between working and backup paths in the diversification formulation used for path protection. In order to make restoration and protection results comparable, the same hop constraints have been imposed on working and backup paths also with restoration.

For each of our test instances, Table 8.1 shows the number of nodes, potential links, and demands, respectively, together with the average node degree $\bar{d} = 2|E|/|V|$ and the number $|\mathcal{D}_e|$ of available link designs, which is the same for all links of an instance. In all computational tests, full restoration or protection of all failing flow in any single link or node failure state is assumed. In order to be able to compare optimal solutions, relatively small networks with 10–20 nodes have been chosen.

Many computational studies are based on randomly generated problem instances. Experience shows, however, that these often exhibit structural differences compared to real-world planning problems. This is particularly true for demand patterns. Most of our test instances, provided to us by network operators, are practical SDH-, WDM-, and leased line planning problems which reflect the different cost structures and demand patterns arising in these planning scenarios. In some of the instances, a few links have been added to make sure that the network is still connected in any single link or node failure situation.

The longest computation time was about 36 hours. However, most instances could be solved to proven optimality within one hour on a Linux machine with 1 GB of RAM and a 1.7 MHz processor. In fact, the algorithm often found good solutions after a short time, spending most of the time on finding slightly

Table 8.1: Characteristics of the test instances

Name	$|V|$	$|E|$	$|D|$	$\bar{d}$	$|\mathcal{D}_e|$
g1	10	25	29	5.0	2
g2	12	19	27	3.2	4
g3	15	22	13	2.9	3
g4	15	24	105	3.2	7
g5	18	26	62	2.8	9
g6	18	32	62	3.6	9
g7	20	32	119	3.2	6
g8	14	21	91	3.0	5
g9	17	28	58	3.3	3

better solutions and proving optimality. All linear programs were solved using CPLEX 9.0 [CPLEX 9.0, 2003].

The column generation approach proved to be well scalable. Whereas the computation times raised almost linearly with small hop limits, they were nearly constant for larger hop limit values. In contrast, enumerating all paths up to a given length leads to an exponential growth in computation time.

In all figures presented in the following, the solution values are scaled such that 100 corresponds to the optimal network cost when *all* routing paths are allowed, regardless of their length. To facilitate the interpretation of the results, we define an additional cost of 10% for a hop-limited solution to be *acceptable*.

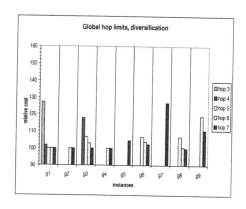

Figure 8.4: Global hop limit, diversification

Global hop limit.   For each of our nine test instances, Figure 8.4 shows the relative network cost with diversification when a global hop limit between

3 (leftmost bar) and 7 (rightmost bar) is imposed on all routing paths (notice that the relative cost scale starts at 90, not at 0).

Figure 8.4 reveals that quite often, high hop limits are needed to obtain a feasible solution at all. In five out of the nine instances, there is a demand which needs a path of length at least 6, and in another two instances, at least hop limit 5 is needed. These long paths are usually due to a "central" node whose failure implies a long detour for some demands.

Another interesting observation is that whenever a feasible solution is found with paths of length ℓ, hop limit $\ell + 1$ leads to an acceptable solution with our test instances. This leads to a natural iterative algorithm: start with a small hop limit and raise it until a feasible solution is found. Going one step further, chances are good to obtain an acceptable solution.

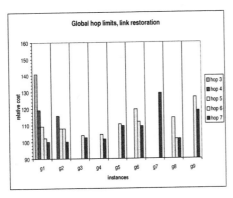 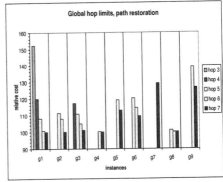

Figure 8.5: Global hop limit, link and path restoration

In a similar way, Figure 8.5 shows the results for link and path restoration with a global hop limit. The figures show that in many cases (five out of nine instances with link restoration, four instances with path restoration), paths of length 6 are needed to obtain a feasible solution. Contrary to diversification, we have not observed any rule of thumb which could give us a hint about the quality of a solution without calculating a lower bound. Even high hop limits can lead to expensive solutions. In several cases, even paths of length 7 are by far not sufficient to find an acceptable solution. Overall, cost sensitivity with respect to hop limits is quite similar for link and path restoration.

As these results indicate, global hop limits are not the best choice to define a good set of routing paths. The problem is that a global hop limit does not take any information on the network size or of the distance between given nodes into account. It can be expected that for larger networks, the global hop limit which is needed to obtain a feasible solution will rise even more, unless the density of the network increases at the same time. Notice that both a larger hop limit and increased density make it difficult if not impossible to enumerate all routing paths.

Demand-dependent hop limit.   Apparently, hop limits should reflect properties of the network such as its size or density. One way to achieve this is to use demand-dependent hop limits: for a given value k, a hop limit of k plus the number of links in a shortest hop path between the demand end nodes is imposed on each demand.

For diversification, the shortest hop distance in the NOS is used for all paths of a demand since it is not known in advance which paths will be used for backup purposes. For restoration, the hop limits for backup paths are defined with respect to the shortest hop distances in the corresponding failure states.

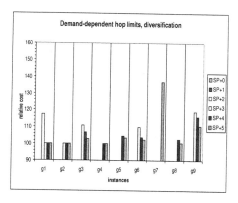

Figure 8.6: Demand-dependent hop limit, diversification

Figure 8.6 shows the relative cost for each instance with diversification, imposing demand-dependent hop limits. Again, 100 corresponds to the optimal network cost when *all* routing paths are allowed, i.e., the values are comparable to those in Figure 8.4. The leftmost bar for each instance shows the result for $k = 0$, which implies that each demand is routed on one or more shortest hop paths. The next bars represent the relative cost if $k = 1, \ldots, 5$ additional hops are allowed.

Again, we see that a high hop limit ($k \geq 4$) is often needed for feasibility. This is again due to nodes whose failure implies a detour for some demands which is much longer than a shortest hop path in the NOS. On the other hand, the smallest hop limit for which a feasible solution exists leads to an acceptable solution in five out of nine cases. Increasing this hop limit by 1, an acceptable solution is found in all cases but one. In summary, the behavior of the network cost with respect to changing hop limits is very similar to the one observed with global hop limits.

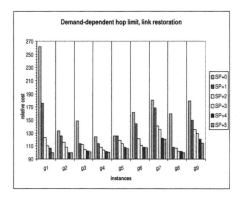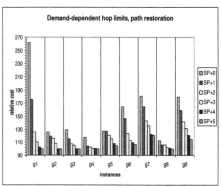

Figure 8.7: Demand-dependent hop limit, link and path restoration

Figure 8.7 shows the results for link and path restoration with demand-dependent hop limits (note the different scale of the cost axis). The values are comparable to those in Figure 8.5.

Contrary to diversification, a restriction to shortest paths always leads to a feasible solution with restoration by definition of the restricted path set, provided that sufficiently large link capacities are available. However, with both link and path restoration, high hop limits are needed to obtain acceptable solutions. In four out of the nine instances, $k \geq 4$ is needed, and in two cases, even $k = 5$ still leads to more than 10% additional network cost. Even more than with global hop limits, the sensitivity of network cost with respect to to changing hop limit values is very similar for both restoration concepts.

A result that we had expected in its tendency but not to that extent is the cost of a shortest path routing. It always incurs more than 10% additional cost, and on instance g1, it is 161% more expensive than a solution where all paths are admissible! Both with link and path restoration, a shortest path routing leads to more than 60% additional cost in four out of our nine instances.

In some of the instances (including g1), not all of the potential links are actually needed in a cost optimal solution with respect to all paths. This partially explains the bad performance of a shortest hop routing (as well as a shortest path routing with respect to kilometer length or any other metric link weights): if the direct link between the end nodes of a demand exists, it is the unique shortest path. This leads to some positive capacity on most links and consequently to high network cost.

4. Conclusion

In this paper, we have studied the impact of varying hop limits on the overall network cost in the planning of a telecommunication network. Based on our mixed-integer linear programming model which integrates topology, link capacity, and routing decisions, we have solved nine problem instances to optimality using a branch-and-cut framework and column generation for working and restoration paths. For each of these instances, we have considered three different classes of admissible path sets and three survivability concepts. Based on optimal solutions, we have compared the overall network cost without restrictions on the admissible paths to the network cost with hop-limited paths, either with demand-dependent or with global hop limits.

As principal conclusion, hop limits should be avoided if the technology allows it. For many of the instances considered in our tests, a global hop limit of six links or a demand-dependent hop limit of four links in addition to the shortest hop count are needed to obtain an acceptable solution. Enumerating all paths up to these hop limits can already exceed available time and memory even for small, sparse networks. Instead, column generation can be employed to deal with all routing paths.

If hop limits are technologically unavoidable or desired for ease of management, the following rules of thumb have proven to be useful:

Path protection Starting with a shortest path routing, the hop limit can be raised until the first feasible solution is found. Further incrementing the hop limit by 1 for each demand often leads to a solution which is at most 10% more expensive than an optimal solution without path length restrictions.

Restoration Both with link and path restoration, demand-dependent hop limits should be used which allow at least four hops in addition to the shortest hop count. In contrast, both global hop limits and a shortest path routing often induce infeasibility or very high network cost.

In any case, the additional network cost caused by hop limits cannot be predicted in advance. Neither network size, nor density, nor the number of demands or the number of installable link designs have been reliable indicators on our test instances.

Acknowledgments

This work has been supported by the DFG Research Center MATHEON, Berlin, www.matheon.de. We thank the reviewers for their valuable comments.

References

Balakrishnan, A. and Altinkemer, K. (1992). Using a hop-constrained model to generate alternative communication network design. *ORSA Journal on Computing*, 4(2):192–205.

Benders, J. (1962). Partitioning procedures for solving mixed-variables programming problems. *Numerische Mathematik*, 4(1):238–252.

CPLEX 9.0 (2003). *ILOG CPLEX 9.0 Reference Manual*. Information available at http://www.cplex.com.

Dahl, G. and Stoer, M. (1998). A cutting plane algorithm for multicommodity survivable network design problems. *INFORMS Journal on Computing*, 10(1):1–11.

Demeester, P., Wu, T.-H., and Yoshikai, N. (1999). *IEEE Communications Magazine*, 37(8):40–101. Collection of papers on survivable communication networks.

Discnet (2000–2004). DISCNET. atesio GmbH, Germany. www.atesio.de.

Doucette, J. and Grover, W.D. (2001). Comparison of mesh protection and restoration schemes and the dependency on graph connectivity. In *Design of Reliable Communication Networks (DRCN 2001)*, Budapest, Hungary, pages 121–128.

Herzberg, M. and Bye, S. (1994). An optimal spare-capacity assignment model for survivable networks with hop limits. In *IEEE Global Communications Conference (GLOBECOM'94)*, San Francisco, CA, USA, pages 1601–1606.

Iraschko, R., MacGregor, M., and Grover, W.D. (1998). Optimal capacity placement for path restoration in STM or ATM mesh survivable networks. *IEEE Transactions on Networking*, 6(3):325–336.

Iri, M. (1971). On an extension of the maximum-flow minimum-cut theorem to multicommodity flows. *Journal of the Operations Research Society of Japan*, 13(3):129–135.

Murakami, K. (1995). *Survivable Network Management for High-Speed ATM Networks*. PhD thesis, Carnegie Mellon University.

Orlowski, S. (2003). Local and global restoration of node and link failures in telecommunication networks. Diploma thesis, Technische Universität Berlin.

Orlowski, S. and Wessäly, R. (2004). Comparing restoration concepts using optimal network configurations with integrated hardware and routing decisions. In *Journal of Network and System Management*. To appear.

Poppe, F. and Demeester, P. (1998). Economic allocation of spare capacity in mesh-restorable networks: Models and algorithms. In *6th International Conference on Telecommunication Systems (ICTSM 1998), Modeling and Analysis*, Nashville, USA, pages 77–86.

Soni, S., Gupta, R., and Pirkul, H. (1999). Survivable network design: The state of the art. *Information Systems Frontiers*, 1:303–315.

Stoer, M. and Dahl, G. (1994). A polyhedral approach to multicommodity survivable network design. *Numerische Mathematik*, 68:149–167.

Wessäly, R. (2000). *Dimensioning Survivable Capacitated NETworks*. PhD thesis, Technische Universität Berlin.

Xiong, Y. and Mason, L. (1997). Restoration strategies and spare capacity requirements in self-healing ATM networks. In *IEEE Infocom 1997*, Kobe, Japan, pages 353–360.

Chapter 9

COMPACT MODELS FOR HOP-CONSTRAINED NODE SURVIVABLE NETWORK DESIGN: AN APPLICATION TO MPLS

Luís Gouveia[1] , Pedro Patrício[2] and Amaro de Sousa[3]

[1] *CIO and DEIO, Fac. de Ciências da Universidade de Lisboa, BLOCO C6, Piso 4, 1749-016 Lisboa, Portugal, email: legouveia@fc.ul.pt;* [2] *Dept. de Matemática, Universidade da Beira Interior, 6200 Covilhã, Portugal, email: pmendes@noe.ubi.pt;* [3] *Inst. de Telecomunicações, Universidade de Aveiro, 3810–193 Aveiro, Portugal, email: asou@det.ua.pt*

Abstract: In this paper we discuss compact models for a hop-constrained node survivable network design problem. We discuss two models involving one set of variables associated to each path between each pair of demand nodes (a standard network flow model with additional cardinality constraints and a model with hop-indexed variables) and a third model involving one single set of hop-indexed variables for each demand pair. We show that the aggregated more compact hop-indexed model produces the same linear programming bound as the multi-path hop-indexed model. This work is given in the context of the following MPLS network design problem. Given the location of edge nodes, the candidate locations of core nodes and the pairs of locations that can be physically connected, the MPLS network design problem addressed in this paper is the determination of the physical network topology, i.e., the location of core nodes and the connections required between all nodes. The aim of the design task is to determine the least cost network. The physical network must support routing paths between all pairs of edge nodes fulfilling two types of path constraints. The first type is a MPLS hop constraint on the maximum number of edges traversed by each routing path, which guarantees a given packet level quality of service (QoS). The second type is the fault-tolerance constraint. An important component of providing QoS is the service reliability and a fault-tolerance scheme must be present in the network to deal efficiently with failure scenarios. We present computational results, taken from graphs with up to 50 nodes and slightly more than 400 edges.

Key words: MPLS, network design, survivability, hop constraints

1.   INTRODUCTION

In this paper we discuss compact models (that is, models with a polynomial number of variables and constraints) for a hop-constrained node survivable network design problem, which arises in the context of a MPLS network design problem. In recent years, Multi-Protocol Label Switching, or MPLS, has been proposed as the solution to overcome many of the performance and scaling problems that service providers are experiencing in their IP (Internet Protocol) networks. MPLS networks contain network nodes, called Label Switching Routers (LSRs), and network links connecting nodes. MPLS organizes the network in domains. Edge LSRs define the boundaries of the domain and are the traffic demand ingress/egress nodes. Other nodes, named core LSRs, can exist on the network to provide communications between edge LSRs. The forwarding of IP packets from ingress to egress LSRs is done by means of routing paths, called Label Switched Paths (LSPs). In the ingress LSR, incoming IP packets are labeled based on their destination and required quality of service (QoS) and, depending on this classification, are forwarded through the appropriate LSP towards an egress LSR. MPLS enables source based routing, i.e. the forwarding path of a LSP from an ingress router to an egress router is not constrained by the paths of other LSPs, which is the basis for more efficient traffic engineering methods. The reader is referred to Xiao, Hannan and Bailey (2000) for a presentation of the MPLS architecture and to Swallow (1999) for a discussion on the traffic engineering issues.

The success of MPLS is directly related with its capacity of supporting service requirements that the current Internet is not able to do. In this work, we consider two of these requirements.

First, the future Internet must support delay sensitive services like voice or video. For example, in order to have an understandable communication on the traditional telephone networks, the standards require a round trip delay between any two communicating peers not greater then 250 ms for terrestrial communications or not greater than 400 ms when a satellite link is used. An IP packet traveling from ingress to egress undergoes a queuing delay in the transmitting interface of each LSR it traverses. The total delay introduced by the network must be bounded to a maximum time value and in many cases queuing is the dominant source of packet delays. Therefore, bounding the delay can be done by limiting either the size of the queues and the number of queues traversed by each demand. Usually, the queue size is determined by other constraints, which means that, in practice, the maximum delay requirement is obtained by routing the demands through paths that have a maximum number of hops. For example, Parekh and Gallager (1994) show that combining the use of weighted fair queuing scheduling disciplines with leaky bucket traffic shaping at ingress nodes, places a bound on the maximum packet delay which is proportional to the number of LSRs.

Secondly, the future Internet must provide reliable services. This is particularly important on real time services since a service cut of a few seconds might be tolerable when retrieving a Web page but it is totally unacceptable if two persons are talking to each other. A robust scheme for fault-tolerance must be present in the network to deal efficiently with failure scenarios. In this work, two LSPs with node-disjoint paths are considered for each pair of edge LSRs. This method is the basis for many fault-tolerance mechanisms which are robust in the network single failure scenario like the 1+1 protection (the total demand is sent simultaneously through two LSPs), the 1:1 protection (the demand is sent through the working LSP and the protection LSP is used only when the working LSP fails) or the two-path diversity routing (the demand is equally split by the two LSPs; in this case, only half the demand is protected over any single failure).

In this paper, we address the problem of designing an MPLS network domain assuming the network operator knows the location of the edge LSRs, since they are the connection points to the client networks and/or terminal equipment. To define the design problem, we consider also that a set of candidate locations for the core LSR placement is defined, with an associated cost for each location, and that the pairs of locations that can be physically connected are known, with an associated cost for each pair. The network design problem is the determination of the least cost physical network, i.e., the location of core LSRs and the connections to be set up between all LSRs, whose topology includes two hop-constrained node-disjoint paths between each pair of edge LSRs. The rest of the paper is organized as follows. In section 2, we present and compare three Mixed Integer Programming formulations for the problem described above. In section 3, we present the results of our computational experience.

2. MPLS NETWORK DESIGN MODELS

We define the problem in an undirected graph $G = (V,E)$ with $S \subset V$, and S denoting the set of edge LSRs. We shall say that a $(s–t)$–path is a sequence of arcs $\{(i_1,j_1),...,(i_k,j_k)\}$ such that $i_1 = s$, $j_k = t$ and $j_p = i_{p+1}$ for $p = 1,...,k–1$ and that a H–path is a path with at most H hops.

We start by presenting a generic formulation for the problem which involves three sets of variables: the binary variables x_e for all $e \in E$, indicating whether edge e is included in the solution, the binary variables N_i $(i \in V \setminus S)$, which indicate whether a core LSR is put in operation in node i, and the flow integer variables f_{ij}^{pq} indicating the number of paths from node p to q and traversing edge $\{i,j\}$ in the direction from i to j (for simplicity, variables f_{ij}^{pq} with $j = p$ and variables with $i = q$ are not defined):

minimize $\sum_{e \in E} c_e x_e + \sum_{i \in V \setminus S} l_i N_i$

subject   *to*

$$\{(i,j): f_{ij}^{pq} > 0 \quad contains \quad two \quad (p,q) - \mathrm{H} - paths\} \quad for \quad all \quad p,q \in S \quad (1)$$

$$f_{ij}^{pq} + f_{ji}^{pq} \le x_e \quad for \quad all \quad e = \{i,j\} \in E; \quad p,q \in S \qquad (2)$$

$$\sum_{i \in V} f_{ij}^{pq} \le N_j \quad for \quad all \quad j \in V \setminus S; \quad p,q \in S \qquad (3)$$

$$\sum_{i \in V} f_{ij}^{pq} \le 1 \quad for \quad all \quad j \in S \setminus \{p,q\}, \quad p,q \in S \qquad (4)$$

$$x_e \in \{0,1\} \quad for \quad all \quad e = \{i,j\} \in E \qquad (5)$$

$$N_j \in \{0,1\} \quad for \quad all \quad j \in V \setminus S \qquad (6)$$

The objective function is the total cost of the network solution where c_e is the cost of edge e and l_i is the cost of a core LSR on node i. Constraints **(2)** state that if an edge is traversed in some direction, then that edge must be included in the solution. Constraints **(3)** guarantee that a core LSR is put in operation at each visited node of the paths between any pair of nodes $p,q \in S$. These constraints, together with **(4)**, guarantee that the paths are node-disjoint. The problem studied here is a network design problem with node-disjoint hop-constrained paths between specified pairs of nodes. For more on designing networks with node-disjoint (or edge-disjoint) paths between specified pairs of nodes, the reader is referred to Raghavan (1995), Stoer (1992), the references in Raghavan and Magnanti (1997) and the more recent papers by Magnanti and Raghavan (1999) and Balakrishnan, Magnanti and Mirchandani (2004). With respect to designing networks with hop constraints and their applications, the reader is referred to the works by Balakrishnan and Altinkemer (1992), Gouveia (1998), LeBlanc, Chifflet and Mahey (1999) (which present many applications modeled with hop constraints) and the recent work by Gouveia et al. (2003) which also use hop constraints to guarantee maximum delay QoS in a design problem involving MPLS over Optical Networks. Recently, modeling approaches for network design problems with survivability considerations and hop requirements have been given in Orlowski and Wessaely (2004) (which discuss formulations involving an exponentially sized set of variables), Huygens, Mahjoub, and Pesneau, (2004), and Huygens et al. (2004) (the latter two papers discuss formulations with an exponentially sized set of constraints). In this paper we discuss three compact formulations for the MPLS problem discussed above. These formulations can be simply adapted for a general problem with survivability and hop requirements.

Two ways of modeling the non-explicit part of the generic formulation **(1)** are given in the *Table 9-1*. They are based on considering a model for each hop-constrained path between each pair of demand nodes.

Table 9-1. Modeling two Hop-Constrained Paths (from node p to node q) – Part 1

Network Flow Model

$$\sum_{j \in V} y_{ij}^{pqs} - \sum_{m \in V} y_{mi}^{pqs} = \begin{cases} 1, i = p \\ 0, i \neq p, q \quad s = 1, 2; \\ -1, i = q \end{cases}$$

$$\sum_{(i,j):\{i,j\} \in E} y_{ij}^{pqs} \leq H \;, \quad s = 1, 2;$$

$$f_{ij}^{pq} = \sum_{s=1,2} y_{ij}^{pqs}, \; (i,j):\{i,j\} \in E;$$

$$y_{ij}^{pqs}, \; y_{ji}^{pqs} \in \{0,1\}, \; \{i,j\} \in E; \; s = 1,2;$$

$$f_{ij}^{pq}, f_{ji}^{pq} \geq 0 \text{ and integer, } \{i,j\} \in E.$$

Hop-Indexed Model

$$\sum_{j \in V} z_{pj}^{1\,pqs} = 1 \;, \; s = 1, 2;$$

$$\sum_{j \in V} z_{ij}^{2\,pqs} = z_{pi}^{1\,pqs} \;\;, \; i \in V; \; s = 1, 2;$$

$$\sum_{j \in V} z_{ij}^{h+1,\,pqs} - \sum_{m \in V} z_{mi}^{hpqs} = 0, \quad i \neq p; \;\; h = 2,\ldots,H-1; \;\; s = 1,2;$$

$$\sum_{j \in V} z_{jq}^{Hpqs} = 1 \;, \;\; s = 1, 2;$$

$$f_{ij}^{pq} = \sum_{s=1,2} \; \sum_{h=1,\ldots,H} z_{ij}^{hpqs}, \;\; (i,j):\{i,j\} \in E;$$

$$z_{ij}^{hpqs}, z_{ji}^{hpqs} \in \{0,1\}, \;\; \{i,j\} \in E; \;\; h = 1,\ldots,H; \;\; s = 1,2;$$

$$z_{qq}^{hpqs} \in \{0,1\}, \;\; h = 2,\ldots,H; \;\; s = 1,2;$$

$$f_{ij}^{pq}, f_{ji}^{pq} \geq 0 \;\; \text{and} \;\; \text{integer}, \{i,j\} \in E.$$

We let NF^{pq} denote the set of feasible solutions of the Network Flow model, and Hop^{pq} denote the set of feasible solutions of the Hop-Indexed model. We denote by MCF the model obtained by using NF^{pq} for all p,q ($p < q$) in the generic model. Similarly, by using Hop^{pq} we obtain a hop-indexed version of the previous model, the Hop-MCF model. We note that when creating these models, the linking constraints $f_{ij}^{pq} = \sum_{s=1,2} y_{ij}^{pqs}$ and $f_{ij}^{pq} =$

$\sum_{s=1,2} \sum_{h=1,...,H} z_{ij}^{hpqs}$ relating the two sets of variables allow us to rewrite the models, if necessary, without the flow variables f_{ij}^{pq}.

The Network Flow model NF^{pq} uses the variables f_{ij}^{pq} as specified before and variables y_{ij}^{pqs} indicating whether edge $\{i,j\}$, traversed in the direction from i to j, is in the s-th path from node p to node q (for simplicity, variables y_{ij}^{pqs} with $j=p$ and with $i=q$ are not defined). Since the 0-1 variables y_{ij}^{pqs} specify a path between node p and node q, the inequality $\sum_{(i,j):\{i,j\} \in E} y_{ij}^{pqs} \leq H$ in the network flow model restricts the s-th path to contain at most H arcs. This model has been suggested by Balakrishnan and Altinkemer (1992).

Besides the flow variables f_{ij}^{pq}, the Hop-Indexed model Hop^{pq} also uses binary variables z_{ij}^{hpqs} indicating whether edge $\{i,j\}$ is traversed in the direction from i to j and is the hth edge in the s-th (p,q)–H–path. The model contains constraints stating that an arc enters node i in position h in the s-th path if and only if another arc emanates from this node in position $h+1$ in the same path and that one arc enters node q in position H for every path. Note that this model contains "loop" variables z_{qq}^{hpqs} ($h=2,...,H$) with zero cost to model situations when the corresponding path from node p to node q contains fewer than H arcs (that is, $z_{jq}^{hpqs}=1$ for some $j \in V\setminus\{q\}$ and $1 \leq h \leq H-1$). This formulation has been proposed by Gouveia (1998). The equalities $f_{ij}^{pq} = \sum_{s=1,2} \sum_{h=1,...,H} z_{ij}^{hpqs}$ relate the original variables with the extended variables. The Hop-Indexed model Hop^{pq} contains far more variables than the Network Flow model NF^{pq}. However, as the next result shows, its inclusion in the generic formulation (yielding the Hop-MCF model) provides a lower bound which is at least as good as the one obtained by the MCF model (and our computational experience will show that, in general, significant improvements are obtained with the hop-indexed model):

Proposition 1 – The linear programming bound given by Hop-MCF is at least as good as the linear programming bound given by MCF.

Proof: As the two models have similar structures, it is sufficient to compare the submodels, involved in each model, representing the subproblem of the two hop-constrained paths between two nodes p and q. To simplify our argument we replace the arc linking constraints $f_{ij}^{pq} = \sum_{s=1,2} \sum_{h=1,...,H} z_{ij}^{hpqs}$ in the Hop-Indexed model Hop^{pq} with the two sets of arc linking constraints $y_{ij}^{pqs} = \sum_{h=1,...,H} z_{ij}^{hpqs}$ for $s = 1,2$ and $f_{ij}^{pq} = \sum_{s=1,2} y_{ij}^{pqs}$. Note that this modification does not alter the strength of the linear programming relaxation of the hop-indexed submodel Hop^{pq}. However, it enables us to compare the two models, Hop^{pq} and NF^{pq}, in the space of the y variables.

For each s, we let NF^{pqs} denote the set of feasible solutions of the Network Flow model NF^{pq} for the same s, and without the relating constraints $f_{ij}^{pq} = \sum_{s=1,2} y_{ij}^{pqs}$. In the same way, we let Hop^{pqs} denote the set of feasible solutions, for the same s, of the Hop-Indexed model Hop^{pq} and without the constraints $f_{ij}^{pq} = \sum_{s=1,2} \sum_{h=1,...,H} z_{ij}^{hpqs}$. Gouveia (1998) has shown that, for the linear programming relaxations, the projection of the set of feasible solutions of the Hop^{pqs} submodel in the space of the y variables is contained (in general, strictly contained) in the feasible set of the NF^{pqs} submodel. That is, for each s we can view the Hop^{pqs} model as being equal to the NF^{pqs} model augmented with extra constraints (as noted in Dahl and Gouveia (2004), this extra set of constraints is quite simple when $H=2$ and $H=3$ but appears to be rather complicated when $H>3$).

This characterization implies that, for the linear programming relaxations, the projection of the set of feasible solutions of the Hop^{pq} submodel in the space of the f variables is contained (in general, strictly contained) in the projection of the feasible set of the NF^{pq} submodel in the space of the f variables. As a consequence, the linear programming bound given by Hop-MCF is at least as good as the one given by MCF. □

The two models presented before contain two sets of variables for each pair of nodes in S. The path systems for each required path are simply adaptations of systems developed for problems with hop constraints but no survivability requirements. By using the relation $w_{ij}^{hpq} = \sum_{s=1,2} z_{ij}^{hpqs}$ we can obtain a new model using a single set of variables for each demand pair. This Aggregated Hop-Indexed model gives a third way of modeling the non-explicit part of the generic formulation (*Table 9-2*).

Table 9-2. Modeling Two Hop-Constrained Paths (from node p to node q) – Part II

Aggregated Hop-Indexed Model
$\displaystyle\sum_{j \in V} w_{pj}^{1pq} = 2$
$\displaystyle\sum_{j \in V} w_{ij}^{2pq} = w_{pi}^{1pq} \ , i \in V;$
$\displaystyle\sum_{j \in V} w_{ij}^{h+1,pq} - \sum_{m \in V} w_{mi}^{hpq} = 0 \ , \ i \neq p; \ h = 2,...,H-1;$
$\displaystyle\sum_{j \in V} w_{jq}^{Hpq} = 2$
$\displaystyle f_{ij}^{pq} = \sum_{h=1,...,H} w_{ij}^{hpq}, \ (i,j):\{i,j\} \in E;$
$w_{ij}^{hpq}, w_{ji}^{hpq} \in \{0,1,2\}, \ e = \{i,j\} \in E; \ h = 1,..., H;$
$w_{qq}^{hpq} \in \{0,1,2\}, \ h = 2,...,H;$
$f_{ij}^{pq}, f_{ji}^{pq} \geq 0 \ and \ integer, \ e = \{i,j\} \in E.$

We let $AHop^{pq}$ denote the set of feasible solutions of the Aggregated Hop-Indexed model. We denote by AHop-MCF the model obtained by using $AHop^{pq}$ for all p,q ($p < q$) in the generic model. Besides the flow variables f_{ij}^{pq}, this model uses integer variables w_{ij}^{hpq} indicating the number of (p,q)–H–paths including edge $\{i,j\}$, traversed in the direction from i to j, in the hth position. Similarly to the disaggregated model, this model contains "loop" variables w_{qq}^{hpq} ($h=2,...,H$) with zero cost to model situations when some of the (p,q)–H–paths contain fewer than H arcs (that is, $w_{jq}^{hpq} \geq 1$ for some $j \in V \backslash \{q\}$ and $1 \leq h \leq H{-}1$). Again, we note that when creating the AHop-MCF model, the arc linking constraints $f_{ij}^{pq} = \sum_{h=1,2} w_{ij}^{hpq}$ allow us to rewrite the models without the flow variables f_{ij}^{pq}. The fact that the AHop-MCF model is an aggregated version of the Hop-MCF model suggests that it may have a weaker linear programming relaxation. As we show next, the more compact model is as tight as the previous model.

Proposition 2 – The linear programming bound given by Hop-MCF is equal to the linear programming bound given by AHop-MCF.

Proof: Again, as the two models have similar structures, it is sufficient to compare the submodels, involved in each model, representing the subproblem of the two hop-constrained paths between two nodes p and q. We add the aggregating arc constraints $w_{ij}^{hpq} = \sum_{s=1,2} z_{ij}^{hpqs}$ to the Hop^{pq} model and note that this addition does not alter the strength of the corresponding linear programming relaxation.

We show next that the projection of the set of feasible solutions of the linear programming relaxation of Hop^{pq}, in the space of the w variables, equals the set of feasible solutions of the linear programming relaxation of $AHop^{pq}$. The inclusion "$\subseteq$" follows straightforwardly from the equalities $w_{ij}^{hpq} = \sum_{s=1,2} z_{ij}^{hpqs}$. To see that the inclusion "$\supseteq$" also holds we notice that given any feasible solution for the linear programming relaxation of $AHop^{pq}$ we can obtain a feasible solution for the linear programming relaxation of Hop^{pq} by simply setting $z_{ij}^{hpq1} = z_{ij}^{hpq2} = (1/2)w_{ij}^{hpq}$ for arc (i,j) and each h.

This equivalence shows that the projection of the set of feasible solutions of the linear programming relaxation of Hop^{pq}, in the space of the f variables, must be equal to the projection of the set of feasible solutions of the linear programming relaxation of $AHop^{pq}$, into the space of the f variables. As a consequence, the linear programming bound given by Hop-MCF is equal to the linear programming bound given by AHop-MCF.   □

This result gives a clear advantage to the AHop-MCF model. The computational results given in Section 3 confirm these expectations.

We note that the Aggregated Hop-Indexed model $AHop^{pq}$ (without the linking constraints $f_{ij}^{pq} = \sum_{h=1,2} w_{ij}^{hpq}$) is a network flow model on an expanded layered network and so has the advantage that the extreme points of its linear programming relaxation are integer-valued. Thus, the projection of the set of feasible solutions of the linear programming relaxation of the model $AHop^{pq}$ into the space of the f variables is integer. This observation also gives an alternate proof for the "$\supseteq$" inclusion in the previous proposition as it shows that, for each pair of demand nodes, we cannot find a stronger linear representation for the convex hull of the integer solutions described by **(1)**.

We finish this section by making a reference to two variations of the proposed problem and the potential impact of the new model in solving them. One variation requires s ($s > 2$) edge/node disjoint path between some pairs of demand nodes (s-path diversity routing). It is not difficult to see that Proposition 2 holds for this more general case. The aggregated model becomes more and more attractive when s increases. The second variation is suggested in Ben-Ameur (2000). For simplicity, we assume $s=2$ and suppose we introduce different hop limits, $H1$ and $H2$, for the two required paths for each pair of demand nodes. The models of *Table 9-1* are straightforwardly modified for this variation. The interesting fact is that we can replace the flow conservation constraint $\sum_{j \in V} w_{jq}^{Hpq} = 2$ for node q by two constraints $\sum_{j \in V} w_{jq}^{H1pq} = 1$ and $\sum_{j \in V} w_{jq}^{H2pq} = 1$ (the first constraint stating that node q receives an arc in position $H1$ while the second states that the same node receives an arc in position $H2$) in the aggregated model $AHop^{pq}$ of *Table 9-2*, and obtain an aggregated model AHop-MCF for which Proposition 2 is still valid (for simplicity we omit the details of such a proof as it is quite similar to the previous one).

3.   COMPUTATIONAL RESULTS

In the computational results, we have considered five different randomly generated Euclidean graphs. In graphs 1, 2 and 3, we have considered 25 nodes ($|V|=25$) randomly located in a square grid of 4000 by 4000 and in graphs 4 and 5, we have considered 50 nodes ($|V|=50$) randomly located in a square grid of 5000 by 5000. In all cases, the node locations were constrained to a minimum distance of 200. We have included the edges between all pairs of nodes whose distance is not higher than 2000, which resulted in a total number of 127, 129, 131, 407 and 427 edges respectively.

For each graph, some of the randomly generated nodes were selected as edge LSRs (set S) and the remaining nodes were considered as core LSR candidate locations. We have considered the selection of five edge LSRs ($|S|=5$) in graphs 1 and 4 and ten edge LSRs ($|S|=10$) in graphs 2, 3 and 5. In graphs 1, 2, 4 and 5, all edge LSR nodes were selected as the most distant nodes from the Euclidean center of the graph. In graph 3, two edge LSR nodes were considered around the Euclidean center of the graph and the remaining eight edge LSR nodes were selected as the most distant nodes from the Euclidean center. In all problem instances, the cost of putting a core LSR in operation is given by $l_i = 100$, for all $i \in V\backslash S$, and the cost of including an edge $e=\{i,j\}$ in the solution is given by $c_e =$ (Euclidean distance between i and j)/100.

Table 9-3 presents the computational results for H equal to 4, 5 and 6, solved through the branch-and-cut algorithm of CPLEX 7.0 software package with a computational time set to a maximum of two days. For each problem instance, the table presents the Linear Relaxation (LR) bound, the cpu time to determine the LR bound and the cpu time to determine the optimal solution (both in seconds). The "Opt" column shows the cost of the optimal solution. In the problems that were not solved within two days, the table shows the values of the best lower bound and the best solution found. The results were obtained on a Pentium III at 450Mhz with 128Mb of RAM. The value $H=3$ was found not feasible for most of the cases and the value $H=7$ was found to be almost equivalent to the case with no hop constraints.

Table 9-4 shows the computational results using the three models with an elimination procedure to exclude superfluous variables. Consider a commodity (p,q) and an arc (i,j). If for all $r=1,...,H-2$ there is no r–path from p to i and no $(H-r-1)$–path from j to q, then arc (i,j) is not going to be in the H–path from p to q. Thus, the corresponding flow variables in the several models described above can be eliminated. As expected (and confirmed by the results shown in *Table 9-4*), such an elimination test works reasonably well, for instances with H small. A discretized variation of this test also enables us to remove some of the hop-indexed flow variables (for simplicity, we omit details of this variation).

The results shown in these tables confirm that the AHop-MCF model is better than the Hop-MCF model in all problem instances. In both cases (with and without variable elimination), the AHop-MCF model always obtains the optimal solution using less cpu time than Hop-MCF. Moreover, there is one case where the optimal integer solution was obtained with AHop-MCF (graph 3, $H=5$) but not with the less compact Hop-MCF model. In the remaining cases where the optimal solution was not found, the gap between the best solution and the lower bound is always significantly smaller in the results given by the AHop-MCF.

Without variable elimination, the AHop-MCF is clearly better than the MCF model and the differences are higher for lower values of H (an high value of H penalizes the total number of variables included in the AHop-MCF).

Table 9-3. Computational Results

test	grid	|V|	|S|	|E|	H		MCF	Hop-MCF	AHop-MCF	OPT
1	4000	25	5	127	4	LR value	891,5	901	901	904
						LR cpu	7,18	0,9	0,33	
						optimal cpu	662,13	18,21	4,66	
					5	LR value	876,33	888,5	888,5	895
						LR cpu	2,21	8	2,54	
						optimal cpu	712,4	278,05	86,21	
					6	LR value	874	879	879	884
						LR cpu	0,71	8,05	2,51	
						optimal cpu	501,07	1214,58	159,65	
2	4000	25	10	129	4	LR value	872	908	908	910
						LR cpu	188,64	29,85	10,51	
						optimal cpu	2 days 900,9 to 920	702,57	65,84	
					5	LR value	850	871,21	871,21	884
						LR cpu	71,63	211,25	53,9	
						optimal cpu	2 days 867,6 to 973	48598,03	38576,5	
					6	LR value	842	861,72	861,72	872
						LR cpu	14,38	561,32	136,16	
						optimal cpu	2 days 865,09 to 873	76340,91	35313,49	
3	4000	25	8-2	131	4	LR value	935,24	947,72	947,72	952
						LR cpu	212,75	43,66	15,56	
						optimal cpu	2 days 951,17 to 978	3791,67	644,31	
					5	LR value	913,26	933,36	933,36	952
						LR cpu	122,04	330,94	110,09	
						optimal cpu	2 days 924,62 to 977	2 days 934,85 to 972	85640,21	
					6	LR value	905	912,96	912,96	unknown
						LR cpu	81,94	559,47	131,83	
						optimal cpu	2 days 912,24 to 965	2 days 919 to 965	2 days 927,7 to 932	
4	5000	50	5	407	4	LR value	1062	1409	1409	1410
						LR cpu	185,58	2,43	1,33	
						optimal cpu	131378,47	3,84	1,49	
					5	LR value	1008,5	1142,27	1142,27	1149
						LR cpu	218,35	88,13	15,1	
						optimal cpu	2 days 1027,55 to 1617	1554,6	377,2	
					6	LR value	981,8	1031,75	1031,75	1040
						LR cpu	157,01	321,41	49,84	
						optimal cpu	2 days 1001,25 to 1072	5212,94	213,72	
5	5000	50	10	427	4	LR value	1173,5	1283	1283	1284
						LR cpu	3248,45	74,53	34,06	
						optimal cpu	2 days l.b.=1189,69	214,37	71,98	
					5	LR value	1117,8	1175	1175	1175
						LR cpu	1340,56	2648,89	721,67	
						optimal cpu	2 days 1127,12 to 1292	2684,5	468,4	
					6	LR value	1095,2	1142	1142	1142
						LR cpu	1266,45	14121,35	2237,68	
						optimal cpu	2 days 1097,79 to 2998	8354,35	1520,93	

Table 9-4. Computational Results with Variable Elimination

test	grid	|V|	|S|	|E|	H		MCF	Hop-MCF	AHop-MCF	OPT
1	4000	25	5	127	4	LR value	901	901	901	904
						LR cpu	0,46	0,55	0,27	
						optimal cpu	3,33	18,75	4,54	
					5	LR value	888,5	888,5	888,5	895
						LR cpu	1,19	5,5	1,8	
						optimal cpu	99,7	300,73	41,72	
					6	LR value	874	879	879	884
						LR cpu	1,22	9,56	2,2	
						optimal cpu	416,14	431,1	142,97	
2	4000	25	10	129	4	LR value	908	908	908	910
						LR cpu	24,43	29,41	10,18	
						optimal cpu	145,15	171,15	221,44	
					5	LR value	862,57	871,21	871,21	884
						LR cpu	62,13	305,88	68,61	
						optimal cpu	2 days 877,46 to 898	62767,13	15776,27	
					6	LR value	846,5	861,72	861,72	872
						LR cpu	25,74	670	163,59	
						optimal cpu	2 days 860,54 to 880	59138,3	20271,83	
3	4000	25	8-2	131	4	LR value	947,72	947,72	947,72	952
						LR cpu	40,66	42,7	15,22	
						optimal cpu	4212,04	3926,86	828,99	
					5	LR value	917,75	933,36	933,36	952
						LR cpu	115,69	326,68	94,84	
						optimal cpu	2 days 928,14 to 984	2 days 939,66 to 965	2 days 947,53 to 956	
					6	LR value	905	912,96	912,96	unknown
						LR cpu	53,33	901,27	115,24	
						optimal cpu	2 days 914,5 to 960	2 days 917,18 to 962	2 days 923,26 to 940	
4	5000	50	5	407	4	LR value	1405	1409	1409	1410
						LR cpu	1,61	2,16	0,9	
						optimal cpu	80,10	3,05	0,95	
					5	LR value	1140,25	1142,27	1142,27	1149
						LR cpu	29,83	102,25	16,05	
						optimal cpu	1616,2	1369,56	303,87	
					6	LR value	1017,5	1031,75	1031,75	1040
						LR cpu	47,39	495,49	79,47	
						optimal cpu	68046,4	2450,15	1255,64	
5	5000	50	10	427	4	LR value	1283	1283	1283	1284
						LR cpu	77,01	71,62	32,32	
						optimal cpu	326,57	211,37	88,93	
					5	LR value	1166,5	1175	1175	1175
						LR cpu	1285,79	3040,75	653,38	
						optimal cpu	116704,81	1930,31	429,88	
					6	LR value	1122	1142	1142	1142
						LR cpu	1100,77	10704,57	1486,53	
						optimal cpu	2 days 1126,25 to 2662	10724,45	1240,09	

Interesting is the fact that the LR bound of the MCF model improves (substantially, in a few cases) for $H=4$ when the elimination test is included (that is, the test corresponds to adding equalities stating that certain variables are equal to zero and the inclusion of such equalities may improve the lower bound) but the same does not happen when the hop-indexed models are involved. To explain this behavior, consider a situation with $H=2$, for a pair of nodes p and q. A fractional extreme point solution of the network flow model for a fixed s is as follows: ½ of the flow goes along a 1-path while the other goes along a 3-path. The test eliminates the middle arc in the 3-path. What is interesting is that such solution is not feasible for the two hop-indexed models, because the hop indexed ranges from 1 to 2. In the hop indexed models, the first arc in the 3-path would have the hop index $h=1$, the second arc would have $h=2$ and the third would have $h=3$ (which is not feasible). Unfortunately, the test does not work as well for the instances with $H=5$.

The computational results of AHop-MCF and MCF models with variable elimination show that in the easier problem instances (the ones with lower solution times), the two models are equivalent since the solution times are of the same scale. However, the AHop-MCF is preferable since it has much lower cpu times in the harder problem instances: all problem instances solved in more than 200 seconds by the MCF model, were solved faster using the AHop-MCF model.

REFERENCES

Balakrishnan, A., and Altinkemer, K. (1992), "Using a Hop-constrained Model to Generate Alternative Communication Network Design", ORSA Journal on Computing, Vol 4, pp 192-205.

Balakrishnan, A., Magnanti, T.L., and Mirchandani, P., (2004), "Connectivity-Splitting Models for Survivable Network Design", Networks, Vol 43, pp 10-27.

Ben-Ameur, W. (2000), "Constrained Length Connectivity and Survivable Networks", Vol 36, pp 17-33.

Dahl, G. and Gouveia, L. (2004), "On the Directed Hop-Constrained Shortest Path Problem", O.R. Letters, Vol 32, pp 15-22.

Gouveia, L. (1998), "Using Variable Redefinition for Computing Lower Bounds for Minimum Spanning and Steiner Trees with Hop Constraints", INFORMS Journal on Computing, Vol. 10, pp 180-188.

Gouveia, L., Patrício, P., de Sousa, A.F. and Valadas, R. (2003), "MPLS over WDM Network Design with Packet Level QoS Constraints based on ILP Models", IEEE INFOCOM, Vol. 1, pp. 576-586.

Huygens, D., Mahjoub, A.R., and Pesneau, P. (2004), "Two Edge-Disjoint Hop-Constrained Paths and Polyhedra" Research Report LIMOS/RR 04-20 from LIMOS, Université Blaise Pascal, Clermont-Ferrand, France, (to appear in SIAM Journal on Discrete Math).

Huygens, D., Labbé, M., Mahjoub, A.R., and Pesneau, P. (2004), "Two Edge-Disjoint Hop-Constrained Paths: Valid Inequalities and Branch-and-Cut" paper presented at Optimization 2004, Lisbon, July 1004 .

LeBlanc, L., Chifflet, J., and Mahey, P. (1999), "Packet Routing in Telecommunication Networks with Path and Flow Restrictions", INFORMS Journal on Computing, Vol. 11, pp 188-197.

Magnanti, T. and Raghavan, S. (1999), "Strong Formulations for Network Design Problems with Connectivity Requirements, Working paper OR 332-99, Operations Research Center, MIT, April 1999.

Orlowski, S., and Wessaely, R. (2004), "The Effect of Hop Limits on Optimal Cost in Survivable Network", ZIB-Report 04-23 (June 2004).

Parekh, A. and Gallager, R. (1994), "A Generalized Processor Sharing Approach to Flow Control in Integrated Services Networks: The Multiple Node Case", IEEE/ACM Transactions on Networking, Vol. 2, No. 2, pp. 137-150.

Raghavan, S., (1995), "Formulations and Algorithms for Network Design Problems with Connectivity Requirements", PhD Thesis, MIT, Cambridge.

Raghavan, S., and Magnanti, T. L., (1997), "Network Connectivity", In M. Dell'Amico, F. Maffiolli and S. Martello, Eds., Annotated Bibliographies in Combinatorial Optimization, pp 335-354, John Wiley & Sons.

Stoer, M. (1992), "Design of Survivable Networks", Lecture Notes in Mathematics, N° 1531, Springer Verlag.

Swallow, G. (1999), "MPLS Advantages for Traffic Engineering", IEEE Communications Magazine, Vol. 37, No. 12, pp. 54-57.

Xiao, X., Hannan, A. and Bailey, B. (2000), "Traffic Engineering with MPLS in the Internet", IEEE Network, Vol. 14, No. 2, pp. 28-33.

Chapter 10

A NOTE ON SEARCH BY OBJECTIVE RELAXATION

S. Raghavan and Daliborka Stanojević

The Robert H. Smith School of Business
University of Maryland
College Park, MD 20742, USA

{raghavan,dstanoje}@rhsmith.umd.edu

Abstract   Salman et al. [1] propose a technique called search by objective relaxation for the local access network design problem. In this note we show that this technique can essentially be considered as a stylized branch-and-bound strategy on a mixed-integer programming formulation for the local access network design problem, wherein only a single type of facility can be installed on an edge. This provides an alternate, and somewhat simpler interpretation of their technique. Given the computational success Salman et al. have had in solving large network design problems with SOR, we examine if similar benefits are reaped with the stylized branch-and-bound strategy on the mixed-integer programming formulation. To this end we provide some computational experiments with this stylized branch-and-bound strategy, and compare it with the direct application of a state-of-the-art mixed-integer programming solver to several alternate formulations for the local access network design problem.

Keywords: integer programming, network design, telecommunications, convex envelopes

1.   Introduction

In the Local Access Network Design (LAND) problem a set of nodes needs to be connected to a backbone network through a single access node. This design problem requires the simultaneous solution of a network loading problem and traffic routing problem. In other words, given the cost and capacity of different transmission facilities (different types of optical cables for example), we need to determine the optimal combination of transmission facilities to be installed at each link and define a routing of traffic so that all the demand in the network is satisfied at minimum cost. Salman et al. [1] describe a novel branch-

and-bound (B&B) strategy termed *Search by Objective Relaxation* (SOR) for this problem. In particular, they describe a relaxation wherein the objective function is approximated by a piecewise convex linear function, that is refined as the B&B algorithm progresses.

In this paper, we show that SOR can be considered as a stylized B&B algorithm on a mixed-integer programming (MIP) formulation of the problem where only a single facility type can be installed on an edge. We show that the objective function refinements within SOR can be mimicked by the addition of an appropriate set of constraints to the B&B tree. The advantage of this approach is that it does not require any explicit change (i.e., refinements) in the objective function coefficients throughout the course of the B&B algorithm (i.e., they occur implicitly within the algorithm). This provides a somewhat simpler interpretation of SOR.

Given the computational success of SOR, we wanted to examine whether applying the stylized B&B algorithm would provide similar results, and improve upon the direct application of a state-of-the-art MIP solver to several alternate formulations for LAND. Consequently, we report on our computational experiments comparing the stylized B&B approach with: SOR (to the extent possible), and the direct application of a state-of-the-art MIP solver to two alternate formulations.

2.   Search by Objective Relaxation

In LAND, we are given a network $G = (V, E)$, with a designated sink node D (the access node) and demand d_i at various nodes of the network that must be transported to this sink node. There are several cable types $q = \{1, \ldots, Q\}$ available for installation on the edges of the network. Each cable type q has a given capacity u_q, and a cost c_q per unit length. In this application it is assumed that the cost structure follows the economies of scale that is common in the telecommunications industry. That is, $u_1 \leq u_2 \leq \ldots \leq u_Q$; $c_1 \leq c_2 \leq \ldots \leq c_Q$; and $\frac{c_1}{u_1} > \frac{c_2}{u_2} > \ldots > \frac{c_Q}{u_Q}$.

Salman et al. point out that one can precompute (via dynamic programming) the optimal combination of cable types for all flow levels. This gives a monotonically increasing step cost function[1] for the flow on any edge in the network (see Figure 10.1). This allows for two possibilities. Modeling the LAND problem as a network flow problem (since there is a single sink for this network it can be modeled with a single commodity) with a nonlinear objective function. Or as a MIP with additional variables to model the nonlinear objective function.

---

[1] We will also refer to the monotonically increasing step cost function as a staircase function.

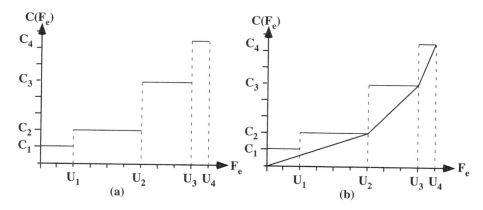

Figure 10.1. An example of a monotonically increasing step cost function (a) and its lower convex envelope (b).

Salman et al. work with the nonlinear network flow model. They approximate the nonlinear step cost function by its lower convex envelope (see Figure 10.1). In other words they solve a relaxation that is a network flow problem with a piecewise linear continuous convex objective function. They refine this approximation within a B&B based procedure. Specifically, at any step in the algorithm they branch on the flow variables in the network flow model. For the flow range for the subproblem, they refine the approximation by recalculating the lower convex envelope over the flow range of the subproblem. As each subproblem in this approach is a network flow problem, that can be solved using a combinatorial algorithm, the authors find that SOR works rapidly and outperforms alternate MIP models for the problem.

An alternative to this approach is to model each of the pieces of the staircase function (obtained by finding the optimal combination of cable types) as new facilities $t = \{1, \ldots, T\}$ with cost C_t and capacity U_t. With this, we can recast the problem as a network loading problem where we are only allowed to install a single facility type on a link.

We show that the linear programming relaxation of the single facility installation model also approximates the staircase function by its lower convex envelope. We then explain how SOR may be viewed as a stylized B&B algorithm on this single facility installation model. In particular, we show how the objective function refinements within the B&B procedure of SOR correspond to the addition of constraints with the single facility installation model.

Croxton et al. [2] show that the linear relaxations of the three commonly used MIP formulations (incremental, multiple choice, and convex combination formulation) for generic minimization problems with a general separable nonconvex piecewise linear costs, are equivalent in feasibility terms and all approximate the cost function with its lower convex envelope. They prove this elegant result using the convex combination formulation. In this paper, we propose an alternative proof that the linear relaxation of the multiple choice formulation (i.e., the model that we refer to as the single facility installation model) for the LAND problem approximates a monotonically increasing step cost function with its lower convex envelope. Although our proof is in the context of the step cost function, with a little effort the proof can be modified to accommodate nonconvex piecewise linear costs. Our proof is based on duality, and uses geometrical arguments that are easy to visualize and perhaps somewhat more intuitive.

The rest of this paper is organized as follows. In Section 3 we show that the linear programming relaxation of the single facility installation model approximates the staircase cost function with its lower convex envelope. We then explain how at each iteration the SOR procedure provides a solution identical to the one obtained by solving the LP relaxation of a version of the single facility installation problem. In Section 4, we apply this result to define a stylized B&B algorithm for the LAND problem that mimics the SOR procedure. In Section 5 we describe our computational experience with the stylized B&B approach. Section 6 provides some concluding remarks.

3.   Relaxation of the Single Facility Installation Problem

To view SOR as a stylized B&B procedure, we first model the staircase cost function as a single facility installation (SFI) problem for a single edge in the network.[2] We show that the LP relaxation of this model approximates the staircase cost function by its lower convex envelope. The SFI model for the staircase cost function (for any given value of flow F_e) may be modeled as follows.

$$\text{Minimize} \quad \sum_{t=0}^{T} C_t Y_e^t \tag{3.1}$$

$$\text{subject to} \quad \sum_{t=0}^{T} U_t Y_e^t \geq F_e \tag{3.2}$$

$$\sum_{t=0}^{T} Y_e^t = 1 \tag{3.3}$$

$$Y_e^t \geq 0 \quad \text{integer} \tag{3.4}$$

In this formulation, the Y_e^t variables indicate the facility type used (of the new facilities defined after finding the optimal combination of cable types for

---

[2]It suffices to focus on a single edge as the objective function is separable by edge.

all the different flow levels). Recall, C_t and U_t represent the cost and capacity of facility type t, while F_e is the level of flow over edge e considered. Note that we have also included an artificial facility of type $t = 0$, with zero cost and capacity, which is used for zero flow levels. Observe that to model the LAND problem, we simply add flow balance constraints, sum the objective over all edges $e \in E$, and add constraints (3.2), (3.3), and (3.4) for all edges in the network. This is described in Appendix B.

If we assign dual variables α and β to constraints (3.2) and (3.3) respectively, then the dual to the LP relaxation of the single facility installation problem (3.1) - (3.4) is:

$$\text{Maximize} \quad F_e \alpha - \beta \tag{3.5}$$
$$\text{subject to} \quad U_t \alpha - \beta \leq C_t \quad \text{for } t = 0, \ldots T \tag{3.6}$$
$$\alpha \geq 0. \tag{3.7}$$

Noting that for $t = 0$, $C_t = U_t = 0$, $U_0 \alpha - \beta \leq C_0$ is simply $-\beta \leq 0$, this can be rewritten as

$$\text{Maximize} \quad F_e \alpha - \beta$$
$$\text{subject to} \quad U_t \alpha - \beta \leq C_t \quad \text{for } t = 1, \ldots, T$$
$$\alpha, \beta \geq 0.$$

The corresponding complementary slackness conditions are:

$$\alpha \left[\sum_{t=0}^{T} U_t Y_e^t - F_e \right] = 0 \tag{3.8}$$

$$Y_e^t [U_t \alpha - \beta - C_t] = 0 \quad \text{for } t = 0, \ldots, T \tag{3.9}$$

When $F_e \leq U_0$, it should be clear that the optimal solution to the LP relaxation of the single facility installation problem is to set $Y_0 = 1$ which is integral. We consider the situation where $F_e > U_0$ and prove that the following algorithm gives the optimal solution to the linear relaxation of the primal problem.

Algorithm 1: Optimal Solution to the LP relaxation of the single facility installation problem

1. Set $t^* = 0$, $t' = 0$
2. While $(F_e > U_{t'})$ do{
3.   Set $t' = \arg\min_{t > t^*} \{ \frac{C_t - C_{t^*}}{U_t - U_{t^*}} \}$
4.   If $(F_e \leq U_{t'})$
5. $Y_e^{t'} = \frac{F_e - U_{t^*}}{U_{t'} - U_{t^*}}; Y_e^{t^*} = \frac{U_{t'} - F_e}{U_{t'} - U_{t^*}};$
6.   else set $t^* = t'$.
7. }

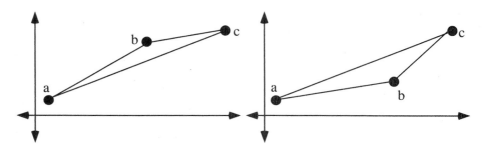

Figure 10.2.   An illustration of Lemma 3.1.

In proving the optimality of the algorithm we will use a simple result from Euclidean geometry (familiar to most high school students) that we state without proof. The validity and correctness should be obvious from Figure 10.2.

LEMMA 3.1 *Given three points $a = (x_a, y_a)$, $b = (x_b, y_b)$, and $c = (x_c, y_c)$ with $x_a < x_b < x_c$, let m_{ab}, m_{bc}, and m_{ac} represent the slope of the lines between points a and b, b and c, and a and c respectively. Exactly one of the following three situations must occur (1) $m_{ab} < m_{ac} < m_{bc}$. (2) $m_{ab} > m_{ac} > m_{bc}$. (3) $m_{ab} = m_{ac} = m_{bc}$. Further, the relationship between the slope of any two of the three lines characterizes which of the three situations occur.*

By way of notation, we denote the point (U_t, C_t) by P_t, and as in Lemma 3.1 the slope between any two points a and b by m_{ab}.

THEOREM 3.2 *Algorithm 1 provides the optimal solution to the LP relaxation of the single facility installation problem.*

Proof: It is straightforward to verify that the algorithm generates a feasible primal solution. To prove optimality of the solution consider the following dual solution.[3]

$$(*) \qquad \alpha = \frac{C_{t'} - C_{t^*}}{U_{t'} - U_{t^*}}; \beta = U_{t^*} \frac{C_{t'} - C_{t^*}}{U_{t'} - U_{t^*}} - C_{t^*}.$$

To verify that this solution is feasible to the dual, first observe by design $\alpha \geq 0$. Now consider the following four cases: (i) $t = t^*$, (ii) $t = t'$, (iii) $t > t^*$, and

---

[3]Notice that the value of α is equal to the slope of the line between P_{t^*} and $P_{t'}$, while the value of β is equal to the negative of the intercept of the line between P_{t^*} and $P_{t'}$. Condition $U_t \alpha - \beta \leq C_t$ says that (U_t, C_t) lies above the line passing through the points P_{t^*} and $P_{t'}$.

(iv) $t < t^*$. In the first two cases, we have that $U_t \alpha - \beta = C_t$, so the solution satisfies the dual constraint (3.6) for $t = t^*$ and $t = t'$.

For the facility types $t > t^*$, we have that $U_t > U_{t^*}$, and verifying inequality, $U_t \alpha - \beta \le C_t$, is equivalent to:

$$U_t \frac{C_{t'} - C_{t^*}}{U_{t'} - U_{t^*}} - (U_{t^*} \frac{C_{t'} - C_{t^*}}{U_{t'} - U_{t^*}} - C_{t^*}) \le C_t$$

$$(U_t - U_{t^*}) \frac{C_{t'} - C_{t^*}}{U_{t'} - U_{t^*}} \le C_t - C_{t^*}$$

$$\frac{C_{t'} - C_{t^*}}{U_{t'} - U_{t^*}} \le \frac{C_t - C_{t^*}}{U_t - U_{t^*}}$$

In other words the slope of the line connecting the points $P_{t'}$ and P_{t^*}, is less than or equal to the slope of the line connecting the points P_t and P_{t^*}. But, given the choice of t' in step 3 of Algorithm 1, this is true for all $t > t^*$. Therefore, for all $t > t^*$, solution (∗) satisfies constraint (3.6).

In the case where $t < t^*$, we have $U_t < U_{t^*}$. Thus, inequality $U_t \alpha - \beta \le C_t$ is equivalent to:

$$\frac{C_{t'} - C_{t^*}}{U_{t'} - U_{t^*}} \ge \frac{C_{t^*} - C_t}{U_{t^*} - U_t} \tag{3.10}$$

In other words the slope of the line connecting the points $P_{t'}$ and P_{t^*}, is greater than or equal to the slope of the line connecting the points P_t and P_{t^*}.

For notational convenience, let $\Gamma = \{z^1, z^2, \ldots, z^l\}$ denote the t^* values selected in the iterations of Algorithm 1 (i.e., z^i is the t^* value selected in iteration i, and the total number of iterations is l). To show that condition (3.10) is true, we consider two cases: (a) t is equal to one of the t^* values selected in the iterations of Algorithm 1, and (b) $t < t^*$ and $t \notin \Gamma$.

In case (a), when $t = z^{l-1}$ (in our notation z^{l-1} denotes the t^* value selected in the previous iteration of Algorithm 1), we know from Step 3 of the algorithm that the slope of the line between points $P_{z^{l-1}}$ and $P_{t'}$ is strictly greater than the slope of the line between points $P_{z^{l-1}}$ and P_{t^*}. Since $U_{z^{l-1}} < U_{t^*} < U_{t'}$, from Lemma 3.1 $m_{P_{t^*} P_{t'}} > m_{P_{z^{l-1}} P_{t'}}$. In other words, $\frac{C_{t'} - C_{t^*}}{U_{t'} - U_{t^*}} > \frac{C_{t^*} - C_{z^{l-1}}}{U_{t^*} - U_{z^{l-1}}}$; or condition (3.10) is satisfied. Repeating this argument for the line segments between points $P_{z^{i-1}}$, P_{z^i}, and $P_{z^{i+1}}$ for $i = 2, \ldots, l - 2$ shows that

$$\frac{C_{z^i} - C_{z^{i-1}}}{U_{z^i} - U_{z^{i-1}}} < \frac{C_{z^{i+1}} - C_{z^i}}{U_{z^{i+1}} - U_{z^i}}, \qquad \text{for } i = 2, \ldots, l - 1. \tag{3.11}$$

Now consider the three points P_{z^i}, $P_{z^{i+1}}$, and P_{t^*} for any i in the range $1, 2, \ldots, l - 2$. From Step 3 of Algorithm 1, $m_{P_{z^i} P_{z^{i+1}}} < m_{P_{z^i} P_{t^*}}$. Since $U_i < U_{i+1} < U_{t^*}$, Lemma 3.1 implies $m_{P_{z^i} P_{t^*}} < m_{P_{z^{i+1}} P_{t^*}}$. Since this is true for any i in the range $1, 2, \ldots, l - 2$

$$m_{P_{z^1} P_{t^*}} < m_{P_{z^2} P_{t^*}} < \ldots < m_{P_{z^{l-1}} P_{t^*}}.$$

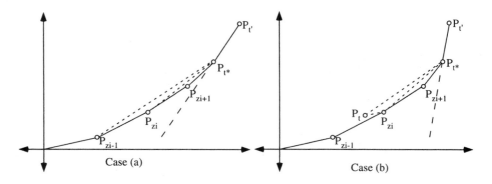

Figure 10.3. Illustration of cases (a) and (b), when $t < t^*$, in the proof of Theorem 3.2. Proving constraint (3.6) is satisfied corresponds to showing the point P_t lies above the line passing through points P_{t^*} and $P_{t'}$.

But, we have already shown that $m_{P_{z^{l-1}}P_{t^*}} < m_{P_{t'}P_{t^*}}$. Which means, $m_{P_{z^i}P_{t^*}} < m_{P_{t'}P_{t^*}}$ for $i = 1, 2, \ldots, l-1$ and condition (3.10) is satisfied for all t in case (a).

Now consider case (b). When $z^{i-1} < t < z^i$, we know from Step 3 of Algorithm 1 that $m_{P_{z^{i-1}}P_{z^i}}$ is less than or equal to $m_{P_{z^{i-1}}P_t}$. (In other words all points P_t with t between z^{i-1} and z^i lie above the line passing through the points $P_{z^{i-1}}$ and P_{z^i}). But, since $U_{z^{i-1}} < U_t < U_{z^i}$, from Lemma 3.1 $m_{P_t P_{z^i}}$ must be less than or equal to $m_{P_{z^{i-1}}P_{z^i}}$. But from equation (3.11) $m_{P_{z^{i-1}}P_{z^i}} < m_{P_{z^i}P_{z^{i+1}}}$. Thus, for $i = l$ (i.e., when $z^{l-1} < t < t^*$), $m_{P_t P_{t^*}} < m_{P_{z^{l-1}}P_{t^*}} < m_{P_{t'}P_{t^*}}$. Further, from the proof of case (a) (or using Step 3 of Algorithm 1) $m_{P_{z^i}P_{z^{i+1}}} < m_{P_{z^i}P_{t^*}}$. Or, $m_{P_t P_{z^i}} < m_{P_{z^i}P_{t^*}}$. Since, $U_t < U_{z^i} < U_{z^{i+1}}$, Lemma 3.1 implies $m_{P_t P_{t^*}} < m_{P_{z^i}P_{t^*}}$. But, we have already shown in case (a) $m_{P_{z^i}P_{t^*}} < m_{P_{t'}P_{t^*}}$. Consequently for $i = 2, \ldots, l-1$ $m_{P_t P_{t^*}} < m_{P_{t'}P_{t^*}}$. This completes the argument that for all t, solution $(*)$ satisfies constraint (3.6), and thus the solution is dual feasible. (Figure 10.3 is helpful in illustrating cases (a) and (b) when $t < t^*$.)

To prove optimality, we show that the primal and dual solutions satisfy complementary slackness.[4] For the primal solution $\sum_{t=0}^{T} U_t Y_e^t - F_e = 0$. So complementary slackness condition (3.8) is always satisfied. In the primal solution $Y_e^t = 0$, except when t is equal to either t^* or t'. In these two cases $U_t \alpha - \beta = C_t$, so complementary slackness condition (3.9) is also satisfied. ∎

---

[4]Alternatively, it is easy to verify that both the primal and dual solution have the same objective value.

Observe that if we run Algorithm 1 with $F_e = U_T$ then we have all the necessary information for solving the problem in the range $U_0 < F_e \leq U_T$. Let $\Gamma = \{z^1, z^2, \ldots, z^l\}$ denote the t^* values selected in the iterations of Algorithm 1, and let $z^{l+1} = T$. Let $\alpha_i = \frac{C_{z^{i+1}} - C_{z^i}}{U_{z^{i+1}} - U_{z^i}}$, and $\beta_i = U_{z^i} \frac{C_{z^{i+1}} - C_{z^i}}{U_{z^{i+1}} - U_{z^i}} - C_{z^i}$. They denote the optimal α and β values specified in Theorem 3.2 when $U_{z^i} < F_e \leq U_{z^{i+1}}$. From Theorem 3.2, the optimal LP objective value for flow F_e in the range $(U_{z^i}, U_{z^{i+1}}]$ is given by $G(F_e) = F_e \alpha_i - \beta_i$. Or $G(F_e)$ is a piecewise linear function. An immediate consequence, is that the LP relaxation of the single facility installation model approximates the staircase objective function by its lower convex envelope.

COROLLARY 3.3 *The LP relaxation of the single facility installation model approximates the step (staircase) function by its lower convex envelope.*

Proof: Let $G(F_e)$ denote the optimal LP objective value for flow F_e. From Theorem 3.2, $G(F_e) = F_e \alpha_i - \beta_i$, for $U_{z^i} < F_e \leq U_{z^{i+1}}$. But, α_i corresponds to the slope of the line between P_{z^i} and $P_{z^{i+1}}$, and β_i its negative intercept. Thus, the point $(F_e, F_e \alpha_i - \beta_i)$ lies on the line between P_{z^i} and $P_{z^{i+1}}$.

Observe, $U_{z^i} \alpha_i - \beta_i = U_{z^i} \alpha_{i-1} - \beta_{i-1}$ for $i = 2, \ldots, l$. Note, from Theorem 3.2 $\alpha_i < \alpha_{i+1}$, or the slope of the pieces strictly increases. In other words, $G(F_e)$ is a piecewise linear and continuous convex function. At $F_e = U_{z^i}$, $G(F_e) = C_{z^i}$. Thus at each of the breakpoints of $G(F_e)$, the value of $G(F_e)$ coincides with the staircase objective function. Finally, from Theorem 3.2 any point P_t with $z^i < t < z^{i+1}$ lies above the line between P_{z^i} and $P_{z^{i+1}}$ (i.e., above $F_e \alpha_i - \beta_i$). Thus, $G(F_e)$ provides a lower bound on the staircase objective function.

In simple terms, $G(F_e)$ is a piecewise linear and continuous convex function, it provides a lower bound on the staircase objective function, and each point where the slope changes corresponds to a point on the staircase objective function. Thus $G(F_e)$ is the lower convex envelope of the staircase objective function. ■

We now consider the situation when the minimum facility type has capacity greater than zero.[5] Consider the situation when $U_0 > 0$. We do not use this in our proof, thus it should be clear that for $U_0 < F_e < U_T$ the previous discussion holds. When $F_e \leq U_0$, the optimal LP objective is C_0 which is exactly equal to the value of the staircase objective function. Since $C_0 = U_0 \alpha_1 - \beta_1$ our previous assertion on the LP approximating the step function by its lower convex envelope holds true.

---

[5]This is pertinent because the SOR procedure refines the convex envelope approximation by considering ranges of the staircase objective function.

In SOR (more details on SOR are given in the next section), when restricting the flow ranges, the objective function is refined by recalculating the lower convex envelope of the staircase function over the flow range of the problem. Each piece of the staircase objective function corresponds to a facility type in the single facility installation model. Consequently, the identical refined approximation can be achieved in the single facility installation model by removing the facility types (or setting the corresponding Y_e^t variable to zero) that are not allowed in a particular subproblem.

4. Search by Objective Relaxation as a Stylized Branch-and-Bound Strategy on the Single Facility Installation Model

We now elaborate further on the branch-and-bound procedure used in SOR and define a corresponding branch-and-bound procedure using an MIP based on the Single Facility Installation Model. We refer to this procedure as SFI B&B. We explain how the branching procedure in SOR can be mimicked in SFI B&B.

The SOR branch-and-bound procedure starts by solving a network flow problem with the original cost function replaced by its lower convex envelope. The cost of the resulting flow levels is then compared to the actual cost for the same flow levels. If the two costs do not match over all edges in the network, the procedure proceeds with the branching steps that refine the objective function for a single edge at the time. The update of the objective function is based on branching into 2 or 3 new problems with different ranges of flow for a given edge. The cost function for each branch is then defined as the lower convex envelope of the staircase cost function over the range of flow specific to the edge we are branching on. The main steps of this procedure are outlined in Figure 10.4.

In Figure 10.4 $C(F_e)$ denotes the staircase cost function and $h(F_e)$ denotes its lower convex envelope. SOR uses a very clever upper bounding strategy that is quite effective. Noting that the solution at any node in the branch-and-bound tree is a feasible flow for the problem, SOR calculates the cost of the feasible flow pattern with the staircase cost function. Salman et al. proposed three possible branching rules for SOR, but only the first rule (Rule 1) was used in their implementations.

The branch-and-bound procedure that we develop in this paper uses a MIP model based on the Single Facility Installation Problem. We refer to this formulation as SFIMIP and provide the complete formulation in Appendix B. Our procedure, SFI B&B, differs from SOR in two main aspects. First, at the root and every other node of the branch-and-bound tree, SOR solves a network flow problem with a piecewise linear cost function. Thus, it explicitly calculates the

Begin
   Root node
      Solve the SOR subproblem (see Appendix for complete formulation)
      with the objective function specified by the lower convex envelope, $h(F_e)$,
      for every edge in the network.
      Set:
      LB = objective value in the optimal solution of the SOR subproblem
      UB $= \sum_{e \in E} l_e C(\overline{F_e})$, where $\overline{F_e}$ is the flow in the optimal solution of
      the SOR subproblem, and $C(\overline{F_e})$ the cost for carrying flow $\overline{F_e}$
      Let V_e and W_e denote lower and upper bounds of flow respectively
   While termination rule is not met
      From all nodes in the current branch-and-bound tree, select the node with
      the minimum lower bound to branch on.
      Select the edge for branching (that is select one of the variables F_e)
      based on the one of the following three rules:
      Rule 1: Select the edge with the most potential improvement, i.e.,
      select $max_{e \in E}(C(\overline{F_e}) - h(\overline{F_e})) * l_e$
      Rule 2: Select the edge whose flow $\overline{F_e}$ has the largest range in the
      corresponding $C(F_e)$.
      Rule 3: Select the edge with maximum flow.
      For the selected edge e^* and its flow F_{e^*}, find the corresponding
      range $(U_i, U_{i+1}]$ in $C(F_e)$.
      If F_{e^*} is at a breakpoint between two facility types $(\overline{F_{e^*}} = U_{i+1})$,
      branch into two problems:
          1. $V_{e^*} \leq F_{e^*} \leq U_{i+1}$
          2. $U_{i+1} < F_{e^*} \leq W_{e^*}$
      Otherwise, branch into three problems:
          1. $V_{e^*} \leq F_{e^*} \leq U_i$
          2. $U_i < F_{e^*} \leq U_{i+1}$
          3. $U_{i+1} < F_{e^*} \leq W_{e^*}$
      For each of the newly created nodes:
         Update $h(F_{e^*})$ by a convex piecewise linear function over the
         corresponding flow range that is permitted on edge e^*.
         Using $h(F_{e^*})$ defined in the previous step, solve the SOR subproblem
         Fathom the node if:
            1. the lower bound at the node is $\geq$ UB,
            2. $C(\overline{F_e}) = h(\overline{F_e})$ $\quad \forall e \in E$,
            3. Relaxation is infeasible.
         If the upper bound at the new node < UB, update UB
         to the upper bound at the new node.
   End
End

Figure 10.4. Steps of SOR procedure.

Branch	SOR	SFI B&B
1	$V_{e^*} \leq F_{e^*} \leq U_i$	$Y_{e^*}^{i+1} = Y_{e^*}^{i+2} = \ldots = Y_{e^*}^T = 0$ $V_{e^*} \leq F_{e^*} \leq U_i$
2	$U_i < F_{e^*} \leq U_{i+1}$	$Y_{e^*}^0 = Y_{e^*}^1 = \ldots = Y_{e^*}^i = Y_{e^*}^{i+2} = \ldots = Y_{e^*}^T = 0$ $U_i < F_{e^*} \leq U_{i+1}$
3	$U_{i+1} < F_{e^*} \leq W_{e^*}$	$Y_{e^*}^0 = Y_{e^*}^1 = \ldots = Y_{e^*}^{i+1} = 0$ $U_{i+1} < F_{e^*} \leq W_{e^*}$

Table 10.1.   SOR and SFI B&B Branching Strategies.

Branch	SOR	SFI B&B
1	$V_{e^*} \leq F_{e^*} \leq U_i$	$Y_{e^*}^{i+1} = Y_{e^*}^{i+2} = \ldots = Y_{e^*}^T = 0$ $V_{e^*} \leq F_{e^*} \leq U_i$
2	$U_i < F_{e^*} \leq U_{i+1}$	$Y_{e^*}^0 = Y_{e^*}^1 = \ldots = Y_{e^*}^i = Y_{e^*}^{i+2} = \ldots = Y_{e^*}^T = 0$ $U_i + 1 \leq F_{e^*} \leq U_{i+1}$
3	$U_{i+1} < F_{e^*} \leq W_{e^*}$	$Y_{e^*}^0 = Y_{e^*}^1 = \ldots = Y_{e^*}^{i+1} = 0$ $U_{i+1} + 1 \leq F_{e^*} \leq W_{e^*}$

Table 10.2.   Improved Lower Bounds in SFI B&B's Branching Strategy.

lower convex envelope of the staircase cost function, and appropriately formulates the (convex cost piecewise linear) network flow problem at each node. Our procedure, instead, solves the linear relaxation of the SFIMIP formulation with no changes in variables or changes in the cost function. The linear relaxation of our model implicitly calculates the lower convex envelope of the staircase cost function. Second, since the subproblem in SOR is a network flow problem, branching takes place over the flow variables (and then the objective function is refined for the flow range). Instead our branching strategy in SFI B&B is performed using the facility installation variables Y_e^t in addition to establishing flow bounds. Our branching strategy on the Y_e^t variables, along with the corresponding SOR rules, is shown in Table 10.1.

Notice, for the both SOR and SFI B&B the branching rules add a strict inequality. When the data for the problem are integer (this is an assumption we can make without loss of generality), the optimal solution will have integral flow variables. With this observation, a constraint of the type $U_{i+1} < F_e$ can be enforced as $U_{i+1} + 1 \leq F_e$ (rather than adding $U_{i+1} + \epsilon \leq F_e$ with a small ϵ value). We make this change in SFI B&B. Table 10.2 displays the resulting branching strategy in SOR B&B.

When lower bounds on flow are imposed, we noticed an important difference between SOR and SFI B&B. Since SOR uses a network flow algorithm, the solution sends flow on only one direction on an edge. However, in the subproblems in SFI B&B when there is a lower bound on the flow on an edge, it is possible for the linear programming solution to send flow on both directions on an edge (i.e., to send flow around a cycle). To prevent this situation, when a non-zero lower bound is imposed for the first time for flow on an edge $e = \{i, j\}$, we create two branches instead of one. One branch imposes the lower bound on the flow variable f_{ij} and sets $f_{ji} = 0$, and the other branch imposes the lower bound on the flow variable f_{ji} and sets $f_{ij} = 0$.

Other than this difference in branching when a non-zero lower bound is imposed for the first time on the flow on an edge, we use the same choices as Salman et al. [1] within the branch-and-bound algorithm. Specifically, we use the same criteria for node and edge selection within the branch-and-bound tree.

5. Computational Experiments

We now report on our computational experiments with SFI B&B. We coded SFI B&B using Microsoft Visual C++ and the CPLEX 7.1 Callable Libraries. We did not use any special purpose code (like COIN-OR) to handle the branch-and-bound tree. We developed our own routines, external to CPLEX, to handle the branching, as well as to manage the branch-and-bound tree. At each node of the branch-and-bound tree, addition of constraints was handled by changing the bounds on the flow and facility choice variables (i.e., the f_{ij} and Y_e^t variables). At each node of the branch-and-bound tree we used the parent basis (as a starting basis for the LP problem at the node) and used CPLEX's default LP settings.

We compared SFI B&B to running CPLEX 7.1 directly on the single facility installation model for the problem. In other words, we let CPLEX determine using its own internal routines how to strengthen and solve the formulation. We refer to this procedure as SFIMIP, and the results obtained in this fashion are presented under the heading SFIMIP. We also compared SFI B&B to using CPLEX directly on an incremental formulation called INCMIP (this is presented in Appendix C). We refer to this procedure as INCMIP, and the results obtained in this fashion are presented under the heading INCMIP. All computational tests were performed on a Sun Microsystems Enterprise 250 with 2x400 MHz processors and 2GB RAM.

We used the same test problems as Salman et al.[6] These instances include four problems originally defined in [3] (problems ARPA, OCT, USA, and RING), four problems originally defined in Salman's dissertation [4] (problems S6, S15, N1, and N3), and twelve problems (5 instances of each) randomly generated in Salman et al. [1]. For the last group of 12 problems the notation e(n)(s)(d) provides summary information on the dataset. n identifies the number of nodes in the graph, s identifies the location of the sink node in

---

[6]We thank Professor Salman for providing us the test problems.

Problem	Solution Procedure	Cable Types 1, 3, 5, 7		Cable Types 1, 2, ..., 9	
		cpu time	Nodes	cpu time	Nodes
e10ch	INCMIP	3.266	498.8	3.426	484.2
	SOR	6.54	1174	2.89	644
	SFI B&B	4.786	623.8	3.168	406.8
e10cl	INCMIP	0.88	184.6	1.268	155.8
	SOR	1.78	506	1.53	454
	SFI B&B	1.544	251.2	1.478	252.2
e10rh	INCMIP	1.84	571.4	2.236	517.8
	SOR	6.21	1499	4.07	1023
	SFI B&B	3.602	594.4	3.35	531.2
e10rl	INCMIP	0.894	572.4	0.984	411.4
	SOR	5.36	1627	3.17	999
	SFI B&B	3.88	780.4	2.546	501.6

Table 10.3. Small Random Instances

the graph with respect to location of other nodes (c - the sink node is located in the center of the graph, and r - location of the sink node in the graph randomly selected), and d identifies level of demand (l - low demand randomly generated between 0 and 30, and h - high demand randomly generated between 0 and 60). The cable data was originally defined in Berger et al. [5]. There are 9 different cable types. We tested the problem sets for two combinations of cable types. In the first combination, all 9 cable types were considered, while in the second set 4 cable types (cable types: 1, 3, 5, 7) were considered.

In all the test instances, we limited the number of new facility types (after solving the dynamic program[7]) by either determining the maximum possible flow through the network (sum of all demands), or by limiting the maximum possible flow to 450 units in the case of 9 cable types, and 500 units in the case of 4 cable types. Limiting the maximum possible flow, and thus the number of new facility types reduces the number of variables in the formulation. We used a 2 hour CPU limit as a termination criteria.

Given the differences in hardware and software used in [1] and in this paper, it is not possible to make a performance comparison of SOR and the SFI B&B procedure. Instead, we provide a rough comparison of the two procedures for small instances where both procedures found the optimum.

Table 10.3 summarizes the average performance of SOR (from [1]), SFI B&B, and running CPLEX on the INCMIP formulation for the 4 small random problem sets (5 instances each). In comparing SFI B&B and INCMIP, it appears that INCMIP outperforms SFI B&B both in running time and the average number of B&B nodes examined. We note that Salman et al. [1] found

---

[7]We actually modeled this problem as an IP and solved it to determine the optimal combination of cable types for the different flow levels.

Prob	Sol. Proc.	Cable Types 1, 3, 5, 7			Cable Types 1, 2, ..., 9		
		cpu time	Nodes	% Gap	cpu time	Nodes	% Gap
S6	INCMIP	99.81	14620	0.00	196.92	22816	0.00
	SFIMIP	500.77	317917	0.00	177.08	104925	0.00
	SFI B&B	165.60	12949	0.00	102.67	7332	0.00
S15	INCMIP	12.03	1374	0.00	29.58	4286	0.00
	SFIMIP	5.89	2610	0.00	8.72	3178	0.00
	SFI B&B	75.49	7389	0.00	148.47	12054	0.00
N1	INCMIP	2869.17	311493	0.00	210.50	18382	0.00
	SFIMIP	7200.00	2992475	1.95	849.83	299699	0.00
	SFI B&B	7200.00	179970	9.89	7200.00	174582	6.79
N3	INCMIP	2190.20	152952	0.00	2906.13	209693	0.00
	SFIMIP	7200.00	2806384	6.44	7200.00	2434000	6.04
	SFI B&B	7200.00	170138	4.57	7200.00	174374	5.34
ARPA	INCMIP	48.62	4250	0.00	95.62	8538	0.00
	SFIMIP	585.56	314648	0.00	3965.77	1989198	0.00
	SFI B&B	122.68	8837	0.00	558.22	29558	0.00
OCT	INCMIP	1044.63	87639	0.00	121.36	8919	0.00
	SFIMIP	7071.97	2682869	0.00	1170.43	478892	0.00
	SFI B&B	1379.09	58525	0.00	732.35	33810	0.00
USA	INCMIP	7200.00	425910	2.17	7200.00	383809	3.19
	SFIMIP	7200.00	2077784	6.40	7200.00	2179235	6.42
	SFI B&B	7200.00	170257	4.74	7200.00	170968	7.05
RING	INCMIP	7200.00	231037	3.42	7200.00	304034	10.52
	SFIMIP	7200.00	1588231	10.50	7200.00	1543161	11.67
	SFI B&B	7200.00	154765	6.74	7200.00	154683	8.08
Ave	INCMIP	2583.06	153659	0.70	2245.01	120060	1.71
	SFIMIP	4620.52	1597865	3.16	3471.48	1129036	3.02
	SFI B&B	3817.86	95354	3.24	3792.71	94670	3.41

Table 10.4. Comparison of SFI B&B, SFIMIP, and INCMIP.

a similar behavior in comparing SOR and INCMIP on small instances. While comparing SOR and SFI B&B, we focus on the number of nodes examined. Surprisingly, SFI B&B examines significantly fewer nodes than SOR. We are not entirely sure why this difference occurs. There may be several possible reasons. First, the number of new facility types used might be different. Second, as explained in Section 4 we have to do some additional branching to ensure that flow is not sent on both directions on an edge. Third, recall since all of the data are integer we enforced the condition $U_i < F_e$ by the constraint $U_i + 1 \leq F_e$. This improved lower bound might perhaps help our implementation examine fewer nodes in the branch-and-bound tree.

We next considered the eight instances S6, S15, N1, N3, ARPA, OCT, USA, and RING. These problems range in size from 15 to 32 nodes, and from 28 to 60 edges. Here we compared SFI B&B to running CPLEX with its default settings on SFIMIP and INCMIP. Table 10.4 displays the results of our comparisons.

From Table 10.4 we see that INCMIP provides the best results in all instances. The comparison with SFIMIP does not provide a clear conclusion. Sometimes SFI provides a significantly better percentage gap[8] than SFI B&B, and sometimes a significantly worse gap. On the other hand, the number of nodes explored by SFI B&B is significantly lower than the number of nodes for SFIMIP in almost all of the instances. The reason for this is not completely clear given that the linear relaxations solved at each node of SFIMIP and SFI B&B have similar structure. One possible explanation for this result could be that the internal handling of all computations for SFIMIP by CPLEX is much more efficient than the custom external computations that we performed within SFI B&B. Another possible explanation could be the automatic generation of cuts performed by CPLEX when solving SFIMIP and INCMIP.

Indeed, we found that if we disable the generation of cuts in CPLEX when solving INCMIP and SFIMIP, the performance of both formulations significantly deteriorates. (Note, in SFI B&B no automatic cut generation takes place). Specifically, over the eight selected instances in the case where there are 4 cable types, the average CPU time for INCMIP increased from 2583.06 seconds to 3369.36 seconds, while the average number of nodes explored increased from 153659 to 306754, and the average gap increased from 0.7% to 1.64%. For the same set of test instances the average CPU time for SFIMIP increased from 4620.52 seconds to 5433.38 seconds, the average number of nodes explored increased from 1597865 to 2606227, and the average gap increased from 3.16% to 9.21%. So, in this case, SFI B&B provides better results than the SFIMIP formulation, but remains worse than the INCMIP formulation. We can also see that, compared to the INCMIP formulation, our SFI B&B procedure explores a significantly lower number of nodes within the prespecified time limit.

Although SFI B&B has a worse average performance than formulations INCMIP and SFIMIP in terms of the gap, we found that it provides the best upper bounds in almost all the instances (the only exception is problem N3 with all cable types, where INCMIP provided the best upper bound). Over all the 16 instances, the SFI B&B upper bound was on average 0.79% better than the upper bound provided by INCMIP and 1.31% better than the upper bound provided by SFIMIP. This suggests that the upper bounding procedure proposed by Salman et al. [1] is indeed very powerful, and rapidly generates high-quality upper bounds for the problem.

---

[8]Gap refers to the percentage gap between the best upper bound and the best lower bound found by the algorithm.

Problem	Sol. Proc.	Cable Types 1, 3, 5, 7			Cable Types 1, 2, ..., 9		
		cpu time	Nodes	% Gap	cpu time	Nodes	% Gap
e20ch	INCMIP	1590.13	148206	0.00	2085.96	139482	0.96
	SFI B&B	4328.8	88727	2.03	4423.21	103453	2.71
e20cl	INCMIP	57.39	8153	0.00	105.59	20147	0.00
	SFI B&B	1606.39	45800	0.81	2225.3	74154	1.17
e20rh	INCMIP	1794.65	173402	0.18	1067.4	141700	0.00
	SFI B&B	4885.06	120833	2.47	5770.31	139281	2.93
e20rl	INCMIP	1913.87	335883	1.30	2308.23	371161	0.70
	SFI B&B	5952.29	153833	6.44	6043.86	160407	6.28
e30ch	INCMIP	7196.47	363889	3.59	7200	424110	7.28
	SFI B&B	7200	149235	6.26	7200	158071	7.26
e30cl	INCMIP	5027.05	445968	5.49	6271.23	629557	10.13
	SFI B&B	7200	165822	10.33	7200	168017	9.73
e30rh	INCMIP	6121.65	314500	3.73	7200	409206	7.83
	SFI B&B	7200	161615	6.05	7200	159349	6.18
e30rl	INCMIP	6867.59	577289	5.49	7200	683812	8.83
	SFI B&B	7200	159922	11.01	7200	168609	10.51
Average	INCMIP	3821.1	295911	2.47	4179.8	352397	4.47
	SFI B&B	5696.57	130723	5.67	5907.84	141418	5.85

Table 10.5. Large Random Instances

Our final set of computational experiments are on a set of large random instances. Here we only compare INCMIP and SFI B&B procedure, since the performance of SFIMIP was significantly worse than INCMIP on the smaller test problems. Table 10.5 summarizes these results. It shows that the average percentage gap provided by the INCMIP formulation was again better than the one provided by SFI B&B. However, SFI B&B examines a significantly smaller number of nodes in the B&B tree. Further, SFI B&B provided upper bounds that are better than INCMIP in 14 instances, and worse in 8 instances. In the remaining 38 instances, INCMIP and SFI B&B provided the same upper bound.

In contrast to our experiments, the computational experiments in [1] indicate a relatively poor performance of the INCMIP formulation for large test instances. This difference in performance could be due to the different computers used in implementation of these procedures, or most likely due to different versions of CPLEX used (we used CPLEX 7.1, while Salman et al. used CPLEX 6.0.1). Another, rather unlikely, possible explanation is that the multicommodity version of INCMIP may have been used instead of the single commodity version (the multicommodity version of INCMIP is described in [1]).

In any event, contrary to our expectations when we started this computational study, SFI B&B did not outperform INCMIP or SFIMIP. However, what is promising is that SFI B&B examines a significantly fewer number of nodes than INCMIP and SFIMIP. Consequently, we believe improvements to the implementation of SFI B&B might yield significantly better computational results. In particular, we believe better handling of data structures used in the course of SFI B&B, and better integration between our branching procedures and the CPLEX environment, will significantly improve the computational results of SFI B&B.

6.   Conclusions

In this paper, we explained how SOR may be viewed as a stylized branch-and-bound procedure on a single facility installation model of the LAND problem. In particular we show that the linear programming relaxation of the single facility installation model also approximates the staircase function by its lower convex envelope. This provides an alternate (and somewhat more geometrical) proof to Croxton et al. [2] in the context of staircase cost functions.

We developed a branch-and-bound procedure called SFI B&B, based on the SFIMIP formulation, that mimics the SOR procedure. Instead of explicitly refining the lower convex envelope, our algorithm implicitly calculates the lower convex envelope of the staircase cost function. We performed computational experiments with SFI B&B and compared it with the application of the state-of-the-art MIP solver CPLEX on two alternate formulations (SFIMIP and INCMIP) of the LAND problem. Contrary to our expectations SFI B&B did not outperform these methods. SFI B&B was superior to SFIMIP when cut generation was disabled within CPLEX. However, it was always worse than INCMIP. We suggest possible computational enhancements to SFI B&B that might make it competitive with INCMIP.

We note that it is easy to establish that the linear programming relaxations of INCMIP and SFIMIP are identical (see Croxton et al. [2] for example). Consequently, it is possible to mimic SOR and SFI B&B using the INCMIP formulation. We call this procedure INC B&B. Since CPLEX performs significantly better on INCMIP than SFIMIP, one possibility would be to run computational experiments on INC B&B and evaluate its performance. We leave this for future research.

Appendix: Formulations for LAND Problem

Notation

l_e - the length of edge $e \in E$
S - set of source nodes,
D - destination (sink) node,
d_k - total demand for traffic originating at node k,
F_e - total flow over edge $e \in E$,
$f_{e,t}$ - total flow over edge $e \in E$ and flow segment that requires use of facility type t,
$f_{e,p}$ - total flow over edge $e \in E$ and piece p of the piecewise linear function,
V_e - the lower bound on flow over edge e,
C_t - cost of facility type t,
U_t - capacity of facility type t,
g_t - incremental cost between facility types $(t-1)$ and t,
r_t - incremental capacity between facility types $(t-1)$ and t,
δ_p - slope of piece p of the piecewise linear approximation of the objective function,
r_p - flow range of piece p of the piecewise linear function.

A: SOR Subproblem Formulation (SORLP)

This formulation is a linear program used in the course of the SOR procedure. It basically solves a single commodity flow problem where traffic is sent from a set of demand sites to a single sink. The objective function of this formulation, however, represents a successively refined lower convex envelope of the staircase cost function. Recall, this is a continuous piecewise linear and convex cost function. Consequently, the number of pieces changes along with changes in the objective function in this formulation. Salman et al. present this formulation as a multicommodity flow model. Here, we describe it in the context of a single commodity (which it would be for the LAND problem). They solve this subproblem efficiently, using the LEDA software for the network flow problem.

$$\text{Minimize} \quad \sum_{e \in E} l_e \left(\sum_{p=1}^{P} \delta_p f_{e,p} + C(V_e) \right)$$

$$\text{subject to} \quad \sum_{j \in V} f_{ij} - \sum_{j \in V} f_{ji} = \begin{cases} d_i & \text{if } i \in S \\ -\sum_{k \in S} d_k & \text{if } i = D \\ 0 & \text{otherwise} \end{cases} \quad \forall i \in V$$

$$f_{ij} + f_{ji} = F_e \qquad \forall e = (i,j) \in E$$

$$\sum_{p=1}^{P} f_{e,p} + V_e = F_e \qquad \forall e = (i,j) \in E$$

$$0 \le f_{e,p} \le r_p \qquad p = 1, ..., P, \forall e = (i,j) \in E$$

$$f_{ij} \ge 0 \qquad \forall e = (i,j) \in E$$

B: SFIMIP Formulation

The SFIMIP formulation builds upon the single-edge formulation described in Section 3. In this formulation, each Y_e^t variable represents a single facility type, and for each edge in the network, we have to select exactly one of the available facility types.

$$\text{Minimize} \quad \sum_{e \in E} l_e \sum_{t=1}^{T} C_t Y_e^t$$

$$\text{subject to} \quad \sum_{j \in V} f_{ij} - \sum_{j \in V} f_{ji} = \begin{cases} d_i & \text{if } i \in S \\ -\sum_{k \in S} d_k & \text{if } i = D \qquad \forall i \in V \\ 0 & \text{otherwise} \end{cases}$$

$$f_{ij} + f_{ji} = F_e \qquad \forall e = (i,j) \in E$$

$$F_e \leq \sum_{t=1}^{T} U_t Y_e^t \qquad \forall e = (i,j) \in E$$

$$\sum_{t=0}^{T} Y_e^t = 1 \qquad \forall e = (i,j) \in E$$

$$f_{ij} \geq 0 \qquad \forall e = (i,j) \in E$$

$$Y_e^t \in \{0,1\} \qquad \forall t = 1, ..., T, e \in E$$

C: INCMIP Formulation

The INCMIP formulation is a single commodity incremental formulation for the LAND problem. In this formulation, each Y_e^t variable corresponds to the *incremental* use of the capacity when facility type t is selected. In other words, if flow is sent on facility type t, then $Y_e^1 = Y_e^2 = \ldots = Y_e^t = 1$ and $Y_e^{t+1} = Y_e^{t+2} = \ldots = Y_e^T = 0$.

$$\text{Minimize} \quad \sum_{e \in E} l_e \sum_{t=1}^{T} g_t Y_e^t$$

$$\text{subject to} \quad \sum_{j \in V} f_{ij} - \sum_{j \in V} f_{ji} = \begin{cases} d_i & \text{if } i \in S \\ -\sum_{k \in S} d_k & \text{if } i = D \qquad \forall i \in V \\ 0 & \text{otherwise} \end{cases}$$

$$f_{ij} + f_{ji} = F_e \qquad \forall e = (i,j) \in E$$

$$F_e \leq \sum_{t=1}^{T} r_t Y_e^t \qquad \forall e = (i,j) \in E$$

$$Y_e^t \geq Y_e^{(t+1)} \qquad \forall e = (i,j) \in E$$

$$f_{ij} \geq 0 \qquad \forall e = (i,j) \in E$$

$$Y_e^t \in \{0,1\} \qquad \forall t = 1, ..., T, e \in E$$

References

[1] Salman, F. S., R. Ravi, and J. Hooker. 2001 Solving the Local Access Network Design Problem. *Technical Report, Purdue University.*

[2] Croxton, K. L., B. Gendron, and T.L. Magnanti. 2003 A Comparison of Mixed-Integer Programming Models for Nonconvex Piecewise Linear Cost Minimization Problems. *Management Science*, Vol. 49, No. 9, pp. 1268 - 1273.

[3] Gavish B. and K. Altinkemer. 1990 Backbone network design tools with economic trade-offs. *ORSA Journal on Computing*, Vol. 2, No. 3, pp. 236 - 252.

[4] Salman F. S. 2000. Selected Problems in Network Design: Exact and Approximate Solution Methods. *PhD Thesis*, Carnegie Mellon University, Pittsburgh.

[5] Berger D. and B. Gendron and J. Potvin and S. Raghavan and P. Soriano. 2000 Tabu search for a network loading problem with multiple facilities. *Journal of Heuristics*, Vol. 6, No. 2, pp. 253 - 267.

Chapter 11

MINIMIZING THE NUMBER OF WAVELENGTH CONVERSIONS IN WDM NETWORKS WITH HYBRID OPTICAL CROSS-CONNECTS

Dirceu Cavendish[1], Aleksandar Kolarov[2], and Bhaskar Sengupta[3]

[1]*NEC Laboratories America*
10080 North Wolfe Road Suite SW3-350
Cupertino, CA 95014, USA
dirceu@sv.nec-labs.com

[2]*NEC Laboratories America*
4 Independence Way
Princeton, NJ 08540, USA
kolarov@nec-labs.com

[3]*ExxonMobil Research and Engineering*
1545 Route 22 East
Annandale, NJ 08801, USA
Bhaskar.Sengupta@exxonmobil.com

Abstract   In this paper, we study routing and wavelength assignment (RWA) tasks in wavelength division multiplexed (WDM) mesh networks with hybrid optical cross-connects (OXCs) devices. We use two optimization criteria: (1) minimize the number of wavelength conversions, and (2) minimize the hop count. For each lightpath request, we solve the routing and wavelength assignment sub-problems as a single problem, rather than as two separate problems. Both problems are solved by a Dijkstra type of algorithm, executed sequentially on one request at a time. We also develop an integer linear programming (ILP) model with the above mentioned objective functions. We conduct a comprehensive simulation study of the performance of the algorithms for different network topologies and traffic scenarios.

Keywords: Wavelength division multiplexing, routing, wavelength assignment, Dijkstra algorithm, integer linear programming.

1.   Introduction and Related Work

Routing and wavelength assignment (RWA) is the procedure by which routing paths are determined and wavelengths are assigned to connections to be provisioned by an optical transport network (OTN). The RWA should be done so as to conserve OTN resources as much as possible, since this may result in a lower blocking probability when additional connections are requested. Designing the system so as to directly minimize blocking probability is quite a difficult problem. So, in this paper, we focus on two different criteria for optimization as follows:

(1) Minimizing the number of wavelength conversions used. This criterion is motivated by the fact that wavelength conversion requires special hardware, involving optical-electrical-optical (OEO) conversions, and hence it consumes expensive network resources. Note that the use of this criterion may result in a connection request to be routed on a long path using one single wavelength along the path, rather than on a short path using different wavelengths on different links.

(2) Minimizing the total hop count used by all lightpaths. Since this is a spatial problem with a finite number of wavelengths available on each link, a shorter path consumes less network resources than a longer path, hence increasing the probability that future requests may find unused network resources.

Wavelength conversion is known to improve network utilization [1]. However, due to several technological limitations and commercial factors, WDM networks are likely to have nodes with limited wavelength conversion capabilities, at least in the foreseeable future. Our problem formulation allows different wavelength conversion capabilities at various nodes, to accommodate facts such as: nodes manufactured by different vendors; nodes manufactured by a single vendor, but operating at different wavelength bands, etc.

The RWA problem takes two flavors: off-line and on-line [2]. In the off-line case, all connection requests are known in advance, thus a routing decision can be made based on the complete knowledge of the traffic to be served by the network. This case models new systems which must be populated according to an initial traffic matrix. In the on-line case, a connection request must be routed and wavelengths assigned independently of other connections, which either have already been assigned or will be assigned in the future. Finding a globally optimal solution for the off-line problem is NP-hard [3]. So one is forced to use algorithms which are sub-optimal but are computationally efficient for the off-line problem. As will be seen later, the algorithms discussed in this paper are particularly well suited for the on-line version of the problem.

Various aspects of the routing and wavelength assignment problem in mesh networks have been addressed in the recent literature. The integer linear programming (ILP) approach to address the RWA problem is considered in [4–7].

Among the RWA problems with no wavelength conversion capability, a quite comprehensive RWA problem formulation is presented in [8, 9]. In [9] the authors developed an integer linear programming model, which for a given set of lightpath requests, determines the routes and assigns wavelengths to the lightpaths so as to minimize the number of ports needed. They described the properties of a node instead of a link as in other ILP formulations for RWA, but they did not consider optical cross-connects with wavelength conversion capability. The authors of [10] presented an ILP formulation of the RWA problem with wavelength conversion, attesting that only very small instances of the problem can be solved optimally. They also introduced a detailed modeling of optical cross-connects (OXCs), including wavelength conversion and multiplexing. They presented a heuristic based on K alternate shortest paths and define a wavelength assignment strategy seeking to minimize the number of conversions needed. In [11], the authors introduced an optical node architecture that deals with multigranularity flows, including fiber, wavelength and waveband. Graph transformation techniques were also used by [12] to solve RWA problems, via minimization of a path cost function which involves link costs with a traversal together with a wavelength conversion components.

Analyzing the approaches of these and other papers, we have come to the following conclusions. An integer linear programming approach is useful for static RWA problems only, and even in that case it is unlikely to be useful for solving large RWA problems with wavelength conversion. Relaxation techniques help with the scalability issue, but it is unclear how network performance gets affected by these techniques. Dijkstra based heuristics is a popular approach, which is not surprising given the low algorithm complexity ($N \log N$). However, these heuristics vary wildly, depending on the definition of the link cost function.

The work presented in this paper differs from previous work in several ways. First, we consider WDM mesh networks with a specified limitation on wavelength conversion capabilities (number of conversions), whereas most of previous work has been on ring networks with heterogeneous wavelength conversion capabilities or on mesh networks with no or a particular type (e.g. full) wavelength conversion capability. Second, we formulate problems with different objectives for optimization, whereas most of the previous work has focused on a single objective. Third, for each of those optimization problems we develop an ILP model. The formulation of the ILP model is unique since it describes a detailed model of optical cross-connects with wavelength conversion capability. Fourth, for each of the objectives outlined earlier, we develop a *sequential* algorithm (by sequential we mean one request considered singly and sequentially). This allows us to use the algorithms for both off-line and on-line RWA problems. Each algorithm, based on the Dijkstra algorithm, solves the routing *and* wavelength assignment sub-problems as a single problem, rather than separating them into a routing and a wavelength assignment sub-problem (e.g., in approaches using alternate paths). Although our basic approach is to use a graph transformation and apply a Dijkstra type algorithm, which may resemble previous work [12], we evaluate various cost functions from a network performance point of view. Our main and unique objective is to understand how a given cost function, network topology and traffic pattern affect the performance of an optical network under the realistic assumption that every network element has diverse and limited wavelength conversion capabilities.

The paper is organized as follows. In Section 2, we state the problem. In Section 3 we present an ILP model with two objective functions: (1) minimize the number of wavelength conversions, and (2) minimize the number of hops. In Sections 4 and 5, we describe the proposed algorithms for solving mesh RWA problems. In Section 6, we evaluate the performance of the proposed algorithms. Conclusions are drawn in Section 7.

2.   Problem Statement

A WDM mesh network of N nodes is modeled as a directed graph $\mathcal{G}(\mathcal{V}, \mathcal{E})$, where $|\mathcal{V}| = N$, and $|\mathcal{E}| = J$. Nodes are labeled by n, where $0 \leq n \leq N - 1$. A link (n, m) connects node n to node m. The presence of link (n, m) in $\mathcal{E}$ means that communication can take place from node n to node m. We represent the graph $\mathcal{G}$ by means of adjacency lists. So, for all $j \in \mathcal{V}$, we define $\mathcal{A}(j)$ to be a subset of $\mathcal{V}$, containing the nodes adjacent to node j, i.e., $n \in \mathcal{A}(j)$ if and only if $(n, j) \in \mathcal{E}$.

A wavelength set $\Lambda = \{0, 1, \cdots, K - 1\}$ of size $|\Lambda| = K$ represents the number of wavelengths (colors) available in the WDM network. For each node j of the mesh network, we specify a number κ_j, which denotes the maximum number of wavelengths which can be converted at node j. An OEO switch fabric at node j has κ_j input-output ports and tunable lasers, and therefore, κ_j is typically a power of 2. This implies that any wavelength in the set Λ can be converted into any other, provided that the number of such conversions is limited to κ_j. Note that this does not imply full wavelength conversion capabilities. In fact our problem reduces to the case of full wavelength conversion capability only when $\kappa_j = K$ for all j. In view of the cost of the OEO switch, we expect κ_j to be much smaller than K.

A request set $\mathcal{R} = \{(s_0, d_0), \cdots, (s_{|\mathcal{R}|-1}, d_{|\mathcal{R}|-1})\}$ is defined as a set of pairs s_i and d_i, of size $|\mathcal{R}|$, representing the source and destination nodes of the connections to be provisioned. We require $s_i \neq d_i$. From an element (s_i, d_i) (also called a connection) of the request set, we must construct a *lightpath* L_i, which is defined as a sequence of vertices $L_i = (s_i, I_i(1), I_i(2), \cdots, I_i(\ell_i), d_i)$, where $\{I_i(j); j = 1, \cdots, \ell_i\}$ represent intermediate nodes in the path from s_i to d_i for request i. Note that it is possible for ℓ_i to be zero. The size of a path

L_i is defined to be the number of vertices minus one, or the number of links contained in the path or $\ell_i + 1$. This definition of lightpath implies that any two adjacent nodes in a lightpath must be a valid link in $\mathcal{E}$.

The coloring of lightpath L is defined as the assignment of wavelength labels to all links of L. A valid coloring must fulfill the following conditions: (a) Every link belonging to each lightpath must be colored. (b) If two consecutive links in a lightpath are colored with different colors, say colors r and s, the node j attached to these two links must be capable of performing this wavelength conversion. This means that the value of κ_j must be greater than or equal to the number of lightpaths that require wavelength conversion at node j. (c) No two distinct lightpaths L_i and L_j, with a common link and in the same direction, can use the same wavelength at this common link. The problem now is to route and color each and every element of the request set so as to optimize one of the criteria mentioned earlier, subject to satisfying the three constraints stated above.

The global optimization problem (when all requests are considered together as in the off-line version of the problem) is NP-hard [3]. In the next section we formulate an integer linear programming (ILP) model with two objective functions: (1) minimize the number of wavelength conversions, and (2) minimize the hop count.

3.   Integer Linear Programming Model

In this section we first describe the OXC model. The nodes in the optical network are hybrid optical devices each consisting of a transparent optical (OOO) and a wavelength opaque (OEO) switch. This architecture is referred to as "hybrid cross-connect". Fig. 11.1 shows the architecture of a hybrid OXC.

Each hybrid node has several ports that are used as terminal points for both external and local add/drop links. Input links are terminated at input ports, and output links are originated from output ports. Local input (add) and output (drop) ports are the part of the OEO switch. We assume that the number of add ports and the number of drop ports are not limited and equal to the number of wavelength requests to be added and dropped at a given OXC, respectively. The number of input and output ports of OEO switch that are used for wavelength conversions when provisioning connections through the OXC is limited to κ ports. The number of input and output ports of OOO switch is limited.

As Fig. 11.1 shows, an optical connection can be provisioned through the hybrid OXC by one of the following ways:

OOO: From a non-local input port to a non-local output port through the OOO
        switch (*no wavelength conversion*);

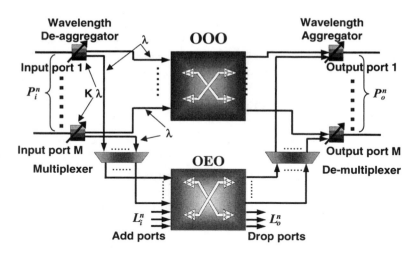

Figure 11.1.   Hybrid OXC architecture.

OEO: From a non-local input port to a non-local output port through the OEO switch (*wavelength conversion*). Note that the maximum number of wavelength conversions is limited to κ;

Drop: From a non-local input port to a local drop port through the OEO switch (*no wavelength conversion*);

Add: From a local add port to a non-local output port through the OEO switch (*no wavelength conversion*).

3.1   Notations

$\mathcal{V}$: Set of network nodes;

N : Number of network nodes;

J : Number of network links;

(n, m) : Link between node n and node m;

$\mathcal{A}(n)$: Set of adjacent nodes to node n;

$\mathcal{P}_i^n$: Set of input ports at node n where incoming links (m, n), $m \in \mathcal{A}(n)$ are terminated;

$\mathcal{P}_o^n$: Set of output ports at node n where outgoing links (n, m), $m \in \mathcal{A}(n)$ are originated;

$\mathcal{P}_i^{n,m}$: Input port at node n where an incoming link from node m is terminated; thus, $\mathcal{P}_i^n = \bigcup_m \mathcal{P}_i^{n,m}$;

$\mathcal{P}_o^{n,m}$: Output port at node n where an outgoing link to node m is originated; thus, $\mathcal{P}_o^n = \bigcup_m \mathcal{P}_o^{n,m}$;

$\mathcal{L}_i^n$: Set of local add ports at node n;

$\mathcal{L}_o^n$: Set of local drop ports at node n;

$\mathcal{PL}_i^n$: $\mathcal{P}_i^n \bigcup \mathcal{L}_i^n$. Set of all input ports (local and non-local) at node n;

$\mathcal{PL}_o^n$: $\mathcal{P}_o^n \bigcup \mathcal{L}_o^n$. Set of all output ports (local and non-local) at node n;

K : Number of wavelengths available in a WDM network;

Λ : Wavelength set $\Lambda = \{0, 1, \cdots, K-1\}$;

k, l, p : Wavelengths from set Λ;

κ_n : Maximum number of wavelengths which can be converted at node n;

η_n : Number of wavelengths converted at node n;

T : Number of node pairs having non-zero traffic demand;

c_t : Number of connection requests to be provisioned between the node pair (s_t, d_t), where s_t and d_t represent the source and destination node, respectively. Note that $0 \le t < T$;

$\mathcal{R}_t$: Set of connection requests $\mathcal{R}_t = \{r_t^0, \cdots, r_t^{c_t-1}\}$ of size c_t, to be provisioned between the node pair (s_t, d_t);

$\mathcal{R}$: Set of all connection requests $\mathcal{R} = \bigcup_t \mathcal{R}_t$, of size $|\mathcal{R}| = \sum_{t=0}^{T-1} c_t$, to be provisioned in a given network topology. Note that $\mathcal{R} = \{r_t^j : 0 \le t < T, 0 \le j < c_t\}$.

3.2   ILP Variables

The following variables describe the properties of the hybrid OXC node.

$W_{r_t^j,i,o}^{n,k,l}$: 1 if at node n a connection request r_t^j $(r_t^j \in \mathcal{R})$ uses wavelength k at input port i $(i \in \mathcal{PL}_i^n)$ and wavelength l at output port o $(o \in \mathcal{PL}_o^n)$; otherwise, it is 0;

The traffic at a node can be drop traffic, through traffic or add traffic. The variable $W_{r_t^j,i,o}^{n,k,l}$ represents drop traffic when $i \in \mathcal{P}_i^n$, $o \in \mathcal{L}_o^n$ (item "Drop"); through traffic when $i \in \mathcal{P}_i^n$, $o \in \mathcal{P}_o^n$ (item "OOO" or "OEO") or add traffic when $i \in \mathcal{L}_i^n$, $o \in \mathcal{P}_o^n$ (item "Add").

Before we define the optimization criteria and constraints, we analyze the number of variables $W^{n,k,l}_{r^j_t,i,o}$. From the range of indexes r^j_t, i, o, n, k, and l, it follows that the number of ILP variables grows approximately as $O(|\mathcal{R}|N(JK/N +|\mathcal{R}|/N)^2)$. In the following analysis we show how the number of ILP variables can be reduced. We examine all possible cases for provisioning a connection request in a hybrid OXC presented in Fig. 11.1.

Let us consider at node n a connection request r^j_t, which is the jth connection request between the node pair (s_t, d_t), $(0 \le t < T, 0 \le j < c_t)$. If node n is the source node of connection request r^j_t $(n = s_t)$, then only variables $W^{n,k,l}_{r^j_t,i,o}$ with indexes $i \in \mathcal{L}^n_i$, $o \in \mathcal{P}^n_o$, $k = 0$, and $l \in \Lambda$ should be consider in the ILP problem. Variables whose indexes i, o, and k are out of given ranges are identically equal to zero. Similarly, if node n is the destination node of connection request r^j_t $(n = d_t)$, then only variables $W^{n,k,l}_{r^j_t,i,o}$ with indexes $i \in \mathcal{P}^n_i$, $o \in \mathcal{L}^n_o$, $k \in \Lambda$, and $l = 0$ should be consider in the ILP problem. Variables whose indexes i, o, and l are out of given ranges are identically equal to zero. Finally, when node n is a "through" node for request r^j_t $(n \ne s_t, n \ne d_t)$, only variables with indexes $i \in \mathcal{P}^n_i$, $o \in \mathcal{P}^n_o$, $k \in \Lambda$, and $l \in \Lambda$ could have non-zero values. If we subtract those non-existing variables, we find that the total number of ILP grows approximately as $O(|\mathcal{R}|(N-2)(JK/N)^2)$, which is a smaller number than $O(|\mathcal{R}|N(JK/N + |\mathcal{R}|/N)^2)$.

The number of ILP variables can be further reduce by provisioning all connection requests between neighboring source and destination nodes on direct links only. For such requests no "through" nodes are considered, and the number of ILP variables is substantially reduced. Note that any solution that minimizes the number of wavelength conversions always attempts to provision requests between neighboring nodes on direct links, because that is the most effective way to utilize network resources.

3.3   Minimizing the Number of Wavelength Conversions

Let η_n be the number of wavelengths converted at node n (see item "OEO"). Our first objective is to minimize the total number of OEO conversions in a WDM network. A path using the smallest number of hops is favored when there is a tie between multiple paths with the same number of wavelength conversions. The first objective function, denoted as Ψ_1, is defined as

$$\Psi_1 = \min \sum_{n \in \mathcal{V}} [\eta_n + \epsilon \omega_n],\qquad(11.1)$$

where

$$\eta_n = \sum_{r^j_t \in \mathcal{R}} \sum_{i \in \mathcal{P}^n_i} \sum_{o \in \mathcal{P}^n_o} \sum_{k \in \Lambda} \sum_{l \in \Lambda, l \ne k} W^{n,k,l}_{r^j_t,i,o},\qquad(11.2)$$

$$\omega_n = \sum_{r_t^j \in \mathcal{R}} \sum_{i \in \mathcal{P}_i^n} \sum_{o \in \mathcal{PL}_o^n} \sum_{k \in \Lambda} \sum_{l \in \Lambda} W_{r_t^j, i, o}^{n,k,l}, \tag{11.3}$$

$$\epsilon < (KN)^{-1}. \tag{11.4}$$

In (11.1), η_n represents the number of OEO conversions at node n, and ω_n represents the number of active wavelengths on the input ports of the same node. The small constant ϵ is used for breaking ties between the paths with the same number of OEO conversions. Note that the sum $\sum_{n \in \mathcal{V}} \omega_n$ represents the total number of hops of provisioned requests. Also, in (11.1) only $W_{r_t^j, i, o}^{n,k,l}$ which are not identically equal to zero (see discussion in Section 3.2) are included in the sum.

3.4   Minimizing the Number of Hops

Our second objective is to minimize the number hops used. A path using the smallest number of conversions is favored when there is a tie between multiple paths with the same number of hops. The second objective function, denoted as Ψ_2, is defined as

$$\Psi_2 = \min \sum_{n \in \mathcal{V}} [\omega_n + \epsilon \eta_n], \tag{11.5}$$

where ω_n, η_n, and ϵ are given in (11.3), (11.2), and (11.4), respectively.

3.5   Constraints

In the formulation of the RWA ILP model, we first specify constraints on traffic flows. Let us consider a set of connection requests $\mathcal{R}_t = \{r_t^0, \cdots, r_t^{c_t-1}\}$ of size c_t, to be provisioned between the node pair (s_t, d_t). Then, the following constraints have to be satisfied at the source and destination nodes, respectively.

$$\sum_{r_t^j \in \mathcal{R}_t} \sum_{i \in \mathcal{L}_i^n} \sum_{o \in \mathcal{P}_o^n} \sum_{k \in \Lambda} \sum_{l \in \Lambda} W_{r_t^j, i, o}^{n,k,l} = c_t \quad n = s_t, \quad 0 \le t < T \tag{11.6}$$

$$\sum_{r_t^j \in \mathcal{R}_t} \sum_{i \in \mathcal{P}_i^n} \sum_{o \in \mathcal{L}_o^n} \sum_{k \in \Lambda} \sum_{l \in \Lambda} W_{r_t^j, i, o}^{n,k,l} = c_t \quad n = d_t, \quad 0 \le t < T. \tag{11.7}$$

Next, we specify the wavelength capacity constraint on both input and output ports of node n.

$$\sum_{r_t^j \in \mathcal{R}} \sum_{o \in \mathcal{PL}_o^n} \sum_{l \in \Lambda} W_{r_t^j, i, o}^{n,k,l} \le 1 \quad n \in \mathcal{V}, i \in \mathcal{P}_i^n, k \in \Lambda, \tag{11.8}$$

$$\sum_{r_t^j \in \mathcal{R}} \sum_{i \in \mathcal{PL}_i^n} \sum_{k \in \Lambda} W_{r_t^j, i, o}^{n,k,l} \le 1 \quad n \in \mathcal{V}, o \in \mathcal{P}_o^n, l \in \Lambda. \tag{11.9}$$

Let us now consider a link (m, n) connecting nodes m and n. Then, for any wavelength l $(l \in \Lambda)$ and request r_t^j $(r_t^j \in \mathcal{R})$ the wavelength continuity constraint on link (m, n) is defined as follows.

$$\sum_{r_t^j \in \mathcal{R}} \sum_{i \in \mathcal{PL}_i^m} \sum_{k \in \Lambda} W_{r_t^j, i, \mathcal{P}_o^{m,n}}^{m,k,l} - \sum_{r_t^j \in \mathcal{R}} \sum_{o \in \mathcal{PL}_o^n} \sum_{p \in \Lambda} W_{r_t^j, \mathcal{P}_i^{n,m}, o}^{n,l,p} = 0$$

$$n, m \in \mathcal{V}, l \in \Lambda. \qquad (11.10)$$

The constraint on the number of OEO conversions at node n (η_n) is defined as follows.

$$\sum_{r_t^j \in \mathcal{R}} \sum_{i \in \mathcal{P}_i^n} \sum_{o \in \mathcal{P}_o^n} \sum_{k \in \Lambda} \sum_{l \in \Lambda, l \neq k} W_{r_t^j, i, o}^{n,k,l} \leq \kappa_n \quad n \in \mathcal{V}. \qquad (11.11)$$

From (11.6) to (11.11) it follows that the total number of constraints grows approximately as $O(3JK)$.

The ILP model just presented can be used to solve RWA problems for networks whose lightpaths must be provisioned for a set of pre-defined requests. This is a common scenario on layered networks, where other circuit and packet technologies run on top of lightpaths. The ILP formulation above provides an efficient traffic engineering solution for avoiding costly wavelength conversion hardware, but it is unlikely to be used for solving large RWA problems with wavelength conversion. Also, in case on-line solutions of the RWA problem are needed, the ILP formulation developed is not applicable firstly because knowledge of the entire request set is not feasible, and secondly because even if that was the case, via reconfiguration of all lightpaths plus a new request, there might not be enough time to solve a large RWA problem every time a new request arrives. For these cases, we need to develop efficient heuristics. In the next two sections, we examine a class of algorithms with polynomial complexity, which are sequential. Sequential optimization problem is likely to occur in many optical networks where connection requests come in one at a time.

4.   Minimizing the Number of Wavelength Conversions

We first describe an algorithm to minimize the number of wavelength conversions used. If there are multiple ways in which this can be achieved, then the algorithm minimizes the length of the lightpath.

We start by renumbering the nodes of the network so that node 0 is the source and node $N - 1$ is the destination node of a lightpath. In the discussion to follow, we refer to this network as the *renumbered* network. Then we replace the renumbered network of N nodes by a *new* network of $(N-1)K+1$ vertices. Note that to avoid confusion between the renumbered and new networks, we use words like *node* and *link* in the context of the renumbered network and correspondingly, we use words like *vertex* and *edge* in the context of the new network throughout this paper. We define the set $V^* = \{1, \cdots, N-1\}$, *i.e.*, $V^* = V - \{0\}$. Node 0 of the renumbered network is left unchanged in the new network, *i.e.*, it is called vertex 0. However, every node j ($j \neq 0$) of the renumbered network is replaced by K vertices of the form $[j, k]$ for $k \in \Lambda$. Every link of the form (n, j) in the renumbered network is replaced by K^2 edges from vertex $[n, k]$ to vertex $[j, l]$ for $n, j \in V^*$ and $k, l \in \Lambda$ in the new network. A link of the form $(0, j)$ in the renumbered network is replaced by K edges from vertex 0 to vertex $[j, k]$ for $j \in V^*$ and $k \in \Lambda$ in the new network. Thus the new network has a total of $(J - |\mathcal{A}(0)|)K^2 + |\mathcal{A}(0)|K$ edges. This number is always upper bounded by JK^2. Fig. 11.2 shows an example of how to construct a new network from a renumbered network. In this example, $N = 4$ and $K = 2$. The renumbered network is shown on the top part of the figure and the corresponding new network is shown in the bottom part. Suppose we want to examine a path in the renumbered network from node 0 to node 1 and then to node 3, using wavelength 1 on the link (0,1) and wavelength 0 on link (1,3). This same path, in the new network is from vertex 0 to vertex [1,1] and then to vertex [3,0]. Notice how as a result of increasing the number of nodes and links in the network, we have been able to include in the vertex label all of the information about the wavelengths used in the path.

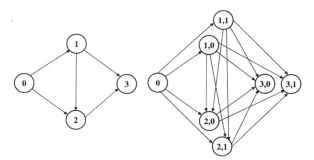

Figure 11.2. An example of a renumbered and new network with $N = 4$ and $K = 2$.

Consider the edge from vertex $[n, k]$ to vertex $[j, l]$ for $n, j \in V^*$ and $k, l \in \Lambda$ in the new network. The meaning of this edge is that if a path contains this link, then the path represents the use of wavelength l on the link (n, j) of the renumbered network and the use of wavelength k in entering node n. Referring to our example in Fig. 11.2, the edge from $[1, 0]$ to $[3, 1]$ in the new network represents the fact that wavelength 0 is used in entering node 1 and wavelength 1 is used in going from node 1 to 3 in the renumbered network. We now place a "cost" on each edge of the new network. The cost of the edge from vertex $[n, k]$ to vertex $[j, l]$ in the new network is denoted by $d(n, k; j, l)$, when $n, j \in V^*$

and $k, l \in \Lambda$. For example, if we are solving the problem of minimizing the number of wavelength conversions for the network of Fig. 11.2, the value of $d(1, 1; 3, 0)$ can be set to 1 to reflect the fact that one wavelength conversion has been used to switch from wavelength 1 to wavelength 0 at node 1. Similarly, for the same network, $d(2, 0; 3, 0) = 0$ to reflect the fact that no wavelength conversion is used. So, if the values of $d(n, k; j, l)$ are set in this manner, we can solve the problem of minimizing the number of wavelength conversions by simply solving a shortest path problem in the new network. There is, however, one difference. In the renumbered network, we are interested in finding an optimum path from node 0 to node 3. In the new network, we are interested in the shortest path from vertex 0 to any element of the set of vertices $\{[3, 0], [3, 1]\}$. In a general setting, this is equivalent to solving a shortest path problem from vertex 0 to the set of vertices of the form $[N - 1, k]$ for $k \in \Lambda$.

To summarize, by increasing the number of nodes and links, we have done away with the need for separately keeping track of the wavelengths and converted the problem to the well-known shortest path problem. Once we have done this, it is easy to see that the Dijkstra algorithm can be used directly on the new network.

Readers interested in the details of the Dijkstra algorithm are referred to [13]. A set $\mathcal{M}$ is used to keep track of the vertices closest to vertex 0. Starting with the empty set, in each iteration of step 4 below, a new vertex is added to the set $\mathcal{M}$. Further, $f(j, k)$ represents the current estimate of the smallest cost of the shortest path from vertex 0 to vertex $[j, k]$ of the new network, when we are restricted to the use of the vertices in the set $\mathcal{M}$ as intermediate nodes. The variables $\Gamma(j, k)$ and $\Pi(j, k)$ keep track of the wavelength used and the node number respectively in the step immediately prior to entering the vertex $[j, k]$ of the new network. Going back again to the example of Fig. 11.2, if the path from vertex 0 to vertex [1,0] and then to vertex [3,1] happens to be an optimal one, then $\Pi(3, 1) = 1$ and $\Gamma(3, 1) = 0$. We first explain the on-line algorithm.

On-line algorithm begin:

Step 1: For all $n, m \in \mathcal{V}$ and $k \in \Lambda$ define $\alpha_{nm}(k) = 1$, if wavelength k is available for use on that link, and 0 otherwise. Usually, $\alpha_{n,m}(k) = 1$ for $k = 0, \cdots, K - 1$ and $(n, m) \in \mathcal{E}$, unless for some reason, certain wavelengths are not available on some links (*e.g.*, out of service). Also, if $(n, m) \notin \mathcal{E}$, then $\alpha_{n,m}(k) = 0$. Let $\beta_k = 1$ for $k = 0, \cdots, K - 1$ - this variable is used to keep track of which wavelengths have been used by any request provisioned so far. Let H denote the total number of hops in all paths selected so far and initialize H to 0. Let ϵ denote a small quantity satisfying $\epsilon < (KN)^{-1}$. For all $j \in \mathcal{V}$, let $\mathcal{A}(j)$ be a subset of $\mathcal{V}$ containing nodes adjacent to node j, *i.e.*, $n \in \mathcal{A}(j)$ if and only if $(n, j) \in \mathcal{E}$. Let $\rho_j = \kappa_j$ for all $j \in \mathcal{V}$ represent the wavelength conversion capability at node j. Select the first request of the ordered request set.

Step 2: Renumber the nodes of the network so that the source node of the request under consideration is numbered 0 and the destination node is numbered $N - 1$. Since this renumbering is a permutation of the indices of the original network, permute the quantities $\alpha_{nj}(k)$, ρ_j and $\mathcal{A}(j)$ in a similar manner, for all $j, n \in \mathcal{V}$. Let the set $\mathcal{V}^* = \{1, \cdots, N - 1\}$, *i.e.*, $\mathcal{V}^* = \mathcal{V} - \{0\}$. Let $\mathcal{W}$ denote the set of all tuples of the form (n, k) where $n \in \mathcal{V}^*$ and $k \in \Lambda$. Let $\mathcal{M}$ denote a subset of $\mathcal{W}$ and initialize $\mathcal{M}$ to the empty set. For all $j \in \mathcal{V}^*$ and $k \in \Lambda$, let $\Gamma(j, k) = 0$ and $\Pi(j, k) = 0$.

Step 3: For all $n \in \mathcal{V}^*$, $j \in \mathcal{A}(n)$ and $k, l \in \Lambda$, let

$$d(n, k; j, l) = \begin{cases} \epsilon \text{ if } k = l \text{ and } \alpha_{nj}(l) = 1, \\ 1 + \epsilon \text{ if } k \neq l, \alpha_{nj}(l) = 1 \text{ and } \rho_n \geq 1, \\ \infty \text{ otherwise.} \end{cases} \quad (11.12)$$

Remark: As described earlier, $d(n, k; j, l)$ is the cost between vertices $[n, k]$ and $[j, l]$ in the new network. Notice that this link cost is set to a small value of ϵ for every link in the path to keep track of the number of hops for the lightpath. Thus a lightpath with m hops will have a cost of $m\epsilon$, if there are no wavelength conversions. This is done so that a path using the smallest number of hops is favored when there is a tie between multiple paths with the same number of wavelength conversions. Also note that the cost is $1 + \epsilon$ when a wavelength conversion is needed (the 1 accounts for the number of wavelength conversions and ϵ is needed to keep track of the number of hops). Finally, note that according to the definition, this cost is infinity in the following cases: (a) wavelength l is not available between nodes n and j or $\alpha_{nj}(l) = 0$ (this could happen if nodes n and j are not adjacent or if wavelength l has been used previously by some other request) and (b) nodes n and j are adjacent, but a wavelength conversion is needed and no wavelength conversion capability is available (ρ_n has dropped to 0).

For all $j \in \mathcal{V}^*$ and $k \in \Lambda$, let

$$f(j, k) = \begin{cases} \epsilon \text{ if } \alpha_{0j}(k) = 1, \\ \infty \text{ otherwise.} \end{cases} \quad (11.13)$$

Remark: As explained earlier, $f(j, k)$ represents the current estimate of the cost of the shortest path from vertex 0 to vertex $[j, k]$ in the new network. In this step, only the immediate neighbors of the source node with available wavelengths have a cost of ϵ, while all other nodes have a cost of infinity. Again, the small cost of ϵ is included in the cost to account for the fact that the path from vertex 0 to vertex $[j, k]$ (where node j is a neighbor of node 0) is exactly one hop long. This is used for breaking ties. Note also that there is no cost associated with wavelength conversion in this initializing step.

Step 4: Let

$$g = \min_{(j,k)\in \mathcal{W}-\mathcal{M}} f(j,k). \tag{11.14}$$

Let (μ,ν) be the value of (j,k) which minimizes (11.14). Resolve ties by first taking the lowest index of the j variable and if ties still remain, then the lowest index of the k variable. Let $\mathcal{M} \leftarrow \mathcal{M}\cup\{(\mu,\nu)\}$. If $\mu = N-1$ then go to step 5; otherwise continue. For all $j \in \mathcal{A}(\mu)$ and $k \in \Lambda$:

$$\text{if } (f(j,k) \quad > \quad f(\mu,\nu) + d(\mu,\nu;j,k)) \tag{11.15}$$
$$\text{then } \{f(j,k) \quad = \quad f(\mu,\nu) + d(\mu,\nu;j,k) \tag{11.16}$$
$$\Pi(j,k) \quad = \quad \mu \tag{11.17}$$
$$\Gamma(j,k) \quad = \quad \nu\}. \tag{11.18}$$

Repeat step 4.

Step 5: Let $m = 1$, $\xi_m = \mu$ and $\phi_m = \nu$. If $f(\xi_m,\phi_m) = \infty$, stop. There is no path available for this request. Select the next request (if any left) from the request set and go to step 2. Otherwise, continue.

$$\text{while } (\xi_m \quad \neq \quad 0)$$
$$\{m \quad \leftarrow \quad m+1$$
$$\phi_m \quad = \quad \Gamma(\xi_{m-1},\phi_{m-1})$$
$$\xi_m \quad = \quad \Pi(\xi_{m-1},\phi_{m-1})\}.$$

Remark: This step computes m, which is the number of nodes in the optimal path (including the source and destination nodes). This step also reconstructs the sequence of nodes and wavelengths used in the optimal path.

Step 6: Let $\alpha_{\xi_{j+1},\xi_j}(\phi_j) = 0$ for $j = 1,\cdots,m-1$. Let $\beta_{\phi_j} = 0$ for $j = 1,\cdots,m-1$. Let $\rho_{\xi_j} \leftarrow \rho_{\xi_j} - \Delta(\phi_{j-1},\phi_j)$ for $j = 2,\cdots,m-1$, where $\Delta(x,y) = 1$ if $x \neq y$ and 0 otherwise. Let $H = H + m - 1$. If requests are left, then pick a new request from the request set and go to step 2. If no requests are left, then stop.

End of the on-line algorithm.

For the request under consideration, the optimal lightpath consists of m nodes and equals $(\xi_m, \xi_{m-1}, \cdots, \xi_1)$, where $\xi_m = 0$ and $\xi_1 = N-1$. The wavelength used on the link (ξ_{i+1}, ξ_i) is ϕ_i for $i = 1,\cdots,m-1$. The number of wavelength conversions needed by the request under consideration is given by $\sum_{i=2}^{m-1} \Delta(\phi_{i-1},\phi_i)$. The variable β_k is 0 if wavelength k has been used by any request provisioned so far and it is 1 otherwise. Hence the number of wavelengths used by all the requests processed so far is given by $K - \sum_{k\in\Lambda}\beta_k$. The hop count for the request under consideration is given by $m - 1$. The hop count of all requests processed so far is given by H. The value of ρ_j for $j = 0,\cdots,N-1$ denotes the wavelength conversion capability still left at node

j, after the processing of all requests so far. This means that no wavelength conversion capability is left at node j if ρ_j has dropped to a value of 0. The value of $\sum_{k \in \Lambda} \alpha_{nm}(k)$ represents the total number of wavelengths left for use on the link (n, m) for all $n, m \in \mathcal{V}$, after taking into account the wavelengths used by all requests processed so far.

Let us now explain the off-line algorithm that is based on the on-line algorithm.

Off-line algorithm begin:

Step 1: First, find the shortest paths for all elements of the request set and then order the elements by the length of their shortest path in non-decreasing order. If ties remain, then order them further by the size of the request. If ties still remain, then order them further by the index of the source node, and then, if ties still remain, by the index of the destination node. Let $\rho_j = 0$ for all $j \in \mathcal{V}$. In other words, do not allow wavelength conversion capability at any node. Proceed with step 2.

Step 2: Sequentially process all ordered requests by the on-line algorithm. Then, set $\rho_j = \kappa_j$ for all $j \in \mathcal{V}$ so that wavelength conversion capability is now available at all nodes. Proceed with step 3.

Step 3: Use the on-line algorithm to process all requests which are blocked in step 2.

End of the off-line algorithm.

5. Minimizing the Hop Count

This method minimizes the number of hops used, one request at a time. If there are multiple ways in which this can be achieved, then it minimizes the number of wavelength conversions. The method of solving the problem is identical to the one presented in Section 4, except step 3, which should be changed to:

Step 3: For all $n \in \mathcal{V}^*$, $j \in \mathcal{A}(n)$ and $k, l \in \Lambda$, let

$$d(n, k; j, l) = \begin{cases} 1 & \text{if } k = l \text{ and } \alpha_{nj}(l) = 1 \\ 1 + \epsilon & \text{if } k \neq l, \alpha_{nj}(l) = 1 \text{ and } \rho_n \geq 1, \\ \infty & \text{otherwise.} \end{cases} \quad (11.19)$$

For all $j \in \mathcal{V}^*$ and $k \in \Lambda$, let

$$f(j, k) = \begin{cases} 1 & \text{if } \alpha_{0j}(k) = 1, \\ \infty & \text{otherwise.} \end{cases} \quad (11.20)$$

In this algorithm, the hop count metric is a simple one which adds a 1 for the use of each hop. Moreover, the use of the small quantity ϵ favors the use of those paths which have the lowest number of wavelength conversions, in case of ties in the hop count.

6.   Performance Analysis

In this section, we report on simulation results about the routing and wavelength assignment (RWA) algorithms for mesh WDM networks introduced earlier. The input of the simulator is the request set, the network topology, and various parameters. The output of the simulator is the provisioned lightpath for each request, which is specified as a sequence of links and their associated wavelength assignments. The simulator keeps track of blocked requests, *i.e.*, those for which no lightpaths could be found.

The performances of the following RWA algorithms are studied:

1 MinConv - minimizes the number of wavelength conversions, one request at a time. If there are multiple ways in which this can be achieved, then the algorithm minimizes the length of the lightpath. We consider the on-line and off-line versions of the MinConv algorithm.

2 MinHop - minimizes the number of hops used, one request at a time. If there are multiple ways in which this can be achieved, then the algorithm minimizes the number of wavelength conversions. Both versions of the algorithm are studied.

We first study how close to the best RWA solution each heuristic algorithm performs, by comparing its performance against the solution of the corresponding ILP formulation of the RWA problem, given in Section 3. Given the complexity of the ILP formulation, only small RWA problems can be handled. Large problems are dealt with in a subsequent subsection, where our heuristics are compared to one another.

6.1   Optimum RWA Solution and Our Heuristics

We use the NSF backbone optical network depicted in Fig. 11.3, which has $N = 14$ nodes and $J = 23$ bidirectional links (the average node degree is 3.29) to compare the performances of the MinConv and MinHop algorithms with the optimum solutions of the corresponding ILP problems, obtained by the CPLEX software tool. Each link has a capacity of 4 wavelengths in each direction ($K = 4$). The size of all OEO switches is set to $\kappa_j = 2$. A traffic matrix is randomly generated based on the uniform distribution. The number of lightpaths requested by any source-destination node pair is in the range $0 - 3$. We simulate different traffic load scenarios by varying the number of requests $|\mathcal{R}| = \{32, 48, 64\}$. We define the following two metrics: the total number of wavelength conversions in the network, denoted by Ω, and the hop count of all requests processed, denoted by H. The results are given in Table 11.1, in which each value for Ω and H is obtained by averaging results from 5 simulation runs.

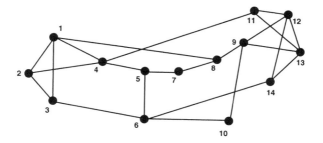

Figure 11.3.   14-node NSFNET network.

Table 11.1.   Results for the optimum and heuristic algorithms.

Metrics	Load		MinConv			MinHop	
Ω, H	$|\mathcal{R}|$	ILP	off-line	on-line	ILP	off-line	on-line
Ω	32	0.0	0.0	0.0	0.0	0.0	0.8
Ω	48	0.0	0.4	2.0	0.0	2.0	2.6
Ω	64	0.0	2.4	3.0	0.0	4.2	4.8
H	32	68.4	69.2	69.8	68.4	69.2	69.4
H	48	104.0	111.2	113.8	104.0	110.0	111.4
H	64	128.0	131.6	137.0	128.0	130.2	133.6

From Table 11.1, we see that the optimum solution obtained from the ILP model with the objective to minimize the number of wavelength conversion (see the MinConv ILP column) is identical to the optimum solution when the objective is to minimize the number of hops (see the MinHop ILP column). The total number of wavelength conversions under either version of the Min-Conv algorithm (off-line or on-line) is larger than the optimum one. The same happens for the hop count of all requests processed. The MinConv algorithm sequentially processes requests, as opposed to the ILP model, which considers all requests at once. Hence, the wavelength assignment under the MinConv algorithm is less efficient than the optimum one, what causes some unnecessary wavelength conversions. The performance of the MinHop algorithm in terms of the number of the wavelength conversions is slightly worse than that of the MinConv algorithm, but in terms of the hop count it is better than that of the MinConv algorithm. As expected, the off-line version of any algorithm processes the requests more efficiently than the on-line version.

6.2   Heuristics' Performance for Large RWA Problems

In the following text we study the previously described heuristic algorithms on two examples of larger networks. In the first example we consider a European optical network (EON) shown in Fig. 11.4, which consists of $N = 19$ nodes and $J = 38$ bidirectional links (the average node degree is 4.00). Each link has capacity of $K = 16$ wavelengths in each direction. The size of OEO switch is set to 2 ($\kappa = 2$), whereas OOO switches are non-blocking.

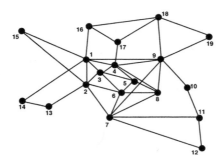

Figure 11.4.   19-node European optical network (EON).

We use two performance metrics for comparison of the RWA algorithms. The first parameter, denoted as η, is the average number of wavelength conversions per node. It is important to keep this metric low because it reduces the actual number of OEO ports used, so that the size of OEO switches is kept small. The second performance metric, denoted by γ, is the average number of hops per request, averaged over all provisioned requests. In both examples all connection requests were successfully provisioned.

In the first example, traffic matrices were generated based on the uniform traffic distribution. Source nodes and destination nodes were randomly selected for the following number of connection requests: $|\mathcal{R}| = \{128, 192, 256\}$. Simulation results for the average number of OEO conversions per node (η), and the average number of hops per request (γ) are shown in Table 11.2. Each value in Table 11.2 is an average of 10 simulations.

Table 11.2 shows that the smallest η is achieved under the off-line version of the MinConv algorithm, but that is only noticeable in the case of the traffic load of 256 requests. The MinConv algorithm minimizes the number of wavelength conversions and in that respect it performs slightly better than the MinHop algorithm. As expected, the off-line version of any algorithm shows a better performance than the on-line version, but the difference is very small. For all algorithms, η is much lower than 2, which is the size of OEO switches, and therefore, adding more of OEO switching capabilities would not yield a better network performance. The MinHop algorithm minimizes the hop count and in

Table 11.2. Results for η and γ in case of EON and uniform traffic distribution.

Metrics	Load	MinConv		MinHop	
η, γ	$\|\mathcal{R}\|$	off-line	on-line	off-line	on-line
η	128	0.000	0.000	0.000	0.000
η	192	0.000	0.000	0.000	0.005
η	256	0.018	0.021	0.153	0.163
γ	128	2.227	2.227	2.227	2.227
γ	192	2.232	2.238	2.232	2.237
γ	256	2.240	2.252	2.232	2.239

that respect it performs better than the MinConv algorithm. The results for γ in Table 11.2 show that the difference is only noticeable in the case of the traffic load of 256 requests. Again, the off-line version shows a better performance than the on-line version.

In the second example we study an American optical network (AON) shown in Fig. 11.5, which consists of 139 nodes and 156 bidirectional links (the average node degree is 2.24). Each link has capacity of 32 wavelengths in each direction. The size of OEO switch is set to 2 ($\kappa = 2$), whereas OOO switches are non-blocking. Traffic matrices were generated based on the Zipf traffic

Figure 11.5. 139-node American optical network (AON).

distribution [14]. In case of the Zipf distribution, the nodes in the network were randomly ranked and the amount of traffic (integer number of lightpath requests) destined for a particular node was set to be inversely proportional to its rank. A source node is then randomly selected for each request. The Zipf distribution is quite common in a wide variety of events (in particular, distribution of Web traffic among popular sites). We simulated different traffic load scenarios by varying the number of lightpath requests: $\|\mathcal{R}\| = \{256, 320, 384\}$. Simulation results are shown in Table 11.3, in which each value is an average of 10 simulations.

Table 11.3. Results for η and γ in case of AON and Zipf traffic distribution.

Metrics	Load	MinConv		MinHop	
η, γ	$|\mathcal{R}|$	off-line	on-line	off-line	on-line
η	256	0.012	0.029	0.095	0.123
η	320	0.045	0.070	0.198	0.238
η	384	0.135	0.177	0.343	0.396
γ	256	12.883	13.041	12.746	12.881
γ	320	12.996	13.223	12.767	13.082
γ	384	13.086	13.676	12.780	13.495

Table 11.3 confirms that the smallest η is achieved under the off-line version of the MinConv algorithm. Also, the off-line version of any algorithm shows a better performance than the on-line version. The OEO switches ($\kappa = 2$) proved to be large enough to handle required wavelength conversions. In general, η is always higher in case of the Zipf distribution than in case of the uniform distribution since in the former case fewer destination nodes receive more requests than in the latter case. Although the results for η in Table 11.2 and Table 11.3 correspond to two different network topologies, the same conclusion is derived when both traffic distributions are studied on either network. This is true for all four algorithms. The smallest γ is achieved under the off-line version of the MinHop algorithm. Table 11.3 shows that use of the sorting algorithm improves the performance of the off-line version of either algorithm.

We have simulated a lot more network topologies and traffic scenarios but due to limited space we are not able to present results from those experiments. The results presented in this paper as well as those not reported here show that if the objective of the network design is to minimize the cost of network switches, then the most suitable algorithm is the MinConv strategy. Otherwise, if the objective of the network design is to minimize the utilization of network links than the MinHop scheme is the most suitable solution. In general, both algorithms find a similar solution to the problem of routing and wavelength assignment of lightpath requests in WDM mesh networks. The off-line versions of the algorithms should be used when all connection requests are known in advance.

7. Conclusions

In this paper, we proposed two different optimization criteria to solve the RWA problem in mesh WDM networks: minimization of the wavelength conversions and minimization of hop count. For each of them, we developed a method of finding the *optimal sequential* solution for the on-line RWA problem, *i.e.,* one request at a time, by using a Dijkstra type algorithm. We also developed an ILP model with two different objective functions. Our unique ILP model can handle a detailed model of hybrid OXC nodes. The solution of the ILP model is a *globally optimal* solution for the off-line RWA problem, although it can only be obtained for relatively small networks, due to its exponential complexity. We found that the method which minimizes the number of wavelength conversions more efficiently uses the network switching resources while the RWA method which minimizes the hop count better utilizes the network links resources.

References

[1] R. Ramaswami and K. N. Sivarajan, "Optical Networks - A Practical Perspective", *Morgan Kaufmann Publishers, Inc*, 2002.

[2] R. Ramaswami and G. Sasaki, "Multiwavelength Optical Networks with Limited Wavelength Conversion", *IEEE/ACM Transactions on Networking*, vol. 6, no. 6, pp. 744-754, Dec. 1998.

[3] B. Mukherjee, "Optical Communication Networks", *McGraw-Hill*, New York, 1997.

[4] M. Alanyali and E. Ayanoglu, "Provisioning Algorithms for WDM Optical Networks", *IEEE/ACM Transactions on Networking*, vol. 7, no. 5, pp. 767-778, Oct. 1999.

[5] D. Banerjee and B. Mukherjee, "A Practical Approach for Routing and Wavelength Assignment in Large Wavelength-Routed Optical Networks", *IEEE Journal on Selected Areas in Communications*, vol. 14, no. 5, pp. 903-908, June 1996.

[6] A. Mokhtar and M. Azizoglu, "Adaptive Wavelength Routing in All-Optical Networks", *IEEE/ACM Transactions on Networking*, vol. 6, No. 2, pp. 197-206, Apr. 1998.

[7] A. E. Ozdaglar, and D. Bertsekas, "Routing and Wavelength Assignment in Optical Networks", *IEEE/ACM Transactions on Networking*, vol. 11, no. 2, pp. 259-272, Apr. 2003.

[8] Y. Xin, G. N. Rouskas, and H. G. Perros, "On the Physical and Logical Topology Design of Large-Scale Optical Networks", *IEEE Journal of Lightwave Technology*, vol. 21, no. 4, pp. 904-905, Apr. 2003.

[9] X. Cao, V. Anand, Y. Xiong, and C. Qiao, "A Study of Waveband Switching With Multilayer Multigranular Optical Cross-Connects", *IEEE Journal of Selected Areas of Communications*, vol. 21, no. 7, pp. 1081-1095, Sep. 2003.

[10] T. Cinkler, D. Marx, C. P. Larsen and D. Fogaras, "Heuristic Algorithms for Joint Configuration of the Optical and Electrical Layer in Multi-Hop Wavelength Routing Networks", in *Proceedings of IEEE Infocom 2000*, Mar. 2000, pp. 1000–1009.

[11] P-H. Ho and H. T. Mouftah, "Routing and Wavelength Assignment with Multigranularity Traffic in Optical Networks", *IEEE Journal of Lightwave Technology*, vol. 20, no. 8, pp. 1292-1303, Aug. 2002.

[12] I. Chlamtac, A. Farago and T. Zhang, "Lightpath (Wavelength) Routing in Large WDM Networks", *IEEE J. on Selected Areas of Communications*, vol. 14, no. 5, pp. 909-913, June 1996.

[13] T. H. Cormen, C. E. Leiserson and R. L. Rivest, "Introduction to Algorithms", *MIT Press*, Cambridge, Massachusetts, 1990.

[14] Y. Ijiri and H. A. Simon, "Skew Distributions and the Sizes of Business Firms", *North-Holland Publishing Company*, 1977.

Chapter 12

AN UNINFORMED BEST FIRST SEARCH BASED WAVELENGTH ASSIGNMENT ALGORITHM TO MINIMIZE THE NUMBER OF SONET ADMs IN WDM RINGS

J. Sethuraman, Ambuj Mahanti and Debashis Saha
Management Information Systems Group, Indian Institute of Management Calcutta, D.H. Road, Joka, Kolkata-700104, INDIA

Abstract: In WDM rings, determining the minimum number of ADMs is NP-Hard. The best known algorithm namely, least interference heuristic gives optimal results in only 77% cases. In this paper, we analyze the problem and propose an exact algorithm called uninformed best first search (UBFS). Computational experiments are provided.

Key words: WDM rings, ADM, Group path, UBFS

1.   INTRODUCTION

Wavelength division multiplexing (WDM) rings are increasingly deployed to support SONET/SDH self healing rings. One of the fundamental network design problem for WDM networks is the wavelength assignment problem. Wavelength assignment problem in optical networks is due to the wavelength division multiplexing technology employed in them. For setting up several lightpaths or connections that share a fiber, the bandwidth of the fiber needs to be partitioned into several channels. In each channel, the allotted bandwidth can be used at a unique wavelength which can be shared by many non-overlapping lightpaths. Many studies have attempted to address this problem[1-3]. However it has been observed that

- Most of the WDM systems are under deployed; meaning many wavelengths within a fibre are not fully utilized.
- TDM line terminal equipments like ADMs (Add/Drop Multiplexers) contribute heavily towards network cost[4,5].

Hence wavelength minimization which has been extensively studied in the past is no more attractive from a service provider's point of view. TDM line terminal equipments like ADMs cost as high as US $40,000 -$200,000[6]. In this paper we deal with the problem of minimizing the number of ADMs in WDM rings. In a WDM ring supporting multiple SONET/SDH rings, the SONET ADMs are needed to terminate lightpaths. Every lightpath requires two ADMs, one at each end of the lightpath. Although the origin node only needs the downstream ADM function and the termination node only needs the upstream ADM function, full ADMs are installed on both nodes to complete the protection path around the ring. The ADM minimization problem is to assign wavelengths to a set of lightpaths by making non-overlapping adjacent lightpaths share an ADM, thereby reducing the number of ADMs used. The task is to minimize the total number of ADMs used in the network. It has previously been shown that ADM and wavelength minimization are intrinsically different problems[4]. Though the problem has been proved to be NP hard[7] and there exist a number of fast heuristics, there is a need for an efficient formulation of the problem which can further reduce the number of ADMs in a reasonable amount of time. This paper tries to bridge this gap by giving an efficient formulation followed by an optimal algorithm to solve it. The algorithm suggested is of slowly growing exponential complexity. Since it is a one time investment decision facing the service providers during the pre-deployment stage of the WDM optical networks, a good quality solution can drastically reduce their CAPEX (CAPital EXpenditure) investment.

2.   PROBLEM DEFINITION

Two lightpaths, $LP_i = (s_i, t_i)$ and $LP_j = (s_j, t_j)$ can share an ADM if and only if the following two conditions are satisfied:
1. LP_i and LP_j are assigned the same wavelength,
2. LP_i and LP_j are adjacent lightpaths, i.e., $s_i = t_j$; or $s_j = t_i$.

Figures 12.1 and 12.2 show an example of ADM sharing. In figure 12.1, two lightpaths $LP_1 = (a, b)$ and $LP_2 = (b, c)$ are assigned different wavelengths and 4 ADMs are needed to support them. In figure 12.2, the ADM at node b is shared by both the lightpaths and in total only 3 ADMs are needed. Lightpaths (a, b) and (b, c) are assigned the same wavelength. Thus we find that proper wavelength assignment techniques are needed to minimize the requirement of ADMs.

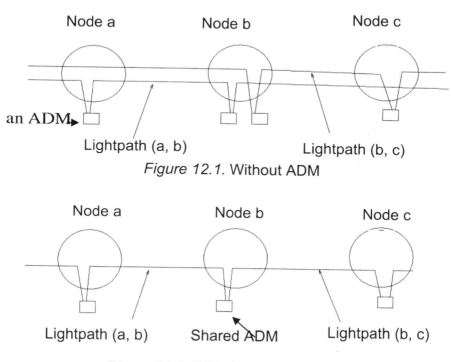

Figure 12.1. Without ADM

Figure 12.2. With ADM sharing

Liu et al.[7] show that the optimal wavelength assignment problem to minimize the number of SONET ADMs is NP-hard. In this paper we give a set covering formulation of the problem and propose an uninformed best first search algorithm to find the optimal number of ADMs. The paper begins with notation, definitions and comments on ADM sharing in Section 3. Related work is described in Section 4, followed by a discussion on our proposed study in Section 5. Section 6 gives a new problem formulation and presents an uninformed best first search algorithm. Section 7 talks about experimental setup and results. Section 8 provides conclusions and scope for future work.

3. NOTATIONS AND DEFINITIONS

Assume a Wavelength Division Multiplexed (WDM) ring network consisting of N optical nodes labeled from 0 to (N-1) in clockwise order. Let M be a set of lightpaths $\{(s_i, t_i) \ 1 \le i \le |M|\}$, where the lightpath (s_i, t_i) is the arc in a ring from s_i to t_i in clockwise direction. We call s_i the origin (or source) node and t_i the termination (or destination) node. A wavelength assignment to a set of lightpaths is valid if any two overlapping lightpaths are assigned different wavelengths. The assumption is that lightpaths can be routed only in clockwise direction.

We consider following assumptions as described in the earlier study[8].
1. The set of lightpaths is known apriori i.e. static wavelength assignment.
2. Lightpaths are routed clockwise on the ring.
3. A lightpath cannot be split.

3.1 Definitions

Adjacent lightpaths: Two lightpaths (s_i, t_i) , (s_j, t_j) are said to be adjacent if $s_i = t_j$; or $s_j = t_i$.

Length of a lightpath: The length of a lightpath $LP_i = (s_i, t_i)$ is; t_i-s_i if $t_i > s_i$; and $N + t_i$-s_i if $t_i < s_i$.

Group path: A group path is a collection of lightpaths such that:
- Every lightpath is an adjacent lightpath.
- No two lightpaths in a group overlap.

Circular group path: A circular group path is a group path in which collection of lightpaths form a complete circle; i.e. destination of the last lightpath will be the same as the source of first lightpath.

Non-circular group path: Any group path which is not a circular group path is called a non-circular group path.

Order of a group path: If a group path contains K lightpaths, it is called a group path of order K, where K ranges from 1 to the size of the ring i.e. N. Group paths of order 1 are individual lightpaths.

3.2 Comments on ADM sharing

Let the size of the ring be N; let the total number of lightpaths be denoted by M; let the total number of lightpaths in a group path, called its order, be denoted by K; let the total number of ADMs shared be denoted by ADM_{Sh}; and let the total number of ADMs used be denoted by ADM_{Us}.

We now make a set of propositions which are clear from the statements in most cases.

Proposition 1: The sum of number of ADMs used and the number of ADMs shared is twice the number of Lightpaths, i.e. $ADM_{Sh} + ADM_{Us} = 2M$.

Proposition 2: The upper bound on number of ADMs used (ADM_{Us}) is 2M.

Proposition 3: The number of ADMs shared (ADM_{Sh}) can never exceed M.

Proposition 4: The number of ADMs used (ADM_{Us}) should be at least M.

We can summarize the above propositions 1, 2, 3, and 4 as follows

$$0 \leq ADM_{Sh} \leq M,$$

$$M \leq ADM_{Us} \leq 2M.$$

Proposition 5: Each group path can have atmost N lightpaths.

Proposition 6: A group path with N lightpaths always forms a circular group path.

Proposition 7: A group path of order K can be a circular group path iff it uses K ADMs.

In a circular group path every lightpath has to share an ADM. It means they have to share as many ADMs as the number of lightpaths in the group path which is nothing but K.

Suppose if K ADMs are used, using proposition 1, we can say that it shares K ADMs. K ADMs can be shared only if every lightpath shares an ADM. This is possible only if the group path is circular.

Proposition 8: The number of ADMs used by a non-circular group path of order K is always (K+1).

Proposition 9: The number of ADMs shared is equal to number of ADMs used iff set of lightpaths form a circular group path.

4.   RELATED WORK

In deploying WDM rings, equipments like ADMs significantly contribute towards capital expenditure for service providers. Hence algorithms for minimizing the number of ADMs have generated significant interest in the last few years. There are some heuristic algorithms which have been proposed to solve this problem. But none of them can guarantee optimal solution in all cases. Presently there are 5 heuristics namely,

1. Cut-First[4]
2. Assign-First[4]
3. Iterative Merging[7]
4. Iterative Matching[7]
5. Breadth first least interference heuristic[8].

In Table 12.1 below, we give a brief description of each of these five heuristic methods.

HEURISTIC	DESCRIPTION/MERITS
Cut-First Heuristic[4]	This algorithm starts at some node and cuts all the lightpaths that pass through it into two segments. Then it sweeps the ring in a clockwise direction and whenever it encounters a lightpath that originates at some node k it strives to allocate a wavelength that has been used by another lightpath which had terminated before reaching node k.
Assign-First Heuristic[4]	The Assign-First wavelength assignment heuristic avoids ADM creation by skipping the cut step in the Cut-First algorithm. Initially, assign all lightpaths that originate at or crossover node 0. Then greedily node by node, from node 1 to node (N-1), as in the Cut-First assign the rest of the lightpath heuristic.
Iterative Matching[7]	Initially there are $|M|$ segments, with each segment consisting of one lightpath. At each step, at each node i a bipartite graph G_i (U_i, V_i, E_i) is constructed, where 1. U_i is the set of segments ending at node i; 2. V_i is the set of segments starting at node i; 3. For any $u \in U_i$ and $v \in V$ $(u_i, v_i) \in E_i$ if and only if u and v do not overlap with each other. Maximum matching of G_i is found. Then pick the node at which size of the maximum matching is the largest, and merge the segments according to the maximum matching at this node. This procedure is repeated until no matching can be found any more. This algorithm has polynomial run-time.
Iterative Merging[7]	At the beginning of the algorithm there are $|M|$ segments, with each segment consisting of one lightpath. At each step, one of the following three possible operations is performed in decreasing priority: Operation-1. Merge two non-circle segments into a circle segment. Operation-2. Split a noncircle segment into two non-circle segment and then merge one of them with another non-circle segment into a circle segment.0

	Operation-3. Merge two noncircle segments into a larger non-circle segment. Operation 1 decreases the number of non-circle segments by two and Operation 2 and Operation 3 both decrease the number of noncircle segments by one. Thus, the algorithm terminates after $\|M\|$ -1 steps.
Breadth First Least Interference Heuristic[8]	This algorithm is based on greedy breadth first technique where the algorithm tries to find as many circles as possible using the set of lightpaths.The algorithm consists of two steps • Fist step is to explicitly find as many circle segments as possible. • In the second step a heuristic called the least interference heuristic is used to find more lightpaths that can share ADMs This is the best known algorithm having complexity of $\|M\|^4$ and giving optimal result in 77% cases.

Table 12.1. Summary of existing algorithms

Studies have shown that iterative merging algorithm is about 40% more effective than assign-first heuristic and about 10% more effective than the iterative matching heuristic[7]. Breadth first least interference heuristic[8] is the only heuristic that has been compared with optimal solution and gives optimal results in 77 % of the cases.

5.   PROPOSED STUDY

Observation: *Circle forming strategy doesn't ensure optimal result always.*

The Breadth first least interference technique[8,9] always tries to find as many circles as possible in a greedy manner. It might miss out those circles that lead to optimal solution because the algorithm doesn't do an exhaustive search[8].Even iterative merging algorithm[7] also gives highest priority to circle formation.

However authors have failed to notice that Circle forming strategy by itself doesn't lead to optimal solution always. We here prove that non-circular group paths can at times give optimal result which makes the problem hard to solve.

Lemma: *Non-circular group paths can at times give optimal solution than circle forming strategy*[7,8]

Proof: There may be possibilities of non-circular group paths which may be optimal.

(E.g.) Given T= {(0, 1), (0, 5), (1, 3), (1, 8), (4, 0), (6, 8), (7, 2), (8, 0))

Using BFLI, Iterative merging the result will form a circle using (0, 1), (1, 8), (8, 0).The rest of the lightpaths can't share any ADMs.So the total count of ADM is 13. Whereas there is a better solution to this problem by merging following lightpaths;

(6,8), (8,0),(0,5) & (0,1),(1,3), (4,0).

Therefore the total count of ADMs is only 12. Hence non-circular group paths may give better solutions than circular group paths.

□

We now propose a new exact best first search based technique to solve the problem of minimizing of number of ADMs in WDM rings. Our algorithm contains two steps:

1. Formation of group paths.
2. Select a feasible set with a minimum number of ADMs, where a feasible set is a collection of group paths such that every lightpath occurs only once in the total collection of group paths.

We show experiments results of UBFS in comparison with two of the five algorithms mentioned in Section 4, namely Iterative Merging and Breadth First Least Interference (BFLI) Heuristic. The reasons for choosing these two algorithms are:

- BLFI performs the best among all the five and gives optimal results in 77% cases[8].
- Iterative Merging is 40% more effective than Assign-First Heuristic and about 10% more effective than Iterative Matching[7].

5.1   Algorithm to form group paths

Our algorithm to form all possible group paths is very similar to the algorithm of forming all possible circles as explained in an earlier study[8].We will now describe the procedure for finding all the group paths starting from each lightpath.

Find_All_Group_Paths (lightpath: startpath)

(1) Create a segment, S, containing startpath.

(2) Insert S into the queue

(3) While (queue is not empty) do

(4)   Seg = dequeue ()

(5)   Let Seg.start be the starting node of Seg.

         Let Seg. end be the ending node of Seg

(6)   for each lightpath p that starts from Seg.end do

(7)   if (p and Seg form a circular group path) then

(8)   Put the circle in a list called CLOSED.

(9)   else

             if (p is adjacent with Seg) then

(10)   Merge p and Seg to form 'p + Seg'

               insert 'p + Seg' into the queue

               Put 'p + Seg' in CLOSED.

(11)   end if

(12)   end if

(13)   end for

(14) end while

5.1.1   Example for formation of group paths

To find all group paths which begin from a given lightpath, the algorithm takes the lightpath as a parameter and determines if there are group paths that can be formed beginning from the lightpath.

Consider the following set of lightpaths {(2,4), (4,6), (5,1), (7,3)}.Then the steps for group path formation algorithm are as follows:

  i.   Create a segment S, containing the first lightpath (2,4) as startpath.

  ii.   Put S into the queue.

  iii. If the queue is non-empty then do the following steps,

  iv.   Deque () the first element from the queue and call it as Seg.

  v.   Consider the Seg = (2,4), where Seg.start =2 & Seg.end =4.

vi.   For every lightpath p starting with Seg.end i.e. 4, do the following steps.

vii.   There is no possibility for circular group path formation with Seg = (2,4).

viii.   Nothing is put in CLOSED since no circle is formed from Seg= (2,4).

ix.   Else look for a lightpath p such that p is adjacent with Seg. We find a lightpath p i.e. (4,6) is adjacent with Seg= (2,4).

x.   Merge Seg = (2,4) and p i.e. (4,6).Put 'p + Seg' i.e. [(2,4) (4,6)] in a list called CLOSED and insert it into the queue.

xi.   End of step (x).

xii.   End of step (ix).

xiii.   End for at step (vi).

Next pass of the loop at (iii)

iv   Deque () first element from the queue and call it as Seg i.e. Seg = (2,6) .

v   Consider the Seg = (2,6), where Seg.start =2 & Seg.end =6.

vi   For every lightpath p starting with Seg.end i.e. 6, do the following steps.

vii   We find no possibility for circular group path formation with Seg = (2,6).

viii   Nothing is put in CLOSED since no circular group path is formed from Seg= (2,6).

ix   Else look for a lightpath p that is adjacent with Seg. We do not have any lightpath p which is adjacent to Seg= (2,6).

x   Nothing is inserted into the queue.

xi   End of step (x).

xii   End of step (ix)

xiii   End for at step (vi).

iii   Now the queue is empty, so we have finished finding all possible group paths starting from a single lightpath (2,4).

Repeat the steps for the rest of the lightpaths (4,6),(5,1) and (7,2).We find that there is no possibility of additional group paths starting with (4,6).Similar is the case with remaining lightpaths (5,1) and (7,2). Finally we have set of all group paths in CLOSED as follows : [(2,4),(4,6)], [(2,4)], [(4,6)], [(5,1)], [(7,3)].

6.   PROBLEM FORMULATION

M: $M = \{1, 2, 3...\}$ is a finite set of lightpaths.
S: S is the set of all group paths G_j, $j \geq 1$
$N = |S|$

Consider a tuple $T_j = (G_j, C_j)$, where G_j is a group path and C_j is the number of ADMs for this group path. Let $x_j = 1$ if the jth group path in S with cost C_j is selected and $x_j = 0$, otherwise. Define a_{ij} to be 1 if the jth group path in S contains the element (lightpath) $i \in M$. The problem of minimizing the number of ADMs can now be formulated as a set covering problem as follows:

$$Min \sum_{j=1}^{N} C_j x_j$$
$$s.t. \sum_{j=1} a_{ij} x_j = 1 \ \forall i \in M$$
$$x_j = 0,1; \ G_j \in S; 0 \leq j \leq N.$$

6.1   State space description

State or Node (n): A set of non-overlapping group paths is called a state or node 'n'.
Start node (s): Null.
Child of a node n: A node containing all the group paths present in n and augmented with another non-overlapping group path.
A goal node: A set of non-overlapping group paths covering all the light paths.

6.2   Uninformed Best First Search (UBFS)

The UBFS works much in the similar way as the A* (A star) algorithm[10,11]. It however does not have a heuristic function to estimate its proximity with a goal state/node.

6.3   UBFS Algorithm

1. *Put all group paths as nodes in a list called open.*
2. *While open is not empty*
   - *Select a node n from open, which has minimum average number of ADMs per lightpath.*
   - *If n is goal node then stop, else remove n from open and put it in a list called CLOSED. Generate the children of n and put them in open.*

6.4   Optimality proof

UBFS starts with a list of all possible group paths, and then builds search trees out of each explored node (initially each node contains one possible group path) by creating children that contain exactly one additional non-overlapping group path. By always selecting the node with minimum average number of ADMs to be explored next, the algorithm is guaranteed to reach the optimal solution.

6.5   State space formulation with an example

Consider the following set of lightpaths {(2,4) , (4,6) , (5,1) ,(7,3)} Following is set of all group paths [(2,4),(4,6)], [(2,4)], [(4,6)], [(5,1)], [(7,3)] generated from given lightpaths (using the procedure in sub-section 5.1). Figure 12.3 depicts the state space.

UBFS (Uninformed Best First Search Algorithm):

1. All the group paths [(2,4),(4,6)], [(2,4)], [(4,6) ,[(5,1)], [(7,3)] are put in open.
2. Group path [(2,4),(4,6)]$^{3/2}$, which requires minimum average number of ADMs, is selected first. It is put in CLOSED. Then we generate its children [(2,4),(4,6),(5,1)] & [(2,4),(4,6),(7,2)] and put them in open.
3. The search continues in this fashion and finally a goal node [(2,4)(4,6),(5,1),(7,3)]$^{7/4}$ is selected and then the search terminates. The optimal number of ADMs needed for the problem is 7.

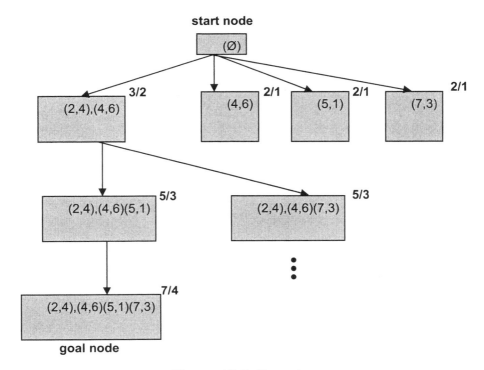

Figure 12.3. Search space

7.   EXPERIMENTAL SETUP AND RESULTS:

To evaluate the performance of the algorithms, we conducted experiments on a 1.6 GHz Pentium IV machine with 1GB RAM. We are assuming that the network consists of 16 nodes (16 is recommended for SONET rings). Now for problems of varying size (i.e. with different number of lightpaths), we randomly generate lightpaths with source and destination pairs. In this process we have used the lightpath generator used by Xin Yuan et al[8].The results reported in Table 12.2 are average of 25 randomly generated problems of each size. The first column shows the problem size i.e. the number of lightpaths.The second, third, and fourth columns show average number of ADMs obtained by Iterative Merging, Least Inference Heuristic, and UBFS algorithms respectively. Fifth column shows the average time taken by UBFS to reach the optimal solution.

It is found that UBFS always outperforms the existing heuristics in terms of average number of ADMs needed. This is true for all our experiments which include problems of size ranging from 8 to 30 lightpaths.

Number of LPs	Avg ADM by Iterative Merging Algorithm	Avg ADMs by Least Inference Heuristic	Avg ADMs by UBFS Algorithm
8	12.9	12.8	12.7
10	16.2	16.0	15.8
15	24.75	24.55	24.3
20	33.2	33.0	32.8
25	39.65	39.4	39.15
30	47.75	47.35	47.1

Table 12.2. Experimental results

The two heuristics Iterative Merging and Least Interference have been so designed that they take greedy steps to arrive at some sub-optimal solution almost immediately and requiring little storage.UBFS on the other hand require few seconds to few minutes to run for problems of sizes 8-30 lightpaths as shown in the table above. UBFS ensures optimality by always making node selections on the basis of minimum average number of ADMs and hence it is always bound to require more memory than the existing techniques. The results seem encouraging and the challenge is to modify UBFS so that it can give quick optimal solutions for problems of much larger size.

8.   CONCLUSION

Efficient wavelength assignment algorithms have to be developed to minimize the system cost in WDM rings. We have suggested an uninformed best first search algorithm that always finds optimal number of ADMs. Future scope of this work should be aiming to develop informed search based algorithms to handle huge number of Lightpaths.We hope this paper would motivate to deploy A* type efficient Artificial Intelligence (AI) algorithms[10] to solve similar problems.

REFERENCES

[1] R. Barry and P. Humblet, "Models of Blocking Probability in All-Optical networks with and without Wavelength Changers", *IEEE JSAC: Special Issue on Optical Networks*, vol. 15, no. 5, pages 858-867, 1996.

[2] I. Chlamtac, A. Ganz and G. Karmi, "Lightnets: Topologies for High-Speed Optical Networks", *IEEE/OSA Journal on Lightwave Technology*, vol. 11, No.5/6, pages 951-961, 1993.

[3] M. Kovacevic and A. Acampora, "Benefits of Wavelength Translation in All Optical Clear-Channel Networks", *IEEE JSAC: Special Issues on Optical Networks*, vol. 14, no. 5, pages 868-880, 1996.

[4] O. Gerstel, P. Lin and Sasaki "Wavelength Assignment in a WDM Ring to Minimize Cost of Embedded SONET Rings", *IEEE INFOCOM*, pages 94-101, 1998.

[5] O. Gerstel, G. Sasaki and R. Ramaswami, "Cost Effective Traffic Grooming in WDM Rings", *IEEE INFOCOM*, pages 69-77, 1998.

[6] A. Tofanelli, M. De Bartoli, R. Girardi, G.Guerricchio, "Fixed Network access technology olutions",*telecomitalialab.com* Report, 2001.

[7] L. Liu, X. Li, P Wan and O. Frieder, "Wavelength Assignment in WDM Rings to Minimize SONET ADMs", *IEEE INFOCOM*, pages 1020-1025, 2000.

[8] Xin Yuan and Amit Fulay, "Wavelength Assignment to Minimize the Number of SONET ADMs in WDM Rings," *Journal of Photonic Network Communications*, Volume 5, Number 1, pages 59-68, January 2003.

[9] Xin Yuan and Amit Fulay, "Wavelength Assignment to Minimize the Number of SONET ADMs in WDM Rings", *IEEE International Conference on Communications*, pages 2917-2921, 2002.

[10] Dechter, R., and Pearl, J, "Generalized Best-First Search Strategies and the Optimality of A*", *Journal of the Association for Computing Machinery*, Vol. 32, No. 3, pp. 505-536, 1985.

[11] Bagchi, A. and Mahanti, A, "Search Algorithms under Different Kinds of Heuristics – A Comparative Study", *Journal of the Association for Computing Machinery* Vol.30, No.1, pp. 1-21, 1983.

Chapter 13

DISTRIBUTED CONTROL OF FLOW ON NETWORKS OF GENERAL TOPOLOGY

Yi-Ju Chao and Blaise Morton
Morton Consulting Corporation, Minnetonka, MN, USA

yiju@mortoncorp.com

blaise@mortoncorp.com

Abstract   This paper presents a routing control method for packet-switched networks using an algebraic-topological framework. Our approach is a two-step paradigm. The outer loop control finds the global optimal steady-state routing strategy consistent with the average network inputs and outputs. The inner-loop control corrects for deviations from the steady-state flow by using high-bandwidth, real-time feedbacks of queueing states. The resulting formulation in the algebraic-topological framework allows us to find acyclic (loop-free) stable solutions that are optimal with respect to cost functions. We show how these optimal solutions may be computed using distributed algorithms, where each node updates its own routing table autonomously based on local information. Simulation results for 10-node and 100-node examples are shown to validate the algorithm concept.

Keywords: Distributed control, Routing, Quadratic cost function, Steady-state routing strategy, Dynamic inversion, Algebraic topology, Graph theory

1.   Introduction

We consider routing problems for packet-switched networks. This type of problem is abstracted into a graphical model with a typical network structure. We assume a network is composed of nodes and links interconnecting them. Multiple classes of packets are routed through the network. Each packet enters the network through a node, which is called the source node for the packet, and is destined to another node where it leaves the network. A packet enters into the network without pre-defined route to its destination node. For a string of packets, a node may be a source node, a destination node, or, if neither of these, a router. Each node has its own routing table to decide the route of each packet as a function of destination node as well as class.

Our approach to design the routing policy for packet-switched networks is a two-step paradigm:

1. Outer-loop control - find the global optimal steady-state routing strategy consistent with the average network inputs and outputs.

2. Inner-loop control - correct for deviations from the steady-state flow by using high-bandwidth, real-time feedback of queueing states.

This control framework is proposed in our earlier paper [1]. That paper introduces an algebraic-topological framework to describe network models. In it we show that the steady-state routing solution is characterized by a manifold of dimension $L = M - N + 1$ (i.e. Euler's Formula) where M is the number of links and N is the number of nodes. A general global optimal cost function is solved over the L-dimensional manifold. Furthermore, a dynamic-inversion strategy to correct the deviations from the steady-state flows is proposed.

In this paper we extend the control method in two directions:

1. A systematic way to solve the global optimal steady-state routing solutions for quadratic cost functions on networks of general topology.

2. A system of distributed algorithms which implements the above control paradigm, where each network node updates its own routing table autonomously based on local information.

In the first direction we design a first-order dynamic system which has trajectories on the space of cycles, a subspace of the link space, which we formally call the space of 1-chains. The system drives the states of the network to an equilibrium that optimizes a cost function. The algebraic-topological structure provides the geometric framework in which the tangent vector to the flow is the projection of the gradient of the cost function in the space of cycles. Here we consider only quadratic cost functions, the result for general cost functions will be developed in a later paper.

In the second direction we generate distributed algorithms by taking advantage of the local operators that arise in algebraic topology, namely the boundary operator, coboundary operator, and Laplacian. There are two parts to the system of distributed algorithms. One part of the algorithm is to obtain routing tables at each network node so that network flows will achieve optimal network performance. For this purpose, we introduce the concept of "potential" functions distributed on network nodes. The potential functions are analogous to the potential functions of electric-circuit networks [10]. At every iteration step, a node computes its own potential value, and then uses its own potential value and those of its neighbor nodes to compute the directions and the magnitudes of network flow on its neighbor links. This computation does not need to be performed synchronously by the network nodes. The potential function on the nodes is not unique, so the iterative algorithm does not always provide a convergent series for the potential. The iterative algorithm does provide a convergent series for the flows on the links, however. The convergence is proved in our main theorems 13.13 and 13.14.

The other part of the system is to obtain a routing adjustment at each node to compensate for the variation of traffic input. The objective is actually to load-balance queues among network nodes. We use the Laplacian, which is a local operator, to achieve this objective. This inner-loop adjustment can be computed asynchronously. The use of graph or weighted Laplacian to achieve load-balanced queues at nodes is an established technique for parallel and distributed computing systems in computer science, for example, [21], [22], [19]. Recently the graph Laplacian has also been used to reach consensus between network nodes in control of vehicle formation problems, for example, [23], [24], and [25].

We further show that our routing solution, computed by the proposed system of distributed algorithms, produces acyclic flows, even though distributed algorithms are applied to obtain the routing tables. This is due to a graceful connection between the node space and link space arising as a consequence of the adjoint relation between the boundary and coboundary operators.

Our approach is more flexible than the traditional Multicommodity Flow Problem applied to routing problems for data networks [3], [4], [5], [6], [7], etc. This multicommodity flow approach to the network routing problem is to optimize the cost of flow from source node to target node with respect to a cost function, which usually represents the delay on the selected path. Our formulation distinguishes packets by their target nodes, but not their source nodes. We see this as a more natural formulation of packet-switched networks because routers do not need to have the knowledge of the whole path of a packet and, at minimum, only need to know target-node addresses for forwarding the packet. In our method optimal flow solutions on links for general cost functions are obtained without the restriction of single-path routing. The optimal solution may even take advantage of multi-path routing. We can also accommodate, if desired, end-to-end in-sequence delivery for a packet flow. One way to achieve this is to have the router read a flow identifier and forward packets of the same flow to only one downstream node, while the router assigns packets of different flows to different downstream nodes proportionally, so that the flows of steady-state routing solutions are well approximated.

Our algorithm can be implemented with little more information than is used in the Bellman-Ford algorithm, Dijkstra's algorithm, and the Floyd-Warshall algorithm [2]. All these methods can be implemented in distributed algorithms and only require minimal control information exchanged, mainly between neighbor nodes. Bellman-Ford and Dijkstra's algorithms are asynchronous while our algorithm is partly asynchronous. In our approach, the header of each packet requires the same minimum amount of information necessary for the purpose of routing – the address of its destination node. The only extra information we assume, compared with the referenced methods, is some estimate of expected flow between sources and destinations. We make good use of this information if we have it, but we can use a default (light-loading) assumption if no information is available.

The problems of end-to-end flow control and admission control based on the proposed control methodology are not addressed in this paper. In our view, these types of control should be based on the performance requirements of the underlying network layer. In reality, routers more adapted to traffic conditions tend to update routing tables more often; therefore, an end-to-end flow may often change its path, even for OSPF. It may be possible to use established techniques, for example, utility and/or pricing models for end-to-end flow control, [12], [13], [14], [15] in our network design. If so, the equivalence between different network formulations for packet-switched networks, the path-link matrices adopted in the references and our algebraic-topological formulation, should be established.

We specifically address the case of quadratic cost functions on network links. First, a closed-form routing solution for quadratic cost functions can be obtained because the topological structure of the graph makes easy to work with quadratic cost functions. Secondly, if we view weights on network links as resistance in electric-circuit networks and network flows as currents, the quadratic cost function on network links is an analogous to the dissipated power of electric-circuit networks. This type of cost function is the simplest to analyze and requires less computational complexity in this framework. See [16] for a broad view of quadratic cost functions applied to networks.

This paper is organized as follows. Section 2 introduces fundamental notation and theory of algebraic topology. Section 3 considers the optimization problem for a nominal steady-state routing solution. Quadratic cost functions are discussed separately. Section 4 presents the dynamic-inversion method. Distributed control algorithms for computing the nominal steady-state routing solution and the dynamic routing adjustments are respectively presented in Section 5. Section 6 shows simulation results on aperiodic networks and bipartite networks. The results are summarized in Section 7.

2.   Network Theory

The network considered is abstracted into a topological graph G with N nodes and M links interconnecting them.

Our description of graphs is based on standard graph-theoretic concepts [8], [9]. Basic notation is presented in our early paper [1]. In this paper the notation of algebraic-topological network theory is extended to a scaled version by considering general weights on links, which might represent bandwidths or cost functions or other such things. The scaled algebraic-topological notation naturally brings up interesting theorems that will be helpful to our control strategy.

Let the N nodes be labelled by $a(i)$ for $i = 1, \cdots, N$. Nodes $a(i)$ for $i = 1, \cdots, N$ are connected by links $b(j)$ for $j = 1, \cdots, M$. We do not allow a link $(a(i), a(i))$ leading from a node to itself, so all the links are of the form $b(j) = (a(j_1), a(j_2))$ with $j_1 \neq j_2$.

We will distinguish $(a(j_1), a(j_2))$ and $(a(j_2), a(j_1))$; the distinction is a matter of orientation. Packets can flow in either direction through any link. The choice of orientation can be changed at will, in order to suit whatever problem is studied, but a standard default is that the link $b(j) = (a(j_1), a(j_2))$ is *directed positively* if and only if $j_1 < j_2$. To represent a message flow from $a(j_2)$ to $a(j_1)$ on link $(a(j_1), a(j_2))$ with $j_1 < j_2$, we use a negative coefficient whose magnitude represents the amount of flow.

The flows of networks are described in the following graph theoretic language. Let C_0 denote the set of zero-chains, defined to be the set of all summations (13.1)

$$C_0 = \{\sum_{i=1}^{N} f(i)a(i) \,|\, f(i) \in \mathbf{R}\}, \tag{13.1}$$

where the coefficients $f(i)$ lie in the set of real numbers $\mathbf{R}$. Let C_1 denote the set of 1-chains, defined to be the set of all summations (13.2)

$$C_1 = \{\sum_{i<j}^{N} g(i,j)(a(i), a(j)) \,|\, g(i,j) \in \mathbf{R}\}, \tag{13.2}$$

where the coefficients $g(i,j)$ lie in the set of real numbers $\mathbf{R}$. Notice that in (13.2) the summation is over the $\frac{N(N-1)}{2}$ terms because of $i < j$. An important defining condition for C_1 is that the coefficient $g(i,j)$ must be zero when $a(i)$ and $a(j)$ are not connected by links. For oriented models we identify $(a(i), a(j)) = -(a(j), a(i))$.

Each link $(a(i), a(j))$ is associated with a positive constant, $B_{ij} = B_{ji} > 0$, representing the bandwidth or the "weight" of the link. For a pair of nodes $a(k)$ and $a(l)$ without a link connecting them we let $B_{kl} = 0$; otherwise $B_{kl} > 0$.

For given $B = (B_{ij})$, there are two important linear operators between the spaces C_0 and C_1. The *boundary* operator $\partial_B : C_1 \mapsto C_0$ and the *coboundary* operator $\delta_B : C_0 \mapsto C_1$ are defined by (13.3) and (13.4), respectively,

$$\partial_B(\sum_{i<j}^{N} g(i,j)(a(i),a(j))) = \sum_{i<j}^{N} g(i,j)B_{ij}(a(j) - a(i)) \qquad (13.3)$$

and

$$\delta_B(\sum_{i=1}^{N} f(i)a(i)) = \sum_{i=1}^{N} \sum_{a(j)\in N(a(i))} f(i)B_{ij}(a(j),a(i)), \qquad (13.4)$$

where $N(a(i)) = \{a(j)|a(j)$ is a neighbor node of $a(i)\}$. The neighbor nodes of $a(i)$ are those nodes $a(j)$ that share a link with the node $a(i)$. For the case that $B_{ij} = 1$ for a connected pair of nodes $a(i)$ and $a(j)$ and $B_{ij} = 0$ for a disconnected pair of nodes $a(i)$ and $a(j)$, the above defined operators are consistent with the standard boundary operator, ∂, and the standard coboundary operator, δ, respectively, [8] and [9].

The relation of the scaled operators defined in this paper to the standard operators is established in the following lemma.

LEMMA 13.1 *For any $B = (B_{ij})$ with $B_{ij} = B_{ji} \geq 0$, the following are satisfied:*

1 $\forall X \in C_1$, $\partial_B(X) = \partial(B.*X)$

2 $\forall Y \in C_0$, $\delta_B(Y) = B.*\delta(Y)$

where for $A, B \in C_1$, $A.*B$ denotes the element-by-element product of A and B.

Proof. Easy computation.

We introduce inner products $<,>_0$ on C_0 and $<,>_1$ on C_1 by definitions (13.5), (13.6)

$$< a_i, a_j >_0 = \begin{cases} 1, & if \ i = j \\ 0, & otherwise \end{cases} \qquad (13.5)$$

and

$$< (a_i,a_j),(a_k,a_l) >_1 = \begin{cases} 1, & if \ i = k, j = l, for \ i < j, k < l \\ 0, & otherwise \end{cases} \qquad (13.6)$$

and extending linearly, i.e., for

$$F = \sum_{n=1}^{N} f(n)a(n) \in C_0$$

and

$$G = \sum_{n=1}^{N} g(n)a(n) \in C_0,$$

we have

$$< F, G >_0= \sum_{n=1}^{N} f(n)g(n), \qquad (13.7)$$

and for

$$H = \sum_{n<m}^{M} h(n,m)(a(n), a(m)) \in C_1$$

and

$$K = \sum_{n<m}^{M} k(n,m)(a(n), a(m)) \in C_1,$$

we have

$$< H, K >_1= \sum_{n<m}^{M} h(n,m)k(n,m). \qquad (13.8)$$

For $F = \sum_{n=1}^{N} f(n)a(n) \in C_0$, we define the C_0-norm

$$\|F\|_{C_0} =< F, F >_0^{1/2}= \left[\sum_{n=1}^{N} f(n)^2 \right]^{1/2}. \qquad (13.9)$$

For $H = \sum_{n<m=1}^{N} h(n,m)(a(n), a(m)) \in C_1$, we define the C_1-norm

$$\|H\|_{C_1} =< H, H >_1^{1/2}= \left[\sum_{n<m}^{N} h(n,m)^2 \right]^{1/2}. \qquad (13.10)$$

We also introduce a linear "Laplacian" operator, defined to be $L_B = \partial_B \circ \delta_B :$ $C_0 \mapsto C_0$. With respect to the natural basis of C_0 the matrix of L_B is (13.11)

$$L_B = \begin{pmatrix} \sum_{j \neq 1}^{N} B_{1j}^2 & -B_{12}^2 & \cdots & -B_{1N}^2 \\ -B_{21}^2 & \sum_{j \neq 2}^{N} B_{2j}^2 & \cdots & -B_{2N}^2 \\ \vdots & \vdots & \ddots & \vdots \\ -B_{N1}^2 & -B_{N2}^2 & \cdots & \sum_{j \neq N}^{N} B_{Nj}^2 \end{pmatrix}, \qquad (13.11)$$

so for $X = \sum_{j=1}^{N} X(j)a(j) \in C_0$, the i-th entry of $L_B(X)$ is

$$L_B(X)(i) = \sum_{j=1}^{N} L_B(i,j)X(j)$$

for $i = 1, \cdots, N$. One important property of L_B is that the eigenspace of zero for connected networks is a one-dimensional space.

$$Ker(L_B) = \{\sum_{i=1}^{N} fa(i) : f \in \mathbf{R}\}.$$

The Laplacian is very important to our distributed control theory, as we will see in later sections.

The following lemma relates ∂_B, δ_B and L_B.

LEMMA 13.2 *For $X_1, X_2 \in C_1$ and $Y \in C_0$, we have the following equalities:*

1 $< \partial_B(X_1), Y >_0 = < X_1, \delta_B(Y) >_1$

2 $< \delta_B(X_1), \delta_B(X_2) >_1 = < L_B(X_1), X_2 >_0 = < X_1, L_B(X_2) >_0$

Proof. The proof is an easy computation.

As a consequence of the second item of the above Lemma and positive semi-definiteness of L_B, it will be true for connected networks that the kernel of L_B is one-dimensional and is equal to $ker(\delta_B)$.

The *degree* operator $deg : C_0 \mapsto \mathbf{R}$ is defined as usual:

$$deg(\sum_{i=1}^{N} f(i)a(i)) = \sum_{i=1}^{N} f(i). \tag{13.12}$$

The space of *cycles* of the network is characterized as follows. Given an $N \times N$-matrix as before, define the set of cycles $Z_B \in C_1$ to be the subset of C_1 mapped to zero by the boundary operator, ∂_B,

$$Z_B = ker(\partial_B : C_1 \mapsto C_0) = \{c \in C_1 : \partial_B(c) = 0\}. \tag{13.13}$$

This definition of cycle is different from that of the standard definition, i.e. z satisfies $\partial(z) = 0$. The coefficient of each link $(a(i), a(j))$ of cycle z_B is scaled by $1/B_{ij}$; however, the set of links that form a cycle is the same. Our new definition agrees with the standard one when all nonzero $B_{ij} = 1$.

We restrict our attention to *connected* networks, i.e. networks for which there is a path (a sequence of links) connecting any pair of nodes. Two operators: *inclusion $i : Z_B \mapsto C_1$* and $[\times \sum a(n)] : \mathbf{R} \mapsto C_0$ are defined:

$$i(z) = z \ \forall z \in Z_B,$$

and

$$[\times \sum a(n)](f) = \sum_{n=1}^{N} fa(n) \ \forall f \in \mathbf{R}.$$

We introduce a definition for a sequence of mappings $(g_i : \Omega_{i-1} \to \Omega_i)$ for $i = 1, 2, \cdots$

$$\cdots \Omega_{i-1} \xrightarrow{g_i} \Omega_i \xrightarrow{g_{i+1}} \Omega_{i+1} \xrightarrow{g_{i+2}} \Omega_{i+2} \cdots \qquad (13.14)$$

DEFINITION 13.3 *A sequence of linear operators is called "exact" if and only if "image of g_i = kernel of g_{i+1}" in Ω_i.*

Consider a connected network. It is a small modification of a standard result that the sequences of operators (13.15) and (13.16) are exact:

$$0 \to Z_B \xrightarrow{i} C_1 \xrightarrow{\partial_B} C_0 \xrightarrow{deg} \mathbf{R} \to 0 \qquad (13.15)$$

and

$$0 \to \mathbf{R} \xrightarrow{[\times \sum a(i)]} C_0 \xrightarrow{\delta_B} C_1 \to C_1/\delta_B(C_0) \to 0 \qquad (13.16)$$

The proof that the above sequences are exact is in Appendix A.

As a consequence of (13.15) we can compute

$$dim(Z_B) = dim(C_1) - dim(C_0) + 1 = M - N + 1, \qquad (13.17)$$

and from (13.16) we find

$$dim(\delta_B(C_0)) = dim(C_0) - 1 = N - 1; \qquad (13.18)$$

so in fact we find

$$dim(Z_B) + dim(\delta_B(C_0)) = M = dim(C_1). \qquad (13.19)$$

Equation (13.17) is known as Euler's formula.

Now we present some lemmas that will be useful for our design of network control. By "$\oplus$" we mean orthogonal direct sum.

LEMMA 13.4 $C_0 = ker(deg) \oplus ker(\delta_B)$

Proof. For $x \in C_0$ we have the following decomposition

$$x = [x - \frac{deg(x)}{N}e] + \frac{deg(x)}{N}e$$

where $e = \sum_{n=1}^{N} a(n)$. It is easy to check that $x - \frac{deg(x)}{N}e$ belongs to $ker(deg)$ and $\frac{deg(x)}{N}e$ belongs to $ker(\delta_B)$ by the exactness (13.16). It is also true that if $x \in ker(deg) \cap ker(\delta_B)$, then we have $x = \sum_{n=1}^{N} fa(n)$ for some $f \in \mathbf{R}$ and $deg(x) = \sum_{n=1}^{N} f = Nf = 0$; therefore, we have $x = 0$. To show orthogonality, note that for a single node a we have $deg(a) = 1$, so $< a - \frac{1}{N}e, \frac{1}{N}e > = \frac{1}{N} - (\frac{1}{N^2})N = 0$, and we extend linearly. Q.E.D.

LEMMA 13.5 $C_1 = \delta_B(C_0) \oplus Z_B$

Proof. For $g \in Z_B$ and $f \in C_0$, we have

$$< g, \delta_B(f) >_1 = < \partial_B(g), f >_0 = < 0, f >_0 = 0$$

so Z_B and $\delta_B(C_0)$ are orthogonal. But we also know that the inner product $<, >_1$ is positive definite, so the intersection of Z_B and $\delta_B(C_0)$ is zero. By equation (13.19) we know the dimensions of these two spaces are complementary, so $C_1 = \delta_B(C_0) \oplus Z_B$. Q.E.D.

LEMMA 13.6 *Let $K \in C_0$ be the kernel of $deg : C_0 \mapsto \mathbf{R}$. There is a unique invertible mapping $A_B : K \mapsto K$ such that $\partial_B \circ \delta_B \circ A_B = Identity : K \mapsto K$.*

Proof. By the exactness of (13.16) we know that $\delta_B : K \mapsto C_1$ is injective. But we also know that $\delta_B(C_0)$ is orthogonal to $Z_B = ker(\partial_B)$, so $\partial_B \circ \delta_B : K \mapsto C_0$ is also injective. Finally, by the exactness (13.15) we know that composition $\partial_B \circ \delta_B$ maps K into K, so $\partial_B \circ \delta_B$ is a full rank map, hence invertible. Put $A_B = (\partial_B \circ \delta_B)^{-1}$. Q.E.D.

The point of Lemma 13.6 is that $A_B = L_B^{-1}$ is well-defined on K, i.e. for $X \in K$, $L_B \circ A_B(X) = X$ is satisfied.

LEMMA 13.7 *For any $X \in C_0$, $A_B \circ L_B(X)$ is well-defined and we have $A_B \circ L_B(X) = X - \frac{deg(X)}{N}e$, where $e = \sum_{n=1}^{N} a(n)$.*

Proof. The mapping $A_B \circ L_B(X)$ is well-defined because $deg \circ L_B(X) = 0$ by the exactness of (13.15). We see $A_B \circ L_B(X) - (X - \frac{deg(X)}{N}e)$ is in both $Ker(deg)$ and $Ker(L_B)$. The eigenspace of L_B for the eigenvalue 0 is one-dimensional, which is $\sum_{i=1}^{N} fa(i)$ for $f \in \mathbf{R}$; therefore, we have $Ker(deg) \cap Ker(L_B) = 0$, which implies $A_B \circ L_B(X) = X - \frac{deg(X)}{N}e$. Q.E.D.

Next, we introduce the notion of an "acyclic" one-chain.

DEFINITION 13.8 *A one-chain $T = \sum_{i<j} t_{ij}(a(i), a(j))$ is acyclic provided that there is no $z = \sum_{i<j} z_{ij}(a(i), a(j))$ in $ker(\partial_B)$ satisfying*

1 for all (i, j), $|t_{ij} - z_{ij}| \leq |t_{ij}|$, and

2 there exists one (i, j), $|t_{ij} - z_{ij}| < |t_{ij}|$.

In other words, an acyclic one-chain T has the property that it cannot be made smaller, in a uniform and element-by-element sense, by subtracting cycles. These acyclic one chains represent flows having the property that packets never get caught in endless loops.

THEOREM 13.9 *Let* $U \in Ker(deg)$ *and* A_B *be the mapping of lemma 13.6. Then* $T = \delta_B(A_B(U))$ *satisfies*

1 $\partial_B(T) = U$, *and*

2 T *is acyclic.*

Proof. It is easy to see $\partial_B(T) = U$ by lemma 13.6. To show T is also acyclic we verify that T satisfies the algebraic condition. By construction we know that T is orthogonal to Z_B (because $T \in \delta_B(C_0)$ and lemma 13.5), hence for any $z \in Z_B$ we know that

$$\|T + z\|_1^2 = \|T\|_1^2 + \|z\|_1^2 \geq \|T\|_1^2,$$

so it is not possible to reduce any of the magnitude of the coefficients of T while leaving the other magnitudes unchanged. Q.E.D.

Now, we have the following characterization.

THEOREM 13.10 *For* $U \in Ker(deg)$, *any one-chain* T *satisfying* $\partial_B(T) = U$ *is characterized as follows:*

$$T = \delta_B(A_B(U)) + \sum_{l=1}^{L} c_l z_l$$

for some $c_l \in R$ *and* $\{z_1, \cdots, z_L\}$ *is a basis of the space of cycles* Z_B.

Proof. The fact that any solution of $\partial_B(T) = U$ is $T = \delta_B(A_B(U)) + z$ for some $z \in Z_B$ follows from lemma 13.5 and $\partial_B(z) = 0$. Since Z_B is an L-dimensional space, therefore there is a basis $\{z_1, \cdots, z_L\}$ of Z_B st. $z = \sum_{l=1}^{L} c_l z_l$. Q.E.D.

2.1   Iterative Method for the Inverse of Laplacian

This subsection presents the theorems that provide iterative methods to compute the inverse of Laplacian in a distributed way.

First, we denote D^{-1} to be a diagonal matrix with its i-th diagonal being the inverse of the i-th diagonal of L_B. We also denote the identity matrix by I. We define $L'_B = D^{-1} L_B =$

$$L'_B = \begin{pmatrix} 1 & -\dfrac{B_{12}^2}{\sum_{j \neq 1}^{N} B_{1j}^2} & \cdots & -\dfrac{B_{1N}^2}{\sum_{j \neq 1}^{N} B_{1j}^2} \\ -\dfrac{B_{21}^2}{\sum_{j \neq 2}^{N} B_{2j}^2} & 1 & \cdots & -\dfrac{B_{2N}^2}{\sum_{j=2}^{N} B_{2j}^2} \\ \vdots & \vdots & \ddots & \vdots \\ -\dfrac{B_{N1}^2}{\sum_{j \neq N}^{N} B_{Nj}^2} & -\dfrac{B_{N2}^2}{\sum_{j=1}^{N} B_{Nj}^2} & \cdots & 1 \end{pmatrix}. \qquad (13.20)$$

Note that $I - L'_B$ is a Markov matrix. Furthermore, the eigenvalues of L'_B are the same as the eigenvalues of $D^{1/2}L'_B D^{-1/2}$, which is symmetric, so all eigenvalues of $I - L'_B$ are real. Before stating the main theorems, we introduce the following preliminary results. We consider every link is bidirectional; therefore, the Laplacian is symmetric and all its eigenvalues are real. Recall the definition that a Markov matrix is irreducible if some power of it has all entries strictly larger than zero.

LEMMA 13.11 *$I - L'_B$ is irreducible if and only if the graph is connected.*

Proof. See Appendix Section 4 of [27].

LEMMA 13.12 *For connected graphs, $I - L'_B$ is either aperiodic or periodic with period 2.*

Proof. Here we use the fact that the eigenvalues of $I - L'_B$ are real, so the graph is periodic if and only if ± 1 are the only eigenvalues of magnitude 1 by Theorem 4.7 of the Appendix of [27]. Q.E.D.

According to Frobenius-Perron Theorem [27] and [28], if $I - L'_B$ is aperiodic, there is a unique eigenvalue with magnitude 1 and the magnitudes of the other eigenvalues are strictly less than 1. We consider two cases for connected networks:

1 Aperiodic graphs with unidirectional or bidirectional links (Theorem 13.13).

2 Periodic graphs with bidirectional links and thus with period 2 (Theorem 13.14).

THEOREM 13.13 *Suppose $I - L'_B$ is aperiodic. For $u \in Ker(deg) \subset C_0$, let $z = D^{-1}u$. Then, the following iterative limit*

$$\phi(z) = \lim_{k \to \infty} \sum_{j=1}^{k} \delta_B (I - L'_B)^j z + \delta_B(z) \in Im(\delta_B) \subset C_1$$

is well-defined and acyclic. Moreover, the following equality is true

$$\partial_B \phi(z) = u.$$

Proof. Assume $I - L'_B$ is aperiodic. By Frobenius-Perron theorem, we know that $I - L'_B$ has a single eigenvalue 1 and all the other eigenvalues $|\lambda_i| \leq m < 1$, for $i = 2, ..., N$. Note that if we place the eigenvalues of $I - L'_B$ in order of decreasing magnitude on the diagonal, then we have

$$\Lambda = \begin{pmatrix} 1 & \cdots & \cdots & \cdots \\ 0 & \lambda_2 & \cdots & \cdots \\ \vdots & \vdots & \ddots & \vdots \\ 0 & 0 & \cdots & \lambda_N \end{pmatrix},$$

where $\lambda_i \geq \lambda_{i+1}$. Let $e = (1, ..., 1)'$ be the eigenvector of 1 and w_i be the eigenvector of λ_i for $i = 2, ..., N$. Let

$$W = (e, w_2, \cdots, w_N).$$

For any integer $j > 0$ we have

$$(I - L_B')^j W = W\Lambda^j$$

and for any vector z there is a coefficient vector c such that $z = Wc$, and

$$(I - L_B')^j z = W\Lambda^j c.$$

But we know $\delta_B(e) = 0$, so for all j, we have

$$\delta_B((I - L_B')^j)z = (\delta_B e, \delta_B w_2, \cdots, \delta_B w_N)\Lambda^j c$$

$$= (0, \delta_B w_2, \cdots, \delta_B w_N) \begin{pmatrix} 1 & \cdots & \cdots & \cdots \\ 0 & \lambda_2^j & \cdots & \cdots \\ \vdots & \vdots & \ddots & \vdots \\ 0 & 0 & \cdots & \lambda_N^j \end{pmatrix} c,$$

which has magnitude less than

$$||(\delta_B w_2, \cdots, \delta_B w_N)|| ||m|^j|| ||c||,$$

which converges to 0 as $j \to \infty$.

Furthermore, for all z we have

$$\sum_{j=0}^{\infty} \delta_B(I - L_B')^j z = (\delta_B w_2, \cdots, \delta_B w_N) \sum_{j=0}^{\infty} \begin{pmatrix} \lambda_2 & \cdots & \cdots \\ \vdots & \ddots & \vdots \\ 0 & \cdots & \lambda_N \end{pmatrix}^j \tilde{c},$$

where $c = \begin{pmatrix} c_1 \\ \tilde{c} \end{pmatrix}$, converges to the 1-chain $\phi(z)$.

Observe the following equalities

$$\partial_B \phi(z) = \partial_B(\delta_B w_2, \cdots, \delta_B w_N) \sum_{j=0}^{\infty} \begin{pmatrix} \lambda_2 & \cdots & \cdots & \cdots \\ 0 & \lambda_3 & \cdots & \cdots \\ \vdots & \vdots & \ddots & \vdots \\ 0 & 0 & \cdots & \lambda_N \end{pmatrix}^j \tilde{c}$$

$$= (L_B w_2, \cdots, L_B w_N) \sum_{j=0}^{\infty} \begin{pmatrix} \lambda_2 & \cdots & \cdots & \cdots \\ 0 & \lambda_3 & \cdots & \cdots \\ \vdots & \vdots & \ddots & \vdots \\ 0 & 0 & \cdots & \lambda_N \end{pmatrix}^j \tilde{c}.$$

Since we have

$$D^{-1}L_B W = W(I - \Lambda),$$

so equivalently

$$L_B W = DW(I - \Lambda);$$

therefore,

$$\partial_B \phi(z) = (L_B w_2, \cdots, L_B w_N) \sum_{j=0}^{\infty} \begin{pmatrix} \lambda_2 & \cdots & \cdots & \cdots \\ 0 & \lambda_3 & \cdots & \cdots \\ \vdots & \vdots & \ddots & \vdots \\ 0 & 0 & \cdots & \lambda_N \end{pmatrix}^j \tilde{c}$$

$$= D(w_2, \cdots, w_N) \begin{pmatrix} (1-\lambda_2)\sum_{j=0}^{\infty}\lambda_2^j & \cdots & \cdots \\ \vdots & \vdots & \ddots & \vdots \\ 0 & 0 & \cdots & (1-\lambda_N)\sum_{j=0}^{\infty}\lambda_N^j \end{pmatrix} \tilde{c}$$

$$= D(w_2, \cdots, w_N)\tilde{c} = D(z - ec_1).$$

Q.E.D.

THEOREM 13.14 *Suppose* $I - L_B'$ *is of period 2. For* $u \in Ker(deg) \subset C_0$, *let* $z = D^{-1}u$. *Then, the following limits* $\phi_1(z)$ *and* $\phi_2(z)$

$$\phi_1(z) = \lim_{k\to\infty} \sum_{j=1}^{2k} \delta_B(I - L_B')^j z + \delta_B(z) \in Im(\delta_B) \subset C_1$$

$$\phi_2(z) = \lim_{k\to\infty} \sum_{j=1}^{2k+1} \delta_B(I - L_B')^j z + \delta_B(z) \in Im(\delta_B) \subset C_1$$

are well-defined and acyclic. Moreover, let

$$x = (\phi_1(z) + \phi_2(z))/2,$$

then we have

$$\partial_B(x) = u.$$

Proof. Because $I - L_B'$ is irreducible and of period 2, it has two one-dimensional eigenspaces for eigenvalues 1, -1 and the all other eigenvalues $|\lambda_i| \le m < 1$, for $i = 3, \cdots, N$. Let the eigenspace decomposition be

$$(I - L_B')W = W\Lambda,$$

where

$$\Lambda = \begin{pmatrix} 1 & 0 & \cdots & \cdots & \cdots \\ 0 & -1 & 0 & \cdots & \cdots \\ 0 & 0 & \lambda_3 & \vdots & \vdots \\ 0 & 0 & \cdots & \ddots & \vdots \\ 0 & 0 & \cdots & \cdots & \lambda_N \end{pmatrix}$$

and

$$W = (e, w_2, w_3, \cdots, w_N).$$

It is still true that for any vector z we have a unique coefficient vector c such that $z = Wc$ and

$$(I - L'_B)^j z = W\Lambda^j c.$$

Again, we have

$$\delta_B(I - L'_B)^j z = (\delta_B w_1, \delta_B w_2, \cdots, \delta_B w_N)\Lambda^j c$$

$$= (0, \delta_B w_2, \cdots, \delta_B w_N) \begin{pmatrix} 1 & 0 & \cdots & \cdots & \cdots \\ 0 & (-1)^j & 0 & \cdots & \cdots \\ 0 & 0 & \lambda_3^j & \vdots & \vdots \\ 0 & 0 & \cdots & \vdots & \vdots \\ 0 & 0 & \cdots & \cdots & \lambda_N^j \end{pmatrix} c,$$

but it is no longer true that $\|\delta_B(I - L'_B)^j z\| \to 0$ as $j \to \infty$. However, for any integer $k > 0$, both the limits

$$\phi_1(z) = \lim_{k \to \infty} \sum_{j=1}^{2k} \delta_B(I - L'_B)^j + \delta_B(z)$$

and

$$\phi_2(z) = \lim_{k \to \infty} \sum_{j=1}^{2k+1} \delta_B(I - L'_B)^j + \delta_B(z)$$

exist. Let $x = (\phi_1(z) + \phi_2(z))/2$. By a computation similar to that of Theorem 13.13, we can show

$$\delta_B(x) = u.$$

Q.E.D.

The idea of the proof in Theorem 13.13 for aperiodic graphs is well known and is proved, for example, in [24]. The result in Theorem 13.14 for periodic graphs appears to be new, however, so we give the constructive proof in some detail.

There are applications where, for a given a 0-chain u on network nodes, there is a need to have a distributed computation for obtaining the flow (1-chain) T on network links that will satisfy $\partial_B T = u$ on network nodes ([1], [24] and [26]). Theorem 13.13 and 13.14 show constructive, distributed and iterative methods to establish the desired network flow. The solution flow T is also acyclic, i.e., it has no closed loop.

Example 2.1 Let B be all one for connected pairs of nodes and all zero for disconnected pairs of nodes. The simplest nontrivial aperiodic graph is the triangle $(a(1), a(2), a(3))$. The eigenvalues of $(I - L')$ are $1, -\frac{1}{2}, -\frac{1}{2}$. If we pick $u = a(1) - a(2)$ in Theorem 13.13, we find $z = \frac{a(1)-a(2)}{2}$ and

$$\phi(z) = [-(a(1), a(2)) + \frac{1}{2}(a(2), a(3)) + \frac{1}{2}(a(3), a(1))] \sum_{j=0}^{\infty} (-\frac{1}{2})^j$$

$$= \frac{2}{3}[-(a(1), a(2)) + \frac{1}{2}(a(2), a(3)) + \frac{1}{2}(a(3), a(1))].$$

Example 2.2 Let B be all one for connected pairs of nodes and all zero for disconnected pairs of nodes. The simplest nontrivial periodic graph is the square $(a(1), a(2), a(3), a(4))$. The eigenvalues of $(I - L')$ are 1, -1, 0, and 0. If we pick $u = a(1) - a(2) + a(3) - a(4)$ in Theorem 13.14 then $z = \frac{u}{2}$, $(I - L')z = -z$ so $\phi_1(z) = \delta(z) = \frac{\delta(u)}{2}$, $\phi_2(z) = 0$, and $x = \frac{1}{4}\delta(u)$. Then,

$$\partial(x) = \frac{L(u)}{4} = u,$$

as claimed.

3.   Nominal Steady-State Routing Solution

The first step of the proposed control strategy is to obtain a nominal steady-state solution by optimizing a cost function defined on the network routing solutions T. The methods of Theorem 13.13 and 13.14 will be used to produce such solutions in a distributed way.

Packets are distinguished by their classes as well as their destination nodes. We assume there are K types of packets and each type is destined to node $a(N_k)$, for $k = 1, \cdots, K$. Let $U^k \in C_0$ denote the k-type packet exogenous input rate at network source nodes, and $deg(U^k)$ denote the packet output rate leaving from the network node $a(N_k)$, and let $T^k \in C_1$ denote the routing flow rates on network links. A essential network stability condition is for $k = 1, \cdots, K$,

$$\partial(T^k) + U^k - deg(U^k)a(N_k) = 0. \qquad (13.21)$$

The above equation is a consequence of law of conservation. The derivation of this equation can be found in [1].

We define the K-vectors with elements from C_1 as follows:

$$C_1^K = \{\sum_{m=1}^M f_m b(m) : f_m = (f_m^1, \cdots, f_m^K), f_m^k \in \mathbf{R}\}.$$

The routing flow rates of all types of packets are represented by

$$T = (T^1, \cdots, T^k, \cdots, T^K) \in C_1^K,$$

where

$$T^k = \sum_{i<j} T_{ij}^k(a(i), a(j)).$$

Let $F : C_1^K \to R$ be a cost function of packet flows on network links. We assume F is a positive, differentiable and convex function. The local cost of packet flows on a link is often only associated with local state information of packet flows; otherwise, more state information should be communicated between network nodes. We also assume the link cost only depends on the magnitude of flow and increases with respect to the flow magnitude. Also we do not allow packet flows of the same type on opposite directions over a link because this will create unnecessary routing loops; however, a link may have different directions of packet flows of different types.

The cost function described in the algebraic-topological framework is as follows. Pick an orientation for each link; for convenience, we assume the orientation of a link is $(a(i), a(j))$ with $i < j$. Since the cost function F is defined with respect to flow magnitude, we do not distinguish $F(T_{ij}^k)$ and $F(T_{ji}^k)$, i.e.,

$$F(T_{ij}^k) = F(T_{ji}^k) = F(|T_{ij}^k|).$$

However, we need to distinguish the derivatives of $F(T)$ with respect to T_{ij}^k and T_{ji}^k. For $i < j$, we denote the derivative of F with respect to T_{ij}^k to be $\frac{\partial F}{\partial T_{ij}^k}$ and the derivative of F with respect to T_{ji}^k is defined to be $-\frac{\partial F}{\partial T_{ij}^k}$, i.e.

$$\frac{\partial F}{\partial T_{ij}^k} = -\frac{\partial F}{\partial T_{ji}^k}.$$

This means $\frac{\partial F}{\partial T_{ij}^k}$, related to flows of type k from node $a(i)$ to node $a(j)$, is the same as $-\frac{\partial F}{\partial T_{ji}^k}$, related to a "virtual" negative flow from $a(j)$ to $a(i)$. Also since we assume F increases with respect to the flow magnitudes, for a positive flow of type k on link $(a(i), a(j))$, the first-order derivative $\frac{\partial F}{\partial T_{ij}^k}$ should be positive, and $\frac{\partial F}{\partial T_{ji}^k}$ should be negative as well. For $k = 1, \cdots, K$, we denote the gradient of F in C_1 to be

$$\frac{dF}{dT^k} = \sum_{i<j} \frac{\partial F}{\partial T_{ij}^k}(a(i), a(j)).$$

A standard example of $F(T)$ used in optimal routing problem for data network is introduced

$$\sum_{(i,j)} \frac{\sum_{k=1}^{K} |T_{ij}^k|}{C_{ij} - \sum_{k=1}^{K} |T_{ij}^k|}, \qquad (13.22)$$

where C_{ij} is the bandwidth of link (i, j), which approximates the average number of queued packets at each node by a M/M/1 queue, based on the Kleinrock independent approximation [2].

The optimization problem is formulated as follows:

$$\text{Minimize } F(T) \qquad (13.23)$$

$$\text{subject to } U^k + \partial(T^k) - deg(U^k)a(N_k) = 0, \forall k = 1, \cdots, K. \qquad (13.24)$$

The above optimization can be solved by a gradient search, making use of $\frac{dF}{dT^k}(T(t))$. In distributed computation, the value of $\frac{dF}{dT^k}(T(t))$ should be obtained locally; otherwise, significant amounts of information about the values of $\frac{dF}{dT^k}(T(t))$ must be exchanged between network nodes. One frequently-encountered cost function is the total communication delay on links , e.g. [18], [20] or [17]. This type of delay function is the summation of the delays for different classes of traffic on different links, in the context of our framework, which means that the gradient $\frac{dF}{dT^k}(T(t))$ at a given link does not depend on other links, but different types of packet flows on the same link will interact with each other.

Our formulation is different from the classical *multicommodity flow problem*, which is widely used in optimization of flows for data networks, for example, [3], [4], [5],[6], [7], [12], [13] and [14]. In these articles, the cost is optimized subject to flow rates of predetermined paths of given pairs of source nodes and target nodes. The network topology is described by path-link matrices, whose entry (i, j) is 1 if link i is on path j; otherwise, (i, j) is 0 if link i is not on path j. We provide an alternative formulation to the *multicommodity flow problem* by formulating the problem on the link space using algebraic-topological notation. In our formulation, network nodes only see the combined rate of arriving flows of the same destination nodes as well as classes, but without having to know their paths and their source nodes. The packet conservation law is formulated by use of the boundary operator, ∂. One advantage of this approach is that in some cases the optimization of our formulation is over a much smaller state space than the traditional one which is formulated on path spaces. For example, consider a network of N nodes, there are $N(N-1)/2$ possible source-destination (SD) pairs and each SD pair may have many possible paths. The size of our formulation, where no path is predetermined, is bounded by $N(N-1)/2$. This approach may also provide a more natural way to formulate connectionless packet flows through networks because no path needs to be pre-determined.

A framework to solve the optimization problem "Minimize F(T)" (13.23) for general cost functions will be the subject of another paper. If one chooses linear cost functions for F(T) in (13.23) then methods from linear programming can be used to compute solutions. The OSPF solution commonly used for Internet routing can be obtained from a linear cost function. Here, however, we focus on quadratic cost functions. One key advantage of quadratic cost functions is that optimal solutions are unique, and closed-form expressions for the solutions can be found (see (13.26) below).

One previous research paper that addresses optimization of quadratic cost functions on networks, with applications to electric circuits, is [16]. The use of quadratic cost functions for optimal control problems has a long history in the control community – see [30] for a reference to the early (1971) literature and an elementary discussion of the quadratic regulator problem. Our parameters B (link weights) can be viewed as design parameters that the design engineer can tweak to create optimal routing solutions with varying properties. One may wonder how best to choose the weights B. The answer is that, in some problems, such as electric power distribution, there are parameters that naturally suggest themselves (e.g. the electrical resistances or impedances of the links); but in general there is no best way to pick the weights. In fact, practical network design problems usually cannot be reduced to the optimization of a single cost function. For example, it is not enough simply to minimize delay or packet drop rates. Often, engineers use cost-function-based methodologies by adjusting the weights iteratively, in search of a solution that represents an acceptable trade among multiple competing objectives.

One other point worth mentioning is that linear cost functions lead to uni-path routing, as in OSPF, while quadratic and high-power cost functions lead to multi-path routing which facilitates load balancing among network nodes (see more discussion later in Section 4 Dynamic Inversion). This general observation suggests that the best choice of cost function might depend on network loading. When loading is light it might be best to use a linear function F(T), but when loading is heavy and congestion becomes a problem it might be better to use a quadratic or higher-order function. See the pentagon example in [1] (Table 14.1). The best choice of cost functions and weight parameters depends on system objectives, network resources and operational environment.

3.1   Quadratic Cost Functions

The quadratic link cost function has a particular algebraic-topological expression, that gives a closed-form optimal solution. However, the optimal solution provides multi-path routing solutions, which might not be suitable in some real-world scenarios.

Our analysis still assumes K types of packets distinguished by their classes as well as their destination nodes. The network is modeled by a weighted graph where each link $(a(i), a(j))$ with respect to type k packets is weighted by B_{ij}^k with $B_{ij}^k = B_{ji}^k$, and B_{ij}^k is defined to be zero if there is no link connecting node $a(i)$ and node $a(j)$. The weight B_{ij}^k usually represents a performance parameter, e.g., delay parameter or guaranteed bandwidth.

We consider the optimization problem with a quadratic cost function:

$$\text{Minimize } F(T) = \sum_{k=1}^{K} \sum_{i<j} \left(\frac{T_{ij}^k}{B_{ij}^k}\right)^2 \text{ over } T \qquad (13.25)$$

subject to $\partial(T^k) + U^k - deg(U^k)a(N_k) = 0, \forall k = 1, \cdots, K.$

We denote

$$\frac{T^k}{B^k} = \sum_{i<j} \frac{T_{ij}^k}{B_{ij}^k}(a(i), a(j)),$$

which is an element-by-element fraction. By Theorem 13.10 we have the following decomposition

$$\frac{T^k}{B^k} = \delta_{B^k}(X^k) + z_{B^k},$$

for some $z_{B^k} \in Z_{B^k}$, and some $X^k \in C_0$, where X^k can be found by the following steps. Applying ∂_{B^k} on the above equation leads to

$$\partial_{B^k}\left(\frac{T^k}{B^k}\right) = \partial_{B^k}(\delta_{B^k}(X^k) + z_{B^k}) = \partial_{B^k}(\delta_{B^k}(X^k)).$$

We also notice

$$\partial_{B^k}\left(\frac{T^k}{B^k}\right) = \partial T^k = deg(U^k)a(N_k) - U^k.$$

By Lemma 13.6 and the above equations we have

$$X^k = A_{B^k}(deg(U^k)a(N_k) - U^k).$$

Next, we solve the optimization problem of (13.25). First, notice

$$\left\|\frac{T^k}{B^k}\right\|^2 = \left\|\sum_{i<j} \frac{T_{ij}^k}{B_{ij}^k}(a(i), a(j))\right\|^2 = < \delta_{B^k}(X^k) + z_{B^k}, \delta_{B^k}(X^k) + z_{B^k} >_1$$

$$=< \delta_{B^k}(X^k), \delta_{B^k}(X^k) >_1 + < z_{B^k}, z_{B^k} >_1 \geq < \delta_{B^k}(X^k), \delta_{B^k}(X^k) >_1 .$$

Therefore, the minimum is achieved when the following is true

$$\frac{T^k}{B^k} = \delta_{B^k}(A_{B^k}(deg(U^k)a(N_k) - U^k)).$$

The optimal routing solution is

$$\hat{T}^k = B^k . * \delta_{B^k}(A_{B^k}(deg(U^k)a(N_k) - U^k)), \forall k = 1, ..., K, \qquad (13.26)$$

which is acyclic by Theorem 13.9.

Moreover, the total minimal cost is (by lemma 13.2)

$$\sum_{k=1}^{K} < \delta_{B^k}(X^k), \delta_{B^k}(X^k) >_1$$

$$= \sum_{k=1}^{K} < L_{B^k}(A_{B^k}(deg(U^k)a(N_k) - U^k)), A_{B^k}(deg(U^k)a(N_k) - U^k) >_0$$

$$= \sum_{k=1}^{K} < deg(U^k)a(N_k) - U^k, A_{B^k}(deg(U^k)a(N_k) - U_k) >_0 .$$

In the routing solution (13.26), A_{B^k} is the only global operator. However, we can use a distributed algorithm to construct the solution based on Theorem 13.13 and 13.14. The algorithm is described in Section 5.

4.   Dynamic Inversion

This section proposes an inner-loop control method to dynamically adjust routing flow rates to compensate for second-order variations of traffic inputs. The inner-loop control uses a linear control law called dynamic inversion to determine routing flow-rate adjustments. The proposed method has several desirable properties. First, the adjusted routing solution still produces acyclic flows. Second, the inner-loop control preserves stability of network states. Third, the inner-loop control can be computed in a distributed algorithm, where each node updates its own routing table autonomously. Finally, it helps to achieve load-balanced queues among network nodes.

We consider a routing flow-rate adjustment of $\bar{T}^k$, where $\bar{T}^k$ is the steady-state routing solution as designed in the previous section. Our inner-loop control is restricted to a subset of network links $D_1 \subset C_1$, where D_1 is support of $\bar{T}^k$ minus the links to the target node $a(N_k)$, i.e. the set of links over which type-k packets flow, excluding the links to the target node. The subset of nodes incident to D_1 is denoted by D_0, where type-k packets communicate, excluding the target node $a(N_k)$.

Let $\bar{Q}^k(i)$ denote the expected queue length in the nominal network steady state for type-k packets at node $a(i) \in D_0$. The expected queue length depends on $\bar{T}^k$ and can either be associated with buffer size requirements or the mean queue length for stochastic models. The measurements of queue length of type-k packets at the node $a(i)$ is denoted by $Q^k(i)$. Note that it is up to network designers to choose the parameter $\bar{Q}^k(i)$, which may represent another objective, for example, minimizing delay or packet drop rates. The inner-loop controller described later in this section will drive the queue state to satisfy (13.31). Which criterion to choose – load-balancing, minimizing delay, or minimizing packet drop rates – is not the focus of this controller. Load-balancing may be preferred in terms of minimizing the workload of the controller because it mainly adjusts for the second-order variations of traffic inputs. If other criteria are used, the controller might also have to compensate the first-order means of traffic inputs.

Our control command is designed from the following dynamic-inversion equation (13.27) over D_0

$$\frac{dQ^k}{dt}(t) = -\epsilon_k L_B(Q^k(t)/\bar{Q}^k) \tag{13.27}$$

for some $\epsilon_k > 0$, a constant representing the rate of desired convergence to the nominal steady-state solution. For nodes $a(j) \notin D_0$ we simply let

$$\frac{dQ^k}{dt}(t) \equiv 0$$

at node $a(j)$. We denote the above control system as

$$\frac{dQ^k}{dt} = -\epsilon_k L_B(Q^k/\bar{Q}^k) \in C_0.$$

Under this control law the system dynamic is described by

$$\frac{dQ^k}{dt} = U^k - deg(U^k)a(N_k) + \partial(T^k) \tag{13.28}$$

and

$$\frac{dQ^k}{dt} = -\epsilon_k L_B(Q^k/\bar{Q}^k), \tag{13.29}$$

where (13.28) is a consequence of conservation law and its derivation can be found in [1]. By setting the right-hand sides of (13.28) and (13.29) equal, the system dynamic can be realized by solving the following equation for T^k

$$\epsilon_k L_B(Q^k/\bar{Q}^k) + U^k - deg(U^k)a(N_k) + \partial(T^k) = 0.$$

The above equation can be solved explicitly for T^k, and its solution is

$$T^k = B. * \delta_B A_B(deg(U^k)a(N_k) - U^k) + \sum_{l=1}^{L} c_l z_l + \epsilon_k B. * \delta_B(Q^k/\bar{Q}^k),$$

for some constant $c_1, \cdots, c_L$ and where $(z_1, \cdots, z_L)$ is a basis of the space of cycles Z_B. We denote the routing adjustments by

$$\Delta T^k = \epsilon_k B. * \delta_B(Q^k/\bar{Q}^k).$$

The control law (13.27) has the following desired properties:

1. Since $deg(\epsilon_k L_B(Q^k(t)/\bar{Q}^k)) = 0$ for all $Q^k(t)$, the desired dynamic can be achieved by having ΔT^k satisfy $\partial(\Delta T^k) = -\epsilon_k L_B(Q^k/\bar{Q}^k)$. The routing adjustment of the dynamic (13.27) can be realized by having

$$\Delta T^k = \epsilon_k B. * \delta_B A_B L_B(Q^k(t)/\bar{Q}^k)) = \epsilon_k B. * \delta_B(Q^k(t)/\bar{Q}^k)),$$
(13.30)

which is computed only by local operators and needs only local information.

2. Since the eigenspace of the eigenvalue zero of L_B is a one-dimensional space, which is $\sum_{i=1}^N fa(i)$ for $f \in \mathbf{R}$, the dynamic equation load-balances queues among network nodes. In other words, the control dynamic will drive the queuing state at nodes $\in D_0$ to

$$\frac{Q(i)}{\bar{Q}(i)} = \frac{Q(j)}{\bar{Q}(j)}$$
(13.31)

for nodes $a(i) \neq a(j)$. When the queuing states are not load-balanced, (13.29) automatically tries to balance them. When the queuing states are load-balanced, the control is turned off and (13.21) is satisfied.

3. The new routing solution is still acyclic because it is in the image of δ_B.

4. The new routing solution $\Delta T^k + \bar{T}^k$ still satisfies the network stability equation (13.21).

5.   Distributed Control Algorithms

The network theory developed in the previous sections can be computed by distributed algorithms. The algorithm is composed of two parts: computation for the nominal steady-state routing solutions, and computation for dynamic routing solutions to load balance queues among network nodes.

5.1   Steady-State Routing

Recall that the optimal nominal steady-state routing solution is

$$\hat{T}^k = \lim_{k \to \infty} B^k. * \delta_{B^k}(\sum_{j=0}^k (I - L'_{B^k})^j D^{-1}(\deg(U^k)a(N_k) - U^k)).$$
(13.32)

Our distributed algorithm is based on the above iterative computation. Before performing the iteration, the values of $deg(U^k)$ should be known by its destination node $a(N_k)$. This can be achieved by communicating a type of control frame carrying the information for U^k.

In the distributed algorithm, each node performs the following steps to obtain the steady-state routing solution for type-k packets.

1 At time 0, let $P(0) = -D^{-1}(\deg(U^k)a(N_k) - U^k)$.

2 At each iterative step h, $P(h)$ is computed by

$$P(h) = P(0) + (I - L'_{B^k})P(h - 1).$$

3 Some criterion is used to decide whether or not the iterative algorithm has converged. For example, the following criterion is used for the simulation results of Section 6. Denote $P(i, h)$ to be the value obtained in step 2 for node $a(i)$ at timestep h. Node $a(i)$ computes the flow for each of its neighbor link $(a(i), a(j))$ as follows:

$$T_{ij}(h) = (B^k_{ij})^2(P(j, *) - P(i, h)),$$

where $P(j, *)$ is the most recent value, which may not be obtained at timestep h, for node $a(j)$. The above formula is consistent with (13.32). The algorithm has converged if for all links $(a(i), a(j))$

$$|T_{ij}(h + 1) - T_{ij}(h)| \le \epsilon,$$

for some $\epsilon > 0$. In Section 7 we say a little about the convergence rate of the algorithm.

In this algorithm, each network node receives the update values of P from its neighbor nodes, and then uses the update values iteratively to compute its own value for P. This part of the algorithm can be performed asynchronously between network nodes.

The routing solution $\hat{T}^k$ often implies multi-path routing in the case of a quadratic cost function. Some example implementations of this multi-path routing scheme are described as follows. Node $a(i)$ looks at the flow rates to all the downstream nodes $a(j) \in N^-(a(i))$, and then establishes a percentage of flow rates for each downstream node. The percentage to a given downstream node is the ratio of its flowrate of the given downstream node to the total downstream flow rates. Once the percentages are computed, node $a(i)$ forwards packets to different downstream nodes proportionally based on weighted round-robin or probabilistic-distribution methods, etc.

As network size grows, it might become a problem that the number of routing paths increase. If desired, a hierarchy can be imposed on the network domain such that routing paths for a class of traffic are restricted to a subnetwork. This is achieved by imposing additional boundary conditions.

Even though multi-path routing may be implemented, the possibility of end-to-end in-sequence delivery of a packet flow is not necessarily restricted. To enable end-to-end in-sequence delivery we need only make changes at the network layer. End-to-end in-sequence deliveries can be maintained if each router node distinguishes packets by a flow identifier and the router routes packets of the same flow to only one downstream node.

5.2 Dynamic Routing Using Queuing Feedback

Queues may build up at network nodes for various reasons. First, traffic inputs to the network tend to have variations. Second, communication links have finite bandwidth, therefore outstanding packets on links are queued at nodes.

The inner-loop control adjusts the routing solution based on equation (13.30)

$$\Delta T^k = \epsilon_k B. * \delta_B A_B L_B(Q^k(t)/\bar{Q}^k)) = \epsilon_k B. * \delta_B(Q^k(t)/\bar{Q}^k)).$$

The steps to compute the dynamic routing adjustments are described as follows.

1 Each node measures the queuing lengths either periodically or on an event-triggered basis. The ratio of the queuing lengths to the expected queuing lengths $Q/\bar{Q}$ are then computed.

2 A type of control frame carrying the values of $Q/\bar{Q}$ are communicated between neighbor nodes.

3 Each node $a(i)$ computes its routing adjustments by equation (13.30). Note that this is a distributed algorithm because there are only local operators in equation (13.30) and only local information is exchanged between neighbor nodes.

4 Each node updates its own routing table based on the routing adjustments.

The algorithm is distributed and does not rely on any global information; only queuing information is exchanged between neighbor nodes. This algorithm is executed more often than the one for the nominal steady-state routing solution.

6. Simulation Results

6.1 Aperiodic Networks

We simulate the algorithm in section 5.1 in a network with 10 nodes. As shown in Fig. 13.1, the exogenous input rates are 2 units at node 1, 3 units at

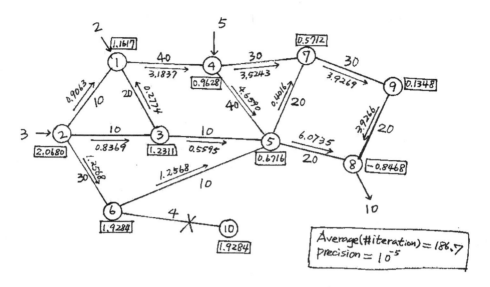

Figure 13.1. An aperiodic 10-node Network

node 2, 5 units at node 4, and the output rate at the target node 8 is 10. The weights on links are symmetric, for example, the weight from node 1 to node 2 is 10, and that from node 2 to node 1 is the same. The initial condition for potential values is 2 at node 1, 3 at node 3 and 5 at node 4, and -10 at node 8, and 0 at the other nodes. The simulation result shows the converged potentials at each node. Notice that the source nodes, nodes 1, 2, and 4, have the highest potentials and the target node 8 has the lowest potential. The flow on a link is always from the node with a higher potential to that with a lower one and the magnitude of the flow is the potential difference divided by the weight on the link. Notice that there should not be flow between node 10 and node 6 because the potentials at node 6 and node 10 are equal; otherwise, a cycle including node 6 and node 10 is created. The average number of iteration at each node for achieving 10^{-5} precision is 186.7. This result shows the multi-path routing feature. This simulation also validates the acyclic property.

Figure 13.2 shows an aperiodic network with 100 nodes. The network is not planar. Some nodes, for example, node 54, node 90, are not connected to the network. The initial condition for potentials are 0.2 at node 1, 0.3 at node 2, 0.5 at node 32, 0.8 at node 42, 0.1 at node 55, 0.3 at node 64, 0.6 at node 91, -2.8 at node 99, and 0 at the other nodes. The average number of iteration at each node for achieving 10^{-5} precision is 562.13. Figure 13.3 shows the corresponding network flow for Figure 13.2. The result also validates the desired properties as mentioned previously.

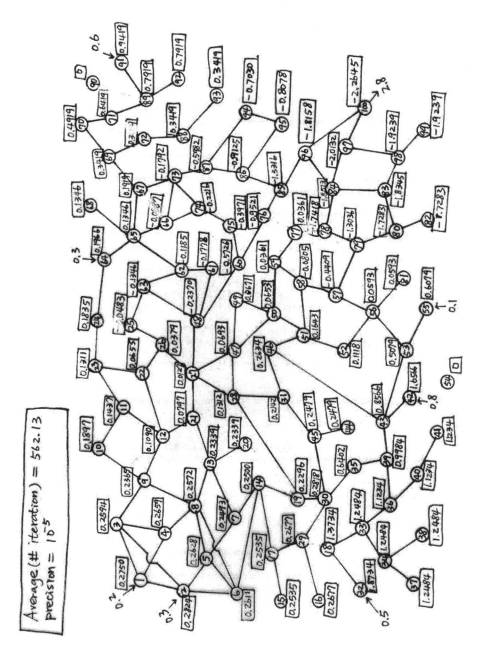

Figure 13.2. The potentials of an aperiodic 100-node network

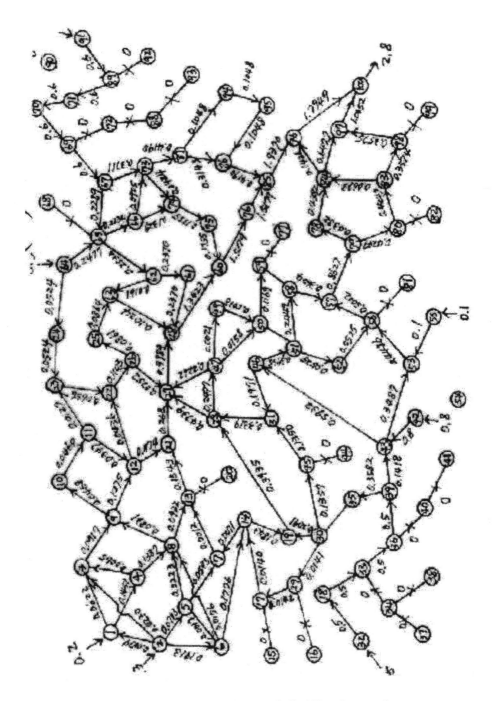

Figure 13.3.   The flow of the aperiodic 100-node network

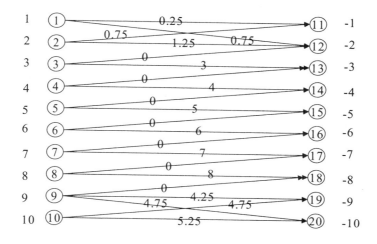

Figure 13.4. A network of Period 2

6.2 Networks of Period 2

Fig 13.4 shows a network of period 2, where nodes at one side only communicate to nodes of the other sides. The potentials at node i is i for $i = 1, ..., 10$, and the potentials at node i is $10 - i$ for $i = 11, ..., 20$. The simulation result shows the flow that results the given potentials at nodes.

Fig 13.5 shows another network of period 2. The potentials are 2 at node 1, -1 at node 2, 4 at node 3, -3 at node 4, -1 at node 5, and -1 at node 6. The simulation result also shows the flow that results the given potentials at nodes.

7. Summary

In our previous paper [1] we showed how routing problems for packet-switched networks could be formulated and solved using methods from the algebraic topology of 1-complexes [9]. The approach in [1] provided a nice theoretical framework but it did not address a number of practical issues, the most notable of which was the use of global network state information in the optimization and feedback computations. In this paper we extend from the previous paper in two ways:

1 Removing the need for global state feedback, and

2 Building more of the framework needed for distributed computation and cost-function optimization.

We remove the need for global state feedback by demonstrating in Theorems 13.13 and 13.14 an iterative, distributed algorithm that performs the necessary

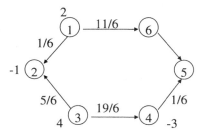

Figure 13.5. Another network of period 2. $u = 2a_1 - a_2 + 4a_3 - 3a_4 - a_5 - a_6$. $T = \frac{1}{6}(a_1, a_2) + \frac{5}{6}(a_3, a_2) + \frac{19}{6}(a_3, a_4) + \frac{1}{6}(a_4, a_5) + \frac{5}{6}(a_6, a_5) + \frac{11}{6}(a_1, a_6)$. $\delta T = -u$.

computations. The convergence of this iterative algorithm is almost an immediate consequence of the diagonal dominance of the Laplacian operator. The problem of periodicity that arises in some network topologies forces us to consider the Frobenius-Perron Theory [27], [28] in full generality. Note that the algorithm in Theorem 13.14 can be applied to both periodic and aperiodic cases, so it can be applied uniformly in cases where the global network topology is unknown.

The iterative algorithm converges geometrically, with the error in the j-th iteration proportional to m^j, where m is the second largest eigenvalue of $(I - L'_B)$ in the aperiodic case and the third largest eigenvalue of $(I - L'_B)$ in the periodic case. Thus, convergence is fastest when the non-unitary eigenvalues are close to zero. The relation between the topology of a graph and the spectrum of its Laplacian is an area of active research [29] that might provide useful insight in performance analysis of the iterative algorithms presented in Section 2.

In Section 3 we turn our attention to the problem of optimal steady-state routing control of networks. Our discussion of the optimization problem is limited to explaining how the algebraic-topological machinery can be used to formulate problems of this type, and to obtain closed-form solutions for quadratic cost functions on network links. This framework can be extended to solving the optimization of a general cost function with flow costs on links. The key approach is to construct a first-order linear dynamic system on the space C_1^K, where the tangent vector of the trajectory is the projection of the gradient of the general cost function to the space of cycles. This is consistent with our earlier characterization in Theorem 13.10 that the set of solutions of (13.24) is the linear space of an acyclic flow and the basis of the space of cycles. This method can also be generalized to a general cost function with flow costs on links and load costs at nodes, for example, the type of load balancing problem for parallel computation considered in [18]. The key approach is still to use an appropriate first-order linear dynamic system in the product space of C_1^K and C_0^K as long as the specified boundary condition is satisfied. The key question of all the above problems is whether it can be computed in a distributed way. This relies on constructing an iterative matrix that can be represented by local operators. In the cases we have investigated, the iterative matrices can be constructed from the boundary operator ∂, the coboundary operator δ, and δA, where δA is a global operator that can be computed by iterations of local operators according to Theorems 13.13 and 13.14.

Section 4 shows how to dynamically compensate for second-order variations of traffic inputs while maintaining stability. The criterion chosen in this paper is to load balance queues, weighted by $\bar{Q}$, at network nodes. Even though the discussion focuses on a quadratic cost function, the use of the Laplacian can be extended to other network routing designs based on other type of cost function.

In Section 5 we show how the network control can be performed in a distributed and asynchronous way. The first part incorporates the optimal steady-state solution for the quadratic cost problem for links, which uses the iterative algorithm based on local data from Section 2 to approximate the global optimum solution. Then, to balance the queue lengths at nodes, we incorporate inner-loop feedback by using a distributed algorithm that is asynchronous and depends only on local information.

In Section 6 we presented some examples to show that the distributed algorithm has potential to solve problems of realistic size. We considered both periodic and aperiodic examples. As mentioned before, the convergence of the algorithm is geometric with parameter m. This rate may nonetheless be slow if the parameter m is very close to 1, which presumably can occur if the network topology is bad. We did not look for nor did we consider pathological cases. In the future we will consider more detailed performance analysis.

In summary, our outer-loop control is over the cycle space, which is orthogonal to the image of the coboundary operator, and of dimension $M - N + 1$ (Lemma 13.5). The load-balancing objective we adopt here, implemented via dynamic inversion, is just one way to use coboundary feedback. The general point is that coboundary feedback provides $N - 1$ degrees of freedom, as can be seen in Lemma 13.4, which is exactly the number required to make all queue lengths a fixed percentage higher or lower than their nominal, steady-state values. The load-balancing control objective is expressed in equation (13.31). According to the fundamental dynamic equation (14.23) in [1], the law of conservation for one type of message is

$$\frac{dX(t)}{dt} = \partial(T(t)) + U(t) - deg(U(t))a(N), \qquad (13.33)$$

where $X(t)$ is the quantity of messages served or queued at nodes at time t, $T(t)$ is the flow on links at time t, $U(t)$ is the input rate at time t, and $a(N)$ is the destination node. For fixed input rate U, the above equation has M degrees of freedom. Thus it is possible to achieve optimal steady-state message flows and, at the same time, use load-balancing to compensate for transient message-rate variations. However, after doing that we have used up all available degree of freedom to control the flows because $M = (M - N + 1) + (N - 1)$. If the network is congested, which is possible if the traffic input is too heavy, the only way to decongest the network is to use flow control or admission control to decrease the input rate U. The input rate U is in the node space of dimension N. Because the coboundary feedback control gives us control over $N-1$ degrees of freedom, the admission/flow control is reduced to a residual one-dimensional space that can be identified with the kernel of the coboundary operator (see Lemma 13.4 again). In the context of load-balancing objective, the remaining degree of freedom can be thought of as the average queue length over all the nodes in the network.

Appendix

LEMMA A.1 *The following sequences are exact.*

$$0 \to Z_B \xrightarrow{i} C_1 \xrightarrow{\partial_B} C_0 \xrightarrow{deg} \mathbf{R} \to 0$$

$$0 \to \mathbf{R} \xrightarrow{[\times \sum a(i)]} C_0 \xrightarrow{\delta_B} C_1 \to C_1/\delta_B(C_0) \to 0$$

Proof. The first sequence is exact because, for $x \in Z_B$, by the definition of Z_B,

$$\partial_B(x) = 0$$

and for $y = \sum_{i<j} y_{ij}(a(i), a(j)) \in C_1$,

$$deg\partial_B(y) = deg(\sum_{i<j} y_{ij} B_{ij}(a(j) - a(i))) = \sum_{i<j}^{N} y_{ij} B_{ij} - \sum_{i<j}^{N} y_{ij} B_{ij} = 0.$$

To prove the second sequence exact, we consider for $r \in \mathbf{R}$

$$\delta_B[\times \sum a(i)](r) = \delta_B(\sum_i^N ra(i)) = \sum_i^N \sum_{a(j) \in N(a(i))} r B_{ij}(a(j), a(i)) = 0.$$

The last equality follows from $(a(i), a(j)) = -(a(j), a(i))$ and $B_{ij} = B_{ji}$. Q.E.D.

References

[1] Chao, Yi-Ju, Morton B., A framework for analysis and control of communication networks, *Telecommunications Network Design and Management* edited by G. Anandalingam and S. Raghavan, Chapter 14, p 273-301, (Kluwer Academic Publishers, 2002).
[2] Bertsekas, D., Gallager, R. *Data Networks*, Prentice Hall, 1992.
[3] Bertsekas, D., Optimal routing and flow control methods for communication networks, *Analysis and Optimization of Systems* edited by A. Bensoussan and J. L. Lions, (New York: Springer-Verlag, 1982).

[4] Tsai, W. K., Antonio, J. and Huang, G. M., Complexity of gradient projection method for optimal routing in data networks, IEEE/ACM Transactions on Networks, VOL. 7, NO. 6, December 1999.

[5] Moy, J. T. *OSPF Anatomy of an Internet Routing*, Reading, MA: Addison-Wesley, 1998.

[6] Reeves, D. S. and Salama, H. F., A distributed algorithm for delay-constrained unicast routing, IEEE/ACM Transactions on networking, VOL. 8, NO. 2, April 2000.

[7] Rastogi, R., Breitbart, Y., Garofalakis, M. and Kumer, A., Optimal configuration of OSPF aggregates, IEEE/ACM Transactions on networking, VOL. 11, NO. 2, April 2003.

[8] Gordan, M., Minoux, M., *Graphs and Algorithms*. Wiley, 1984.

[9] Lefschetz, *Topology*. Second Edition. Chelsea publishing, 1956.

[10] Bollobas, B. *Modern Graph Theory*, 1998, Springer-Verlag, New York.

[11] Wilkinson, J. H., *The Algebraic Eigenvalue Problem*, 1965, Oxford.

[12] Kelly, F. P., Maulloo, A. and Tan, D., Rate control for communication networks: shadow precess, proportional fairness and stability, Journal of Operations Research Society, VOL. 49, NO. 3., pp. 237-252, March 1998.

[13] Low, S. H. and Lapsley, D., Optimization flow control, I: basic algorithm and convergence, IEEE/ACM Transactions on Networking, VOL. 7, NO. 6, pp. 861-874, December 1999.

[14] Low, S. H., Paganini, F. and Doyle, J. C., Internet congestion control, IEEE Control Systems Magazine, pp. 28-43, February 2002.

[15] Johari, R. and Tan, D., End-to-end congestion control for the Internet: delays and stability, IEEE/ACM Transactions on Networking, 9 (2001) 818-832.

[16] Bott, R. and Duffin J., On the algebra of networks, Transactions of the American Mathematical Society, VOL 74, NO 1, pp. 99-109, January 1953.

[17] Boulogne, T., Altman, E., Kameda, H., and Pourtallier, O., Mixed equilibrium (ME) for multiclass routing games, IEEE Transactions on Automatic Control, VOL.47, NO.6, June 2002.

[18] Li, J, and Kameda, H., Load balancing problems for multiclass jobs in distributed/parallel computer systems, IEEE Transactions on Computers, VOL.47, NO.3, March 1998.

[19] Herlihy, M. and Rajsbaum, S., On computer science today - recent trends and developments, *Lecture Noted in Computer Science #1000* edited by Jan van Leeuwen, ISBN-3-54060105 (Springer-Verlag, 1996).

[20] Ross, K. W. and Yao, D. D., Optimal load balancing and scheduling in a distributed computer system, J. ACM, VOL.38, NO. 3, pp. 676-690, July 1991.

[21] Kumer, V., Grama, A. Y. and Vempaty, N. R., Scalable load balancing techniques for parallel computers. Journal of Parallel and Distributed Computing, pp. 8-12 (1994).

[22] Willebeek-LeMair, M. and Reeves, A. P., Strategies for dynamic load balancing on highly parallel computers, IEEE Transactions on Parallel and Distributed Systems, 4(9): 979-993 (1993).

[23] Olfati-Saber, R. and Murray, R. M., Consensus protocols for networks of dynamic agents, American Control Conference, Pasadena, California, June 2003.

[24] Fax, A. and Murray, R. M., Information flow and cooperative control of vehicle formations, The 15th IFAC World Congress, June 2002.

[25] Fax A. and Murray, R. M., Graph Laplacian of vehicle formations, The 15th IFAC World Congress, June 2002.

[26] Sunil Kandukuri and Stephen Boyd, Optimal power control in interference limited fading wireless channels with outage probability, IEEE Transactions on Wireless Communications, pp. 46-55, Vol 1 No 1, Jan 2002.

[27] Erhan Cinlar, *Introduction to Stochastic Processes*, 1975, Prentice-Hall.

[28] Richard S. Varga, *Matrix Iterative Analysis*, 2nd Ed., 2000, Springer.

[29] Fan R. K. Chung, *Spectral Graph Theory*, 1997, AMS.

[30] Kailath, Thomas. *Linear Systems*, Prentice Hall, 1980.

Chapter 14

A COMBINATORIAL APPROXIMATION ALGORITHM FOR CDMA DOWNLINK RATE ALLOCATION

R.J. Boucherie[1], A.F. Bumb[1], A.I. Endrayanto[1] and G.J. Woeginger[2]

[1]*Stochastic Operations Research Group, Department of Applied Mathematics, University of Twente, P.O.Box 217, 7500 AE Enschede, the Netherlands. E-mail: {r.j.boucherie, a.f.bumb, a.i.endrayanto}@math.utwente.nl*

[2]*Combinatorial Optimization Group, Department of Mathematics and Computing Science, Eindhoven University of Technology, P.O.Box 513, 5600 MB, Eindhoven, the Netherlands. E-mail: gwoegi@win.tue.nl*

Abstract   This paper presents a combinatorial algorithm for downlink rate allocation in Code Division Multiple Access (CDMA) mobile networks. By discretizing the coverage area into small segments, the transmit power requirements are characterized via a matrix representation that separates user and system characteristics. We obtain a closed-form analytical expression for the so-called Perron-Frobenius eigenvalue of that matrix, which provides a quick assessment of the feasibility of the power assignment for a given downlink rate allocation. Based on the Perron-Frobenius eigenvalue, we reduce the downlink rate allocation problem to a set of multiple-choice knapsack problems. The solution of these problems provides an approximation of the optimal downlink rate allocation and cell borders for which the system throughput, expressed in terms of utility functions of the users, is maximized.

Keywords: CDMA, feasibility transmit power, downlink rate allocation, multiple-choice knapsack, approximation scheme

1.   Introduction

One of the most important features of future wireless communication systems is their support of different user data rates. As a major complicating factor, due to their scarcity, the radio resources have to be used very efficiently.

In Code Division Multiple Access (CDMA) systems, transmissions of different terminals are separated using (pseudo) orthogonal codes. The impact of multiple simultaneous calls is an increase in the interference level, that limits the capacity of the system. The assignment of transmission powers to calls is an important problem for network operation, since the interference caused by a call is directly related to the power. In the CDMA downlink, the transmission power is related to the downlink rates. Hence, for an efficient system utilization, it is necessary to adopt a rate allocation scheme in the transmission powers assignment.

The downlink rate assignment problem has been extensively studied in the literature [3, 6, 12, 14, 16]. In [6], Duan et al. present a procedure for finding the power and rate allocations that minimizes the total transmit power in one cell. In [12], Javidi analyzes several rate assignments in the context of the trade-off between fairness and over-all throughput. The rates are supposed to be continuous and the algorithms proposed for the rate allocation are based on solving the Lagrangean dual. Another approach for joint optimal rates and powers allocation, based on Perron-Frobenius theory, is proposed by Berggren ([3]) and by O'Neill et al. ([14]). Berggren ([3]) describes a distributed algorithm for assigning base station transmitter (BTSs) powers such that the common rate of the users is maximized, while in [14] multiple rates are considered. Again, both algorithms assume continuous rates. In [7], Endrayanto et al. present a model for characterizing downlink and uplink power assignment feasibility, for a single data rate.

In this paper we propose a rate and power allocation scheme for obtaining a close to optimum throughput for the downlink in a Universal Mobile Telecommunication System (UMTS) located on a highway. In accordance with the UMTS standard, the rates are chosen from a discrete set. Our goal is to assign rates to users, such that the utility of the system is maximized. The utility functions describing the satisfaction of the users have a very general form and do not have to satisfy any convexity requirement. For modeling the network, we use the model proposed in [7], which enables a characterization of downlink power feasibility via the Perron-Frobenius (PF) eigenvalue of a suitably chosen matrix. Moreover, an explicit analytical expression for the Perron Frobenius eigenvalue can be obtained. This explicit analytical expression of the PF eigenvalue reduces the rate optimization problem to a series of multiple choice knapsack problems, that can be solved efficiently by standard combinatorial optimization techniques. The algorithm we design is actually a fully polynomial time approximation scheme (FPTAS) for the rate optimization problem. The main advantages of this approach are that, by considering discrete rates, we avoid the rounding errors due to continuity assumptions and that, given an error bound ϵ, we can find a solution of value at least $(1 - \epsilon)$ times the optimum in polynomial time in the size of the input data and $\frac{1}{\epsilon}$. Moreover, the algorithm can be applied for a very large family of utility functions. Furthermore, our results indicate that the optimization problems for different cells are loosely coupled by a single interference parameter. If this parameter were known, the optimization problems for each cell could be independently solved.

The remainder of this paper is organized as follows. In Section 2 we present the model. In Section 3 we charaterise the existence of a downlink power allocation for a given rate allocation via the Perron Frobenius theory. In Section 4 we formulate the rate optimization problem and present a FPTAS for finding a near optimal solution. We conclude our work and present ideas for further research in Section 5.

2. Model

This paper focuses on the modeling of downlink rate allocation in a CDMA system consisting of Base Transmitter Stations (BTSs) along a highway. Specifically, we focus on a two cells model, where only the area between the two base stations is taken into account.

For modeling a cell, we consider the discretized cell model proposed in [7]. This model permits, as we will see below, to characterize analytically the transmit power feasibility for a given rate allocation and users distribution. The discretized cell model can be described as follows. Let X and Y be the two base stations, situated at distance D from each other on a highway. The highway is divided into L small segments, from which segments $\{1, ..., I\}$ are assigned to BTS X and segments $\{I+1, ..., L\}$ to BTS Y. We assume that in each segment, the subscribers are located in the middle of the segment and that they have the same data rate and power. Denote by n_i the number of users in segment $i, i \in \{1, ..., L\}$.

We model the path loss propagation between a transmitter X and a receiver in segment i by a deterministic path loss propagation model of the following form

$$P_i^{rec} = P_i l_{i,X},$$

where $l_{i,X}$ depends only on the distance d_i between the middle of segment i and BTS X, P_i^{rec} is the received power in the i-th segment and P_i is the transmission power towards the $i-th$ segment. If $l_{i,X} = d_i^{-\gamma}$, where $\gamma \geq 0$ is independent on the distance, we obtain the Okumura-Hata model, which performs reasonably in flat service areas (see [1, 10]).

A common measure of the quality of the transmission, is *the energy per bit to interference ratio*, $\left(\frac{E_b}{I_0}\right)$, that, for a user i, say, is defined as (see. e.g. [11])

$$\left(\frac{E_b}{I_0}\right)_i = \frac{W}{R_i} \frac{\text{useful signal power received by user i}}{\text{interference +thermal noise}},$$

where W is the system chip rate and R_i is the data rate in segment i. Under the described path loss model, with users in the same segment having the same power and the same rate and a constant noise N_0, the energy per bit to interference ratio in the segments assigned to BTS X, respectively to BTS Y, becomes

$$\left(\frac{E_b}{I_0}\right)_i = \frac{W}{R_i} \frac{P_i l_{i,X}}{\alpha l_{i,X}(\sum_{j=1}^{I} n_j P_j - P_i) + l_{i,Y} \sum_{j=I+1}^{L} n_j P_j + N_0}, \qquad (14.1)$$

for $i \in \{1, ..., I\}$, respectively

$$\left(\frac{E_b}{I_0}\right)_i = \frac{W}{R_i} \frac{P_i l_{i,Y}}{\alpha l_{i,Y}(\sum_{j=I+1}^{L} n_j P_j - P_i) + l_{i,X} \sum_{j=1}^{I} n_j P_j + N_0}, \qquad (14.2)$$

for $i \in \{I + 1, ..., L\}$, where α is the non-orthogonality factor. In order to ensure a certain quality of service, the energy per bit to interference ratio in each segment i has to be above a prespecified value ϵ_D^*. In the presence of perfect power control, we can actually assume that in each segment i, $\left(\frac{E_b}{I_0}\right)_i = \epsilon_D^*$.

We measure the satisfaction of a user in segment $i, i \in \{1, ..., L\}$ by means of a positive utility function $u_i(R_i)$. For a presentation of the utility functions commonly used in the literature see [17].

Our goal is to allocate rates from a discrete and finite set R=$\{R_1, ..., R_K\}$ to the users such that the total utility, i.e., the sum of the utilities of all users, is maximized under the condition that the prescribed quality of service is met for all users and that a feasible power assignment exists.

3.   Downlink transmit power feasibility

In this section we derive a condition for the existence of a feasible power allocation when the rates allocated to users are known. For this, we will make use of the Perron Frobenius theory (see [15]), by analogy with the characterization of power feasibility for the uplink in [2, 8, 9].

For a rate allocation $r = (r_1, ..., r_L)$, we say that a feasible power assignment exists if there exists a vector $p \in R^L$ verifying the following system

$$\begin{cases} \left(\frac{E_b}{I_0}\right)_i (r,p) = \epsilon_i, \text{ for each user in segment } i, \\ p_i \geq 0 \text{ for each } i \in \{1, ..., L\}, \end{cases} \quad (14.3)$$

Before characterizing the feasibility of system (14.3) we introduce some notations. Let $\mathbf{N} = (n_1, ..., n_L)$, $V(r_i) = \frac{\epsilon_D^* r_i}{W + \alpha \epsilon_D^* r_i}$, $\mathbf{L_X} = (l_1, ..., l_I)$ and $\mathbf{L_Y} = (l_{I+1}, ..., l_L)$, where

$$l_i = \begin{cases} \frac{l_{i,Y}}{l_{i,X}}, \text{ for } i \in \{1, ..., I\}, \\ \frac{l_{i,X}}{l_{i,Y}}, \text{ for } i \in \{I+1, ..., L\}. \end{cases}$$

Based on (14.1) and (14.2), system (14.3) can be rewritten as:

$$\begin{cases} p_i = \alpha V(r_i) \sum_{j=1}^{I} p_j n_j + V(r_i) l_i \sum_{j=I+1}^{L} p_j n_j + V(r_i) l_{i,X}^{-1} N_0, \\ \qquad\qquad\qquad\qquad \text{for } i \in 1, ..., I, \\ p_i = V(r_i) l_i \sum_{j=1}^{I} p_j n_j + \alpha V(r_i) \sum_{j=I+1}^{L} p_j n_j + V(r_i) l_{i,Y}^{-1} N_0, \\ \qquad\qquad\qquad\qquad \text{for } i \in I+1, ..., L, \\ p \geq 0 \end{cases} \quad (14.4)$$

Note that system (14.4) has L equations, besides the positivity constraint of the power vector. Next we show that the feasibility of (14.4) is equivalent to the feasibility of a system with 2 equations (each of them characterizing one cell) and a positivity constraint.

LEMMA 14.1 *System (14.4) is feasible if and only if the following system is feasible:*

$$\begin{cases} \left(1 - \alpha \sum_{j=1}^{I} V(r_j) n_j\right) x - \sum_{j=1}^{I} V(r_j) n_j l_j y = \sum_{j=1}^{I} V(r_j) n_j l_{j,X}^{-1} N_0, \\ - \sum_{j=I+1}^{L} V(r_j) n_j l_j x + \left(1 - \sum_{j=I+1}^{L} V(r_j) n_j\right) y = \sum_{j=I+1}^{L} V(r_j) n_j l_{j,Y}^{-1} N_0, \\ x \geq 0, y \geq 0 \end{cases}$$

$$(14.5)$$

Proof: Let p be a positive solution of (14.4). In system (14.4) multiply each equation with the number of users in the corresponding segment and then add the first I equations and then the other $L - I$. It follows that

$(x, y) = (\sum_{i=1}^{I} n_i p_i, \sum_{i=I+1}^{L} n_i p_i)$ verifies (14.5). Let (x, y) be a solution of (14.5). Define:

$$p_i = \begin{cases} V(r_i)l_i y + \alpha V(r_i)x + V(r_i)l_{i,X}^{-1} N_0, & \text{for } i \in \{1, ..., I\}, \\ V(r_i)l_i x + \alpha V(r_i)y + V(r_i)l_{i,Y}^{-1} N_0, & \text{for } i \in \{I+1, ..., L\}, \end{cases}$$

(14.6)

By simple substitution in (14.4) it can be shown that p is a solution of (14.4). ∎

Lemma 14.1 reduces the amount of calculations involved in characterizing the power feasibility, since it is straightforward to verify that a system with 2 equations in 2 positive variables is feasible.

System (14.5) can be rewritten in the following form:

$$(\mathbf{I} - \mathbf{T}) \begin{pmatrix} x \\ y \end{pmatrix} = \mathbf{c},$$

(14.7)

where

$$\mathbf{T} = \begin{pmatrix} \alpha \sum_{i=1}^{I} V(r_i)n_i & \sum_{i=1}^{I} V(r_i)\, n_i l_i \\ \sum_{i=I+1}^{L} V(r_i)n_i l_i & \alpha \sum_{i=I+1}^{L} V(r_i)n_i \end{pmatrix},$$

$$\mathbf{c} = \begin{pmatrix} \sum_{i=1}^{I} V(r_i)N_0 n_i l_{i,X}^{-1}, \\ \sum_{i=I+1}^{L} V(r_i)N_0 n_i l_{i,Y}^{-1} \end{pmatrix}.$$

Since matrix $\mathbf{T}$ is a non-negative matrix, according to the Perron-Frobenius theorem (see [15]), the feasibility of (14.7) is determined by the Perron- Frobenius (PF) eigenvalue $\lambda(\mathbf{T})$ of the matrix $\mathbf{T}$ i.e.,

$$p \geq \mathbf{0} \text{ exist and } p = (\mathbf{I} - \mathbf{T})^{-1}\mathbf{c} \iff \lambda(\mathbf{T}) < 1.$$

(14.8)

The explicit expression of the PF eigenvalue of $\mathbf{T}$ can be calculated easily

$$\lambda(\mathbf{T}) = \frac{1}{2}(\sum_{i=1}^{I} \alpha V(r_i)n_i + \sum_{i=I+1}^{L} \alpha V(r_i)n_i)$$

$$+ \frac{1}{2}\sqrt{\alpha^2(\sum_{i=1}^{I} V(r_i)n_i - \sum_{i=I+1}^{L} V_i n_i^2) + 4(\sum_{i=1}^{I} V(r_i)n_i l_i)(\sum_{i=I+1}^{L} V_i n_i l_i)}.$$

Further note that the condition $\lambda(T) < 1$ is equivalent with the following system:

$$\begin{cases} \sum_{i=1}^{I} \alpha V(r_i)n_i + \sum_{i=I+1}^{L} \alpha V(r_i)n_i \leq 2, \\ (1 - \sum_{i=1}^{I} \alpha V(r_i)n_i)(1 - \sum_{i=I+1}^{L} \alpha V(r_i)n_i) > (\sum_{i=1}^{I} V(r_i)n_i l_i)(\sum_{i=I+1}^{L} V_i n_i l_i). \end{cases}$$

(14.9)

Since $\sum_{i=1}^{I} \alpha V(r_i)n_i$ and $\sum_{i=I+1}^{L} \alpha V(r_i)n_i$ cannot be both larger then 1 without violating the first inequality of (14.9), system (14.9) is equivalent with

$$\begin{cases} \sum_{i=1}^{I} \alpha V(r_i)n_i < 1, \\ \sum_{i=I+1}^{L} \alpha V(r_i)n_i < 1, \\ (1 - \sum_{i=1}^{I} \alpha V(r_i)n_i)(1 - \sum_{i=I+1}^{L} \alpha V(r_i)n_i) > (\sum_{i=1}^{I} V(r_i)n_i l_i)(\sum_{i=I+1}^{L} V_i n_i l_i). \end{cases}$$

Hence, we have proved the following theorem.

THEOREM 14.2 *For a given rate allocation* r, *a feasible power allocation exists, i.e., system (14.4) is feasible, if and only if*

$$\begin{cases} \sum_{i=1}^{I} \alpha V(r_i)n_i < 1, \\ \sum_{i=I+1}^{L} \alpha V(r_i)n_i < 1, \\ (1 - \sum_{i=1}^{I} \alpha V(r_i)n_i)(1 - \sum_{i=I+1}^{L} \alpha V(r_i)n_i) > (\sum_{i=1}^{I} V(r_i)n_i l_i)(\sum_{i=I+1}^{L} V_i n_i l_i). \end{cases}$$

Theorem 14.2 provides a clear motivation for discretizing the cells into segments, since it facilitates obtaining an analytical model for characterizing the transmit power feasibility for a certain rate allocation and a certain user distribution. Moreover, we observe that the first two conditions we obtained characterize the two cells separately and the third contains products of factors depending only of one cell. In the next section we will show how these nice properties lead to a fast algorithm for finding a close to optimal rate allocation.

4. The rate optimization problem

Let $R = \{R_1, R_2, ..., R_K\}$ be the set of admissible rates, where $R_1 < R_2 < ... < R_K$. The decision of dropping the users of a segment is equivalent with assigning zero rate to the respective segment, case in which $R_1 = 0$.

The problem of allocating rates from the set R to users such that the total utility of the users is maximized, under the condition of ensuring the required Quality of Service and a feasible power assignment, can be formulated as follows:

$$\max \quad \sum_{i=1}^{L} u_i(r_i)$$

$$(P) \qquad \text{s.t.} \quad \left(\frac{E_b}{I_0}\right)_i (r,p) = \epsilon_D^*, \text{ for each user in segment } i,$$

$$r_i \in \{R_1, ..., R_K\}, \text{ for each } i \in \{1, ..., L\},$$

$$p_i \geq 0 \text{ for each } i \in \{1, ..., L\},$$

where r_i, respectively p_i represent the rate, respectively the power allocated to segment i and ϵ_D^* is the threshold for the energy per bit to interference ratio.

We are interested in designing an algorithm for assigning rates to segments in such a way that a throughput of at least $(1 - \epsilon)$ times the optimum is obtained, in a time polynomial in the size of an instance and $\frac{1}{\epsilon}$. Such an algorithm would be a fully polynomial approximation scheme (FPTAS) for problem (P). We distinguish three main steps in the design of the algorithm:

- First we show that finding an optimal solution of (P) can be reduced to solving a set of optimization problems $\{P_1(t), P_2(t)|t \in [t_{min}, t_{max}]\}$, where $P_1(t)$ characterize the first cell, $P_2(t)$ characterize the second cell and the interval $[t_{min}, t_{max}]$ is an interval depending on the system and the user distribution.

- Then we show that $P_1(t)$, respectively $P_2(t)$ are multiple choice knapsack problems, for which efficient algorithms are known.

- Finally, we will prove that, for finding a solution of value at least $(1 - \epsilon)$ times the optimum, for an $\epsilon > 0$, we only have to solve $P_1(t)$ and $P_2(t)$ for $O(\frac{1}{\epsilon})$ t's in $[t_{min}, t_{max}]$. Since to solve $P_1(t)$, respectively $P_2(t)$ we can apply known FPTAS (see e.g. [4]) for the multiple choice knapsack problem, the algorithm we propose is a FPTAS for (P).

We proceed with the first step of the analysis. Theorem 14.2 implies that the optimization problem (14.9) is equivalent with the following problem: (P')

$$\max \sum_{i=1}^{L} u_i(r_i),$$

$$s.t. \quad \sum_{i=1}^{I} \alpha V(r_i)n_i < 1,$$

$$\sum_{i=I+1}^{L} \alpha V(r_i)n_i < 1,$$

$$(1 - \sum_{i=1}^{I} \alpha V(r_i)n_i)(1 - \sum_{i=I+1}^{L} \alpha V(r_i)n_i) >$$

$$(\sum_{i=1}^{I} V(r_i)n_i l_i)(\sum_{i=I+1}^{L} V_i(r_i)n_i l_i) \quad r_i \in \{R_1, ..., R_K\}, i \in \{1, ..., L\}.$$

Note that if the rate assignment in one of the cells is known, the problem of assigning rates to the segments of the other cell reduces to a multiple choice knapsack problem. The multiple choice knapsack problem is a NP-hard problem, for which a FPTAS based on dynamical program ing is proposed in [4]. In a multiple choice knapsack problem the following data are given: the sizes and the profits of a set of objects, which are divided into disjoint classes, and the volume of a knapsack. The goal is to choose the set of objects with maximum profit among the sets of objects that fit into the knapsack and contain one object from each class. If, for example, the rates in the cell assigned to BTS Y were known, then, based on (P'), the problem of allocating rates to the segments in the cell assigned to BTS X becomes:

$$\max \sum_{i=1}^{L} u_i(r_i)$$

$$\sum_{i=1}^{I} V(r_i)n_i(\alpha + l_i \frac{\sum_{i=I+1}^{L} \alpha V(r_i)n_i l_i}{1 - \sum_{i=I+1}^{L} \alpha V(r_i)n_i}) < 1$$

$$r_i \in \{R_1, ..., R_K\}, \text{ for each } i \in \{1, ..., I\}$$

This is a multiple choice knapsack problem with the following data: the objects are the pairs $\{(i,s), i \in \{1, ..., I\}, s \in \{1, ..., K\}\}$, a class consists of the objects corresponding to the same segment, the profit of an object (i,s) is $u_i(R_s)$ and its size is $V(R_s)n_i(\alpha + l_i \frac{\sum_{i=I+1}^{L} \alpha V(r_i)n_i l_i}{1 - \sum_{i=I+1}^{L} \alpha V(r_i)n_i})$. The volume of the knapsack is 1.

Hence, if we knew the rate allocation in one of the cells, we could find a rate allocation for the segments in the other cell by applying an algorithm for the multiple choice knapsack problem. Since this also holds for the case where all the segments in one cell receive zero rate, in the following we may assume that in cell X there is at least one segment which receives non-zero rate.

Under these assumptions, problem (P') can be rewritten as:

$$\max \sum_{i=1}^{L} u_i(r_i)$$

$$(P') \qquad \sum_{i=1}^{I} \alpha V(r_i)n_i < 1 \qquad (14.10)$$

$$\sum_{i=I+1}^{L} \alpha V(r_i)n_i < 1$$

$$\frac{1 - \sum_{i=1}^{I} \alpha V(r_i)n_i}{\sum_{i=1}^{I} V(r_i)n_i l_i} > \frac{\sum_{i=I+1}^{L} V_i(r_i)n_i l_i}{1 - \sum_{i=I+1}^{L} \alpha V(r_i)n_i} \qquad (14.11)$$

$$\sum_{i=1}^{I} r_i > 0 \qquad (14.12)$$

$$r_i \in \{R_1, ..., R_K\}, \text{ for each } i \in \{1, ..., L\}$$

Constraint (14.12) ensures that at least one segment in cell X will receive non zero rate. Remark that the variables and parameters characterizing the two cells are well separated in (P'). This suggests a decomposition of (P') into a set of problems corresponding to the first cell and one corresponding to the second cell. Denote by

$$t_{min} = \min_{r \in R^L} \frac{\sum_{i=I+1}^{L} V_i(r_i)n_i l_i}{1 - \sum_{i=I+1}^{L} \alpha V(r_i)n_i} \quad \text{and} \quad t_{max} = \max_{r \in R^L, r \neq 0} \frac{1 - \sum_{i=1}^{I} \alpha V(r_i)n_i}{\sum_{i=1}^{I} V(r_i)n_i l_i}.$$

From (14.10)-(14.12) follows that (P') is feasible if and only if $\alpha V(R_1) \min_{i \in \{I+1,...,L\}} n_i l_i < 1$ and $t_{min} \leq t_{max}$. In what follows, we suppose that these two conditions are always satisfied.

For each $t \in [t_{min}, t_{max}]$ consider the following problems:

$$\max \sum_{i=1}^{I} u_i(r_i)$$

$P_1(t)$

$$\frac{1 - \sum\limits_{i=1}^{I} \alpha V(r_i) n_i}{\sum\limits_{i=1}^{I} V(r_i) n_i l_i} > t,$$

$$\sum_{i=1}^{I} r_i > 0,$$

$$r_i \in \{R_1, ..., R_K\}, \text{ for each } i \in \{1, ..., I\},$$

and

$$\max \sum_{i=I+1}^{L} u_i(r_i)$$

$P_2(t)$

$$t > \frac{\sum\limits_{i=I+1}^{L} V_i(r_i) n_i l_i}{1 - \sum\limits_{i=I+1}^{L} \alpha V(r_i) n_i},$$

$$r_i \in \{R_1, ..., R_K\}, \text{ for each } i \in \{I+1, ..., L\}.$$

Let OPT denote the optimal value of the optimization problem (P') and $OPT_1(t)$, respectively $OPT_2(t)$, be the optimal values of $P_1(t)$, respectively $P_2(t)$. In the following lemma we prove that we can find OPT by solving $P_1(t)$ and $P_2(t)$ for all $t \in [t_{min}, t_{max}]$.

LEMMA 14.3 $OPT = \max\limits_{t \in [t_{min}, t_{max}]} OPT_1(t) + OPT_2(t)$

Proof: Consider a $t \in [t_{min}, t_{max}]$. Let $(\bar{r}_1, ..., \bar{r}_I)$, respectively $(\tilde{r}_{I+1}, ..., \tilde{r}_L)$, be optimal solutions of $P_1(t)$, respectively $P_2(t)$. Clearly, $(\bar{r}_1, ..., \bar{r}_I, \tilde{r}_{I+1}, ..., \tilde{r}_L)$ is a feasible solution of (P'), and therefore $OPT_1(t) + OPT_2(t) \leq OPT$. We proved that $\max\limits_{t \in [t_{min}, t_{max}]} OPT_1(t) + OPT_2(t) \leq OPT$.

In order to prove the reverse inequality, consider an optimal solution r^* of (P). Let $t = \dfrac{1 - \alpha \sum\limits_{i=1}^{I} V(r_i^*) n_i}{\sum\limits_{i=1}^{I} V(r_i^*) n_i p_i}$. Since $(r_1^*, ..., r_I^*)$ is feasible for $P_1(t)$ and $(r_{I+1}^*, ..., r_L^*)$ is feasible for $P_2(t)$, $OPT \leq OPT_1(t) + OPT_2(t)$. $\blacksquare$

Lemma 14.3 implies that an optimal rate allocation can be found by solving independently the set of optimization problems $\{P_1(t)|t \in [t_{min}, t_{max}]\}$ and $\{P_2(t)|t \in [t_{min}, t_{max}]\}$ where each set characterizes only one cell, the cells interacting only through the parameter t.

Next we show that $P_1(t)$ and $P_2(t)$ are multiple choice knapsack problems, which can be efficiently solved. For this, we rewrite $P_1(t)$ and $P_2(t)$ in the following form:

$$\max \sum_{i=1}^{I} u_i(r_i)$$

$P_1(t)$
$$\sum_{i=1}^{I} V(r_i)n_i(\alpha + l_i t) < 1,$$

$$\sum_{i=1}^{I} r_i > 0,$$

$$r_i \in \{R_1, ..., R_K\}, \text{ for each } i \in \{1, ..., I\},$$

and

$$\max \sum_{i=I+1}^{L} u_i(r_i)$$

$P_2(t)$
$$\sum_{i=I+1}^{L} V(r_i)n_i(\alpha t + l_i) < t,$$

$$r_i \in \{R_1, ..., R_K\}, \text{ for each } i \in \{I+1, ..., L\}.$$

The input to the multiple choice knapsack problems $P_1(t)$, respectively $P_2(t)$ is: the objects are the pairs $\{(i, s), i \in \{1, ..., I\}, s \in \{1, ..., K\}\}$, respectively $\{(i, s), i \in \{I+1, ..., L\}, s \in \{1, ..., K\}\}$; a class consists of the objects corresponding to the same segment; the profit of an object (i, s) is $u_i(R_s)$ and its size is $V(R_s)n_i(\alpha + l_i t)$ for $i \in \{1, ..., I\}$, respectively $V(R_s)n_i(\alpha t + l_i)$ for $i \in \{I+1, ..., L\}$. The volumes of the knapsacks are 1, respectively t. In $P_1(t)$ an extra condition is imposed, namely that the zero rate cannot be allocated to all users in cell X.

Since $P_1(t)$ and $P_2(t)$ are multiple choice knapsack problems, close to optimal solutions can be found by applying for example the FPTAS described in [4]. For an $\epsilon > 0$ and $t \in [t_{min}, t_{max}]$, let $K_1(t, \epsilon)$ and $K_2(t, \epsilon)$, be the value of the solution given by a FPTAS for $P_1(t)$, respectively $P_2(t)$. Hence,

$$K_1(t, \epsilon) \geq (1 - \epsilon)OPT_1(t)$$

and

$$K_2(t, \epsilon) \geq (1 - \epsilon)OPT_2(t).$$

Let t^* be the value for which $OPT_1(t^*) + OPT_2(t^*) = OPT$.

In next lemma we will prove that a feasible solution of (P') of value at least $(1 - \epsilon)OPT$ can be found using only the values $K_1(t, \epsilon)$ and $K_2(t, \epsilon)$, for $t \in [t_{min}, t_{max}]$.

LEMMA 14.4 *For each $\epsilon > 0$, the following relation holds*

$$\max_{t \in [t_{min}, t_{max}]} \{K_1(t, \epsilon) + K_2(t, \epsilon)\} \geq (1 - \epsilon)OPT.$$

Proof: From Lemma 14.3 follows

$$\max_{t \in [t_{min}, t_{max}]} \{K_1(t, \epsilon) + K_2(t, \epsilon)\} \geq K_1(t^*, \epsilon) + K_2(t^*, \epsilon)$$

$$\geq (1 - \epsilon)OPT_1(t^*) + (1 - \epsilon)OPT_2(t^*)$$
$$\geq (1 - \epsilon)OPT,$$

where for the second inequality we have used that $K_1(t^*, \epsilon)$, respectively $K_2(t^*, \epsilon)$ are values returned by a FPTAS for $P_1(t^*)$, respectively $P_2(t^*)$. ∎

However, if $\epsilon \geq \frac{1}{2}$, in order to find a solution of value $(1 - \epsilon)OPT$ it is not necessary to calculate $\max_{t \in [t_{min}, t_{max}]} \{K_1(t, \epsilon) + K_2(t, \epsilon)\}$. Let $r = \{r_1, ..., r_I\}$ and $r' = \{r_{I+1}, ..., r_L\}$ be two rate allocations that give a total utility for cell 1, respectively cell 2, of value at least $\frac{1}{2}OPT_1(t_{min})$, respectively $\frac{1}{2}OPT_2(t_{max})$. Since $OPT_1(t)$ is a decreasing function and $OPT_2(t)$ is an increasing function, it follows that the rate allocation $r'' = (r_1, ..., r_I, r_{I+1}, ..., r_L)$ gives a total utility of value at least $\frac{1}{2}OPT$. The rate allocations r and r' with the above mentioned properties can be found by applying standard methods (see [4]).

In the sequel, we suppose that $\epsilon < \frac{1}{2}$.

The only bottleneck in finding a solution of (P') of value at least $(1-\epsilon)OPT$ is that we have to calculate $K_1(t, \epsilon)$ and $K_2(t, \epsilon)$ for all $t \in [t_{min}, t_{max}]$. However, as we will see below, we can still obtain a solution close to optimum by analysing only a polynomial number of values of t.

For $\epsilon > 0$, let t_{app} be the value of t for which

$$K_1(t_{app}, \epsilon) + K_2(t_{app}, \epsilon) = \max_{t \in [t_{min}, t_{max}]} \{K_1(t, \epsilon) + K_2(t, \epsilon)\}.$$

Note that $OPT_1(t)$, respectively $OPT_2(t)$ are step functions and have at most 2^{KI}, respectively 2^{KJ} jump points, the number of the possible rate assignments in each cell. Therefore, for finding t_{app}, it would suffice to check only the jump points of the two functions.

Next lemma's further reduce the set of t's that must be considered for obtaining a solution of value at least $(1 - \epsilon)OPT$.

LEMMA 14.5 *For each $\epsilon < \frac{1}{2}$, the following holds*
$$t_{app} \in [t_{min}, t_{max}] \setminus \{t | K_1(t_{app}, \epsilon) < \epsilon K_1(t_{min}, \epsilon)$$
$$and \ K_2(t_{app}, \epsilon) < \epsilon K_2(t_{max}, \epsilon)\}.$$

Proof: Suppose that $K_1(t_{app}, \epsilon) < \epsilon K_1(t_{min}, \epsilon)$
and $K_2(t_{app}, \epsilon) < \epsilon K_2(t_{max}, \epsilon)$. Hence,

$$K_1(t_{app}, \epsilon) + K_2(t_{app}, \epsilon) < \epsilon \left(K_1(t_{min}, \epsilon) + K_2(t_{max}, \epsilon) \right),$$

which, since $\epsilon < \frac{1}{2}$, leads to a contradiction with
$$K_1(t_{app}, \epsilon) + K_2(t_{app}, \epsilon) \geq \quad \frac{1}{2} \left(K_1(t_{min}, \epsilon) + K_2(t_{min}, \epsilon) \right.$$
$$\left. + K_1(t_{max}, \epsilon) + K_2(t_{max}, \epsilon) \right).$$

∎

Consider the sets $A_l(\epsilon)$ and $\overline{A_l}(\epsilon)$, for $l \in \{0, 1, ..., \lfloor \frac{1}{\epsilon} ln \frac{1}{\epsilon} \rfloor + 1\}$ defined as

$$A_0(\epsilon) = \{t | K_1(t_{min}, \epsilon) < K_1(t, \epsilon)\},$$
$$\overline{A_0}(\epsilon) = \{t | K_2(t_{max}, \epsilon) < K_2(t, \epsilon)\},$$
$$A_l(\epsilon) = \{t | (1 - \epsilon)^l K_1(t_{min}, \epsilon) < K_1(t, \epsilon) < (1 - \epsilon)^{l-1} K_1(t_{min}, \epsilon)\},$$
$$\text{for } l \geq 1,$$
$$\overline{A_l}(\epsilon) = \{t | (1 - \epsilon)^l K_2(t_{max}, \epsilon) < K_2(t, \epsilon) < (1 - \epsilon)^{l-1} K_2(t_{max}, \epsilon)\},$$
$$\text{for } l \geq 1.$$

REMARK 14.6 From the fact that $(1 - \epsilon)^{\frac{1}{\epsilon} ln \frac{1}{\epsilon}} < \epsilon$, and from Lemma 14.5 follows that $t_{app} \in \bigcup_{l=0}^{\lfloor \frac{1}{\epsilon} ln \frac{1}{\epsilon} \rfloor + 1} (A_l(\epsilon) \cup \overline{A_l}(\epsilon))$

Further we will prove that by choosing only one element from each set A_l, respectively $\overline{A_l}$, we will not deviate significantly from the optimum. This will reduce the number of t's to consider to at most $\lfloor \frac{2}{\epsilon} ln \frac{1}{\epsilon} \rfloor + 2$.

LEMMA 14.7 *a) If $t_{app} \in A_l(\epsilon)$, then for each $t \in A_l(\epsilon)$, $(1-\epsilon)K_1(t_{app}, \epsilon) \leq K_1(t, \epsilon)$.*
b) If $t_{app} \in \overline{A_l}(\epsilon)$, then for each $t \in \overline{A_l}(\epsilon)$, $(1-\epsilon)K_2(t_{app}, \epsilon) \leq K_2(t, \epsilon)$.

Proof: a) For $l = 0$,

$$K_1(t_{min}, \epsilon) \geq (1-\epsilon)OPT_1(t_{min}) \geq (1-\epsilon)OPT_1(t_{app}) \geq (1-\epsilon)K_1(t_{app}, \epsilon),$$

where for the second inequality we used the monotonicity of OPT_1. For $l \in \{1, ..., \lfloor \frac{1}{\epsilon} ln \frac{1}{\epsilon} \rfloor + 1\}$ the proof follows immediately from the definition of A_l. ∎

Let $J_1(\epsilon)$ be the set containing the maximal element from each nonempty set $A_l(\epsilon)$ and $J_2(\epsilon)$ the set containing the minimal element from each nonempty set $\overline{A_l}(\epsilon)$.

The following lemma shows that in order to find a feasible solution of (P) of value at least $(1 - \epsilon)OPT$ it is enough to calculate $K_1(t, \epsilon')$ and $K_2(t, \epsilon')$ only for $t \in J_1(\epsilon') \cup J_2(\epsilon')$, for a well chosen ϵ'.

LEMMA 14.8 *For $\epsilon' = 1 - \sqrt[3]{1 - \epsilon}$ the following relation holds*

$$\max_{t \in J_1(\epsilon') \cup J_2(\epsilon')} \{K_1(t, \epsilon') + K_2(t, \epsilon')\} \geq (1 - \epsilon)OPT.$$

Proof: We have seen in Remark 14.6 that $t_{app} \in \bigcup_{l=0}^{\lfloor \frac{1}{\epsilon'} ln \frac{1}{\epsilon'} \rfloor + 1} (A_l(\epsilon') \cup \overline{A_l}(\epsilon'))$.
Suppose that $t_{app} \in A_k(\epsilon') \cap \overline{A_l}(\epsilon')$.
Let $t_k = J_1(\epsilon') \cap A_k(\epsilon')$ and $\overline{t_l} = J_2(\epsilon') \cap \overline{A_l}(\epsilon')$.

From Lemma 14.7 follows that

$$K_1(t_k, \epsilon') \geq (1 - \epsilon')K_1(t_{app}, \epsilon') \tag{14.13}$$

and

$$K_2(\overline{t_l}, \epsilon') \geq (1 - \epsilon')K_2(t_{app}, \epsilon'). \tag{14.14}$$

Suppose that $t_k \geq \overline{t_l}$. Since $OPT_2(t)$ is an increasing function, the following relations hold:

$$K_2(t_k, \epsilon') \geq (1 - \epsilon')OPT_2(t_k) \geq (1 - \epsilon')OPT_2(\overline{t_l})$$
$$\geq (1 - \epsilon')K_2(\overline{t_l}, \epsilon'). \tag{14.15}$$

Combining (14.13), (14.14), (14.15) and Lemma 14.4, we obtain

$$K_1(t_k, \epsilon') + K_2(t_k, \epsilon') \geq (1 - \epsilon')(K_1(t_k, \epsilon') + K_2(\overline{t_l}, \epsilon'))$$
$$\geq (1 - \epsilon')^2(K_1(t_{app}, \epsilon') + K_2(t_{app}, \epsilon'))$$
$$\geq (1 - \epsilon')^3 OPT,$$

where the first inequality follows from (14.13), the second from (14.14) and (14.15), and the third from Lemma 14.4. Substituting $\epsilon' = 1 - \sqrt[3]{1 - \epsilon}$ in the last relation, we get

$$\max_{t \in J_1(\epsilon') \cup J_2(\epsilon')} \{K_1(t, \epsilon') + K_2(t, \epsilon')\} \geq (1 - \epsilon)OPT.$$

A similar analysis can be done if $t_k \leq \overline{t_l}$, but based on the monotonicity of $OPT_1(t)$. ∎

Hence, the number of points we are looking at in order to find a solution close to the optimum is reduced to $|J_1(\epsilon)| + |J_2(\epsilon)| = \frac{2}{\epsilon'} ln \frac{1}{\epsilon'} + 2 = O(\frac{1}{\epsilon'} ln \frac{1}{\epsilon'}) = O(\frac{1}{\epsilon} ln \frac{1}{\epsilon})$. Note that the points in $J_1(\epsilon') \cup J_2(\epsilon')$ can be found while running the FPTAS presented in [4] for obtaining $K_1(t_{min}, \epsilon')$, respectively for $K_2(t_{max}, \epsilon')$. This implies that the following procedure is a FPTAS for problem (P):

- Let $\epsilon' = 1 - \sqrt[3]{1 - \epsilon}$.

- Find the sets $J_1(\epsilon')$ and $J_2(\epsilon')$.

- For all $t \in J_1(\epsilon') \cup J_2(\epsilon')$, calculate $K_1(t, \epsilon')$ and $K_2(t, \epsilon')$, by using a FPTAS for the multiple choice knapsack problem.

- Find $t_{app} \in J_1(\epsilon') \cup J_2(\epsilon')$ for which $\max_{t \in J_1(\epsilon') \cup J_2(\epsilon')} \{K_1(t, \epsilon') + K_2(t, \epsilon')\}$ is attained.

- Return the rate allocation obtained by solving $K_1(t_{app}, \epsilon')$ and $K_2(t_{app}, \epsilon')$.

If, for solving the multiple choice knapsack problems, one uses the FPTAS described in [4], which, for a given ϵ, runs in time $O(\frac{K^3 L}{\epsilon})$, then the running time of the algorithm presented above is $O(\frac{K^3 L}{\epsilon^2} ln \frac{1}{\epsilon})$.

We conclude this section with several remarks on the algorithm.

REMARK 14.9 The rate allocation provided in this paper should be seen as an almost optimal allocation (with respect to the utility functions) in an ideal setting. Most notably, it requires the base stations to have perfect and complete information on location and path loss of the mobile terminals. This information is clearly not available at the base station. Implementation of rate allocation in a UMTS system will most likely be based on heuristics that use an approximation of location and path loss. For example, from the required power the base station can approximate the location and path loss. In order to characterize the performance of such a heuristic and of a rate allocation, one can use as a benchmark the ideal solution proposed in this paper.

REMARK 14.10 The aim of this paper is to demonstrate that the rate allocation problem reduces to solving coupled multiple choice knapsack problems. For solving such knapsack problems, various approaches are available in the literature. If one is not necessarily interested in obtaining a FPTAS for the rate allocation problem, one can use other approximation or exact algorithms described in the literature (see *e.g.* [5] for a fast branch and bound algorithm). Clearly, any algorithm for the multiple choice knapsack problem, should take into account the specific choice for the utility function. An extensive treatment of the influence of the utility function on the efficiency of the algorithms for solving the multiple choice knapsack problem is beyond the scope of this paper.

REMARK 14.11 Note that the rate allocation algorithm proposed above can be easily adapted to the case where, for each segment, a different set of rates are required by users. The only change will be in the definition of the classes in the underlying multiple choice knapsack problems. More precisely, if, for a segment i, only the rates in the set $\{R_{k_1}, ..., R_{k_2}\}$, with $k_1, k_2 \in \{1, ..., K\}$ are required, the class of objects corresponding to segment i will become $\{(i, s), s \in \{k_1, ..., k_2\}\}$.

REMARK 14.12 The algorithm presented considers differentiated rate allocation in a two cell UMTS system, which goes beyond results described in the literature that usually consider single cell case (see [6] and [13]). For a UMTS network that covers a road, which is the main application intended in this paper, interference among cells will be most likely restricted to neighbouring cells. The main bottleneck in applying our results for general networks, taking into account interference among more than two cells, is the explicit formula for the Perron-Frobenius eigenvalue that is underlying our decomposition among cells. Developing heuristics for more general networks, based on our results, seems possible.

To this end, let us illustrate a possible heuristic for a three cell system. First consider cells 1 and 2. Once a rate allocation has been determined for cells 1 and 2, consider cell 2 and cell 3 and incorporate the interference from cell 1 as noise. Now consider cell 1 and cell 3 and the interference from cell 2 as noise, etc. This procedure may be followed until sufficient convergence is reached. It is among our aims for further research to develop a fixed point scheme for a multi cell UMTS system.

5.   Summary and Further Research

This paper has provided a combinatorial algorithm for finding a downlink rate allocation in a CDMA network, that, for an $\epsilon > 0$, achieves a throughput of value at least $(1 - \epsilon)$ times the optimum. Based on the Perron-Frobenius eigenvalue of the power assignment matrix, we have reduced the downlink rate allocation problem to a set of multiple-choice knapsack problems, for which efficient algorithms are known. This approach proves to have several advantages. First, the discrete optimization approach has eliminated the rounding errors due to continuity assumptions of the downlink rates. Using our model, the exact rate that should be allocated to each user can be indicated. Second, the rate allocation approximation we proposed guarantees that the solution obtained is close to the optimum. Moreover, the algorithm works for very general utility functions. Furthermore, our results indicate that the optimal downlink rate allocation can be obtained in a distributed way: the allocation in each cell can be optimized independently, interference being incorporated in a single parameter t.

It is among our aims for further research to develop a downlink rate algorithm that takes into account mobility of users and limited transmit powers of cells. We will also focus on how the efficiency of the algorithm may be improved in the case of more structured utility functions.

Acknowledgments

The research is partly supported by the Technology Foundation STW, Applied Science Division of NWO and the Technology Programme of the Ministry of Economic Affairs, The Netherlands.

We are thankful to the anonymous referees for their very useful comments.

References

[1] J.B. Andersen, T.S. Rappaport and S. Yoshida, Propagation measurements and models for wireless communications channels, *IEEE Commun. Mag.,* vol. 33, pp. 42-49, 1995

[2] N. Bambos, S.C. Chen, G. Pottie, Channel access algorithms with active link protection for wireless communication networks with power control, *IEEE/ACM Transactions on Networking,* 8(5), pp. 583–597, 2000.

[3] F. Berggren, Distributed power control for throughput balancing in CDMA systems, in *Proceedings of IEEE PIMRC,* vol. 1, pp. 24-28, 2001.

[4] A.K. Chandra, D.S. Hirschberg, and C.K. Wong, Approximate algorithms for some generalized knapsack problems, *Theoretical Computer Science* 3, (1976) 293-304.

[5] M.E. Deyer, W.O. Riha, J. Walker, A hybrid dynamic-programming/branch-and-bound algorithm for the multiple-choice knapsack problem. *Journal of Computational and Applied Mathematics,* 58 (1995), 43-54.

[6] X. Duan, Z. Niu, J. Zheng, Downlink Transmit Power Minimization in Power-Controlled Multimedia CDMA Systems, in *Proceedings of IEEE 13th Int. Symposium Personal, Indoor and Mobile Radio Communication,* 2002.

[7] A.I. Endrayanto, J.L. van den Berg and R.J. Boucherie, An analytical model for CDMA downlink rate optimization taking into account uplink coverage restrictions, to appear in *Journal of Performance Evaluation*.

[8] J.S. Evans, D. Everitt, Effective Bandwidth-Based Admission Control for Multiservice CDMA Cellular Networks, *IEEE Transactions on Vehicular Technology*, vol.48, pp. 36-46,1999.

[9] S.V. Hanly, Congestion measures in DS-CDMA networks, *IEEE Transactions on Communications*, 47 (3), pp. 426-437,1999.

[10] M. Hata, Empirical formula for propagation loss in land mobile radio services, *IEEE Transactions on Vehicular Technology*, vol. 29, pages 317-325, 1980

[11] H. Holma and A. Toskala, WCDMA for UMTS, John Wiley and Sons, 2000.

[12] T. Javidi, Decentralized Rate Assignments in a Multi-Sector CDMA Network, in *Proceedings of IEEE Globecom Conference*, 2003.

[13] R. Litjens, Capacity allocation is wireless communication networks, PhD. thesis, University of Twente, 2003.

[14] D. O 'Neill, D. Julian and D. Boyd, Seeking Foschini's Genie: Optimal Rates and Powers in Wireless Networks, to appear in *IEEE Transactions on Vehicular Technology*.

[15] E. Seneta, Non-Negative Matrices, London, Allen and Unwin, 1973.

[16] V.A. Siris, Cell Coverage based on Social Welfare Maximization, in *Proceeding of IST Mobile and Wireless Telecommunications Summit Greece*, June 2002.

[17] C. Touati, E. Altman, J. Galtier, Fair power transmission rate control in wireless networks, in *Proceedings of IEEE Globecom* 2002.

Chapter 15

RESOURCE ALLOCATION MODEL FOR ESTIMATING NON-UNIFORM SPATIAL LOADS IN CELLULAR WIRELESS NETWORKS

Hanan Luss

Telcordia Technologies, Piscataway, New Jersey 08854, hluss@telcordia.com

Abstract: Carriers of cellular wireless networks often partition the service territory into small bins in order to monitor and provide adequate service throughout the territory. For example, an area of 50 kilometers by 50 kilometers, served by 500 Base Transceiver Stations (BTS's), may be partitioned into 40,000 bins of 250 meters by 250 meters. Carriers estimate the signal strength from every BTS to every bin. The carriers also collect information regarding the carried load and lost call information at every BTS. This information is useful for planning purposes, including the evaluation and modification of a frequency assignment plan. It is also useful for operational purposes, including balancing loads among the BTS's. However, effective planning and control would be further enhanced by having even more detailed load information, specifically, estimates of the offered load initiated at every bin. In this paper, we propose an equitable resource allocation model to derive such load estimates. The model uses as input offered load estimates at each BTS. Service probabilities that assign the load generated at a bin to multiple BTS's are derived using signal strength information. Demographic data is used to estimate a demand target for each bin. The model uses a performance function for each bin, which represents the weighted, normalized deviation from the demand target. The objective function is a lexicographic minimax objective, where the loads at the BTS's are viewed as resources to be allocated among the bins. The model has an intuitively appealing interpretation, and the relations between this model and a model for point-to-point demand estimation in wire-line networks will be presented. A specialized algorithm can readily generate estimated offered loads for problems with a very large number of bins.

Key words: wireless networks, load estimation, network planning, load balancing, resource allocation, lexicographic minimax optimization

1.   INTRODUCTION

Carriers provide cellular wireless services by partitioning the territory into cells. Ideally, these cells are in the shape of hexagons, however, in practice, topological limitations and other considerations lead to significant variations in the cells' topology. Each cell may be further partitioned into a few (say, 3 or 6) cell sectors. Every cell sector has a Base Transceiver Station (BTS) with multiple transceivers that transmit and receive signals at multiple frequencies. Thus, the BTS serves as the access point for the mobile stations into the telecommunications network. Currently, wireless carriers primarily use second generation cellular systems to provide cellular wireless communications. The most widely used systems are the global system for mobile communications (GSM) , which uses a hierarchy of time division multiplexing access (TDMA) frames, and code division multiple access (CDMA), which is a spread spectrum-based technique. Currently, significant work is underway on the development of the third generation (3G) of cellular wireless communications systems. These systems will provide high-speed wireless communications and support a mix of services, including voice, video, and data at various rates. The interested reader may consult any textbook on cellular wireless networks, for example, Chapter 10 in Stallings (2002).

In order to manage effectively the service offered to mobile stations, carriers often partition the service territory to small "bins" (also called pixels). For example, a territory comprised of a 50 kilometers by 50 kilometers square, and served by, say, 500 BTS's, may be partitioned into approximately 40,000 bins of 250 meters by 250 meters. A carrier then derives, using propagation models and field measurements, the average and standard deviation of the received signal strength at every bin from every BTS. The matrix of expected received signal strength is known as the Received Signal Strength Indicator (RSSI) matrix. A mobile station in a particular bin may be adequately served by multiple BTS's. Typically (e.g., in GSM), a mobile station is served by the BTS that transmits the strongest signal to the mobile location, or, alternatively (e.g., in CDMA), it may be served simultaneously by multiple BTS's that transmit the strongest signals. Some exceptions may occur, for example, when all time slots on the strongest signal are occupied

Figure 1 highlights two bins in the territory. Bin 1 receives signals from four BTS's. The signals are shown as dashed lines, where the line width represents the expected signal strength. Consider bin 1. The expected signal strength received from BTS 1 is the highest, and the expected signal strength received from BTS 4 is the lowest. The expected signal strengths received from BTS's 2 and 3 are between the two extremes. Consider now bin 2. The expected signal strengths received from BTS 3 and BTS 4 are about the same. The expected signal strength received from BTS 2 is somewhat lower. The expected signal strength received from BTS 1 is below a minimal threshold and is therefore not shown. The received signal strength deteriorates very fast with the traveling distance (in general, proportionally to *distance*$^{-d}$ where d is a constant between two to four). Hence, only a small fraction of the BTS's in the territory are candidate servers for a specific bin.

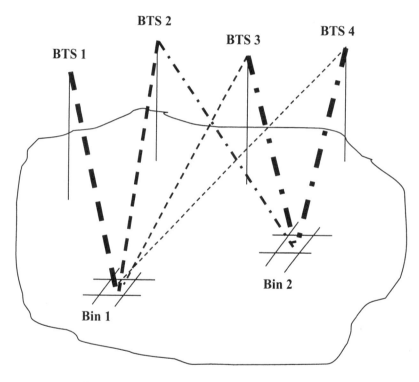

Figure 1. Illustration of Signal Received at Two Bins

Designing and operating a cellular wireless network is quite complex. Carriers continuously collect performance data at every BTS, including data regarding the carried load, blocked calls, dropped calls, quality of connections, etc. Carriers attempt to infer from the data the service provided to different bins in the territory. Today, carriers do not know the load generated at individual bins at different hours of the day. Nevertheless, this information would facilitate better management of network resources and better fine-tuning of different control parameters such as assigned frequencies, signal power levels, handoff decisions, and others. In this paper, we present a method for estimating the loads generated at every bin.

A fundamental problem in GSM networks is the assignment of frequencies to BTS's. The total number of available frequencies is limited, so that each frequency is assigned to multiple BTS's. However, the assignment of these frequencies has to be done so that the interference experienced by the mobile stations is negligible. The frequency assignment problem is a difficult optimization problem; see survey by Aardal et al. (2001). Numerous papers provide algorithms to variations of this problem. All these papers use an aggregation of the bins to a representative expected signal strength matrix among the BTS's. As Bourjolly et al. (2002) describe, the resulting frequency plan should, however, be evaluated at the bin level. For instance, a good plan should have a small fraction of the bins with an unacceptable reception quality. An enhanced evaluation would also take into consideration the loads generated at each bin, so that more attention can be devoted to bins with higher offered loads.

Load management at the BTS's is an important issue for all cellular systems in order to avoid uneven congestion and blocking of call attempts. Carriers can adjust the transmission power from specific BTS's and thus change the area served by these BTS's. By reducing the power transmitted from a certain BTS, some of the bins that were previously served by that BTS will now receive a stronger signal from other BTS's and be served by them. Thus, fine-tuning of power parameters at the BTS's is used to balance the loads served by the BTS's. The load balancing scheme can certainly be enhanced if the offered load of different bins is approximately known for different time intervals during a day and on different days of the week.

We present a model for estimating the offered load generated at every bin. The model uses an equitable resource allocation model; see Luss (1999) for a survey on this topic. The model views offered load estimates at the BTS's as the resources to be allocated among the bins. A mobile station in a specific bin is typically served by the BTS that transmits the strongest signal to the bin. In CDMA systems, in order to achieve better handover performance, mobile stations may be served simultaneously by multiple, typically up to three, BTS's with the strongest signals. We can therefore derive the probabilities that a bin is served by different BTS's, using signal strength information and probabilistic arguments. These probabilities are used to formulate resource constraints, one per BTS. A resource constraint ensures that the computed offered load for a BTS, as a function of the offered load estimates at the bins, does not exceed the estimated offered load at that BTS, where the latter is derived from carried load and lost call measurements. Finally, we use demographic data, such as residence density, business density, and traffic patterns to derive rough approximations of relative demand for wireless service across all bins in the service territory. Many carriers use such demographic data, as well as specialized consulting services, to derive the relative demands. These demands are then adjusted so that their sum over all bins is made equal to the sum of the offered load estimates over all BTS's. The adjusted demands are call *demand targets*.

A precise definition of the objective function of the model will be given in Section 2. The "decision variables" are the unknown offered loads at the bins. A performance function is associated with each bin. This function expresses the weighted, normalized deviation of the unknown bin load from its demand target. A positive deviation implies that the offered load estimate at the bin is below the demand target, while a negative deviation means that the offered load estimate is above the target. The solution to the model provides equitable offered load estimates across all bins in the sense that no performance function value can be decreased (i.e., its bin load estimate increased) without violating a resource constraint or increasing the value of another performance function that is at least as large.

Figure 2 provides a schematic overview of the method. The input uses the three sources described above: received signal strength information at every bin from every BTS, offered load estimates for the BTS's, and approximations of relative demand at the bins. The first two are used to formulate resource constraints, while the third one is used to formulate the objective function. Solution of the model provides equitable offered load estimates for all bins.

The model can be integrated into the planning process and/or the operational process of a carrier. For instance, if used to construct or refine a frequency assignment plan, the model is used only when network changes are planned, for example, once a month. When used, however, for load balancing, the model may be used several times a day in order to change signal power levels.

A related problem in wire-line telecommunications networks is the estimation of point-to-point demands among edge-nodes. In fact, we will show the relations between our model for estimating the bin loads in cellular wireless networks and the model for estimating point-to-point demands in wire-line networks. The first model for point-to-point demand estimation was initially proposed by Kruithof (1937) and modified by Krupp (1979). The method uses only originating and terminating demand measurements at the edge nodes. It applies a matrix balancing technique to modify an initial guess of point-to-point demands to derive a solution that is consistent with the originating and terminating demands. More recent methods make use of more detailed available information, in particular, measurements of loads at the links. Van Zuylen and Willumsen (1980) extend Kruithof's method to that case. Luss and Vakhutinsky (2001) present a resource allocation model to that problem. The method is used to derive point-to-point demands for different services, such as voice, video and data. The paper also provides an extensive list of references and describes different solution approaches that have been proposed. Zhang et al. (2003) present a model for deriving point-to-point demands for an IP network that uses a gravity model to obtain an initial solution, followed by a quadratic programming model that uses link load measurements. The results are used for traffic engineering of an IP network. Significant related work has also been done in the transportation research literature, as estimation of point-to-point traffic is an important input to the planning of transportation networks. A representative reference is Safwat and Magnanti (1988).

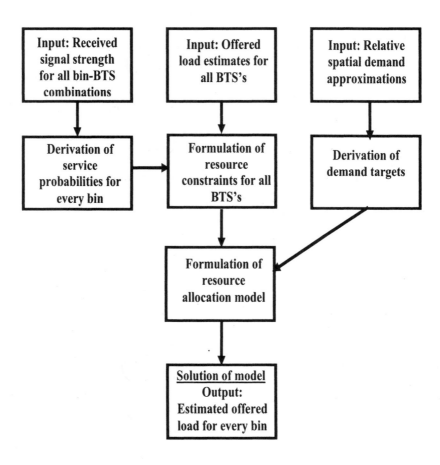

Figure 2. Overview of the method for Bin Load Estimation

2.   THE LOAD ESTIMATION MODEL

We formulate the problem of estimating the offered load at every bin in the service territory as an equitable resource allocation model. As described in the introduction, the model uses as input offered load estimates at the BTS's, data regarding the received signal strength at every bin from every BTS, and an approximation of relative demands across the bins. We use the following notation:

Location parameters
M = Number of BTS's in the service territory.
N = Number of bins in the service territory.
i, k = Indices for BTS's, i (or k) = 1, 2,…, M.
j = Index for bins, j = 1, 2,…, N.

Load and demand target parameters
L_i = Offered load estimate for BTS i. The offered load is derived
                from carried load and lost calls measurements.
e_j = Demand target at bin j.

Demographic data is used to provide an approximation of relative demand for wireless services across the bins. The demographic data may include information on residence density, business density, and traffic pattern. The demand targets are set to be proportional to the relative demands while satisfying

$$\sum_{j=1}^{N} e_j = \sum_{i=1}^{M} L_i .$$

In the absence of sufficient demographic data, the bins can simply be classified into several categories, say, high, medium and low demand, and all bins in the same category would be assigned the same relative demand. The parameters L_i and e_j should be in the same units, such as, bits per second or per minute, number of time slots per second or per minute, and minutes of calls per minute.

Signal strength parameters
The received signal strength at bin j from BTS i is, typically, represented by a random variable with a log-normal distribution. The mean and standard deviation of these variables are obtained through measurements and propagation models. The RSSI input matrix is simply a representation of the

mean signal strengths from any BTS to any bin. Signal strengths are often expressed in decibels, which is a logarithmic scale. One dBm (decibel-miliWatt) is equal to 10log(power expressed in miliWatt). Note that signals expressed in dBm are random variables with a normal distribution. Let:

$f_{ij}(s)$ = The probability density function of the signal s received at bin j from BTS i.

$F_{ij}(S)$ = The probability that the signal strength s received at bin j from BTS i does not exceed S.

p_{ij} = The probability that a mobile station in bin j is served by BTS i.

Assuming that a mobile station is served by the BTS that provides the strongest received signal, and that the signal strengths received are independent variables,

$$p_{ij} = \int_s f_{ij}(s)[\prod_{\forall k,\, k \neq i} F_{kj}(s)]ds, \; i = 1, 2,..., M \text{ and } j = 1, 2,..., N. \quad (1)$$

In practice, we set $p_{ij} = 0$ when the mean signal received at bin j from BTS i is significantly below the largest mean signal received at j (say, by 18 decibels, which implies that it is, on average only about 1.5% of the strongest signal). The positive probabilities are normalized to a sum of one.

Suppose a mobile station is served simultaneously by up to $C \geq 1$ BTS's (e.g., in CDMA systems C is often set equal to 3), and suppose these are the strongest received signals. We need to derive the probability g_{iju} that bin j receives its u-th strongest signal from BTS i. Let $B(j)$ be the subset of BTS's that are candidate to serving mobile stations in bin j (e.g., the expected received signal strength is within 18 decibels of the strongest one). Let B denote a subset of $\{B(j) - i\}$ with $u - 1$ elements. Then,

$$g_{ij1} = \int_s f_{ij}(s)[\prod_{\forall k,\, k \neq i} F_{kj}(s)]ds, \; i = 1, 2,..., M \text{ and } j = 1, 2,..., N, \quad (2a)$$

$$g_{iju} = \sum_{B:\, B \subseteq B(j)} \int_s f_{ij}(s) \prod_{k \in B}[1 - F_{kj}(s)] \prod_{k \in B(j)-B-i} F_{kj}(s)ds, \quad (2b)$$

$$i = 1, 2,..., M, \; j = 1, 2,..., N \text{ and } u = 2, 3,..., C,$$

and

$$p_{ij} = \sum_{u=1}^{C} g_{iju}, \quad i = 1, 2, \ldots, M, \ j = 1, 2, \ldots, N. \tag{2c}$$

Computations of these probabilities can readily be done through numerical integration methods Note that the probabilities p_{ij} can be computed, if desired, for any distribution function.

Decision variables
x_j = Decision variable – the estimated offered load at bin j.
x = Vector of all decision variables, $x = \{x_1, x_2, \ldots, x_N\}$.

The variables x_j are in the same units as the parameters L_i and e_j. We assume that every bin receives a sufficiently strong signal from at least one BTS. Bins that do not receive such a signal are not served by the wireless network and are excluded from the model.

Resource constraints
The offered load estimates for the BTS's serve as resource constraints. Specifically,

$$\sum_{j=1}^{N} p_{ij} x_j \le L_i, \quad i = 1, 2, \ldots, M. \tag{3}$$

The sum in left-hand-side of (3) is the computed offered load that is expected to reach BTS i from all bins. This sum should not exceed the offered load estimate L_i for BTS i.

Performance function
$h_j(x_j)$ = Performance function associated with bin j.

The performance function for bin j measures the weighted normalized deviation of the estimated offered load of bin j from its demand target. Specifically,

$$h_j(x_j) = w_j \frac{e_j - x_j}{e_j}, \quad j = 1, 2, \ldots, N, \tag{4}$$

where the weights $w_j > 0$. Note that $h_j(x_j)$ is strictly decreasing with x_j. When all weights are set equal to one, the performance functions represent normalized deviations from the demand targets. When $w_j = e_j$, for all j, the performance functions represent deviations from demand targets.

The model

An equitable allocation is defined as an allocation of available resources such that no performance function value can be decreased further without either violating at least one of the resource constraints or increasing a performance function of a different bin whose value is at least as large. Since the performance functions are strictly decreasing, an equivalent definition is as follows: None of the bin load estimates can be increased without either violating at least one of the resource constraints or decreasing another bin load estimates with a performance function that is at least as large before the changes.

Note that an equitable allocation attempts to balance normalized deviations from demand targets across all bin load estimates, subject to satisfying the resource constraints. However, an equitable allocation would increase bin load estimates in order to use as much as possible of the available resources, while maintaining equitability as defined above, i.e., as long as it does not lead to a decrease in a bin load estimate with at least an equally large performance function. Hence, performance function values may be negative. The resource parameters are derived from data collected at the BTS's through measurements, hence, it is reasonable to attempt to come as close as possible to satisfying these resource constraints.

Let $h^N(x)$ be a vector of the N performance functions $h_j(x_j)$, where these performance functions are sorted in non-increasing order. That is,

$$h^N(x) = [h_{j_1}(x_{j_1}), h_{j_2}(x_{j_2}), \ldots, h_{j_N}(x_{j_N})], \qquad (5a)$$

where

$$h_{j_1}(x_{j_1}) \geq h_{j_2}(x_{j_2}) \geq \ldots \geq h_{j_N}(x_{j_N}). \qquad (5b)$$

Let x^l be the vector $x \geq 0$ that results in the smallest lexicographic vector $h^N(x)$ among all vectors $x \geq 0$ that satisfy resource constraints (3). The vector x^l provides an equitable allocation of the resources among the N bins, since, by (5), no performance function value can be feasibly decreased without increasing the value of another performance function value that is at least as large. Thus, finding an equitable solution implies finding the smallest lexicographic vector, where the elements of that vector – the performance function values – are sorted in non-increasing order. This is a lexicographic minimax optimization problem; for more details see Luss (1999). Kostreva and Ogryczak (1999) present an axiomatic derivation of lexicographic minimax optimization as an extension of pareto optimality.

The Load Estimation Model (LEM) is formulated as follows:

$$h^N(x^l) = \operatorname*{lexmin}_x [h^N(x)] \tag{6a}$$

so that

$$\sum_{j=1}^{N} p_{ij} x_j \le L_i, \quad i = 1, 2, \dots, M \tag{6b}$$

$$x_j \ge 0, \, j = 1, 2, \dots, N. \tag{6c}$$

Objective function (6a) minimizes lexicographically the vector $h^N(x)$, where $h_j(x_j)$ is given by (4) and $h^N(x)$ is defined by (5). Constraints (6b) ensure that for each BTS, the sum of estimated offered loads at all bins, multiplied by the appropriate probabilities, does not exceed the offered load estimated at the BTS's. Constraints (6c) ensure that all estimated offered loads are nonnegative. Since the functions $h_j(x_j)$ are strictly decreasing, the optimal solution x^l to LEM is unique.

Example
We provide below a small example for illustrative purposes. Consider an example with $M = 3$ BTS's and $N = 6$ bins. The demand targets are $e_j = 150$, 100, 50, 150, 100, 50 for $j = 1, 2, \dots, 6$, respectively. The performance functions are given by (4) with weights $w_j = 1$ for all j. Suppose that resource constraints (3) are:

$$
\begin{array}{llll}
0.5x_1 + & 0.5x_3 + 0.2x_4 + 0.2x_5 & \le 100 \\
0.5x_1 + 0.5x_2 + & 0.8x_5 + 0.2x_6 & \le 200 \\
& 0.5x_2 + 0.5x_3 + 0.8x_4 + & 0.8x_6 & \le 300,
\end{array}
$$

where $x_j \ge 0$ for all j. Thus, for example, as shown by the last column (for $j = 6$), bin 6 is served by BTS 2 with probability $p_{26} = 0.2$ and by BTS 3 with probability $p_{36} = 0.8$. The offered load estimates for the BTS's are 100, 200 and 300 for BTS 1, 2 and 3, respectively.

The lexicographic minimax solution is:

$$x_1^l = 100, \; x_3^l = 33.333, \; x_4^l = 100, \; x_5^l = 66.667,$$

where $h_j(x_j^l) = 0.333$ for $j = 1, 3, 4, 5$ and

$$x_2^l = 161.111, \; x_6^l = 80.556, \text{ where } h_j(x_j^l) = -0.611 \text{ for } j = 2, 6.$$

Thus, for four bins the estimated offered loads are below their demand targets, while for two bins they are above the demand targets. The solution satisfies the resource constraints for BTS's 1 and 2 as equality. It has an excess of 58.333 of the resource associated with BTS 3.

Suppose now that the estimated offered loads at the BTS's at a different time-of-day are changed to 200 for each of the three BTS's. The lexicographic minimax solution is:

$$x_2^l = 85.106, \; x_3^l = 42.553, \; x_4^l = 127.660, \; x_6^l = 42.553,$$

where $h_j(x_j^l) = 0.149$ for $j = 2, 3, 4, 6$, and

$$x_1^l = 144.135, \; x_5^l = 96.090, \text{ where } h_j(x_j^l) = 0.0391 \text{ for } j = 1, 5.$$

Note that now the estimated offered loads for all six bins are below their respective demand targets. The solution satisfies the resource constraints for BTS's 2 and 3 as equality. It has an excess of 61.906 of the resource associated with BTS 1.

3.   THE ALGORITHM

The algorithm for finding the optimal solution to LEM, as formulated by (6), solves repeatedly minimax problems. Upon each minimax solution, some variables are fixed at their optimal values and excluded from the problem, and the amount of available resources is updated. The problem formulation has significant special structure. Each performance function depends on a single decision variable and is strictly decreasing. And, the resource constraints are of the knapsack types (nonnegative coefficients and $\leq$ inequality constraints). For completeness, although not new, we provide a description of the algorithm in the Appendix. The algorithm description follows Luss and Smith (1986) and Luss (1999).

4. THE WIRE-LINE AND CELLULAR WIRELESS MODELS

As discussed in the introduction, the estimation of point-to-point demands among many node-pairs in wire-line networks has been studied extensively. We show below that the bin load estimation model for cellular wireless networks, as formulated by (6), is comparable to the point-to-point demand estimation model in wire-line networks, where the available information is the loads on the links. Specifically, we show that by redefining the parameters used in this paper for LEM, as formulated by (6), we obtain the equitable resource allocation model presented in Luss and Vakhutinsky (2001) for the estimation of point-to-point demands in wire-line networks.

Table 1 highlights the parameter definitions for wireless and wire-line network.

Table 1. Parameter Definitions for Cellular Wireless and Wire-line Networks

Par.	Cellular Wireless Networks	Wire-line Networks
M	Number of BTS's	Number of directed links
N	Number of bins	Number of positive point-to-point demands
I	Index for BTS's	Index for directed links
j	Index for bins	Index for positive point-to-point demands
L_i	Offered load estimate for BTS i	Offered load estimate for link i
e_j	Demand target at bin j	Demand target for point-to-point demand j
p_{ij}	Probability that a mobile station in bin j will be served by BTS i	Probability that point-to-point demand j will be routed on link i
x_j	Decision variable – estimated offered load at bin j	Decision variable – estimated point-to-point demand j
x	Vector of decision variables $x = \{x_1, x_2, \ldots, x_N\}$	Vector of decision variables $x = \{x_1, x_2, \ldots, x_N\}$
$h_j(x_j)$	Performance function for bin j, defined by (4)	Performance function for point-to-point demand j, defined by (4)

For cellular wireless networks, the demand targets e_j are derived from demographic data, and the parameters p_{ij} are derived using probabilistic arguments shown in equations (1) and (2). For wire-line networks, the demand targets e_j are derived from gravity models, Kruithof's method, and demographic data, and the parameters p_{ij} are derived from information regarding the routes used by each of the point-to-point demands and the probabilities of using each of these routes. The parameters L_i are offered loads estimates derived in both cases from carried load measurements and lost call measurements. The parameters for wire-line networks assume asymmetric point-to--point demands and directed links that may have asymmetric loads, which is the case for IP networks. The parameters can readily be defined for networks with symmetric point-to-point demands and symmetric link loads, which is the case for circuit switched networks.

For wire-line networks, resource constraints (6b) state that for every link i, $i = 1, 2,..., M$, the sum of the loads imposed on link i by the point-to-point demands cannot exceed the load L_i on link i. The performance function $h_j(x_j)$, $j = 1, 2,..., N$, is defined by (4) and measures the weighted normalized deviation of estimated point-to-point demand j from its demand target. Thus, formulation (6) is indeed comparable to that provided in Luss and Vakhutinsky (2001) for point-to-point demand estimation in wire-line networks. Note that the latter reference allows for estimation of point-to-point demands for multiple services (e.g., voice, data, and video), while the load measurements L_i are aggregated over all services. Our formulation (6) can readily be extended to handle multiple services offered at the bins, while the load measurements at the BTS's are aggregated over all services, using the same approach. However, this extension is more relevant to wire-line networks than to wireless networks, since in the former case the routing (and hence the probabilities p_{ij}) may depend on the service.

Luss and Vakhutinsky (2001) also present extensive numerical results for large problems, solving problems with about 400,000 positive parameters p_{ij} in about one minute on a SUN Ultra-Enterprise 3000 workstation. Thus, consider, for example, a wireless network that covers a territory of a 50 kilometers by 50 kilometers square, and partitioned into approximately 40,000 bins of 250 meters by 250 meters. Assuming that, on average, a bin may be served by 10 different BTS's, the number of positive parameters p_{ij} is about 400,000. With current computing power, such problems can be solved in negligible time.

We have shown above that the equitable resource allocation models for the wireless and wire-line networks are comparable. Similar arguments can be made for other models used for demand estimation in wireless and wire-line networks. For example, the models of Van Zuylen and Willumsen

(1980) and of Zhang et al. (2003), developed for wire-line networks, can also be adapted for load estimation models in wireless networks. The arguments will be quite similar to those provided above, using appropriate parameter definitions.

ACKNOWLEDGEMENTS

It is my pleasure to thank Ashok Ranade for many helpful discussions on cellular wireless networks. His insights and constructive comments were extremely valuable. Thanks are also due to Arnold Neidhardt for helpful discussions regarding the derivation of the probabilities p_{ij}.

APPENDIX: THE ALGORITHM

The algorithm description follows Luss and Smith (1986) and Luss (1999).

We use I to denote a set of BTS's and J to denote a set of bins. Initially, $I = \{1, 2,..., M\}$ and $J = \{1, 2,..., N\}$. We assume that the input was cleaned up so that $L_i > 0$ for all $i \in I$; for each $i \in I$, $p_{ij} > 0$ for some $j \in J$; and for each $j \in J$, $p_{ij} > 0$ for some $i \in I$. The initial minimax problem to be solved is:

$$V^* = \min_x [\max_j h_j(x_j)] \tag{7a}$$

$$\sum_{j=1}^{N} p_{ij} x_j \le L_i, \quad i \in I \tag{7b}$$

$$x_j \ge 0, \quad j \in J. \tag{7c}$$

It is important to note that problem (7) may have multiple optimal solutions. We need to find the minimal minimax solution vector x^*. Note that x^* is the minimal minimax solution to (7) if $x^* \le x'$, where x' is any other solution to (7). We provide below an outline of an algorithm for solving minimax problem (7). Note that Luss (1999) presents several variations of the algorithm.

The Minimax Algorithm
1. Initialize temporary sets *JTEMP* = *J* and *ITEMP* = *I*.

2. Compute:

$$V_i = \frac{\sum\limits_{j \in JTEMP} p_{ij} e_j - L_i}{\sum\limits_{j \in JTEMP} p_{ij} e_j / w_j} , \quad i \in ITEMP .$$ (8)

Note that V_i is the solution to problem (7) if (7b) includes only a single resource constraint, namely for i, and constraints (7c) are deleted.

3. Find the solution to the relaxed minimax problem, i.e., to problem (7) without constraints (7c):

$$V^R = \max_{i \in ITEMP} [V_i] .$$ (9)

4. If $w_j \geq V^R$ for all $j \in JTEMP$, go to Step 7; otherwise, exclude from $JTEMP$ any $j \in JTEMP$ for which $w_j < V^R$.

5. Update expressions V_i as given by equation (8), for all $i \in ITEMP$, by subtracting from the summations in the numerator and denominator of (8) terms that correspond to j's that were deleted from $JTEMP$ in Step 4.

6. Delete any constraint $i \in ITEMP$ for which all j with $p_{ij} > 0$ were deleted from $JTEMP$. Return to Step 3.

7. Record the minimal minimax solution:

$$V^* = V^R ,$$ (10a)

$$x_j^* = \max[h_j^{-1}(V^*), 0] = \max[e_j(1 - V^* / w_j), 0], \quad j \in J,$$ (10b)

and STOP.

Note that if the w_j's are all the same, then, in Step 4, $w_j \geq V^R$ for all $j \in JTEMP$ in the first iteration. In that case, Step 4 implies that the minimax algorithm finds the optimal solution in a single iteration. Also, as described below in the lexicographic minimax algorithm, we need to compute for each minimax problem only a subset of the variables x_j^*. We now present the algorithm for solving LEM as formulated by (6).

The Lexicographic Minimax Algorithm
1. Formulate the minimax problem (7) with sets I and J and loads L_i.

2. Solve problem (7) using the minimax algorithm. The minimal minimax solution is defined by equations (10). Identify set $R0 = \{i: i \in ITEMP$ and $V_i = V^*\}$. These are resource constraints that are fully used.

3. Identify set $JFIX = \{j: p_{ij} > 0$ for some $i \in R0\}$. Fix $x_j^l = x_j^*$ for all $j \in JFIX$.

4. Delete from J all $j \in JFIX$. If J is now empty, STOP; the lexicographic minimax solution was obtained. If J is not empty, continue with Step 5.

5. Delete i from I if all j with $p_{ij} > 0$ were deleted from J. Update loads
$$L_i \leftarrow L_i - \sum_{j \in JFIX} p_{ij} x_j^l \text{ for all } i \in I. \text{ Return to Step 2.}$$

Suppose, on average, a bin has q positive probabilities p_{ij}. This implies that the number of positive coefficients p_{ij} in resource constraints (6b) is qN. Most of the computational effort on solving the first minimax problem is spent on computing the summations in the V_i's, as given by (8), and subtracting terms from these summations. This effort is in the order of $O(qN)$. Note that at subsequent minimax problems we do not need to compute the summations in (8) by adding again all the terms. Instead, we can use summations computed previously and subtract terms associated with variables that were fixed at their optimal value. Therefore, in all minimax problems solved after the first one, the primary effort is spent on subtracting terms from these summations at a total effort in the order of $O(qN)$. At each minimax problem, the effort in Step 3 on finding V^R is $O(MN)$. Since at each lexicographic iteration at least one variable is fixed, the number of lexicographic iterations is bounded by N, so that the effort on finding V^R over all iterations is $O(MN^2)$. The effort spent on computing the decision variable values, as given by equation (10b), over all minimax problems is $O(N)$. In practice, the computational effort is dominated by the initial computation of the summations in the V_i's and by their subsequent updates at a total effort of $O(qN)$.

REFERENCES

Aardal, K. I., Van Hoesel, S. P. M., Koster, A. M. C. A., Mannino, C., and Sassano, A., 2001, Models and Solution Techniques for Frequency Assignment Problems, Zentrum fur Informationstechnik Berlin (ZIB), ZIB Report 01-40 (also available on http://fap.zib.de).

Bourjolly, J.-M., Dejoie, L., Ding, K., Dioume, O., and Lominy, M., 2002, Canadian Telecom Makes the Right Call, Frequency Allocation in Cellular Phone Networks: An OR Success Story, *OR/MS Today* **29**, April, pp. 40-44.

Kostreva, M. M., and Ogryczak, W., 1999, Linear Optimization With Multiple Equitable Criteria, *RAIRO Operations Research* **33**: 275-297.

Kruithof, J., 1937, Telefoonverkeersrekening, *De Ingenieur* **52**, (8): E15-E25.

Krupp, R. S., 1979, Properties of Kruithof's Projection method, *Bell System Technical Journal* **58**: 517-538.

Luss, H., 1999, On Equitable Resource Allocation Problems: A Lexicographic Minimax Approach, *Operations Research*, **47**: 361-378.

Luss, H., and Smith, D. R., 1986, Resource Allocation among Competing Activities: A Lexicographic Minimax Approach, *Operations Research Letters*, **5**: 227-231.

Luss, H., and Vakhutinsky, A., 2001, A Resource Allocation Approach for the Generation of Service-Dependent Demand Matrices for Communications Networks, *Telecommunication Systems*, **17**: 411-433.

Safwat, K. N. A., and Magnanti, T. L., 1988, A Combined Trip Generation, Trip Distribution, Modal Split, and Trip Assignment Model, *Transportation Science*, **18**: 14-30.

Stallings, W., 2002, *Wireless Communications and Networks*, Prentice Hall, Upper Saddle River, New Jersey.

Van Zuylen, H. J., and Willumsen, L. G., 1980, The Most Likely Trip Matrix Estimated From Traffic Counts, *Transportation Research B*, **14**: 281-293.

Zhang, Y., Roughan, M., Duffield, N., and Greenberg, A., 2003, Fast Accurate Computation of Large- Scale IP Traffic Matrices From Link Loads, *Proceedings of the ACM SIGMETRICS International Conference on Measurement and Modeling of Computer Systems*, San Diego, California, June, pp. 206-217 (also available on www.research.att.com/~duffield/pubs).

Chapter 16

HEAVY TRAFFIC ANALYSIS OF AIMD MODELS

Eitan Altman*
*INRIA,
B.P. 93, 06902 Sophia-Antipolis
Cedex, FRANCE*
eitan.altman@sophia.inria.fr

Harold J. Kushner[†]
*Division of Applied Mathematics, Brown University,
Providence RI 02912, USA*
hjk@dam.brown.edu

Abstract   We study heavy traffic asymptotics of many Additive Increase Multiplicative Decrease (AIMD) connections sharing a common router in the presence of other uncontrolled traffic, called "mice". The system is scaled by speed and average number of sources. With appropriate scalings of the packet rate and buffer content, an approximating delayed diffusion model is derived. By heavy traffic we mean that there is relatively little spare capacity in the operating regime. In contrast to previous scaled models, the randomness due to the mice or number of connections is not averaged, and plays its natural and dominant role. The asymptotic heavy traffic model allows us to analyze buffer and loss management policies of early marking or discarding as a function of the queue size and/or the total input rate and to choose a nearly optimal function via use of an appropriate limiting optimal control problem, captures the essential features of the physical problem, and can guide us to good operating policies. After studying the asymptotics of a large number of persistent AIMD connections we also handle the asymptotics of finite AIMD connections whose number varies as connections arrive and leave. The data illustrate some of the advantages of the approach.

*The work of this author was partially supported by the Euro NGI network of excellence.
[†]The work of this author was supported by contracts DAAD-19-02-1-0425 from the Army Research Office and National Science Foundation Grant ECS 0097447

Keywords: AIMD models, FTP analysis, heavy traffic analysis, approximating
                  delay-diffusions, nearly optimal controls

1.   Introduction

Background and motivation. One of the most active research areas in networking in recent years has been the modeling and analysis of AIMD traffic; e.g., [1–4, 6, 10, 15–18, 20, 21]. When considering a single connection and modeling all other connections through an idealized loss process, simple mathematical formulas for the connection's throughput can be obtained; e.g., [1, 6, 18, 21]. However, it is important in practice to understand the interaction of competing random numbers of connections and the associated system randomness that determines both the throughput as well as the losses suffered by the various connections. One approach is through a fixed point argument; see, e.g., [4]. If the loss rates over the nodes (or links) traversed by the connections are sufficiently small and can be assumed to be additive, an alternative framework can be used where the throughputs of TCP are obtained as the solution of a convex optimization problem and where the loss probabilities are obtained as the Lagrange multipliers [16, 21].

Although the methodologies in these references can be useful due to their simplicity, no dynamical systems description is provided; hence the actual "processes" do not appear, and it is very difficult to add dynamical (say, queue and packet rate dependent) controls to the formulation. The way that packet losses affect individual sources and the consequent effects on the full system are not modeled explicitly, and it is difficult to analyze the oscillations or instabilities that might be caused by delays. They cannot provide a sample-path or transient analysis. Models including some of these features appear in [2, 5] under simplified assumptions on the protocol's behavior (e.g., an assumption in [2] that loss probabilities do not depend on rates, or an assumption in [5] that all connections simultaneously lose a packet when the buffer is full). In order to analyze more complex systems that include buffer management, early marking or discarding, and the impact of the delay in the feedback loop, an alternative line of research has emerged based on fluid models using delay differential equations methodology; see e.g. [8, 17, 21]. In [20], a fluid model of the form of a delayed ordinary differential equation is obtained as a limit of a sequence of suitably scaled physical systems, as the number of connections and the speed of the system grows, and where the randomness is due to the varying number of non-controlled connections. However, there is no randomness in the limit model. More detail on the relations between [20] and our work appears in the Appendix.

Our goal is to analyze heavy traffic approximating models for multiplexing between AIMD and non-controlled traffic, where the losses are a consequence of the actual underlying physical processes, as well as to determine good controls for buffer and loss management. The limit model should retain the main effects of the randomness of the physical processes, which determines the essential features of the buffer and loss processes. The limit model is not deterministic, but it is much simpler to handle than the original discrete stochastic system, and (as seen through numerical examples) it allows us to get good controls for buffer and loss management.

The basic ideas. As with many models for TCP, we will use a "stochastic fluid" model for describing the transmission process; i.e., rather than work explicitly with the widow size; we work with the number of packets that are allowed to be sent per unit time. We consider a model for AIMD traffic in the operating region where the system is near capacity. The analysis will be "asymptotic," as the system grows in speed. In particular, the bandwidth (speed of the router) as well as the mean number of users will be roughly proportional to a parameter n, which is to go to infinity. The analysis will be of the so-called heavy traffic (HT) type [13], which has been of considerable help in studying many complex queueing systems that would be intractable otherwise. Several formulations of the demand process are given. In all cases, there are a certain number of controlled users of the order of n, each having a lot of data to transmit. These share the channel with a large and randomly varying number of users with smaller amounts of data. These are commonly referred to as "mice." They are in the system for too short a time to be controlled, but might take a substantial (40% or more) of the total capacity. While each of the mice (resp., each of the controlled users) has identical statistical properties, this is only for convenience in the numerical analysis: Any number of classes can be handled.

The packets created by the various users enter the system in some random order, then are sent to a buffer via various links, from which they are transmitted. If the buffer capacity is exceeded, then a packet is said to be "lost." Until noted otherwise, the round trip delay α is the same for all AIMD users. The timing of the various rates are as seen at the buffer (not at the sources). They depend on the feedback sent from the buffer α units of time ago, which reached the source t_1 units of time ago, was then acted on and affected the rates at the input to the buffer t_2 units of time later, where $t_1 + t_2 = \alpha$.

We wish to identify a region of operation which is "near capacity" for large n, and a scaling under which the stochastic effects are apparent. One approach to asymptotic analysis is via a fluid model (e.g., [20]). These tend to average or eliminate the effects of stochastic variations in the number of users, mice, data rates, etc. But we are more concerned with demonstrating the actual random processes of losses and buffer content in terms of the random processes of arrivals, data levels, etc.

We are guided by the scaling used for heavy traffic models, as in [13]. There are two related aspects to being "near capacity." One is the difference between the mean packet creation rate and the speed of the system, and the other concerns the buffer size. Suppose that the total mean rate of arrival of packets to the buffer is vn. In order for the system to be in the heavy traffic regime, the speed of exiting the buffer would have to be slightly greater than vn, but not so much faster that the buffer is virtually empty almost all of the time. If the arrival process is the superposition of many independent users, then (loosely speaking) the standard deviation of the "randomness" would be $O(\sqrt{n})$. This suggests that if the system is near capacity at that time, then both the buffer size and the extra capacity would be $O(\sqrt{n})$. If either the buffer or the extra capacity are of a larger order, then the buffer level (scaled by $1/\sqrt{n}$) would go to zero as $n \to \infty$, and there would be no observable packet loss. These are the usual orders in heavy traffic analysis [13]. The amplitude scaling will be $1/\sqrt{n}$.

The heavy traffic regime is one important region of operation, one where small changes in the rates will have major consequences for buffer overflow (i.e, lost packets) and queueing delay. One can view the system as starting much below capacity, with a lower packet rate, and with the rates increasing until capacity is almost reached, at which point the control mechanisms are activated. Our analysis is confined to the time that the system is in this heavy traffic regime. In the comments at the end of Section 3, we will argue formally that the heavy traffic regime is very natural, and that a well regulated system will eventually find itself there. We will also argue formally that one should do the control problem with delays by allowing the controls at t to have some dependence on the path on $[t - \text{delay}, t]$ and controls on $[t - \text{delay}, t)$, although there is no room for a discussion of the delay control problem here.

The controls. There are two classical types of rate control for each user. The first (the AI in AIMD) is the usual simple slow and steady linear increase in the allowed rate of packet creation when there are no buffer overflows. As noted above, in the heavy traffic regime, the number of controlled users is proportional to n on the average, and the excess capacity is $O(\sqrt{n})$. This suggests that the cumulative effect of the first type of control should be a rate increase of $O(\sqrt{n})$ over all controlled users, which implies a rate increase of $O(1/\sqrt{n})$ per user. If it were larger, the system would experience very serious packet losses in short order. Thus we suppose that there is a constant c such that the rate per source increases by $c/\sqrt{n}$. This is the correct order in the heavy traffic regime. See comments at the end of Section 3, where we conjecture that a well regulated system will eventually find itself in this situation.[1] It will turn out that the cumulative effects of this control and of the buffer overflow controls are of the same order. The second type of control (the MD part) is the usual multiplicative decrease when there is a lost packet.

To improve the performance, we also use another type of control, called a *preemptive control*, by which packets are selected at random to be "marked" as they enter the buffer. The chance of being selected depends on the buffer state and/or its input rate, and is a control function to be chosen. (Early discarding or marking has become very popular since it was proposed and deployed in the well known RED buffer management [7, 21].) The selection probability will increase when the system nears a dangerous operating point. There are two choices of how to handle the marked packets. Either they are deleted so that no acknowledgment is sent, or they are not deleted, but "modified" acknowledgments are sent back [19]. In either case, the source rate is decreased in a manner similar to what happens when a packet is lost. This control, which anticipates the possibility of lost packets in the near future, can actually reduce the queueing delay as well as the rate of overflow considerably, with minimal cost in lost throughput. In either case, the use of the preemptive control helps avoid oscillations or instability due to the effects of bursts of lost packets caused by the delays. Here, we work with the second option, and do not delete the selected packets.

Outline of the paper. A general model for the mice is discussed in the next section. Two properties are paramount. One concerns the asymptotic (scaled) total number of packets that have been transmitted by them over any time interval. The other concerns the current rate of creation of packets. The assumptions are intuitively reasonable. To emphasize this, we discuss one particular example in detail, starting from more "physical" assumptions. It is supposed (as is commonly done) that the mice enter with a fixed packet rate (possibly random among the individuals), but that they are in the system for a relatively short time, are not controlled and do not retransmit lost packets.

In Section 3, we consider the case where there are just n controlled users, analogously to the setup in [20]. Each of them has a very large (infinite, here) amount of data to be sent, and is subject to rate control. However, the randomness of the mice process has a significant effect on the total throughput, since it is a major cause of lost packets (buffer overflows), and the consequent rate control. The limit model is a delayed stochastic differential equation with boundary reflection. Note that a delayed reflection term arises. Section 4 considers various extensions of the basic model of Section 2, including the case

---

[1]One could change the model, using fewer sources, each with a higher rate, and allow an accordingly faster increase in the AI control. The analysis would be similar.

where there is no buffer and where the rate for the controlled users changes randomly, perhaps due to reinitializations; this can be useful to model a sequence of TCP connections that are opened consecutively by the application layer, as is the case in the HTTP/1.1 version.

Section 5 deals with the case where the controlled users appear at random, each with a random amount of data to be sent, and vanish when their data has been transmitted. This introduces additional randomness, which (in the asymptotic limit) shows up via the addition of new Wiener processes in the dynamics for the rate process. Data (for small delays) that show some of the advantages of the approach and how to use it effectively are in Section 6.

2.   The Model for the Mice

Recall that we use the name "mice" to describe any set of sources whose transmission rates are uncontrolled and with a relatively small number of packets/source. Various cases where the number of packets goes to infinity as $n \rightarrow \infty$ are covered by the assumptions. We suppose that the total rate at which mice packets are being put into the buffer at time t is $a_m n + \sqrt{n} \xi^n(t)$, where $a_m > 0$ and $\xi^n(\cdot)$ is a random process such that $\int_0^t \xi^n(s)ds$ converges weakly to a Wiener process $w_m(\cdot)$, with variance σ_m^2. The subscript m denotes 'mice." More specifically (where $\Rightarrow$ denotes weak convergence),

$$\frac{(\text{total number of mice packets by } t) - n a_m t}{\sqrt{n}}$$

$$= \int_0^t \xi^n(s)ds = w_m^n(t) \Rightarrow w_m(t), \tag{16.1a}$$

$$\frac{\text{mice rate}(\cdot) - n a_m}{n} = \frac{\xi^n(\cdot)}{\sqrt{n}} \Rightarrow \text{``zero'' process},$$

$$\sup_n E \sup_{s \leq t} \left| \int_0^s \xi^n(\tau)d\tau \right| < \infty, \quad \text{each } t > 0. \tag{16.1b}$$

Equation (16.1a) says that the total mice packet rate is the sum of a "fluid" component and a part that is essentially independent over short and disjoint intervals. It is motivated by the central limit theorem. Owing to the complicated way that packets from different users are scrambled in transmission, it might be hard to say more, or to specify the "mice" model more explicitly. The sizes of the individual mice can grow with n, but slower than $O(n)$. All that we require is that (16.1a, 16.1b) hold. An interesting specific example of a mice process is given next.

Example of a "mice" model. Consider the following example, which was one of the motivations for the general conditions above. The example is meant to be illustrative, and does not exhaust the possibilities. Suppose that the mice arrive as a Poisson process with rate $\lambda_m n$, with each arrival having an exponentially distributed (and independent among arrivals) amount of packets, with mean v_m/μ_m. The packets are put into the system at a rate v_m and each mouse departs at a rate μ_m. μ_m denotes the departure rate of each mouse. The number of active mice at any time is $N_m^n(t)$, which satisfies

$$dN_m^n(t) = n\lambda_m dt - \mu_m N_m^n(t) dt + dM_m^n(t),$$

where $M_m^n(\cdot)$ is a martingale that follows a quadratic variation process $\int_0^t [n\lambda_m + N_m^n(s)\mu_m] ds$. Let us work with the stationary processes. Then $N_m^n(\cdot)/n$ converges weakly to the process with constant values λ_m/μ_m. The rate at which mice packets arrive is $N_m^n(t)v_m$. Write $N_m^n(t) = n\lambda_m/\mu_m + \sqrt{n}\eta_m^n(t)$. Then

$$d\eta_m^n(t) = -\mu_m \eta_m^n(t) dt + dM_m^n(t)/\sqrt{n}.$$

The process $M_m^n(\cdot)/\sqrt{n}$ converges weakly to a Wiener process $\tilde{w}_m(\cdot)$ with variance $2\lambda_m$. The process $\eta_m^n(\cdot)$ converges weakly to $\eta_m(\cdot)$, where $d\eta_m(t) = -\mu_m \eta_m(t) dt + d\tilde{w}_m(t)$. The "noise part" of the arrival rate process for the mice satisfies

$$\xi^n(s) \equiv \frac{v_m N_m^n(\cdot) - n v_m \lambda_m/\mu_m}{\sqrt{n}} \Rightarrow v_m \eta_m(\cdot) \equiv \xi(\cdot).$$

Note that (16.1b) holds.

The variance of (scaled mice packet rate at $t)/\sqrt{n}$ is, asymptotically, $\frac{v_m^2 \lambda_m}{\mu_m}$. The (scaled packet rate) correlation function is this times $e^{-\mu_m t}$. For high speed systems, both μ_m and v_m are large, while the ratio v_m/μ_m (the mean number of packets per mouse) is "moderate." In this case, to show that (16.1a) holds "approximately," write (neglecting the initial condition),

$$\eta_m(t) = \int_0^t e^{-\mu_m(t-s)} d\tilde{w}_m(s),$$

$$\int_0^t \xi(s) ds = v_m \int_0^t \int_0^s e^{-\mu_m(s-\tau)} d\tilde{w}_m(\tau) ds$$

$$= \frac{v_m}{\mu_m} \tilde{w}_m(t) - \frac{v_m}{\mu_m} \int_0^t e^{-\mu_m(t-s)} d\tilde{w}_m(s).$$

The dominant part is the Wiener process. Thus, in (16.1a), $a_m = v_m\lambda_m/\mu_m$ and the variance of the Wiener process is $\sigma_m^2 = 2\lambda_m [v_m/\mu_m]^2$. The stationary variance of the error process (the last term on the right) is $(v_m^2/\mu_m^2)\lambda_m/\mu_m$. For large μ_m and moderate σ_m^2 the error process is close to the "zero" process, in that it converges weakly to it as $\mu_m \to \infty$.

We could also suppose, alternatively, that the individual mice send their packets all at once, but they are interleaved randomly with those from other sources along the way; then we come even closer to (16.1a), (16.1b).

3.   Many controlled Users, Each With Infinite Backlog

In this section, there are a fixed number, namely n, of controlled users, with each having a very large (infinite here, for modeling simplicity) amount of data to be sent. Let $r_i(t)$ denote the rate for controlled source i at time t, and suppose that there are positive a_i such that $a_0 \leq r_i(0) \leq a_1$, so that no single source dominates. Thus $\int_0^t r_i(s)ds$ is the total number of packets generated by controlled source i by time t. Define $\bar{r}^n(t) = \sum_{i=1}^n r_i(t)/n$, and $v_1 = \bar{r}^n(0)$, $v_2 = \sum_i [r_i^n(0)]^2/n$, and $\rho^n(t) = \left[\sum_i r_i(t) - nv_1 \right]/\sqrt{n}$. Thus $\sqrt{n}\rho^n(t)$ is the rate at time t, centered about the initial mean rate nv_1. The analysis commences at the point at which the HT regime is entered.[More on this later.] The service rate (channel speed in packets per second) is assumed to be $C^n = nv_1 + a_m n + b\sqrt{n}$, $b > 0$, which covers the mean requirements (for both persistent connections as well as the mice process) and gives an excess (over the mean requirements) of $b\sqrt{n}$. The buffer size is $B\sqrt{n}$. These are the correct orders in HT analysis [13]. If the buffer or spare capacity were of a larger order, then the number of buffer overflows, asymptotically, would be zero.

When the buffer overflows (i.e., a packet is lost), that packet is assumed to come at random from the various users, in proportion to their individual current rates of packet creation: The various users (mice and controlled) would send their packets in some order, and the order would be more or less scrambled in the course of transmission, so that buffer overflows can be assigned at random to the various users.

As noted in the introduction, the standard multiplicative decrease control is activated by lost packets. I.e., there is some constant $\kappa \in (0,1)$ such that, if the dropped packet at time $t - \alpha$ was from connection i, then the rate $r_i(t-)$ at $t-$ is changed to $r_i(t) = (1 - \kappa)r_i(t-)$.

The "preemptive" control. The performance would be improved if the sources were also signaled to reduce their rates as the buffer level or total input rate increases, but before actual buffer overflow. The type of control, called the *preemptive control,* attempts to do just this, analogously to what is done in the RED system. It selects packets on arrival, either at random or in some deterministic way according to the chosen control law. For notational simplicity, we suppose that the selection is done randomly. The probability that a packet entering the buffer at time t is selected is $u(t)/\sqrt{n}$, where $0 \leq u(\cdot) \leq u_{\max} < \infty$ is a measurable control function, and is to be selected. The selected packets could be deleted as if there was an overflow. A preferable alternative, which we use, does not delete the packets, but returns a modified acknowledgment, which is used to reduce the flow at the source, similarly to what would happen if the packet were actually lost [19]. Let $\mathcal{F}_t^n$ denote the minimal σ-algebra that measures the systems data to time t. Then $u(\cdot)$ is $\{\mathcal{F}_t^n, t < \infty\}$-adapted; i.e.,

$u(t)$ depends only on available data. We suppose that there is a $\kappa_1 \in (0,1)$ so that if a packet from source i is selected at time $t - \alpha$, then $r_i(t) = (1 - \kappa_1)r_i(t-)$. This preemptive control is to be chosen by the system designer and, when suitably selected, it can have a major beneficial effect on the overall operation.

Buffer input-output equations. We have

$$\rho^n(t) = \rho^n(0) + ct - [\text{overflow control effects}] \atop -[\text{preemptive control effects}], \tag{16.2}$$

Let $x^n(t)$ denote $1/\sqrt{n}$ times the number of buffered packets at time t. Then

$$x^n(t) = x^n(0) + [(\text{total input - total output - overflow}) \text{ by } t] / \sqrt{n}.$$

If the buffer is not empty, then its output rate is C^n. For modeling purposes, it is convenient to use this output rate all the time, even if the buffer is empty. Then we must correct for the "fictitious" outputs when the buffer is empty. This is done by adding an "underflow" correction term $L^n(t)$ (which is the number of fictitious outputs sent when the buffer is empty) as is usual in heavy traffic analysis [13]. Let $U^n(\cdot))$ denote $1/\sqrt{n}$ times the buffer overflow. Now, using the definition of $C^n, \rho^n(\cdot)$, and the mice model (16.1a), we can write

$$x^n(t) = x^n(0) + \int_0^t [\rho^n(s) - b + \xi^n(s)] \, dt - U^n(t) + L^n(t). \tag{16.3}$$

The limit dynamical equations. The following theorem gives the HT limits, and identifies the limit control system. Define $\hat{u}^n(t) = \int_0^t u^n(s)ds$.

Theorem 1. *Assume the mice model* (16.1a), (16.1b), *that* $C^n = nv_1 + a_m n + \sqrt{n}b$, *and that* $\sup_n |\rho^n(0)| < \infty$. *Then the sequence* $\{x^n(\cdot), \rho^n(\cdot), \hat{u}^n(\cdot), w_m^n(\cdot), L^n(\cdot), U^n(\cdot)\}$ *is tight in the Skorohod topology. For any weakly convergent subsequence, there is a process* $u(\cdot)$ *such that the weak sense limit* $(x(\cdot), \rho(\cdot), \hat{u}(\cdot), w_m(\cdot), L(\cdot), U(\cdot))$ *satisfies*

$$d\rho(t) = cdt - v_2 \left[\frac{\kappa}{v_1 + a_m} dU(t - \alpha) + \kappa_1 u(t - \alpha)dt \right], \tag{16.4}$$

$$x(t) - x(0) = \int_0^t [\rho(s) - b] \, ds + w_m(t) + L(t) - U(t), \tag{16.5}$$

where $\hat{u}(t) = \int_0^t u(s)ds$. *Let* $\mathcal{F}_t$ *denote the minimal σ-algebra that measures* $(x(s), \rho(s), w_m(s), u(s - \alpha), L(s), U(s), s \le t)$. *Then* $w_m(\cdot)$ *is an $\mathcal{F}_t$-Wiener process with variance* σ_m^2, $0 \le u(t) \le u_{\max}$, *and* $u(t)$ *is* $\{\mathcal{F}_t, t < \infty\}$-*adapted, so that it depends only on available data.*

Comment on the limit equations. Equations (16.4) and (16.5) are suggestive even for more general models. They capture much of the essence of the AIMD and the preemptive control mechanisms, and retain the fundamental role of the randomness, all for an aggregated and scaled system. Equations (16.4) and (16.5) identify the correct limit control system. The asymptotic effects of the overflow and preemptive controls are in the given form. The control is admissible in that it is a delayed nonanticipative (with respect to the Wiener process $w_m(\cdot)$) function satisfying the appropriate bounds.

Proof. It follows from the proof of the reflection mapping theorem in [13, Theorems 3.4.1, 3.5.1] that there is a constant C such that, for each $0 \leq T_0 < T < \infty$,

$$(L^n(T) - L^n(T_0)) + (U^n(T) - U^n(T_0))$$
$$\leq C \sup_{T_0 \leq t \leq T} \left[x^n(T_0) + \int_{T_0}^t [\rho^n(s) + \xi^n(s)]\, ds \right]. \tag{16.6}$$

By the assumption on $\rho^n(0)$, $\sup_n E \sup_{s \leq t} \rho^n(s) < \infty$ for each t. By this, the second line of (16.1b), and (16.6), we have $\sup_n EU^n(t) < \infty$. Thus the number of buffer overflows on any bounded interval is $O(\sqrt{n})$. Thus, since the association of overflow with source is random, we can neglect the possibility that any one source will have more than one overflow on any finite interval.

The Lipschitz condition in (16.6) and the tightness criterion in [13, Theorem 2.5.6] or [11, Theorem 2.7b] assures that the sequence $\{x^n(\cdot), \rho^n(\cdot), U^n(\cdot), L^n(\cdot)\}$ is tight in the Skorohod topology. The sequence $\{\hat{u}^n(\cdot)\}$ is obviously tight since $0 \leq u^n(t) \leq u_{\max}$. The fact that some arguments are delayed is irrelevant.

We next approximate the overflow control effects in (16.2). Suppose that there is a single overflow at time $t - \alpha$. I.e., $\sqrt{n}dU^n(t - \alpha) = 1$. Let $I_i^n(t - \alpha)$ denote the indicator function of the event that the overflow is associated with controlled source i. Then $r_i(t) = r_i(t-)(1 - \kappa I_i^n(t - \alpha))$ and

$$\frac{1}{\sqrt{n}} \sum_{i=1}^n [r_i(t) - r_i(t-)] = -\kappa \sum_{i=1}^n r_i(t-)I_i^n(t - \alpha)dU^n(t - \alpha). \tag{16.7}$$

The user with the lost packet is selected at random, with the probability that controlled user i is selected being (its rate divided by the total rate, all at $t - \alpha$)

$$f_i^n(t - \alpha) = \frac{r_i(t - \alpha)}{\sum_j r_j(t - \alpha) + na_m + \sqrt{n}\xi^n(t - \alpha)}. \tag{16.8}$$

Use (16.8) to center (16.7) about the conditional mean (given the $r_j(t - \alpha)$, $\xi^n(t - \alpha)$, and that $dU^n(t - \alpha) > 0$), and rewrite the right hand side of (16.7) as

$$-\kappa \sum_{i=1}^{n} r_i(t-) \frac{r_i(t-\alpha)dU^n(t-\alpha)}{\sum_j r_j(t-\alpha) + na_m + \sqrt{n}\xi^n(t-\alpha)} + dM_1^n(t), \quad (16.9)$$

where $M_1^n(\cdot)$ is the martingale

$$\int_0^t \kappa \sum_{i=1}^{n} r_i(s-)\left[f_i^n(s-\alpha) - I_i^n(s-\alpha)\right] dU^n(s-\alpha).$$

By the random association of buffer overflow to user, we can show that

$$E|M_1^n(t)|^2 = O(1)E\sum_{s\leq t}|dU^n(s)|^2 = O(1/\sqrt{n})EU^n(t).$$

Hence $M^n(\cdot)$ converges weakly to zero, and the left hand term of (16.9) can be used for (16.7), as $n \to \infty$.

It was seen that we can neglect the possibility that any one source is associated with more than one overflow on any finite interval. Thus, in evaluating the left hand term of (16.9), we can suppose that $r_i(t-\alpha) = r_i(t-)$. Using this and (16.1b), and dividing each part of the term

$$\frac{\sum_i r_i(t-)r_i(t-\alpha)}{\sum_j r_j(t-\alpha) + na_m + \sqrt{n}\xi^n(t-\alpha)}$$

by n, we see that it converges weakly to the constant process, with values $v_2/[v_1 + a_m]$, as $n \to \infty$. The above computations imply that, as $n \to \infty$, the buffer overflow control term in (16.2) is well approximated by $(\kappa v_2/[v_1 + a_m])U^n(t-\alpha)$.

Now, we turn our attention to approximating the effects of the preemptive control. Redefine $I_i^n(t)$ to be the indicator of the event that a packet selected at time t came from controlled source i. Define $R^n(t-\alpha) = \sum_j r_j(t-\alpha) + na_m + \sqrt{n}\xi^n(t-\alpha)$, the total (unscaled) packet arrival rate at time $t-\alpha$. Let $J^n(t)$ denote the number selected by t. Then

$$\frac{\kappa_1}{\sqrt{n}} \sum_i [r_i(t) - r_i(t-)] = \frac{\kappa_1}{\sqrt{n}} \sum_i r_i(t-)I_i^n(t-\alpha)dJ^n(t-\alpha). \quad (16.10)$$

The mean rate at which packets are selected at time $t-\alpha$ is

$$\frac{u(t-\alpha)}{\sqrt{n}}R^n(t-\alpha). \quad (16.11)$$

We can model the random selection times as the jump times of a jump process with conditional jump rate $u^n(t)R^n(t)/\sqrt{n}$ at time t. Thus on any finite interval there are only $O(\sqrt{n})$ selections, and the event that more than one comes from the same source can be neglected. Thus, if a selection at $t - \alpha$ comes from source i, we can suppose (without loss of generality) that $r_i(t-) = r_i(t - \alpha)$. The rest of the development is similar to that for the effects of the overflow control, but with $J^n(\cdot)$ replacing $U^n(\cdot)$. Thus, by centering $I^n_i(t - \alpha)$ at its conditional mean $f^n_i(t - \alpha)$, we have the representation of (16.10) as

$$\frac{\kappa_1}{\sqrt{n}} \sum_i \frac{r_i(t-)r_i(t - \alpha)}{R^n(t)} dJ^n(t - \alpha) + dM^n_p(t), \qquad (16.12)$$

for a martingale $M^n_p(\cdot)$. The quadratic variation of the martingale is $O(1/\sqrt{n})$, hence it converges weakly to zero as $n \to \infty$. Now centering dJ^n about its conditional mean yields the approximation to the left hand term of (16.12) as

$$\frac{\kappa_1}{\sqrt{n}} \sum_i \frac{r_i(t-)r_i(t - \alpha)}{R^n(t)} \frac{u^n(t - \alpha)R^n(t - \alpha)}{\sqrt{n}} dt + dM^n_q(t), \qquad (16.13)$$

where $M^n_q(\cdot)$ is a martingale whose quadratic variation is also $O(1/\sqrt{n})$, hence it is asymptotically negligible.

By what has been said,

$$v_2\kappa_1 \int_0^t u^n(s - \alpha)ds$$

approximates the effects of the preemptive control for large n. Now, with these asymptotic representations for the effects of the controls, we see that the limit of any weakly convergent subsequence of $\{x^n(\cdot), \rho^n(\cdot), \hat{u}^n(\cdot), U^n(\cdot), L^n(\cdot), w^n_m(\cdot)\}$, satisfies (16.4) and (16.5). The Wiener property of $w_m(\cdot)$ is just the assumption (16.1a), (16.1b). The fact that it is an $\{\mathcal{F}_t, t < \infty\}$-Wiener process is proved using standard methods; for example see [13, Theorem 6.1.2]. The limit $\hat{u}(\cdot)$ is absolutely continuous with respect to Lebesgue measure, with derivative bounded by $u_{\max}$; hence the asserted process $u(\cdot)$ exists.

Cost functions and nearly optimal controls for the physical system. In order to assure good performance of the AIMD connections, the buffer management would implement control $u(\cdot)$. The quantities to penalize in the cost are queueing delay (measured by $x(\cdot)$), the loss of throughput due to the control (measured by $-\rho(\cdot)$), and buffer overflow (measured by $U(\cdot))^2$. Let us work with a discounted cost criterion, where $\beta > 0$ can be as small as we wish,

---

[2]Penalizing buffer overflow may be important for several reasons. First, if the mice correspond to real time applications, then these applications will suffer due to losses. Secondly, the AIMD themselves may correspond to real time applications which are "TCP friendly", in which case lost packets are typically not retransmitted. Losses due to overflow then again degrade the quality of the communication.

$c_0 > 0$, and the $k_i(\cdot) \geq 0$ are Lipschitz continuous:

$$W(u) = \beta E \int_0^\infty e^{-\beta t} \left([k_1(x(t)) - k_2(\rho(t))] \, dt + c_0 dU(t) \right). \quad (16.14)$$

The possibility that the $k_i(\cdot)$ are nonlinear can be useful, since (e.g.) we might wish to heavily penalize long queues, but not be too concerned with short queues.

Using the methods of heavy traffic analysis for controlled problems [13], it can be shown that the optimal costs for the physical problem converge to the optimal cost for the limit problem. If the delay is zero, then the optimal control for the limit problem is of the switching curve type: $u(x, \rho)$ takes the maximum value on one side of a switching curve and is zero on the other, and the switching curve is smooth. The switching curve character for $\alpha = 0$ follows from a formal examination of the Bellman equation for the optimal value, since the control appears linearly in the dynamics and does not appear in the cost. The smoothness was implied by the numerical computations. See, for example, Figure 1. Such switching optimal controls are nearly optimal for the physical system for large n. We note that the cost (16.14) is well defined, since it can be shown that $E|\rho(t)| + EU(t) \leq a_1 + a_2 t$, for some $a_i \geq 0$.

We shall also consider an ergodic cost criterion

$$\gamma(u) = \lim_{T \to \infty} E \frac{1}{T} \left[\int_0^T (k_1(x(t)) - k_2(\rho(t))) \, dt + c_0 U(T) \right] \quad (16.15)$$

At present, there is little theory concerning stability or ergodicity theory for delayed reflected diffusions such as ((16.4), (16.5)), or ((16.5), (16.26)) for the model of Section 5. If the delay is zero then, for any feedback control $u(\cdot)$, stability can be shown and the model ((16.5), (16.26)) can be shown to have a unique invariant measure; see, e.g., [13, Chapter 4]. In the numerical computations (where zero delay was always used), we were always able to compute an optimal control for the ergodic cost criterion (with cost and control well approximated by those for the discounted problem for small β), and both stability and convergence to the stationary distribution under the optimal (or other reasonable) controls were apparent.

Comments on the heavy traffic regime. First, we comment on the control $u(t - \alpha)$ in (16.4). Suppose that there is a cost function of either the type (16.14) or (16.15). Owing to the delay, the optimal control $u(t)$ will not be simply a function of $(x(t), \rho(t))$, but rather a function of the path segment $\{x(s), \rho(s), t - \alpha \leq s \leq t\}$ [9, 22]. Although there is some progress with numerical methods for computing and approximating optimal $u(\cdot)$ when $\alpha > 0$, good algorithms are not yet available. Controls $u(t)$ that depend just on the value of $(x(t), \rho(t))$ are subject to oscillations. Those that depend as well on the recent past can avoid oscillations, since they "remember" recent control values and can select the current value accordingly. It is likely that using the full potential of the delay dynamical system can improve the operation and keep the system in the heavy traffic regime. Following are some conjectures. They are reasonable, but unproved at this time.

Suppose that the system starts far from the heavy traffic regime, and that the "slow" increase in packet rate is initially $\bar{c}$ for *each* of the n users. Then the total increase in the rate for the persistent connections is $n\bar{c}$. Capacity will be reached quickly. One can try to pose a control problem with another preemptive control, where losses are penalized heavily. One expects that (roughly speaking) at a time t when the average rate reaches a level where approximately α units of time later, it will be within $O(\sqrt{n})$ of capacity, this control starts to act, and selects packets for the modified acknowledgment. The packet rate into the buffer will keep increasing until the rate reducing effects of the feedback reach the buffer α units of time later. After time t, since the control "knows" the recent state values, it knows how many packets it has already selected, and adjusts new selections accordingly. The $\sqrt{n}$ level is used because that represents the effects of the randomness. The control will start to act when asserted since otherwise there will be large losses. It is reasonable to expect that such behavior would avoid oscillations and bring the system to the heavy traffic regime, where an additional fine control can be exerted. Similar comments apply to the case where the delay depends on the user. We conjecture that a fuller development and exploitation of control theory when the controls are delayed will have a major impact.

4.   Extensions of the Model of Section 3

No Buffer. Suppose that there is no buffer, so that if the total current packet rate exceeds the channel speed, then the excess packets are rejected. The forms of the input processes and channel speed (service rate) are as in the last section, but in lieu of (16.1a), (16.1b), we assume that $\xi^n(\cdot)$ converges weakly to a process $\xi(\cdot)$, as in the example in Section 2. Since there is no buffer to overflow, the "reject" process $U^n(\cdot)$ needs to be defined. Define

$$
\begin{aligned}
y^n(t) &= \left[C_n - \left(\sum_i r_i(t) + a_m n + \sqrt{n}\xi^n(t) \right) \right] \Big/ \sqrt{n} \\
&= [b - \rho^n(t) - \xi^n(t)],
\end{aligned}
\tag{16.16}
$$

the scaled difference between the channel speed and input packet rate at t. Then the scaled number of rejected packets is

$$
U^n(t) = \int_0^t [y^n(s)]^- \, ds = \int_0^t [\xi^n(s) + \rho^n(s) - b]^+ \, ds
\tag{16.17}
$$

Suppose that the correlation time of $\xi^n(\cdot)$ is short (e.g., large μ_m in the special mice model) of Section 2. Then a law of large numbers argument can be used to show that $\xi^n(t)$ can be "integrated out" of (16.17), in that, as $n \to \infty$ and the correlation time goes to zero, the integrand can be replaced by the average over $\xi^n(t)$. This simplifies the expression for $U^n(\cdot)$, and the limit equation for the scaled and centered rate process $\rho^n(\cdot)$ is

$$\dot{\rho}(t) = cdt - v_2 \left[\frac{\kappa}{v_1 + a_m} \dot{U}(t - \alpha) + \kappa_1 u(t - \alpha)dt \right], \qquad (16.18)$$

where $\dot{U}(t) = E_\rho \left[\xi(t) + \rho(t) - b \right]^+$, and the expectation is over the $\xi(t)$. Then we have a deterministic limit, which is not a priori obvious. The randomness due to the mice in the arrival process does not appear explicitly in (16.18), but it affects the value of the expectation that yields the overflow rate $\dot{U}(t)$.

Let us look a little more closely at the example in Section 2. As $\mu_m \to \infty$, we would also have that $v_m \to \infty$, to keep the total mean data per mouse from going to zero. If we suppose that $\lambda_m(v_m/\mu_m)$ is bounded, then the stationary variance of $\xi(\cdot)$ would be $O(v_m)$, which implies that the excess capacity factor b would have to be $O(\sqrt{v_m})$, if large loss rates are to be avoided. This is useful scaling information. It is hardly surprising, since we no longer have the buffer to "integrate" the mice process, and we must deal directly with the large variations in the $\xi^n(\cdot)$ instantaneous rate process. In order to avoid huge losses, the excess capacity must be some large constant times the standard deviation of this process.

Finally, we note that the value of an optimal control at time t for the limit process (which will be applied at time $t + \alpha$) need only depend on $\rho(s), t - \alpha \le s \le t$. Since such controls are nearly optimal for the physical process in heavy traffic, we see that an nearly optimal control can depend only the rate $\rho^n(\cdot)$ on $[t - \alpha, t]$, and not on the more rapidly changing "mice" process $\xi^n(\cdot)$.

Analogous results holds for the model of Section 5, but there the randomness due to the arrival and departure processes of the controlled users remains in the limit. As for the case of concern above, only the $\xi^n(t)$ process would be "integrated out."

Random $r_i(0)$. In the rest of this section, we suppose that there is a buffer, as in the problem of Section 3. Suppose that the initial values of the rates are random, identically distributed, and mutually independent, with $E r_i(0) = v_1$ and $E[r_i(0)]^2 = v_2$. Then all the asymptotic results continue to hold.

Randomly changing rates. In some internet applications, where a user sends a sequence of consecutive TCP connections, the rate of transmission is reinitialized for each new TCP transfer (e.g. HTTP/1.1). We next propose a model of which this scenario is a special case. Suppose that the users change the packet transmission rates at random, and each with rate λ_0. The new rates (which are uniformly bounded) are chosen randomly with the same first two moments.

More precisely, there are mutually independent Poisson processes $P_i(\cdot)$ all with rate λ_0. When $P_i(\cdot)$ jumps, the rate for user i is replaced. The set of replacements, over all users and time, is mutually independent, and independent of all other "driving" processes. Let q denote the canonical rate replacement, and define $v_1 = Eq$, $v_2 = Eq^2$, $\bar{v}_2 = E[q - v_1]^2 = v_2 - v_1^2$, and $Q^n(t) = \sum_i r_i(t)$. Then

$$dQ^n(t) =$$
$$\sqrt{n}\, cdt - [\text{effects of controls}] - \lambda_0 \left[Q^n(t) - nv_1\right] dt + dM_r^n(t), \tag{16.19}$$

where the martingale $M_r^n(\cdot)$ can be shown to have quadratic variation process

$$\lambda_0 \int_0^t \sum_i E\left[r_i(s) - q\right]^2 ds$$
$$= \lambda_0 n \int_0^t \left[\frac{\sum_i r_i^2(s)}{n} - \frac{2v_1 \sum_i r_i(s)}{n} + v_2\right] ds, \tag{16.20}$$

where the expectation is over q only. Recall the definition $\rho^n(t) = [Q^n(t) - nv_1]/\sqrt{n}$. It can be shown that $\rho^n(\cdot)$ is tight and that the limit of any weakly convergent subsequence satisfies

$$d\rho(t)$$
$$= cdt - v_2 \left[\frac{\kappa}{v_1 + a_m} dU(t - \alpha) + \kappa_1 u(t - \alpha) dt\right] - \lambda_0 \rho(t) dt + dw_r(t), \tag{16.21}$$

where the Wiener process $w_r(\cdot)$ has variance $2\lambda_0 \bar{v}_2$. The limit system equations are (16.5) and (16.21). The control is as in Theorem 1.

Delay depending on the user. Up to now, all users had the same delay. The general theory can handle user-dependent delays. Suppose that user i has delay $\alpha_i \le D < \infty$. Let the buffer overflow at time s with a packet from user i. The information will reach user i at time $s + t_{1,i}$. Thus, at time t, user i receives information concerning overflows at time $t - t_{1,i}$, and its response reaches the buffer $t_{2,i}$ units of time later, with $t_{1,i} + t_{2,i} \equiv \alpha_i$. This leads to $dU^n(t - \alpha)$ in the ith summand in (16.9) being replaced by $dU^n(t - \alpha_i)$. To simplify matters in this brief presentation, first suppose that all initial rates are equal: $r_i(0) = v_1$. Then, for large n, the main term in (16.9) is approximately

$$-\kappa \sum_{i=1}^n r_i(t-) \frac{r_i(t - \alpha_i) dU^n(t - \alpha_i)}{\sum_j r_j(t - \alpha_i) + na_m + \sqrt{n}\xi^n(t - \alpha_i)}$$

$$\approx -\frac{\kappa v_1^2}{a_m + v_1} \frac{1}{n} \sum_{i=1}^n dU^n(t - \alpha_j).$$

More succinctly, with $\beta^n(\cdot)$ being a measure with mass $1/n$ at α_i, write

$$\frac{v_1^2}{n} \sum_{i=1}^{n} dU^n(t - \alpha_i) = v_1^2 \int_0^D dU^n(t - \alpha)\beta^n(d\alpha).$$

Suppose that the distribution of delays $\beta^n(\cdot)$ converges weakly to a distribution $\beta(\cdot)$. Then the $dU(t - \alpha)$ in (16.4) is replaced by $\int dU(t - \alpha)\beta(d\alpha)$. All else remains the same. If the $r_i(0)$ are not all equal, then redefine $\beta^n(\cdot)$ to have weight $r_i^2(0)/n$ at α_i, suppose that $\beta^n(\cdot) \Rightarrow \beta(\cdot)$, and replace the right side of the last expression by $\int_0^D dU(t - a)\beta(d\alpha)$. Details of the proof are omitted.

5. A Stochastic Process of Finite AIMD Connections

In the model of Section 3, the number of users is fixed at n. Now, we consider a model where the controlled users arrive independently and randomly and leave at random, with the arrival process is independent of the mice process. New users come from an unlimited population, with (Poisson) arrival rate λn. Each new user comes with an exponentially distributed number of data packets, each with mean v_1/μ, and independent of the mice process and arrival times.[3]

With this model, as with the previous ones, the buffer overflows (i.e., packet losses) are created by the physical process and not imposed. Note that the mean amount of data in a new source does not depend on n. The parameter n scales the system speed and mean number of users only.[4] The source (i.e., the user) stays "active" until all data is sent, and then disappears. Time is still measured at the buffer and the mice model is (16.1a), (16.1b). For simplicity, suppose that the initial rate of each new controlled source is v_1.

First suppose that there are no controls (constant transmission rate from each source) and buffer overflows are not retransmitted. Then the packets are sent

---

[3]Exponential distribution of interarrival times and session duration are more appropriate for telephone calls than for data connections. Thus this model is expected to be more useful for VoIP applications that use TCP friendly mechanisms to regulate their rate. The "exponential" assumptions can be helpful even for the data connections for some preliminary dimensioning purposes.

Non exponential distributions can be handled as well, with an increase in the dimensionality of the limit model. For example, a k-stage Erlang model would require a k-dimensional process to represent the rate process. The mathematical development and results are similar. This higher dimensionality is a handicap for numerical computations, say via the Markov chain approximation method [12], or a pathwise approximation method. But it is not a serious handicap for simulation. Indeed, simulating the approximating limit model is substantially simpler than simulating the physical process, when there are very many users.

Experimentation with the basic model can lead to insights that are useful for more general cases. For example, numerical results for the basic model with no delay indicate that threshold controls, based on the rate only, provide good approximations to the values obtained by optimal controls. This observation provides a basis for getting good controls, which would be very hard to compute otherwise, for more general large size systems.

[4]The rate of arrivals of new users can be a smaller order of n, and then they would each have an amount of data that would depend on n. E.g., rate of arrival $O(\sqrt{n})$, with data $O(\sqrt{n})$. In this case the rate of work on each source is $O(\sqrt{n})$, so that the average sojourn in the system is still $O(1)$.

from each active source to the buffer at a rate v_1. The mean time that a source is active is $1/\mu$, and the total rate at which the sources drop out at t is $\mu N^n(t)$, where $N^n(t)$ denotes the number of active sources. The (stationary) mean number of sources in the system is $n\lambda/\mu$. Hence, the analog of the channel speed C^n of Section 3 is $C^n = v_1 n[\lambda/\mu] + a_m n + b\sqrt{n}$, where, again, $b\sqrt{n}$ denotes the excess capacity over the mean rate $n[v_1\lambda/\mu + a_m]$. On departure of a user, its rate v_1 is lost.[5] We suppose that $1/\mu$ is large enough relative to the delay α so that there is enough time for many round trips.

Now suppose that the input rates from the non-mice sources are actually controlled. There are several approaches that one can take for the source departure process. One approach supposes that the departure rate (of an AIMD connection) is μ, and does not depend on the current packet transmission rate for the source. Then the lost packet rate if connection i leaves is $r_i(t)$. This situation arises when the AIMD connections correspond to real time applications that have a dynamic compression rate (which is then "TCP friendly"). In these applications, lost packets are not retransmitted (the possibility of lost packets might be anticipated in the coding). For simplicity in the development, this is the approach that will be taken. [6]

The dynamics and limit for the rate process. The details are similar to those in Section 3, except for the treatment of the randomness due to the arrivals and departures for the controlled users, and we will concentrate on this point. Write $N^n(t) = n\hat{N} + \sqrt{n}\nu^n(t)$, $\hat{N} = \lambda/\mu$. Since the user arrival process is Poisson and the departure rate per user is constant,

$$dN^n(t) = \lambda n\, dt - \mu N^n(t)\, dt + dM_a^n(t) - dM_d^n(t). \qquad (16.22)$$

Here $M_a^n(\cdot)$ is the martingale associated with the arrival process and has quadratic variation process $n\lambda t$, and $M_d^n(\cdot)$ is the martingale associated with the departure process and has quadratic variation process $\mu \int_0^t N^n(s)\, ds$. For simplicity, suppose that $N^n(\cdot)$ is stationary. It follows from this, (16.22), and the cited values of the quadratic variations, that the sequence $N^n(\cdot)/n$ converges weakly to a process with constant value $\hat{N} = \lambda/\mu$, as $n \to \infty$. Also, $\nu^n(\cdot)$ satisfies

$$d\nu^n(t) = -\mu\nu^n(t)\, dt + [dM_a^n(t) - dM_d^n(t)]/\sqrt{n}. \qquad (16.23)$$

---

[5] Strictly speaking a source should not depart until an acknowledgment of its last transmission has been received. But our approximation to the actual departure rule has little effect, since the order of lost packets is still $O(\sqrt{n})$, and μ is large.

[6] An alternative approach replaces the value of μ by a time varying quantity to reflect the fact that even if the service rate per source changes the total amount of data per source doesn't. For example, if the allowed data rate for an AIMD connection is cut in half due to an increase in the number of sources, then the value of the connection departure rate for that source should be cut in half. The mathematical development of this situation is much harder.

The quadratic variation of the scaled martingale term in (16.23) is $\lambda t + \mu \int_0^t N^n(s)ds/n$, which converges weakly to $2\lambda t$. The sequence $\nu^n(\cdot)$ converges weakly to $\nu(\cdot)$, where

$$d\nu(t) = -\mu\nu(t)dt + dw(t), \qquad (16.24)$$

where $w(\cdot)$ is a Wiener process with variance 2λ.

Returning to the rate process, write $\sum_i r_i(t) = Q^n(t) = n\hat{R} + \sqrt{n}\rho^n(t)$, where $\hat{R} = v_1\lambda/\mu$. The process $Q^n(\cdot)$ satisfies

$$dQ^n(t) = \lambda v_1 n dt - \mu Q^n(t)dt + c\sqrt{n}dt - $$
$$\text{[effects of overflow and preemptive controls]} + v_1 dM_a^n(t) - dM_{d,1}^n(t), \qquad (16.25)$$

where $M_{d,1}^n(\cdot)$ is the martingale associated with the "rate departure" process and it has quadratic variation process $\mu \int_0^t \sum_i r_i^2(s)ds$. This, divided by n, converges weakly to the process with values $v_1^2 \lambda t$, as $n \to \infty$. Finally, following the procedure used in the proof of Theorem 1, it is not hard to show that $\rho^n(\cdot) \Rightarrow \rho(\cdot)$, where

$$d\rho(t) = -\mu\rho(t)dt + [\lambda/\mu]cdt - \frac{v_1^2\kappa[\lambda/\mu]}{v_1[\lambda/\mu] + a_m}dU(t-\alpha)$$
$$+ v_1^2\kappa_1[\lambda/\mu]u(t-\alpha)dt + v_1 dw. \qquad (16.26)$$

Approximations to the optimal via the limit model. The limit system equations are (16.5) and (16.26). The comments made after Theorem 1 concerning the convergence of the optimal costs for the physical problem to that for the limit also hold here.

6.   Numerical Data: Optimal Preemptive Controls

It is not possible at present to conveniently compute good approximations to optimal policies when there is a delay in the control, although there is promising work being done on the development of numerical algorithms. Because of this, in the numerical discussion to follow we set $\alpha = 0$. The results still shed light on the system behavior when the delay is small relative to the time constant in (16.4) or (16.26).

Numerical results were obtained for the optimal control and costs for the model of Section 5 with the cost function being either (16.14) or (16.15), with $k_1(x) = c_1 x$, $k_2(\rho) = c_2\rho$. The results for the two cost functions were nearly the same when $\beta \leq .02$, and the ergodic case will be described. The numerical method was the Markov chain approximation method [12], which is the most versatile current approach for controlled reflected diffusions. Only a few details can be given here. Use $c = 1, \lambda/\mu = 4, b = 1, v_1 = 1.5, a_m = 4, \kappa = \kappa_1 = .5$,

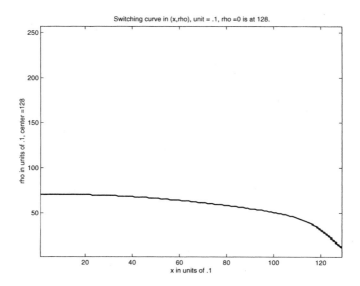

Figure 16.1. A switching curve; no delay.

$\sigma_m^2 = 4$. Since there is no delay the control is a function of $(\rho(t), x(t))$. We used the bound $0 \leq u(x, \rho) \leq 1$. The buffer capacity is $12.8\sqrt{n}$ packets, and $c_0 = 100, c_1 = 1, c_2 = 5$, reflecting our desire to penalize lost packets most heavily. The mice account for about 40% of the traffic and the system is quite "noisy," since the variances of the Wiener processes driving (x, ρ) are $(9, 4.5)$.

The optimal preemptive controls are determined by a switching curve: $u(x, \rho) = 0$ below the curve and equals its maximum value above the curve. The curve obtained for our example in the asymptotic regime is given in Figure 1. As we see, in (x, ρ) space, the curve is initially (for small x) almost a straight line with a slightly decreasing slope as x increases. As the buffer fills up, the slope becomes sharply more negative, as expected. The optimal cost for the problem with preemptive control was about 1/10th of that without. In general, The values of the cost components (stationary mean values of $x(t), \rho(t)$, and $\lim_{t \to \infty} EU(t)/t$ are more significant than the optimal cost, since they give us information on the tradeoffs. Optimal control is not of interest for its own sake, but rather for the information provided on good design, and tradeoffs among the cost components as the weights change.

For the uncontrolled problem, the sum of the buffer overflow rate for all users was $5.35\sqrt{n}$, vs. $0.28\sqrt{n}$ under the optimal control for the given cost coefficients. The mean queue was virtually full for the uncontrolled case, compared to an average of one-third full under optimal control. The total input rate for the controlled users was reduced by an average of $0.36\sqrt{n}$ under optimal preemptive control, compared with an increase of $6.3\sqrt{n}$ with no control. Thus to get an improvement in overflow of about 20 times cost a fractional reduction in the throughput of $(6.3 + 0.36)/[(v_1\lambda/\mu) + a_m]\sqrt{n}) = 0.666/\sqrt{n}$.

If the buffer size is increased, its average percentage occupancy is about the same (queue size is not weighted heavily), the average $E\rho$ increases, and the average overflow rate does not change dramatically (e.g., doubling the buffer only halves the overflow, under our parameters). The optimal system adapts to an increased buffer size mainly by increasing the average flow, keeping the queue size roughly in proportion to the buffer size, an interesting fact in itself. Of course, a larger weight on x will reduce the average queue size.

These numbers illustrate the type of tradeoffs that are possible. One pays for reduced overflow by reduced packet rate. But the packet rate is reduced only where it does the most good. The tradeoffs vary with the cost coefficients. To use the method effectively, one makes a series of runs, varying the coefficients c_i This yields a set of possible tradeoffs between the competing criteria. In each case, the tradeoff is under an optimal control. The approach to the use of numerical methods and heavy traffic approximations is similar to what was done for the problem of input control of a multiplexer system in [14]. A comparison with threshold controls shows that the effects of the optimal control can be well approximated by a threshold control depending on ρ only, for appropriate values of the threshold. The cost components for the no control, optimal, and threshold cases are summarized in Table 1. If the threshold controls are activated only when the buffer exceeds some modest level, their performance is even better. Keep in mind that the described optimal control and costs are for a very heavy weight on overflow.

Table 1. Cost components.			
under run type	buf overflow/$\sqrt{n}$	Ex	$E\rho$
no cont.	5.35	11.92	6.35
opt. cont.	.28	4.4	-.36
thresh $\rho = 0$	.69	7.6	1.46
thresh $\rho = -1$	.48	6.4	.98
thresh $\rho = -3$	.33	4.9	.2

Appendix

Comparison With a Fluid Model

Reference [20] also concerned a limit approximation for large systems and justified the use of a delayed deterministic differential equation as an approximation for a certain class of problems. Since there are major differences between that work and this, apart from the different scaling, and since that paper is the main other current work on the use of limit-delay equations for AIMD models, a brief discussion of some of the differences is worthwhile.

In the basic model of Section 3, capacity (i.e., bandwidth) scales linearly with n, and so does the number of sources. The packet rate for each source is $O(1)$. Our general approach also allows the possibility that the number of sources grows more slowly with n, with the packet rate per source growing accordingly faster. While there are no explicit capacity constraints in [20], it is clear that the bandwidth (BW) is proportional to their n^2, and we use this fact below. They use a fixed number of connections of the order of $\sqrt{BW}$ (and no analog of the models of Sections 4 and 5), each sending packets at rate $O(\sqrt{BW})$. The number of mice connections grows linearly with $\sqrt{BW}$, and so does the rate of each mouse. Time is divided into "decision intervals" of length $O(1/\sqrt{BW})$, and the rates are (perhaps unrealistically) averaged over these successive intervals before feedback and decisions. This averaging over $O(\sqrt{BW})$ packets before feedback effectively eliminates the randomness due to the mice. We work closer to system capacity where the effects of random variations are greater, and it is the true instantaneous randomness that causes the losses and activates the controls.

The total overall rates of increase of the packet rate due to the slow additive control is the same here and in [20]. In [20] the "slow constant rate of increase of the packet rate" of each connection in the nth model (the one corresponding to n TCP connections) increases by $1/n$ per each time slot, so that in terms of real time the total rate of increase does not depend on n. Thus the total rate of increase is of the order of $\sqrt{BW}$, as in our case. In our model, the packet loss of each AIMD source is random and determined by the loss process associated with that source. This is in conformance with the objectives of buffer management schemes [7]. In [20], in contrast, all AIMD sources have the same instantaneous dynamics, hence identical losses. An important advantage of the work in [20] is that the model, being deterministic, is much simpler. Hence, under its assumptions, one can more conveniently explore some of the effects of delays.

References

[1] E. Altman, K. Avratchenkov and C. Barakat, "A stochastic model of TCP/IP with stationary random losses", *ACM SIGCOMM 2000*.

[2] F. Baccelli and D. Hong, "A.I.M.D, Fairness and Fractal Scaling of TCP Traffic" Technical Report, April 2001, RR-4155, INRIA Rocquencourt, France, 2001.

[3] S. Ben Fredj, T. Bonald, A. Proutiere, G. Regnié and J. W. Roberts, "Statistical bandwidth sharing: a study of congestion at flow level", *SIGCOMM'*, 2001.

[4] T. Bu and D. Towsley, "Fixed point approximation for TCP behaviour in an AQM network", *ACM SIGMETRICS*, June 2001.

[5] P. Brown, "Resource sharing of TCP connections with different round trip times", *IEEE Infocom*, Mar 2000.

[6] V. Dumas, F. Guillemin and P. Robert, "A Markovian analysis of AIMD algorithms", *Advances in Applied Probability*, 34(1) 85-111, 2002.

[7] S. Floyd and V. Jacobson, "Random Early Detection gateways for Congestion Avoidance" *IEEE/ACM Transactions on Networking*, 1(4):25–39, 1993.

[8] C. Hollot, V. Misra, D. Towsley and W.-B. Gong, "A control theoretic analysis of RED" IEEE INFOCOM, 2001

[9] A. Ichikawa, "Quadratic control of evolution equations with delays in control" *SIAM J. Control and Optim.* 20:645–668, 1982.

[10] P. Kuusela, P. Lassila, J. Virtamo, "Stability of TCP-RED Congestion Control", in proceedings of ITC-17, Salvador da Bahia, Brasil, Dec. 2001, pp. 655-666.

[11] T.G. Kurtz. *Approximation of Population Processes*, volume 36 of *CBMS-NSF Regional Conf. Series in Appl. Math.* SIAM, Philadelphia, 1981.

[12] H.J. Kushner and P. Dupuis, *Numerical Methods for Stochastic Control Problems in Continuous Time*, Springer-Verlag, Berlin and New York, 1992: Second edition, 2001

[13] H.J. Kushner. *Heavy Traffic Analysis of Controlled Queueing and Communication Networks*. Springer-Verlag, Berlin and New York, 2001.

[14] H.J. Kushner, D. Jarvis, and J. Yang. Controlled and optimally controlled multiplexing systems: A numerical exploration. *Queueing Systems*, 20:255–291, 1995.

[15] T.V. Lakshman and U. Madhow, "The performance of TCP/IP for networks with high bandwidth-delay products and random loss", *IEEE/ACM Transactions on Networking*, Jun 1997.

[16] S. H. Low, "A Duality Model of TCP and Queue Management Algorithms", ITC Specialist Seminar on IP Traffic Measurement, Modeling and Management, September 18-20, 2000, Monterey, CA. To appear IEEE/ACM Trans. on Networking, 2003.

[17] Laurent Massoulie, "Stability of distributed congestion control with heterogeneous feedback delays", IEEE Transactions on Automatic Control 47(2002) 895-902.

[18] J. Padhye, V. Firoiu, D. Towsley, and J. Kurose, "Modeling TCP throughput: A simple model and its empirical validation", *ACM SIGCOMM*, Sep 1998.

[19] K. K. Ramakrishnan, S. Floyd, and D. Black, "The Addition of Explicit Congestion Notification (ECN) to IP" RFC 3168, Proposed Standard, September 2001, available at ftp://ftp.isi.edu/in-notes/rfc3168.txt

[20] S. Shakkottai and R. Srikant. "How good are deterministic fluid models of internet congestion control." In *Proc., IEEE INFOCOM, 2002*, New York, 2002. IEEE Press.

[21] R. Srikant. *The Mathematics of Internet Congestion Control*. Birkhäuser, Boston, 2003.

[22] R. B. Vinter and R. H. Kwong. "The infinite time quadratic control problem for linear systems with state and control delays: An evolution equation approach." *SIAM J. Control and Optim.* 19: 139–153, 1981.

Chapter 17

UNRELIABLE COMPONENTS WITH FAST REPAIR AND DYNAMIC NETWORK RESTORATION

Kostas N. Oikonomou

AT&T Labs–Research
Middletown, NJ 07748, U.S.A.

ko@research.att.com

Abstract   We study the probability distributions, over a given time interval, of the downtime and number of failures of a reference connection in a communications network. These distributions are necessary for setting service-level agreements for the connection, or for imposing requirements on the equipment so that the service objectives can be met.

The model for the connection consists of two switches or routers, the intermediate equipment lumped into the "transport", and the connection's environment, which provides restoration with a certain probability and within a certain time bound. In addition to the downtime and event distributions, we derive a fundamental relationship between the probability with which a downtime objective can be met and the restorability provided by the network.

Our basic building block is a 2-state semi-Markov process with a mixture repair time distribution, which allows us to model transports with many failure modes, each with its own repair characteristics. One of the repair modes is fast repair by the network (restoration). Our results are analytical, in the form of bounds, or numerical, obtained by fast Laplace transform inversion.

1.   Introduction

Consider two nodes in a communications network and the equipment on the path that connects them. Assume that switches or routers are located at the nodes, and refer to the equipment on the connecting path as the "transport"; see Fig. 7.1. Such a connection, consisting of two end routers/switches and a transport, may be considered typical or worst-case for a network of interest; we will use the term *reference* connection.

While the behavior of a reference connection can be studied from many different viewpoints, this paper addresses the reliability aspects. The components of the connection are subject to failure, and when the transport fails the switches attempt to restore the connection by finding another path through the network; this restoration succeeds with a certain probability, the network *restorability*. Otherwise the transport has to be repaired. We will study the probability distribution of the *downtime* of the connection over some time interval, and the distribution of the *number of failures* of the transport over that interval. These interval distributions are necessary when one wants to assess the probability that the reference connection meets some objectives (service-level agreements, SLAs)[1], to set such objectives for the connection, or to see what equipment reliabilities are needed in order to achieve the service objectives.

To put the reference connection viewpoint in context, the performance and reliability of a network, defined as the behavior of a performance measure over a set of failure states, is most properly investigated by looking at the entire network. The literature on this is large; [S&G] is an overview of Markov models at the network level, and [B&R] is a detailed exposition of such a model for a private network. A reference connection model is useful when information on the entire network is not available, as in the initial phases of a design, but one wants to assess the reliability of various alternatives for a path between two nodes. Even when the complete network design is available, one may want to use a reference connection model to answer detailed questions such as "what is the p.d. of the downtime?", which may be too difficult with a model for an entire network. On the other hand, care is needed in drawing conclusions about the entire network from a connection-level model, as the network cannot be taken to be a set of (independent) reference connections.

Typically, reference connection models are set up as a "main" path and one, or a set of, "backup" paths. The backup paths may be (pre) defined by the restoration scheme, or chosen as representative by the modeller. Instead, the model described here considers only one path and abstracts the rest of the network into two parameters, the restorability r and the restoration time τ, the idea being that a restoration path may be found anywhere within the network. The pros and cons of this abstraction are discussed in §7.

---

[1]Steady-state distributions are often used for this purpose, as an easy approximation to the interval distributions.

The basic failure-and-repair models used in this paper are two-state semi-Markov processes. Times between failures are distributed exponentially, whereas repair times have more general, gamma-based distributions. The most interesting abstraction is the model for the transport, which, from the viewpoint of the traffic carried by the connection, is an unreliable component with the possibility of fast repair (restoration by the network). This model is a 2-state semi-Markov process with *mixture* repairs, studied in §2. The repair distribution is a mixture of "fast" repairs, occurring with probability r and assumed to complete within a small constant time, and "slow" repairs, occurring with total probability $1 - r$ and defined by a mixture of gamma densities. This mixture represents the situation in which there are many types of failures, each handled by a different repair mode.

The distribution of the time this process spends in the down state over $[0, T]$ is studied in §3, and both exact results (only one gamma component) and lower and upper bounds are derived. It is shown that under fairly typical conditions, the probability of fast repair (network restorability r) imposes a simple *upper bound* on the probability with which a downtime objective can be met: e.g. to meet a downtime objective with 95% confidence, network restoration must be at least 97.5% successful. In §4 we turn to the number of failures of the process modelling the transport, and calculate the distribution of the number of any individual type of failure (marginal distribution), as well as the joint distribution of all the various types of failures during $[0, T]$. If a one-time cost is associated with each failure event, these distributions also allow us to calculate the cost or loss associated with the failures.

The routers, viewed as relatively reliable components, are modelled by a simpler semi-Markov process with exponential failures and gamma repairs, reviewed in §5. To obtain the downtime of the connection from the downtimes of its constituents, upper and lower bounds on the downtime of a series connection of arbitrary components are described in §6. Finally, an example analysis of a reference connection with calculations of downtime distributions and of distributions for the numbers of failures is given in §7.

From the methodological viewpoint, it is possible to study the distributions of central interest in an almost *analytical* manner by (1) staying within the well-studied *2-state* semi-Markov process framework with exponential failure distributions, (2) by using *mixtures* to represent complicated repair mechanisms that would otherwise require extra states, and (3) in the case of the downtime, handling the series connection of components by upper and lower *bounds*. The distribution of the number of failures of each component is most conveniently approached by (4) *numerical inversion* of Laplace transforms.

Proofs of all analytical results are given in the Appendix.

2. Two-state semi-Markov process with mixture repairs

Consider a two-state semi-Markov (alternating renewal) process, and let $F(t)$ and $R(t)$ be the *distributions* of the holding times in the "up" and "down" states (F for failure, R for repair). The basic results for this process have been derived in [B&H], and are originally due to Takács as referenced there. If $d(T)$ is the time spent by the process in the "down" state over $[0, T]$, then[2]

$$\Pr\big(d(T) \leq t\big) = \sum_{k=0}^{\infty} R^{(k)}(t)(F^{(k)}(T-t) - F^{(k+1)}(T-t)), \qquad (2.1)$$

where $F^{(k)}(\cdot), R^{(k)}(\cdot)$ are the k-fold convolutions of F, R with themselves[3] and $F^{(0)} \equiv 1, R^{(0)} \equiv 1$, whereas $F^{(1)} \equiv F, R^{(1)} \equiv R$. This fundamental relation has been proved many times in the literature; the best treatment is in [M].

If $\nu(T)$ is the number of times the "down" state is entered during $[0, T]$, assuming the process is "up" at 0, then with $H = R \star F$, the distribution of the length of an up-down cycle,

$$\Pr\big(\nu(T) = k\big) = (F \star H)^{(k-1)}(T) - (F \star H)^{(k)}(T). \qquad (2.2)$$

One might wonder about results on probability *densities* instead of distributions. The advantage of expressions such as (2.1) and (2.2) is that certain quantities are known to be ≤ 1 and decreasing with increasing k, thus making approximations and bounds much easier. See [P], [SSR], and [C] for density results.

---

[2] Precisely, $d(T)$ is the integral over $[0, T]$ of the indicator function of the "down" state of the process.

[3] The convolution of distributions F and G is denoted $F \star G$. The more usual convolution of densities f and g is denoted $f * g$. The convolution of F and G is the Stieltjes integral $\int_0^t F(t-\tau)\, dG(\tau) = \int_0^t G(t-\tau)\, dF(\tau)$. If F has a density f, the last integral reduces to $\int_0^t G(t-\tau)f(\tau)\, d\tau$. See [F2], V.4.

2.1   Exponential time to failure

It is commonly assumed that the time to failure is exponentially-distributed. This is a very good assumption for reliable systems[4]. When the p.d. of the time to failure is $\mathcal{E}(x \mid \lambda) = \lambda e^{-\lambda x}$, it is well-known that $F^{(k)}(x) - F^{(k+1)}(x) = (\lambda x)^k e^{-\lambda x}/k!$, i.e. the number of failures in time x is Poisson-distributed, so (2.1) becomes

$$\Pr\big(d(T) \le t\big) = \sum_{k=0}^{\infty} R^{(k)}(t) e^{-\lambda(T-t)} \frac{\lambda^k (T-t)^k}{k!}. \tag{2.3}$$

This sum can be approximated to within any desired ε by stopping the summation when $R^{(k+1)}(t)\bar{\gamma}(k+1, \varphi) < \varepsilon$, where $\varphi = \lambda(T-t)$ and $\bar{\gamma}(\cdot, \cdot)$ is the incomplete gamma function defined in §17.A.1.

Bounds on the sum (2.3) can be found by noting that if Φ, Ψ are any distributions, $(\Phi \star \Psi)(t) = \int_0^t \Phi(t-x)\, d\Psi(x) < \Phi(t) \int_0^t d\Psi(x) = \Phi(t)\Psi(t)$. It follows that $R^{(k)}(t) < R^k(t)$, and so with $\varphi = \lambda(T-t)$,

$$e^{-\varphi}\left(1 + \varphi R(t) + \frac{\varphi^2}{2} R^{(2)}(t)\right) \le \Pr\big(d(T) \le t\big) \le e^{-\varphi(1-R(t))}. \tag{2.4}$$

These bounds are well-known; see e.g. [A&J], [F&Y]. They are tight when $\varphi \ll 1$, i.e. for systems that don't fail often in $[0, T]$, and when φ is sizeable but $\varphi R(t) \ll 1$.

Another known fact ([B&H] Theorem 1, again originally due to Takács) is that as $T \to \infty$, the distribution of $d(T)$ tends to the normal:

$$\begin{aligned} \frac{d(T) - \mu_d}{\sigma_d} &\xrightarrow{\mathcal{D}} N(0, 1), \\ \mu_d = \frac{\mu_R T}{\mu_F + \mu_R}, \quad \sigma_d^2 &= \frac{(\mu_F^2 \sigma_R^2 + \mu_R^2 \sigma_F^2)T}{(\mu_F + \mu_R)^3}, \end{aligned} \tag{2.5}$$

with μ_F and μ_R the means, and σ_F^2, σ_R^2 the variances of the failure and repair distributions.

2.2   Mixture time to repair

We will study the case of the above process in which the time to repair is a mixture of an impulse (delta function) and of a number of gamma

---

[4]It is justified by limit theorems stating that the passage time to a rare set in a Markov chain is approximately exponential (see [K]), and by similar results for more general processes (see [Ge]).

densities. Then the p.d. of the time to repair, of which R is the c.d.f., is

$$\rho(t) = r\delta(t - \tau) + (1 - r)\sum_i c_i G(t \mid a_i, \mu_i), \tag{2.6}$$

where τ is a constant, $G(t \mid a, b)$ is the gamma density $\frac{b^a}{\Gamma(a)}t^{a-1}e^{-bt}$, and $\sum_i c_i = 1$. The interpretation of eq. (2.6) that we will adopt is that r is the probability of a *fast* repair, requiring a relatively short time τ. Now suppose there are various failure modes, with rates $\lambda_1, \lambda_2, \ldots$; if we set $c_i = \lambda_i/\sum_j \lambda_j$, then $(1 - r)c_i$ is the probability of the ith *slow* repair mode (or "long failure"), requiring a gamma-distributed time. §12.4 of [M&W] discusses the use of the gamma density in repair models. One of its appealing features is that when $a > 1$, gamma repair has a rate that initially increases with time but then eventually stabilizes, which is what one would expect from an intelligent repair person or mechanism.

3.   Time spent in the "down" state

Let t be an *objective* which we want the downtime $d(T)$ of the process over $[0, T]$ to meet with some (high) probability. In most of this section we will use (2.6) in the generic form

$$\rho(t) = r\delta(t - \tau) + (1 - r)m(t), \tag{3.1}$$

where $m(\cdot)$ denotes some (possibly mixture) density.

3.1   A one-component mixture

This case is instructive because the exact solution is easy to compute, albeit not expressible in closed form. When there is only one component $G(t \mid a, \mu)$ in (2.6), the Laplace transform of $\rho(t)$ is $R(s) = re^{-\tau s} + (1 - r)\mu^a/(s + \mu)^a$, so

$$R^k(s) = \sum_{i=0}^{k} \binom{k}{i} r^{k-i}(1 - r)^i e^{-(k-i)\tau s} \frac{\mu^{ai}}{(s + \mu)^{ai}}.$$

Inverting this,

$$\rho^{(k)}(t) = r^k \delta(t - k\tau) +$$
$$\sum_{i=1}^{k} \binom{k}{i} r^{k-i}(1 - r)^i G\big(t - (k - i)\tau \mid ai, \mu\big)u(t - (k - i)\tau),$$

$\delta(\cdot)$ and $u(\cdot)$ being the unit impulse and unit step, and then integrating,

$$R^{(k)}(t) = r^k u(t - k\tau) + \sum_{i=\max(1,k-n)}^{k} \binom{k}{i} r^{k-i}(1-r)^i \,\bar{\gamma}\big(ai, \mu(t - (k-i)\tau)\big),$$

(3.2)

where $n = \lfloor t/\tau \rfloor$ and $\bar{\gamma}(\cdot, \cdot)$ is the regularized incomplete gamma function (see §17.A.1). $\Pr(d(T) \le t)$ can be computed from (3.2) with error $\le \varepsilon$ by accumulating the terms in the sum (2.3) while $R^{(k+1)}(t)\,\bar{\gamma}(k+1, \varphi) > \varepsilon$, where $\varphi = \lambda(T-t)$. Note that the sum over i in (3.2) has at most $n+1$ terms, no matter what k is. The exact results for the special cases $r = 0$ and $r = 1$ are easy: for $r = 0$ we have the classic exponential failure, exponential repair result given in [B&H], and for $r = 1$ the answer is $\sum_{k \le t/\tau} e^{-\varphi} \varphi^k / k! = \bar{\Gamma}(n+1, \varphi)$, as can be seen from (2.3).

Fig. 3.1 shows plots of $\Pr(d(T) \le t)$ vs. t when $T \gg t$.

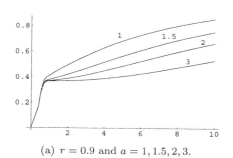

(a) $r = 0.9$ and $a = 1, 1.5, 2, 3$.

(b) Detailed view of $a = 1.5$ showing the step structure due to the constant τ.

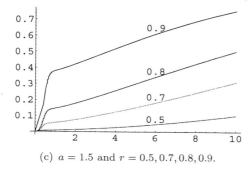

(c) $a = 1.5$ and $r = 0.5, 0.7, 0.8, 0.9$.

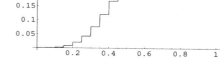

r	$\Pr(d(8760) < 8)$
0	0.0022
0.5	0.0713
0.7	0.244
0.8	0.424
0.9	0.689

(d) Values at $t = 8$.

Figure 3.1. $\Pr(d(T) \le t)$ vs. t for $T = 8760$, $\lambda = 1/876$, $\mu = 1/4$, $\tau = 0.05$.

3.2 Network restorability and downtime objectives

In this section we derive some fundamental relationships among the network restorability, transport failure modes and repair times, and downtime objectives. Suppose we have an unreliable transport, i.e. one that is expected to fail a few times over $[0, T]$. Then

Lemma 3.1. *Assume that $\tau < t \ll T$. Define $\varphi = \lambda(T - t)$, approximately equal to the expected number of failures of the transport in $[0, T]$. Then, for an unreliable transport* [5]

$$\Pr\big(d(T) \leq t\big) < R(t) + \varepsilon_0,$$

and for an even less reliable transport

$$\Pr\big(d(T) \leq t\big) < R^2(t) + \varepsilon_1,$$

where $R(\cdot)$ is the distribution corresponding to the density $\rho(\cdot)$, and

$$\varepsilon_0 = (1 - r)e^{-\varphi}, \qquad \varepsilon_1 = (1 - r^2)(\varphi + 1)e^{-\varphi}.$$

Essentially, this says that if the transport is unreliable, the downtime objective cannot be met with probability greater than that of completing a repair in time less than the objective. And if the transport is even less reliable, the objective cannot be met with probability greater than the square of the probability of repair. The accuracy of these statements is examined in Table 3.1. When $t > \tau$, $R(t) = r + (1 - r)M(t)$. An

		\multicolumn{4}{c}{φ}
		5	6	7	10
$r = 0.8$	ε_0	$1.3 \cdot 10^{-3}$	$5 \cdot 10^{-4}$	$1.8 \cdot 10^{-4}$	$9.1 \cdot 10^{-6}$
	ε_1	0.0145	$6.2 \cdot 10^{-3}$	$2.6 \cdot 10^{-3}$	$1.8 \cdot 10^{-4}$
$r = 0.9$	ε_0	$6.8 \cdot 10^{-4}$	$2.5 \cdot 10^{-4}$	$9.1 \cdot 10^{-5}$	$4.5 \cdot 10^{-6}$
	ε_1	$7.7 \cdot 10^{-3}$	$3.3 \cdot 10^{-3}$	$1.4 \cdot 10^{-3}$	$9.5 \cdot 10^{-5}$

Table 3.1. The accuracies of the bounds of Lemma 3.1.

interesting special case arises when $r \gg (1 - r)M(t)$, i.e. when the probability of fast repair (successful network restoration) is much higher than the probability that restoration fails and *slow* repair is finished within t. In that case $R \approx r$ in Lemma 3.1, and we can state that

---

[5] i.e. the 2-state semi-Markov process of §2.1 and §2.2.

> The probability of meeting the downtime objective of an unreliable transport cannot exceed the network restorability, and for an even more unreliable transport the square of the network restorability.

Equivalently, to meet the downtime objective with probability p, the network restorability must be at least p, or $\sqrt{p}$. Finally, it is clear that all the statements above apply a fortiori to the probability that a connection including such a transport meets its downtime objective.

As an example, consider a transport that is expected to fail about 10 times in $[0, T]$ and slow repair times are exponentially-distributed with a mean of 4 hrs. Then $\varphi = 10$, $M(t) = 1 - e^{-t/4}$, and $R(t) = r + (1 - r)(1 - e^{-t/4})$. The exact value of $\Pr\bigl(d(T) \leq t\bigr)$ is computed by the results of §3.1, and Fig. 3.2 illustrates the above discussion. The condition $M(t) \ll r/(1-r)$ is satisfied as long as t is not too large, and then the r^2 (and r) bound obtains.

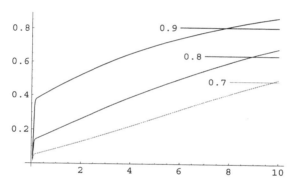

Figure 3.2. $\Pr\bigl(d(T) \leq t\bigr)$ vs. t to illustrate the r^2 bound, with $r = 0.9, 0.8, 0.7$, $T = 8760$, $\lambda = 1/876$, $\tau = 0.01$, and exponential slow repairs with $\mu = 1/4$.

3.3   Lower and upper bounds

Here we develop lower and upper bounds $\underline{P}(t, T)$ and $\overline{P}(t, T)$ on $P(t, T) = \Pr\bigl(d(T) \leq t\bigr)$. The emphasis is on analytical forms, as opposed to calculational procedures[6].

The bounds hold without any assumptions on the magnitudes of the parameters, but they are constructed to become tighter as r approaches 1, which is the case of interest for fast repair of a relatively unreliable system. We develop the bounds in terms of an arbitrary density $m(t)$,

---

[6]If one just wants to find the value of $\Pr(d(T) < t)$ at a specific t, it is easier to compute it straight from (2.3) using numerical Laplace inversion (see §4) to find the value of $R^{(k)}(\cdot)$ at t.

and then particularize them to the case of a gamma mixture. First we have a lower bound better than that of (2.4):

Lemma 3.2. *With the repair time density (3.1) and* $\varphi = \lambda(T - t)$,

$$\underline{P}(t,T) = e^{-(1-r)\varphi}\bar{\Gamma}(n+1, r\varphi) +$$

$$e^{-\varphi}\left((1-r)\varphi \sum_{k=0}^{n} \frac{(r\varphi)^k}{k!} M(t-k\tau) + \frac{(1-r)^2\varphi^2}{2} \sum_{k=0}^{n} \frac{(r\varphi)^k}{k!} M^{(2)}(t-k\tau)\right),$$

where $n = \lfloor t/\tau \rfloor$, $M(t)$ *is the distribution corresponding to* $m(t)$, *and* $M^{(2)}(t)$ *is* $(M \star M)(t)$.

This expression can be viewed as an expansion to order 2 on the number of failures in $[0, T]$ that are not "covered" by the fast repair. $\underline{P}(t,T)$ equals $P(t,T)$ in some boundary cases: when $t = 0$, the value being $e^{-\lambda T}$, and when $r = 1$, the value being $e^{-\varphi} \sum_{0 \le k \le \lfloor t/\tau \rfloor} \varphi^k/k!$.

To know how well $\Pr(d(T) \le t)$ is approximated by $\underline{P}(t,T)$ we need a bound on the difference. We develop a bound which is often significantly better than the straightforward upper bound of (2.4) by exploiting the concept of log-concavity. Recall that a function is log-concave if its log is a concave function[7]. Considering t and τ to be given and fixed, define

$$\alpha = \frac{M(t-\tau)}{M(t)} < 1, \qquad \beta = \frac{M^{(2)}(t-\tau)}{M^{(2)}(t)} < 1 \qquad (3.3)$$

if $M(\cdot)$ is log-concave, and $\alpha = \beta = 1$ otherwise. For example, the exponential distribution is log-concave, and so is the gamma if $a \ge 1$. Then it is shown in the Appendix that for any $j \ge 1$

$$M(t - j\tau) \le \alpha^j M(t), \qquad M^{(2)}(t - j\tau) \le \beta^j M^{(2)}(t), \qquad (3.4)$$

with $\alpha, \beta < 1$ if $M(\cdot)$ is log-concave. With these definitions we have the following improvement to the upper bound of (2.4):

Lemma 3.3. *With* α, β *as in (3.3),*

$$\overline{P}(t,T) = \underline{P}(t,T) +$$

$$e^{-(1-\alpha\beta r)\varphi} \frac{M(t)}{\sqrt{M^{(2)}(t)}}(\sinh \omega - \omega) + e^{-(1-\beta^2 r)\varphi}\left(\cosh \omega - 1 - \frac{\omega^2}{2}\right),$$

where $\omega = (1-r)\varphi\sqrt{M^{(2)}(t)}$.

---

[7] The relevant properties of log-concavity are summarized in §17.A.2.

This result can be extended to apply to a much wider class of distributions:

Lemma 3.4. *Suppose that $M(x)$, while not log-concave itself, is a mixture $\sum_i c_i P_i(x)$ of log-concave distributions $P_i(\cdot)$. Define α_i by (3.3) with P_i in place of M. Also define*

$$\beta_{ij} = \frac{(P_i \star P_j)(t - \tau)}{(P_i \star P_j)(t)}.$$

Then Lemma 3.3 holds for $M(\cdot)$, with $\alpha = \max_i \alpha_i$, $\beta = \max_{i,j} \beta_{ij}$, $\alpha, \beta < 1$.

In some situations, the limiting case of very fast restoration is of interest. We then have

Corollary 3.5. *When $\tau = 0$,*

$$\underline{P}(t, T) = e^{-(1-r)\varphi}\left(1 + (1 - r)\varphi M(t) + \frac{(1 - r)^2 \varphi^2}{2} M^{(2)}(t)\right),$$

$$\overline{P}(t, T) = \underline{P}(t, T) + e^{-(1-r)\varphi}\left(\frac{M(t)}{\sqrt{M^{(2)}(t)}}(\sinh \omega - \omega) + \cosh \omega - 1 - \frac{\omega^2}{2}\right).$$

The bounds of Lemmas 3.2, 3.3, and 3.4 are valid no matter what the density $m(t)$ in (3.1) is. For the gamma mixture of (2.6) we have

$$M(t) = \sum_i c_i \bar{\gamma}(a_i, \mu_i t), \tag{3.5}$$

$$M^{(2)}(t) = \sum_i c_i^2 \bar{\gamma}(2a_i, \mu_i t) +$$

$$2\sum_{i<j} \frac{c_i \mu_i^{a_i} c_j \mu_j^{a_j}}{\Gamma(a_i + a_j)} \int_0^t x^{a_i + a_j - 1} e^{-\mu_i x} \, {}_1F_1\left(a_j, a_i + a_j, (\mu_i - \mu_j)x\right) dx,$$

where ${}_1F_1(a, b, z)$ is the hypergeometric function. It is evident from (3.5) that the difficulty in adding one more term to $\underline{P}(t, T)$ has to do with the expression for $M^{(3)}(t)$. However, $\sum_i c_i^3 \bar{\gamma}(3a_i, \mu_i t)$ is an immediate part of $M^{(3)}(t)$, and an easy improvement is obtained by taking this term into account in Lemma 3.2[8]. In case $m(t)$ is a mixture of exponentials, setting all a_i to 1 in (3.5) yields

$$M(t) = 1 - \sum_i c_i e^{-\mu_i t}, \tag{3.6}$$

$$M^{(2)}(t) = 1 - \sum_i c_i^2 e^{-\mu_i t}(1 + \mu_i t) - 2\sum_{i<j} \frac{c_i c_j}{\mu_j - \mu_i}\left(\mu_j e^{-\mu_i t} - \mu_i e^{-\mu_j t}\right).$$

---

[8] All the other parts of $M^{(3)}$ are also positive, hence the lower bound is preserved.

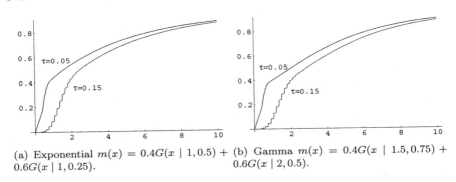

(a) Exponential $m(x) = 0.4G(x \mid 1, 0.5) +$ (b) Gamma $m(x) = 0.4G(x \mid 1.5, 0.75) +$
$0.6G(x \mid 1, 0.25)$. $0.6G(x \mid 2, 0.5)$.

Figure 3.3. $\underline{P}(t, T)$ vs. t for exponential and gamma mixtures with component means of 2 and 4, and $T = 100$, $r = 0.9$, $\lambda = 0.1$.

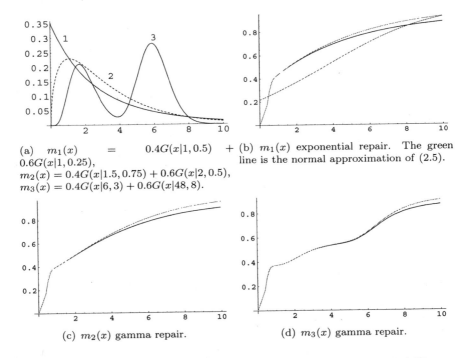

(a) $m_1(x)$ $=$ $0.4G(x|1, 0.5)$ + (b) $m_1(x)$ exponential repair. The green
$0.6G(x|1, 0.25)$,   line is the normal approximation of (2.5).
$m_2(x) = 0.4G(x|1.5, 0.75) + 0.6G(x|2, 0.5)$,
$m_3(x) = 0.4G(x|6, 3) + 0.6G(x|48, 8)$.

(c) $m_2(x)$ gamma repair.   (d) $m_3(x)$ gamma repair.

Figure 3.4. $\underline{P}(t, T)$ and $\bar{P}(t, T)$ vs. t for $T = 100$, $r = 0.9$, $\lambda = 0.1$, $\tau = 0.05$.

Fig. 3.3 illustrates the lower bound of Lemma 3.2 for 2-component mixtures of exponentials and gammas. In both cases the components have means of 2 and 4. In general the closeness of $\underline{P}(t, T)$ and $\overline{P}(t, T)$ to one another depends on (1) the value of $M(\cdot)$ at t, the downtime objective, and (2) on whether $M(\cdot)$ is log-concave or not. The exponential $M(\cdot)$ of (3.6) represents a worst case w.r.t. (1): with t fixed, $M(t)$

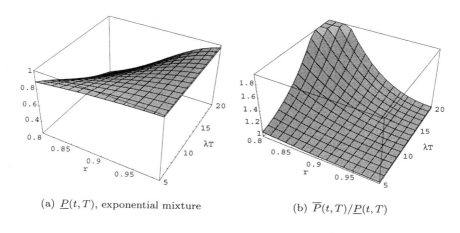

(a) $\underline{P}(t,T)$, exponential mixture   (b) $\overline{P}(t,T)/\underline{P}(t,T)$

Figure 3.5. The approximation $P(t,T) \approx \underline{P}(t,T)$ for the exponential mixture of Fig. 3.3(a). Results for the gamma mixture of Fig. 3.3(b) look similar, but $\overline{P}(t,T)/\underline{P}(t,T)$ is smaller.

decreases when the mode $(a-1)/\mu$ of $G(x \mid a,\mu)$ moves from 0 to values > 0. To offset this, the exponential $M(\cdot)$ is log-concave (see §17.A.2). On the other hand, a mixture of gammas does not, in general, have a log-concave distribution, but things otherwise being equal (equal means with the exponentials, say), will exhibit a smaller $M(t)$. Further, the gamma distribution with $a \geq 1$ *is* log-concave (see §17.A.2), so Lemma 3.4 applies to a mixture of gammas.

Fig. 3.4 shows the bounds on $P(t,T)$ for the mixtures of Fig. 3.3 as well as for a mixture of two well-separated gammas (two distinct slow repair modes), and illustrates considerations (1) and (2) above. Finally, Fig. 3.5 depicts the relative error in approximating $P(t,T)$ by $\underline{P}(t,T)$ as a function of r and $\lambda T \approx \varphi$. Even though the error can be high, it is so in the region of low $P(t,T)$, which is not the region of interest when t is an objective that, presumably, has to be met with high probability.

4.   Number and cost of failures

If n failures occur in $[0,T]$, i.e. the semi-Markov process of §2 enters the "down" state n times, the probability that k of them require long repair ("long failures") is $\Pr(k \mid n) = \binom{n}{k}(1-r)^k r^{n-k}$. Let $\ell(T)$ be the number of long failures in $[0,T]$; then $\Pr(\ell = k) = \sum_n \Pr(\ell = k \mid \nu = n) \Pr(\nu = n)$; so the problem reduces to finding $\Pr(\nu(T) = n)$, where $\nu(T)$ is defined in (2.2).

While one may think of a number of ways to approach this computation[9], there is an almost ideal method, which is exact, relatively easy,
and direct: calculating directly from (2.2) via fast *numerical inversion*
of Laplace transforms by the method described in [A&W]. With $\nu(T)$
and $\ell(T)$ as above, recall that $H(t) = (R \star F)(t)$. Then it follows from
(2.2) that

$$\Pr(\nu(T) = n) = \mathcal{L}^{-1}\left(\frac{1}{s}F(s)\big(1 - H(s)\big)H^{n-1}(s)\right),$$

where $H(s) = F(s)R(s)$, and consequently

$$\Pr(\ell(T) = 0) = \sum_{n=0}^{\infty} r^n \Pr(\nu = n) = 1 - (1-r)\mathcal{L}^{-1}\left(\frac{F(s)}{s(1 - rH(s))}\right),$$

$$\Pr(\ell(T) = m) = (1-r)^m \mathcal{L}^{-1}\left(\frac{F(s)\big(1 - H(s)\big)H^{m-1}(s)}{s\big(1 - rH(s)\big)^{m+1}}\right), \quad m \geq 1$$

$$\Pr(\ell(T) > m) = (1-r)^{m+1}\mathcal{L}^{-1}\left(\frac{F(s)H^m(s)}{s\big(1 - rH(s)\big)^{m+1}}\right), \quad m \geq 1, \quad (4.1)$$

where all transforms are transforms of densities, and all inversions are
evaluated at T.

Recall from §2.2 that each component of the repair time p.d. corresponds to a particular type of failure. A simple extension of the above
argument allows us to find the joint p.d. of the various types of long
failures, as well as the p.d. of long failures of a particular type. Given
a total of n failures (of all types) in $[0, T]$, let ℓ_i count the number of
long failures of the ith type. If there are u types of long failures, then
$\Pr(\ell_1 = k_1, \ldots, \ell_u = k_u \mid \nu = n) = \binom{n}{k_0, k_1, \ldots, k_u}r^{k_0}((1-r)c_1)^{k_1} \cdots ((1-r)c_u)^{k_u}$, where $k_0 = n - k_1 - \cdots - k_u$ is the number of short failures
and the c_i are the coefficients in (2.6). Further, $\Pr(\ell_i = k_i \mid \nu = n) = \binom{n}{k_i}\big((1-r)c_i\big)^{k_i}\big(1 - (1-r)c_i\big)^{n-k_i}$. For example, with $u = 2$ we get

$$\Pr(k_1, k_2 \mid n) = \binom{n}{k_0, k_1, k_2}\left(\frac{1-r}{r}\right)^{k_1+k_2}c_1^{k_1}c_2^{k_2}r^n,$$

---

[9]Analytical results for exponential and constant repairs are in [B&H] and [P]. More general
and less tractable exact results are in [C]. One could also try an extensive analysis of the sort
of §3. Approximate results are: asymptotic normality via the renewal process ([F1], [F2]),
and asymptotic Poisson p.d. ([A&J]).

and therefore[10]

$$\Pr(k_1, k_2) = \frac{(k_1 + k_2)!}{k_1! k_2!} (1 - r)^{k_1 + k_2} c_1^{k_1} c_2^{k_2}$$

$$\mathcal{L}^{-1} \left(\frac{F(s)\big(1 - H(s)\big) H(s)^{k_1 + k_2 - 1}}{s\big(1 - r H(s)\big)^{k_1 + k_2 + 1}} \right), \quad (4.2)$$

where F, H are as in (4.1). These results are illustrated in §7.

Now suppose that a certain one-time *cost* or *loss* is associated with each type of failure event, e.g. disrupting a sensitive application, having to raise an alarm, or initiating a diagnostic procedure. It is then clear that the results just presented also allow us to calculate the p.d. of the cost or loss incurred because of failures of the transport over the interval $[0, T]$. (The component of the loss that depends on the duration of the failure is addressed by the results of §3 on the downtime.)

Finally, on a methodological note, numerical Laplace inversion has recently been used in interesting ways to compute passage-time densities in very large Markov chains: see [BDK] and [H&K][11].

5. Reliable components with gamma repair

It follows from (2.3) that if $\rho(t) = G(t \mid a, \mu)$, then

$$\Pr\big(d(T) \le t\big) = e^{-\varphi} \left(1 + \varphi \bar{\gamma}(a, \mu t) + \frac{\varphi^2}{2} \bar{\gamma}(2a, \mu t) \right) + \varepsilon_3(t), \quad (5.1)$$
$$\text{where} \quad \varepsilon_3(t) < \big(1 - e^{-\varphi}(1 + \varphi + \varphi^2/2)\big) \bar{\gamma}(3a, \mu t).$$

The exact result is known from §3.1, but this analytic approximation is needed for convolution calculations of the type given in §6. If $\varepsilon_3(x)$ is negligible for all $x \le t$, where t is the objective, one can assume $P(t) = \underline{P}(t)$ for this component, $\underline{P}(t)$ being the r.h.s. of (5.1).

6. Downtime of a series connection: bounds

Given a component or system that is either in an "up" or in a "down" state, let $d(T)$ denote the total time it spends in the down state over $[0, T]$. Let $P(t, T) = \Pr\big(d(T) \le t\big)$, which we will sometimes abbreviate to $P(t)$. We then have[12]

---

[10]Write the multinomial coefficient as $\binom{n}{k_1 + k_2} \frac{(k_1 + k_2)!}{k_1! k_2!}$ and then use the fact that $\sum_n \binom{n}{m} z^n = z^m/(1 - z)^{m+1}$.

[11]Passage times are easier to compute than the sojourn times of §3.

[12]This must be well-known, but I don't know of a reference.

Lemma 6.1. *Let $C_1, \ldots, C_n$ be independent two-state components connected in series. Let C_i spend time $d_i(T)$ in the "down" state over $[0, T]$, and let $d(T)$ be the downtime of the entire system over $[0, T]$. Then for any $t \leq T$*

$$(P_1 \star P_2 \star \cdots \star P_n)(t) \leq \Pr\big(d(T) \leq t\big) \leq P_1(t) P_2(t) \cdots P_n(t),$$

where $\star$ denotes convolution of distributions (defined in §2).

For two components this says that $\Pr\big(d_1 + d_2 \leq t\big) \leq \Pr\big(d \leq t\big) \leq \Pr\big(d_1 \leq t\big) \Pr\big(d_2 \leq t\big)$. Each of the bounds is tight: the lower bound is attained when none of the down intervals of C_1 and C_2 overlap, and the upper bound is attained when all of the down intervals coincide. The usefulness of Lemma 6.1 is that it holds *irrespective* of the random processes that govern the behavior of the components. Further, if $d_i(T)$ is known only by bounds on its p.d., as was the case in §3, Lemma 6.1 is usable in the form

Corollary 6.2. *If $\underline{P}_2(t) \leq \Pr\big(d_2(T) \leq t\big) \leq \overline{P}_2(t)$, then $(P_1 \star \underline{P}_2)(t) \leq \Pr\big(d(T) \leq t\big) \leq P_1(t) \overline{P}_2(t)$.*

This follows from the definition of convolution of distributions.

To put Lemma 6.1 and the results we derive from it in perspective, suppose the 2-state components are Markov. Then $\Pr\big(d(T) \leq t\big)$ can be found exactly, by combining the Markov processes into a single Markov process and then using, e.g., the methods of [C], or, in some cases, those of [S]. Nevertheless, in all but the simplest models, numerical evaluation will be necessary. If, however, the component processes are semi-Markov, they do not combine to form another semi-Markov process, but a more complicated *generalized* semi-Markov process (GSMP, see [Gl]), which can only be handled numerically. Apart from the above, there are also asymptotic results of analytical, or almost analytical form: one type is based on the compound Poisson process for reliable components (Ch. 4 of [A&J]), and another on asymptotic normality (§2.1).

7.   Reference connection model

7.1   Model

Fig. 7.1 shows our reference connection model. This model involves a number of idealizations and approximations. First, some components appearing in the connection might be more complex Markov models; they can be approximated by 2-state components using the exponentiality results of [K] and the methods of [BDK]. The abstraction of a connection's environment into r, $m(\cdot)$, and τ deserves most of the attention. We discuss r and τ separately.

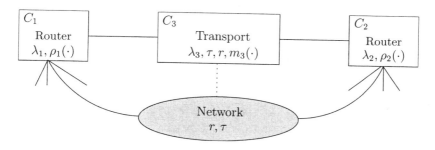

Figure 7.1. A reference connection and its environment.

(a) Representing restoration by the probability r is sound if the connection is part of a large network with many paths between nodes, but loses validity if the network is too "lean". (b) In reality, r is not a number, but a function of the state of the entire network. Estimation of this function requires methods beyond the scope of this paper, but some dependence on the state of the network can be taken into account by treating r as an uncertain quantity, described by an appropriate probability distribution. (c) As presented here, fast repair assumes that the transport path is replaced by a path of identical characteristics; that is not unreasonable as far as slow repair modes and times go, but a desirable extension to the model would be to allow other failure rates for the replacement paths, to reflect dependence on the state of the entire network.

Turning to τ, this time really depends on the routers or switches, on details of the restoration protocol, and on the precise failure event in the network, but experience and simulations with IP and ATM networks show that, in comparison with the slow repairs, it is safe to assume that network restoration completes in time bounded by a small constant.

7.2   Reliability analysis

Suppose that over the time period $T = 1\,\text{year}$ the two routers or switches are not very likely to fail, whereas the transport is expected to fail a few times. Then we can represent the routers by the reliable components with gamma repair of §5, and the transport by the unreliable component with fast + gamma mixture repair of §3. The failure rate for the transport is taken to be the sum of the failure rates of its constituent equipment, assuming that each of them is small.

With the components C_1, C_2, C_3 representing the routers and the transport, the end-to-end downtime will satisfy

$$(P_1 \star P_2 \star \underline{P_3})(t) \le P(t) \le P_1(t)P_2(t)\overline{P_3}(t). \tag{7.1}$$

To avoid using bounds on P_1, P_2, assume, in addition, that the downtime objective t is of the order of a few hours, $\ll T$. If so, taking $P_i(t) = \underline{P}_i(t)$ for $i = 1, 2$ as suggested at the end of §5, we can evaluate the convolution with just one numerical integration by finding the density $p_1 * p_2$. Differentiating (5.1) under the assumptions $t \ll T$ and $\varphi_i = \lambda_i T$ is independent of t we get

$$(p_1 * p_2)(t) = e^{-(\varphi_1 + \varphi_2)} \Big(\delta(t) + \varphi_1 G(t \mid a_1, \mu_1) + \varphi_2 G(t \mid a_2, \mu_2) +$$

$$\frac{\varphi_1^2}{2} G(t \mid 2a_1, \mu_1) + \frac{\varphi_2^2}{2} G(t \mid 2a_2, \mu_2) + \varphi_1 \varphi_2 H(t \mid a_1, a_2) +$$

$$\frac{\varphi_1^3}{6} G(t \mid 3a_1, \mu_1) + \frac{\varphi_2^3}{6} G(t \mid 3a_2, \mu_2)$$

$$+ \frac{\varphi_1 \varphi_2^2}{2} H(t \mid a_1, 2a_2) + \frac{\varphi_1^2 \varphi_2}{2} H(t \mid 2a_1, a_2) + O(\varphi_1^2 \varphi_2^2) \Big),$$

where

$$H(t \mid \alpha_1, \alpha_2) = \frac{\mu_1^{\alpha_1} \mu_2^{\alpha_2}}{\Gamma(\alpha_1 + \alpha_2)} e^{-\mu_1 t} {}_1 F_1 \big(\alpha_2, \alpha_1 + \alpha_2, (\mu_1 - \mu_2) t \big).$$

With this, (7.1) can be evaluated as

$$\int_0^t \underline{P}_3(t - x)(p_1 * p_2)(x) \, dx \le P(t) \le P_1(t) P_2(t) \overline{P}_3(t), \qquad (7.2)$$

where P_1, P_2 are given by (5.1) and $\underline{P}_3, \overline{P}_3$ by Lemmas 3.2 and 3.3 in conjunction with (3.5). (Using Laplace transforms on the l.h.s. of (7.1) is an appealing alternative, but finding the transform of $\underline{P}_3(\cdot)$ is the stumbling block.)

Example.   To illustrate the above results, consider a situation where all of the network equipment is given, its reliability is known, and the network repair policies are also known. The question is "what *restorability* does the network (design, architecture) have to provide so that a worst-case connection has downtime no more than 4 hrs. per year with 90% confidence?"

The parameters of the reference connection are given in Table 7.1. The end routers have about 15 minutes per year expected downtime (failure of the entire router). The transport fails in two modes, one with a 2 hr. MTTR and one with a 6 hr. MTTR; its repair time p.d. is shown in Fig. 3.4a.

Fig. 7.2a shows the bounds on the downtime of the connection, calculated by (7.2) for two values of restorability r. It can be seen that

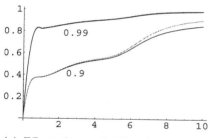

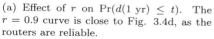

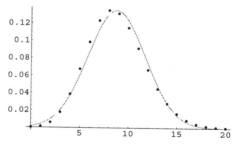

(a) Effect of r on $\Pr(d(1 \text{ yr}) \le t)$. The $r = 0.9$ curve is close to Fig. 3.4d, as the routers are reliable.

(b) Exact $\Pr(\nu(1 \text{ yr}) = n)$ for $r = 0.9$ and 0.99 by (4.1), and asymptotic normal approximation.

Figure 7.2. Distribution of the end-to-end downtime and of the number of *all* transport failures over $T = 1$ yr. $= 8760$ hrs.

$r = 0.99$ is almost adequate for the objective $\Pr(d \le 4) \ge 0.9$. Fig. 7.2b shows the distribution of the number of failures of the transport. Note that $\nu(T)$ is practically independent of r. The asymptotic normal approximation shown, which is remarkably good, is found by the methods of [F1] XIII, §6, and [F2] XI, §5, using the first-order limiting mean and variance of $\nu(T)$. Finally, using (4.2), Fig. 7.3 shows the (marginal) probability distributions of the three types of long failures of the transport (all, type 1, type 2). It can be seen that it is unlikely that there will be more than 2 long failures in a year, whereas it is very likely that there will be between 5 and 12 failures in all (Fig. 7.2b).

To round out the picture, Table 7.2 gives the joint distribution of the type-1 and type-2 long failures.

8. Conclusion

We studied aspects of the performance and reliability of a reference connection in a communications network by using the abstraction of an unreliable component subject to exponential failures and a mixture of fast and slow repairs, the first corresponding to restoration by the

Routers	Transport	
$\lambda_{1,2} = 1/140160$	$\lambda_3 = 1/1000$	
$\rho_{1,2}(x) = G(x \mid 1.5, 0.375)$	$\tau = 1/30$	
	$m_3(x) = 0.4G(x \mid 6, 3) + 0.6G(x \mid 48, 8)$	

Table 7.1. Parameters for the network model of Fig. 7.1 for $T = 1$ year $= 8760$ hrs. All times are in hours.

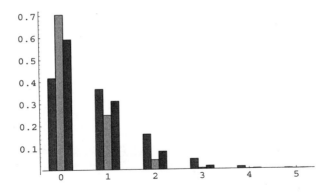

Figure 7.3. Distribution of the various types of *long* transport failures over $T = 1$ yr for $r = 0.9$. The bars in a group are $\Pr\big(\ell(T) = k\big)$, $\Pr\big(\ell_1(T) = k_1\big)$, $\Pr\big(\ell_2(T) = k_2\big)$.

		m_2				
		0	1	2	3	4
	0	0.41660	0.21888	0.057494	0.010067	0.001322
	1	0.14592	0.07666	0.020134	0.003525	0.000463
m_1	2	0.02555	0.01342	0.003525	0.0006171	0.000081
	3	0.00298	0.00157	0.000411	0.000072	$9.4 \cdot 10^{-6}$
	4	0.00026	0.00014	0.000036	$6.3 \cdot 10^{-6}$	$1.9 \cdot 10^{-6}$

Table 7.2. Joint distribution $\Pr\big(\ell_1(T) = k_1, \ell_2(T) = k_2\big)$ of the two types of *long* transport failures over $T = 1$ yr for $r = 0.9$.

network, and the second corresponding to manual repairs represented by gamma densities.

Whereas numerical or simulation methods could provide some of the results obtained here, the analytical approach taken provides additional insight, e.g. in the role of network restorability in meeting connection-level reliability objectives, the improved bounds using log-concavity, and better understanding of the behavior of the various distributions over different regimes of the parameters.

Appendix

1.   Notation for gamma functions

The two incomplete gamma functions are $\gamma(a, x) = \int_0^x u^{a-1} e^{-u}\, du$, and $\Gamma(a, x) = \int_x^\infty u^{a-1} e^{-u}\, du$. The "regularized" versions are given by $\bar{\gamma}(a, x) = \gamma(a, x)/\Gamma(a)$ and $\bar{\Gamma}(a, x) = \Gamma(a, x)/\Gamma(a)$. The two-argument incomplete gamma function is $\Gamma(a, x, y) = \int_x^y u^{a-1} e^{-u}\, du$, and the regularized version is $\bar{\Gamma}(a, x, y) = \Gamma(a, x, y)/\Gamma(a)$. If $G(x$ |

$a, b)$ is the gamma density, then $\bar{\Gamma}(a, bt) = \int_t^\infty G(x \mid a, b)\, dx$, $\bar{\gamma}(a, bt) = \int_0^t G(x \mid a, b)\, dx$ and $\bar{\Gamma}(a, bt_1, bt_2) = \int_{t_1}^{t_2} G(x \mid a, b)\, dx$. Also, $\sum_{k=0}^n y^k/k! = e^y \bar{\Gamma}(n+1, y)$.

2.   Log-concavity

Mathematically, whereas a function F is concave iff $F\left(\frac{x+y}{2}\right) > \frac{F(x)+F(y)}{2}$, F is log-concave iff $F\left(\frac{x+y}{2}\right)^2 > F(x)F(y)$. An alternative necessary and sufficient condition is $F''F < (F')^2$. This implies that: (a) if F is > 0, then F is concave $\Rightarrow$ F is log-concave. So every concave distribution is also log-concave. On the other hand, the gamma distribution with $a \geq 1$ can be shown to be log-concave, but not concave. (b) The distribution corresponding to a mixture of exponential densities is log-concave.

Two other useful facts are (a) the distribution corresponding to a log-concave density is log-concave ([PPT] Theorem 13.20); (b) the convolution of two log-concave distributions is also log-concave ([PPT] Corollary 13.27). For more on log-concavity see Ch. 5 of [K].

In reliability terms, a distribution $M(\cdot)$ is IFR $\Leftrightarrow$ the *complementary* distribution $1 - M(\cdot)$ is log-concave ([B&P], Ch. 3, Defn. 5.5 and Theorem 5.6). Recall that $M(x)$ is IFR (increasing failure rate) if for any fixed $z > 0$, $\Pr(x > y + z)/\Pr(x > y) \searrow$ as $y \nearrow$.

3.   Proofs

Proof of Lemma 3.1.   The proof is based on the fact that $R^{(k)}(x) < R^k(x)$ as pointed out in §2.1, and $R(x) < 1$. Using this in (2.3) we get

$$\Pr\bigl(d(T) \leq t\bigr) < e^{-\varphi}\left(1 + \varphi R(t) + R^2(t) \sum_{k=2}^\infty \frac{\varphi^k}{k!}\right).$$

Using abbreviated notation, it follows that

$$\begin{aligned}
P &< e^{-\varphi}\left(1 + R\varphi + R^2\bigl(1 - (\varphi+1)e^{-\varphi}\bigr)\right), \\
&< (\varphi+1)e^{-\varphi} + R^2\bigl(1 - (\varphi+1)e^{-\varphi}\bigr), \\
&= R^2 + (\varphi+1)e^{-\varphi}(1 - R^2) < R^2 + \varepsilon_1,
\end{aligned}$$

since $R > r$ when $t > \tau$. The proof of the $R + \varepsilon_0$ bound is similar.

Proof of Lemma 3.2.   The proof is based on Laplace transforms. Letting $R(s) = \mathcal{L}(\rho(t))$, it follows from (3.1) that

$$R^k(s) = \sum_{i=0}^k \binom{k}{i} r^{k-i}(1-r)^i e^{-(k-i)\tau s} M^i(s),$$

where $M(s) = \mathcal{L}(m(t))$, and $M^0(s) \equiv 1$. Let $m^{(i)}(t)$ be the i-fold convolution of the density $m(t)$ with itself. Inverting the above transform,

$$R^{(k)}(t) = r^k u(t - k\tau) + \sum_{i=1}^k \binom{k}{i} r^{k-i}(1-r)^i \int_0^{t-(k-i)\tau} m^{(i)}(x)\, dx.$$

If $M^{(i)}(t)$ is the distribution corresponding to $m^{(i)}(t)$, we now have $R^{(k)}(t) > \underline{R}^{(k)}(t)$, where

$$\underline{R}^{(k)}(t) \;=\; r^k u(t - k\tau) + k r^{k-1}(1-r)M(t-(k-1)\tau) + \frac{k(k-1)}{2} r^{k-2}(1-r)^2 M^{(2)}(t-(k-2)\tau),$$

and since $\underline{P}(t,T) = e^{-\varphi} \sum_{0 \le k \le \infty} \underline{R}^{(k)}(t)\varphi^k/k!$, the result of the lemma follows. Noting that $\underline{R}^{(0)}(t) = 1$, $\underline{R}^{(1)}(t) = R(t)$, and $\underline{R}^{(2)}(t) = R^{(2)}(t)$, $\underline{P}(t,T)$ is tighter than the l.h.s. of (2.4), as claimed.

When $m(t)$ is a gamma mixture, $M^{(1)}(t) = M(t)$ is given by the first line of (3.5). The expression for $M^{(2)}(t)$ in the second line involves the convolution of two gamma densities $G(x \mid a_1, \mu_1)$ and $G(x \mid a_2, \mu_2)$.

Proof of (3.4).   Clearly $M(t-2\tau) = \alpha(t-\tau,\tau)\alpha(t,\tau)M(t)$. But $\alpha(t-\tau,\tau) < \alpha(t,\tau) = \alpha$, since this is equivalent to $M(t-2\tau)M(t) < M^2(t-\tau)$, which holds if $M(x)$ is log-concave (see §17.A.2). Hence $M(t-2\tau) < \alpha^2 M(t)$, and the generalization is easy. As pointed out in §17.A.2, the convolution of two log-concave distributions is also log-concave. Hence the proof just given also applies to $M^{(2)}(x)$.

Proof of Lemma 3.3.   Referring to the proof of Lemma 3.2, here we want to bound the error incurred by taking $R^{(k)}(t)$ to be $\underline{R}^{(k)}(t)$. This error is $\varepsilon_3(k)$:

$$\sum_{i=\max(3,k-n)}^{k} \binom{k}{i} r^{k-i}(1-r)^i M^{(i)}(t-(k-i)\tau) < \sum_{i=3}^{k} \binom{k}{i} r^{k-i}(1-r)^i M^{(i)}(t-(k-i)\tau)$$

We want to evaluate $e^{-\varphi}\sum_k \varepsilon_3(k)\varphi^k/k!$. Noting that

$$\sum_{k\ge 3}\sum_{3 \le i \le k} f(i,k) = \sum_{i\ge 3}\sum_{k\ge i} f(i,k),$$

the inner sum becomes

$$\left(\frac{1-r}{r}\right)^i \frac{1}{i!} \sum_{k=i}^{\infty} \frac{(r\varphi)^k}{(k-i)!} M^{(i)}\big(t-(k-i)\tau\big). \tag{3.1}$$

From this point on, the improvement over the straightforward bound following from $M^{(i)}(z) < M^i(z)$ and $M(z-z') < M(z)$ is obtained by using the fact that $M^{(2)}(z)$ is available, and by (3.4). So first assume that i is odd in (3.1). Then $M^{(i)}(z) < \big(M^{(2)}(z)\big)^{\lfloor i/2 \rfloor} M(z)$. For brevity, set $M^{(2)}(t) = x^2$, $M(t) = y$. Then $M^{(i)}\big(t-(k-i)\tau\big) < \beta^{(k-i)\lfloor i/2 \rfloor} x^{2\lfloor i/2 \rfloor} \alpha^{k-i} y$ and (3.1) is less than

$$\left(\frac{1-r}{r}\right)^i \frac{1}{i!} \frac{x^{2\lfloor i/2 \rfloor} y}{\alpha^i \beta^{i\lfloor i/2 \rfloor}} \sum_{k=i}^{\infty} \frac{\left(r\varphi\alpha\beta^{\lfloor i/2 \rfloor}\right)^k}{(k-i)!} = \left(\frac{1-r}{r}\right)^i \frac{1}{i!}\, y x^{2\lfloor i/2 \rfloor} (r\varphi)^i e^{r\varphi\alpha\beta^{\lfloor i/2 \rfloor}}.$$

A similar development leads to the fact that when i is even (3.1) is bounded by

$$\left(\frac{1-r}{r}\right)^i \frac{1}{i!}\, x^i (r\varphi)^i e^{r\varphi\alpha\beta^{i/2}}.$$

So finally we have to evaluate the sums

$$\frac{y}{x}\sum_{j=1}^{\infty}\frac{\left((1-r)\varphi x\right)^{2j+1}}{(2j+1)!}e^{r\varphi\alpha\beta^{j}} \quad \text{and} \quad \sum_{j=2}^{\infty}\frac{\left((1-r)\varphi x\right)^{2j}}{(2j)!}e^{r\varphi\beta^{j}}.$$

The result of the lemma follows by pulling out the factors $e^{r\varphi\alpha\beta}$ and $e^{r\varphi\beta^2}$ to put upper bounds on these sums[13]. There is obviously room for improvement in the bound.

Proof of Lemma 3.4.   With $M(x)=\sum_{i}c_{i}P_{i}(x)$ and $\alpha_{i}=P_{i}(t-\tau)/P_{i}(t)$, we have $M(t-\tau)=\sum_{i}c_{i}\alpha_{i}P_{i}(t)\le\alpha\sum_{i}c_{i}P_{i}(t)=\alpha M(t)$. Now $M^{(2)}(x)=\sum_{i,j}c_{i}c_{j}(P_{i}\star P_{j})(x)$ is a mixture of log-concave distributions (§17.A.2). So by what we just proved, $M^{(2)}(t-\tau)\le\beta M^{(2)}(t)$, where β is as defined in the Lemma.

Proof of Lemma 6.1.   Taking T as given and fixed, the lemma states that

$$\Pr(d_{1}+\cdots+d_{n}\le t)\le\Pr(d\le t)\le\Pr(d_{1}\le t)\cdots\Pr(d_{n}\le t),$$

and it suffices to prove this for $n=2$. The upper bound is easy: $d\le t\Rightarrow d_{1}\le t\wedge d_{2}\le t$ (proof by contradiction), and so $\Pr(d\le t)\le\Pr(d_{1}\le t)\Pr(d_{2}\le t)$.

The lower bound may seem obvious. Nevertheless, a formal proof is useful. First we establish $d\le d_{1}+d_{2}$; then $d_{1}+d_{2}\le t\Rightarrow d\le t$, and so $\Pr(d_{1}+d_{2}\le t)\le\Pr(d\le t)$. To establish $d\le d_{1}+d_{2}$, think of the "trajectories" of C_{1},C_{2} over $[0,T]$ as rectangular 0–1 waveforms $a(t)$ and $b(t)$. Then the waveform describing the series connection is $a(t)b(t)$, and we want to show that

$$T-\int_{0}^{T}a(t)b(t)\,dt\le T-\int_{0}^{T}a(t)\,dt\ +\ T-\int_{0}^{T}b(t)\,dt.$$

This is equivalent to $\int(1-a(t)b(t))\,dt\le\int(2-a(t)-b(t))\,dt$, which will hold if for any x, $a(x)+b(x)-a(x)b(x)\le1$; but this is true since $a(x),b(x)$ are either 0 or 1.

References

[A&J]   T. Aven, U. Jensen. *Stochastic Models in Reliability*. Springer-Verlag, 1999.

[A&W]   J. Abate, W. Whitt. *Numerical Inversion of Laplace Transforms of Probability Distributions*. ORSA Journal on Computing, 7, 1995.

[BDK]   J.T Bradley, N.J. Dingle, P.G. Harrison and W.J. Knottenbelt. *Exact Aggregation Strategies for Semi-Markov Performance Models*. Proc. International Symposium on Performance Evaluation of Computer and Telecommunication Systems (SPECTS 2003), Montreal, Canada, 2003.

[B&H]   R. E. Barlow, L. C. Hunter. *Reliability Analysis of a One-Unit System*. Operations Research, vol. 9, 1961.

[B&P]   R. E. Barlow, F. Proschan. *Statistical Theory of Reliability and Life Testing*. To Begin With, MD, 1981.

[B&R]   M. Balakrishnan, A. Reibman. *Reliability Models for Fault-Tolerant Private Network Applications*. IEEE Transactions on Computers, Vol. 43, No. 9, September 1994.

---

[13]Since $y<1$, the ratio y/x does not exceed $1/x$.

[C]   A. Csenki. *Dependability for Systems with a Partitioned State Space–Markov and Semi-Markov Theory and Computational Implementation.* Lecture Notes in Statistics vol. 90, Springer-Verlag, 1994.

[F1]   W. Feller. *An Introduction to Probability Theory and Its Applications.* Vol. I, 3d Ed., John Wiley, 1968.

[F2]   W. Feller. *An Introduction to Probability Theory and Its Applications.* Vol. II, 2nd Ed., John Wiley, 1971.

[F&Y]   K. Funaki, K. Yoshimoto. *Distribution of Total Uptime during a Given Time Interval.* IEEE Transactions on Reliability, Vol. 43, No. 3, 1994.

[Ge]   I. B. Gertsbakh. *Statistical Reliability Theory.* Marcel Dekker, 1989.

[Gl]   P.W. Glynn. *A GSMP Formalism for Discrete Event Systems.* Proceedings of the IEEE, Vol. 77, No. 1, 1989.

[H&K]   P. G. Harisson, W. J. Knottenbelt. *Passage Time Distributions in Large Markov Chains.* Proceedings of ACM SIGMETRICS 2002, Marina Del Rey, California.

[K]   J. Keilson. *Markov Chain Models—Rarity and Exponentiality.* Springer-Verlag, 1979.

[M]   E. J. Muth. *A Method for Predicting System Downtime.* IEEE Transactions on Reliability, Vol. R-17, No. 2, June 1968.

[M&W]   H. F. Martz, R. A. Waller. *Bayesian Reliability Analysis.* Krieger, 1991.

[P]   P. J. Pedler. *Occupation Times for Two State Markov Chains.* Journal of Applied Probability, vol. 8, 1971.

[PPT]   J. Pečarić, F. Proschan, Y. Tong. *Convex Functions, Partial Orderings, and Statistical Applications.* Academic Press, 1992.

[S]   B. Sericola. *Interval-Availability Distribution of 2-State Systems with Exponential Failures and Phase-Type Repairs.* IEEE Transactions on Reliability, Vol. 43, No. 2, June 1994.

[S&G]   E. de Souza e Silva, H. R. Gail. *Performability Analysis of Computer Systems: from model specification to solution.* Performance Evaluation 14, 1992.

[SSR]   S. K. Srinivasan, R. Subramanian, K. S. Ramesh. *Mixing of Two Renewal Processes and Its Applications to Reliability Theory.* IEEE Transactions on Reliability, Vol. R-20, No. 2, May 1971.

Chapter 18

MULTIPLE SERVICE CLASSES FOR RATE ADAPTIVE STREAMS

Steven Weber[1] and Gustavo de Veciana[2]

[1] *Dept of ECE, Drexel University, Philadelphia PA 19104*
sweber@ece.drexel.edu

[2] *Dept of ECE, UT-Austin, Austin TX 78712*
gustavo@ece.utexas.edu

Abstract   Our previous work [19–21] investigated optimal support of rate adaptive multi-media streams. In particular, we identified the optimal distribution of network bandwidth among competing streams, i.e., the optimal *adaptation policy*, which maximized our Quality of Service (QoS) metric, defined as the client average normalized time-average subscription level. The optimal adaptation policy (for a single link) was identified as granting the maximum subscription level to as many small volume streams as possible and granting the minimum subscription level to the remaining large volume streams, where stream *volume* is the product of the stream duration and the maximum subscription level, i.e., the number of bits associated with the stream at its finest resolution encoding. This type of *volume discrimination* may prove unsatisfactory to clients of large volume streams with heterogeneous QoS requirements.

   In this work we introduce a link architecture supporting multiple service classes, where each service class is characterized by a distinct QoS guarantee. Intuitively, large volume streams, which would suffer under the volume discriminatory nature of the optimal adaptation policy for a single service class, might be willing to pay a price to obtain a higher degree of QoS protection offered by a "premium" service class. We introduce a capacity scaling appropriate for studying large numbers of clients sharing large capacity links. We identify the optimal adaptation policy for a link supporting multiple service classes, and obtain closed form expressions for the asymptotic QoS within each class under the optimal adaptation policy. We demonstrate that the same asymptotic QoS can be obtained under an appropriately designed admission control policy which eliminates the need for dynamic adaptation. Finally, we compare the benefits of offering multiple service classes over a single service class architecture in a case study which investigates how to multiplex small volume audio streams and large volume video streams on a congested link.

1. Introduction

Multimedia streams are *rate adaptive* in that media information may be encoded at a variety of resolutions, where the appropriate resolution for a streaming client may vary in time, depending on the current level of network congestion. That is, clients may *dynamically adapt* their subscription level among the set of stream encodings offered by the media server in response to network congestion or lack thereof. In particular, streaming clients may wish to increase their subscription level if extra capacity becomes available along their route, or may wish to decrease their subscription level at the onset of congestion.

From a systems engineering perspective, it is natural to investigate optimal dynamic adaptation policies, i.e., to identify the optimal instantaneous subscription level assignment for each active stream which maximizes the client average Quality of Service (QoS). Our previous work [19–21] identifies optimal adaptation policies when QoS is defined as the time–average normalized subscription level of a typical client. In particular, our analysis proves the intuitive fact that client average QoS is maximized by granting precedence to small volume streams over large volume streams, where stream volume is the product of the stream duration and the maximum subscription level, i.e., the total number of bits associated with the full encoding of the stream.

Because the client average QoS is maximized under policies which discriminate against large volume streams, such a policy is likely to prove unsatisfactory for clients with heterogeneous QoS requirements. That is, a large volume stream may require a high degree of QoS which it is unlikely to receive if the network employs optimal adaptation. Such clients would benefit from multi–service networks, where the network offers a discrete set of service classes offering different guarantees on QoS. The large body of work on DiffServ and IntServ network architectures demonstrates that multi–service networks are of great interest, but to date there has been no work we are aware of discussing multi–service networks for rate adaptive streams.

In Section 3 we introduce our model for rate adaptive streams and propose a link architecture consisting of a set of service classes characterized by a distinct QoS guarantee. We introduce a capacity scaling appropriate for studying large capacity asymptotics in Section 4. The optimal adaptation policy, which maximizes the overall client average QoS subject to the service class QoS guarantees and the link capacity constraint, is identified in Section 5. We also develop closed form expressions for the asymptotic client average QoS in each class under the optimal adaptation policy. Section 6 introduces an admission control policy which obtains the same asymptotic QoS as the optimal adaptation policy, but without the need for dynamic adaptation. We study the potential benefits of a multiple service class link architecture in a case study on how to best share link capacity among audio and video streams in Section 7. All proofs are found in the appendix.

2. Related Work

The "client" versus "system" views can be used to classify related work in the area of supporting rate adaptive multimedia streams. Representative papers investigating the client perspective include [15, 14]. The work in [15] investigates optimal policies for streams to dynamically adapt the fraction of their available bandwidth given to base and enhancement layers. In [14] the authors propose a TCP-friendly congestion control scheme for rate adaptive video which makes smart use of buffering to absorb short time scale congestion.

Papers investigating the system perspective include [1, 6, 10, 3]. The work presented in [1] and [6] uses an almost identical model for QoS as ours, but neither investigates optimal adaptation, which is central to our effort. In [10], the authors offer a system level analysis of rate adaptive streams, but in a static context, i.e., a fixed number of streams. Also related is [3], which investigates a model where the server dynamically adjusts the number and rate of each subscription layer in response to congestion feedback. We feel such server adaptive models are of less interest than client adaptive models because the former does not generalize well to multicast scenarios. Our other work in this field [19, 20] also takes a system perspective.

Another body of work addresses distributed algorithms for rate adaptive multimedia streams. Representative papers include [2, 8, 7]. The work in [2] analyzes the performance of a rate adaptation algorithm where clients probe the network to determine congestion and then adjust their subscription level accordingly. In [8], the authors contrast a server which adapts the compression level of the stream to match with client requirements versus a server which provides a fixed set of encodings. Finally, [7] proposes a distributed algorithm for layered media with emphasis on efficient use in a multicast scenario.

A different approach to the problem of admission control is taken in [12] which identifies competitively optimal admission policies; it might be interesting to extend this work to the rate-adaptive case.

The field of media quality assessment has developed several metrics for media quality versus encoding rate [16, 11, 17, 13, 5, 4, 9]. These "distortion measures", e.g., sum of squared differences (SSD), mean squared error (MSE), peak signal to noise ratio (PSNR), are quantifiable means of assessing quality, but their correlation to human subjective evaluation is tenuous due to the complexities in the human psychovisual system [17]. These metrics are in general nonlinear functions of the encoding rate, but linear approximations to these functions would seem reasonable within a range of interest.

3.   The Model

We use uppercase letters to denote random variables, and let the corresponding lowercase letters denote the corresponding known quantities, unless specified otherwise.

We define the *stream volume* as the product of the maximum subscription level and the stream duration. Thus, client i in class k with maximum subscription level $S_{i,k} \sim F_{S_k}$ and stream duration $D_{i,k} \sim F_{D_k}$ has a stream volume $V_{i,k} = S_{i,k} D_{i,k}$. This is simply the number of bits associated with the stream when encoded at the finest resolution offered by the content provider.

We investigate a multiple service class link architecture where each service class is characterized by a distinct guarantee on the instantaneous normalized subscription level for all streams in the class. Specifically, the link offers a set of K service classes, for some fixed integer K, characterized by scalars $(\alpha_k, k = 1, \dots, K)$ with $\alpha_k \in (0, 1)$. We assume $0 < \alpha_1 < \dots < \alpha_K < 1$. Each client i in class k is assured, at each time t, of receiving an instantaneous subscription level $S_{i,k}(t)$, such that $S_{i,k}(t) \geq \alpha_k S_{i,k}$, where $S_{i,k}$ is the maximum subscription level offered by the content provider. Equivalently, the *normalized instantaneous subscription level* $\frac{S_{i,k}(t)}{S_{i,k}}$ is guaranteed to exceed the class k QoS guarantee α_k.

Classes offering higher QoS guarantees, i.e., larger α_k, would naturally need to be priced to ensure client service class selection aligns with actual client QoS requirements. The demand for service under each class is modeled as a vector of mean arrival rates $(\lambda_k, k = 1, \dots, K)$. We will actually use a capacity scaling where we linearly scale the arrival rates and the link capacity to infinity, so the mean arrival rates are best thought of as relative intensities. Different service classes will attract different types of streams. We model this by allowing the distribution on the maximum subscription level and the distribution on stream duration to be class specific. In particular, we let F_{S_k} and F_{D_k} denote the CDF for the maximum subscription level and stream duration of class k streams. Note that the maximum subscription level represents the finest granularity encoding offered by the content provider. We denote the means of these subscription levels as $\sigma_k = \mathbb{E}[S_k]$ and $\delta_k = \mathbb{E}[D_k]$.

We assume that the maximum subscription level and stream duration are independent random variables for each stream. The volume distribution for class k streams, denoted F_{V_k}, is therefore given by

$$F_{V_k}(v) = \int_0^\infty F_{S_k}(\frac{v}{d}) dF_{D_k}(d) = \int_0^\infty F_{D_k}(\frac{v}{s}) dF_{S_k}(s). \qquad (18.1)$$

We will also have cause to use a related distribution, which we term the *typical time distribution*. For an arbitrary random variable X with CDF F_X we define the random variable $\hat{X}$ as having a CDF given by $F_{\hat{X}}(x) = \frac{1}{\mathbb{E}[X]} \int_0^x w \, dF_X(w)$. For the case of stream durations and stream volumes, the above CDF corresponds to the distribution of a stream when the system is viewed at a typical time [18]. The distribution of stream durations when viewed at a typical time is "stretched", giving a higher probability of seeing longer duration streams than shorter duration streams. Intuitively, when viewing the system at a typical time, you are more likely to see longer duration streams than shorter duration streams. Stream volumes are also "stretched" because stream volumes are functions of stream durations. We will write $\hat{D}_k$ and $\hat{V}_k$ for class k stream durations and volumes when doing a typical time analysis, with the understanding that $\hat{D}_k \sim F_{\hat{D}_k}$ and $\hat{V}_k \sim F_{\hat{V}_k}$.

We assume each content provider makes available a discrete set of *offered subscription levels*, denoted S. If the maximum subscription level offered by the content provider is S then the set of offered subscription levels is assumed to be aligned with the set of service classes offered by the link, i.e., $S = (\alpha_1 S, \dots, \alpha_K S, S)$. Thus a client, i, of this stream choosing service class k' might receive an instantaneous subscription level $S_{i,k'}(t) \in (\alpha_k S, k = k', \dots, K) \cup S$. That is, a client choosing service class k' will receive a service level $\alpha_{k'}$ or better. The set $(\alpha_k S, k = k', \dots, K) \cup S$ is the set of service levels with service qualities at or exceeding $\alpha_{k'}$.

We will investigate *adaptation policies*, denoted π, where an adaptation policy simply assigns each active stream an instantaneous subscription level such that i) the assigned subscription level is offered by the content provider, ii) the assigned subscription level satisfies the client's service class guarantee, and iii) the aggregate subscription levels don't exceed the link capacity.

We define the Quality of Service (QoS) metric for an adaptation policy, denoted $\mathbb{E}^0[Q^\pi]$, as

$$\mathbb{E}^0[Q^\pi] = \mathbb{E}^0[\frac{1}{D} \int_0^D \frac{S^\pi(t)}{S} dt]. \tag{18.2}$$

Here, the notation $\mathbb{E}^0[\cdot]$ denotes an expectation taken as a client average, defined as

$$\mathbb{E}^0[Q] = \lim_{n \to \infty} \frac{1}{n} \sum_{i=1}^n \int_{-\infty}^\infty Q_i(t) dt,$$

where $Q_i(t)$ is the instantaneous QoS of client i at time t, and is assumed to be zero outside client i's tenure in the system. The notation $S^\pi(t)$ denotes that the instantaneous subscription level for a typical stream will depend on the adaptation policy. The quantity Q^π is therefore the time-average normalized subscription level. Note that a client, say i, of class k, with maximum subscription level $S_{i,k}$, is guaranteed to obtain a QoS $Q_{i,k}^{\pi} \in [\alpha_k, 1]$. Thus the service class guarantee can be thought of as the ratio of the total number of bits received by the client, $\int_0^{D_{i,k}} S_{i,k}^{\pi}(t)$, divided by the total number of bits associated with the maximum subscription level, $S_{i,k}D_{i,k}$.

One way of thinking about rate adaptation is as a means of trading off high subscription levels for low blocking probabilities. A loss network servicing non-adaptive media streams encoded only at their maximum subscription level guarantees a high subscription level for all admitted streams, but the blocking probability may be quite high. Offering reduced quality encodings and using the encodings for congestion control allows for lower blocking probabilities because admitted streams can be adapted to lower subscription levels during congestion in order to free up capacity for newly arriving streams. We make the assumption that the link admits as many streams as possible while still respecting the QoS guarantee of each stream already admitted. That is, a stream in class k' with maximum subscription level s is admitted onto the link provided

$$\sum_{k=1}^{K} \sum_{i=1}^{n_k(t)} \alpha_k s_{i,k} + \alpha_{k'} s \leq c, \tag{18.3}$$

where c is the link capacity and $n(t) = (n_k(t), k = 1, \dots, K)$ is the number of active streams in each service class. We will consider a slightly different admission policy in Section 6.

In summary, our multiple service class link architecture model consists of the following components for each service class: i) a guarantee on the normalized subscription level, α_k, ii) an arrival rate, λ_k, iii) a duration distribution F_{D_k} with mean $\mathbb{E}[D_k] = \delta_k$, and iv) a maximum subscription level distribution F_{S_k} with mean $\mathbb{E}[S_k] = \sigma_k$. In addition, each service class has associated with it i) a volume distribution F_{V_k}, ii) a typical time volume distribution $F_{\hat{V}_k}$ derived from F_{V_k}, and iii) a typical time duration distribution $F_{\hat{D}_k}$ derived from F_{D_k}. Each client receives a time-varying instantaneous subscription level $S_{i,k}^{\pi}(t)$ where instantaneous subscription level assignments depend on the policy π, the set of subscription levels made available by the content provider, and the service class guarantee. Each client receives a QoS $Q_{i,k}^{\pi}$ defined as the time-average normalized subscription level, and we seek the policy π which maximizes the overall client-average QoS, $\mathbb{E}^0[Q^{\pi}]$, subject to the governing constraints.

4.   Capacity scaling for multiple service classes

Let the vector of random variables, $\mathbf{N}(t) = (N_k(t), k = 1, \dots, K)$, denote the instantaneous number of streams active at time t in each service class. Recall that $\delta_k = \mathbb{E}[D_k]$ denotes the average duration of a class k stream and $\sigma_k = \mathbb{E}[S_k]$ denotes the average maximum subscription level of a class k

stream. We denote the *minimum and maximum offered loads for class k* as $\underline{\rho}_k = (\lambda_k \delta_k)(\alpha_k \sigma_k)$ and $\bar{\rho}_k = (\lambda_k \delta_k)\sigma_k$ respectively. Thus, the minimum offered load for class k is the product of the average number of class k streams, i.e., $\mathbb{E}[N_k(t)] = \lambda_k \delta_k$ (in a low blocking regime), times the class k average minimum subscription level $\alpha_k \sigma_k$. Similarly, the maximum offered load is the product of the average number of class k streams times the class k average maximum subscription level. We define the *overall minimum and maximum offered loads* as $\underline{\rho} = \sum_{k=1}^{K} \underline{\rho}_k$ and $\bar{\rho} = \sum_{k=1}^{K} \bar{\rho}_k$ respectively. We define the *overall adaptivity* as the ratio of the overall minimum offered load over the overall maximum offered load, i.e., $\alpha = \underline{\rho}/\bar{\rho}$.

Consider a sequence of links, indexed by m, where we linearly scale the arrival rate vector and the link capacity as follows. The arrival rate vector on the mth link is $\boldsymbol{\lambda}(m) = (\lambda_k(m), k = 1, \ldots, K)$ and $\lambda_k(m) = m\lambda_k$. We denote the per class and overall minimum and maximum offered loads on the mth link as $\underline{\rho}_k(m), \bar{\rho}_k(m), \underline{\rho}(m), \bar{\rho}(m)$ respectively. Note that the overall adaptivity α is independent of m under this scaling. The link capacity on the mth link is $c(m) = \gamma \bar{\rho}(m)$ for some $\gamma > 0$.

We define three *capacity scaling regimes* which depend on the overall adaptivity α and are parameterized by γ. These regimes are $i)$ the *overloaded regime*, parameterized by $\gamma < \alpha$, $ii)$ the *rate adaptive regime*, parameterized by $\alpha \leq \gamma \leq 1$, and $iii)$ the *underloaded regime*, parameterized by $\gamma > 1$. In the overloaded regime the provisioned capacity is inadequate to handle the overall minimum offered load, i.e., $c(m) = \gamma \bar{\rho}(m) < \alpha \bar{\rho}(m) = \underline{\rho}(m)$. In the underloaded regime the provisioned capacity exceeds the overall maximum offered load, i.e., $c(m) = \gamma \bar{\rho}(m) > \bar{\rho}(m)$. Finally, in the rate adaptive regime the provisioned capacity lies between the overall minimum and maximum offered loads. We will show that the rate adaptive regime is the primary regime of interest.

5. Optimal adaptation policy for multiple service classes

In this section we identify the optimal adaptation policy for multiple service classes. Our objective is to maximize the *overall client average time-average normalized subscription level*, $\mathbb{E}^0[Q]$. The following theorem states the optimal adaptation policy is to sort all the active streams by stream volume and grant the maximum subscription level to as many small volume streams as possible while respecting the per-class minimum subscription level guarantees and the link capacity constraint. We denote the optimal multi-class adaptation policy as π_m. We let $n(t) = \sum_{k=1}^{K} n_k(t)$ denote the total number of active streams on the link. We denote the instantaneous subscription level assignment under the optimal multi-class adaptation policy as $\mathbf{s}^{\pi_m}(t) = (s_{i,k}^{\pi_m}(t), i = 1, \ldots, n_k(t), k =$

$1, \ldots, K$). Note that the stream durations for all active streams are assumed *known*, hence $D_{i,k} = d_{i,k}$ for $i = 1, \ldots, n_k(t)$ and for $k = 1, \ldots, K$.

THEOREM 18.1 *The optimal multi-class adaptation policy,* π_m, *which maximizes the overall client average time-average normalized subscription level,* $\mathbb{E}^0[Q]$, *is the instantaneous allocation,* $\mathbf{s}^{\pi_m}(t) = (s_{i,k}^{\pi_m}(t), i = 1, \ldots, n_k(t), k = 1, \ldots, K)$, *at each time t which solves the following integer programming problem:*

$$\max_{\mathbf{s}(t)} \quad q_{agg}(t) = \sum_{k=1}^{K} \sum_{i=1}^{n_k(t)} \frac{s_{i,k}(t)}{s_{i,k} d_{i,k}} \tag{18.4}$$

$$s.t. \quad \sum_{k=1}^{K} \sum_{i=1}^{n_k(t)} s_{i,k}(t) \leq c,$$

$$s_{i,k}(t) \in (\alpha_l s_{i,k}, l = k, \ldots, K) \cup s_{i,k},$$

$$\forall i = 1, \ldots, n_k(t), k = 1, \ldots, K.$$

COROLLARY 18.2 *There exists a near optimal multi-class adaptation policy, denoted* $\tilde{\pi}_m$, *with instantaneous allocation* $\mathbf{s}^{\tilde{\pi}_m}(t)$ *with* $s_{i,k}^{\tilde{\pi}_m}(t) \in \{\alpha_k s_{i,k}, s_{i,k}\}$ *for each* $i = 1, \ldots, n_k(t)$ *and each* $k = 1, \ldots, K$. *In particular, define* $q^{\pi_m}(t)$ *and* $q\tilde{\pi}_m$ *as the expected customer average QoS under allocation* π_m *and* $\tilde{\pi}_m$ *respectively. Then the relative difference between these allocations goes to 0 as* $n(t) \to \infty$, *i.e.,*

$$\frac{q^{\pi_m}(t) - q^{\tilde{\pi}_m}(t)}{q^{\pi_m}(t)} \leq \frac{\kappa_m}{n(t)}, \tag{18.5}$$

for $\kappa_m < \infty$. *An expression for* κ_m *is found in the proof.*

Sort the active streams by volume, indexed by j, so that stream (i, k) is labeled j if stream (i, k) has the jth smallest volume out of all the active streams. Thus, $s_1 d_1 < \ldots < s_{n(t)} d_{n(t)}$. *The allocation under the near optimal multi-class adaptation policy is given by*

$$s_j^{\tilde{\pi}_m}(t) = \begin{cases} s_j, & j = 1, \ldots, \bar{n} - 1 \\ a_j s_j, & j = \bar{n}, \ldots, n(t) \end{cases}, \tag{18.6}$$

where $\bar{n}$ *equals*

$$\bar{n} = \max\{m \mid \sum_{j=1}^{m-1} s_j + \sum_{j=m}^{n(t)} a_j s_j \leq c\}. \tag{18.7}$$

The theorem states that the near optimal adaptation policy is to grant the maximum subscription level to as many small volume streams, regardless of their service class, while reserving enough capacity to service the remaining larger volume streams at the minimum subscription level satisfying their class QoS guarantee. The corollary presents the near optimal policy which has the important characteristic of only utilizing the minimum and maximum subscription levels offered by the content provider, i.e., intermediate subscription levels are never utilized. This policy is near optimal only because there may be some unused capacity under this allocation which one or two streams could benefit from by using an intermediate subscription level. The bound in the corollary shows that the relative difference in the objective between the near optimal and optimal adaptation policy goes to zero as the number of active streams increases. Thus for large capacity links the difference in the objective under the two policies is negligible.

The next theorem identifies the asymptotic quality of service under the optimal adaptation policy for each service class using the capacity scaling of Section 4. We define the asymptotic expected time-average normalized subscription level for class k streams under the multi-class capacity scaling as $q_k^{\gamma,\pi_m} = \lim_{m\to\infty} \mathbb{E}^0[Q_k^{m,\pi_m}]$, where $\mathbb{E}^0[Q_k^{m,\pi_m}]$ is the expected value of Q on the mth link under policy π_m for class k.

THEOREM 18.3 *The asymptotic expected time-average normalized subscription level for class k streams under the optimal adaptation policy for multiple service classes is*

$$q_k^{\gamma,\pi_m} = \begin{cases} \alpha_k, & \gamma < \alpha \\ 1 - (1 - \alpha_k)\bar{F}_{V_k}(v^*), & \alpha \leq \gamma \leq 1 \\ 1, & \gamma > 1 \end{cases} \tag{18.8}$$

where $\bar{F}_{V_k}(\cdot)$ is the complementary cumulative distribution function and v^* is the unique v solving

$$\sum_{k=1}^{K}(\bar{\rho}_k - \underline{\rho}_k)F_{\hat{V}_k}(v) = \gamma\bar{\rho} - \underline{\rho}. \tag{18.9}$$

Note that the asymptotic QoS for each class k is the class minimum, α_k, when the link is provisioned in the overloaded regime, i.e., $\gamma < \alpha$. This confirms the intuition that the overloaded regime requires admitted streams to stay at their minimum subscription level so as to free up capacity for newly arriving streams. Similarly, the asymptotic QoS for each class k is the maximum, 1, when the link is provisioned in the underloaded regime, i.e., $\gamma > 1$. This confirms the intuition that the underloaded regime allows admitted streams to stay at their maximum subscription level because the link is never congested. Finally, the asymptotic QoS in the rate adaptive regime, i.e., $\alpha \leq \gamma \leq 1$, is a function of the QoS guarantees, the per-class volume distributions, and the scaling parameter. Note that the dependence of the optimal adaptation policy for class k on the stream duration distribution F_{D_k} and the maximum subscription level distribution F_{S_k} is only through the volume distribution F_{V_k}.

6.   Asymptotic optimal admission control for multiple service classes

Note that the optimal adaptation policy potentially requires dynamically adapting each stream's instantaneous subscription level each time a stream arrives or departs. For large capacity links servicing large numbers of streams, however, the ensemble of active streams has a more or less fixed distribution. Thus the instantaneous subscription level under the optimal adaptation policy is unlikely to vary significantly, especially for small or large volume streams. As discussed in [21], streams with a volume near a critical volume threshold may experience rapid changes back and forth between their minimum and maximum subscription level.

We propose an *admission policy* wherein admitted streams are assigned a *fixed* subscription level which they maintain throughout their stay in the system, i.e., no dynamic adaptation is employed. The intuition is simple, small volume streams receive their maximum subscription level and large volume streams receive the minimum subscription level guaranteed by their class. Note that the set of all admission policies is a subset of the set of all adaptation policies because an admission policy in essence makes an adaptation decision only at the time of each stream's admission. Thus, showing that an admission policy obtains the same asymptotic QoS as the optimal adaptation policy means that the admission policy is optimal. The following theorem identifies the optimal volume threshold distinguishing between small and large volume streams, and shows that the asymptotic QoS under the optimal admission policy equals the asymptotic QoS under the optimal adaptation policy, thus proving the stated admission policy is optimal.

THEOREM 18.4 *The multi-service network asymptotic optimal admission control policy, denoted, π_{am}, is a volume threshold policy with optimal volume threshold $v^{\gamma,\pi_{am}}$. The optimal threshold is*

$$
v^{\gamma,\pi_{am}} = \begin{cases} 0, & \gamma < \alpha \\ v^*, & \alpha \le \gamma \le 1 \\ \infty, & \gamma > 1 \end{cases} \tag{18.10}
$$

where v^* is the unique v that solves

$$
\sum_{k=1}^{K} (\bar{\rho}_k - \underline{\rho}_k) F_{\hat{V}_k}(v) = \gamma \bar{\rho} - \underline{\rho}. \tag{18.11}
$$

The optimal admission control policy for client i on class k is to assign the client a subscription level

$$s_{i,k}^{\gamma,\pi_{am}} = \begin{cases} s_{i,k}, & v_{i,k} \le v^{\gamma,\pi_{am}} \\ \alpha_k s_{i,k}, & else \end{cases} . \qquad (18.12)$$

The asymptotic expected normalized subscription level for class k streams under policy π_{am} equals that obtained under the optimal multi-class adaptation policy π_m.

Note that the optimal volume threshold is independent of the service class k, i.e., the network discriminates among streams based on their stream volume, irrespective of their service class.

This result shows that the asymptotic optimal admission control policy is both simple and feasible, provided the statistical characteristics of the maximum subscription level and stream duration are known for each class.

7. Case study: multiplexing audio and video streaming clients

In this section we apply the theorems on optimal multi-class adaptation policies to a case study which investigates how to optimally share link capacity among audio and video streaming clients. The case study will investigate three separate link architectures and compare the resulting QoS. The three link architectures are

- **Single service class sharing.** Audio and video streams share the link capacity and are jointly adapted according to the optimal single class adaptation policy of [21]. All streams, audio and video, are assumed to have a fixed stream adaptivity of $\alpha_1 = \frac{1}{4}$. This policy is obtained by setting all per-class service guarantees to be equal, i.e., $\alpha_k = \alpha$ for each $k = 1, \ldots, K$.

- **Two service class sharing.** The network offers two service classes: a free service class with a guaranteed normalized subscription level of α_1 and a premium service class with a guaranteed normalized subscription level of $\alpha_2 = \frac{3}{4}$. Audio clients will generally subscribe to the free class, relying on volume discrimination to grant them acceptable QoS, while video clients will generally subscribe to the premium class, in order to provide them with QoS protection from volume discrimination.

- **Partitioning.** We partition the link capacity *evenly* into two separate channels, one for audio and one for video. All audio streams share the audio channel and all video streams share the video channel. The streams on each channel are adapted according to the optimal single class adaptation policy of [21]. As in the previous case, audio streams are guaranteed a normalized subscription level of α_1 and video streams are guaranteed a normalized subscription level of α_2.

The three link architectures are illustrated in Figure 18.1.

Simulation parameters

We let 1 denote the free service class for audio streams and 2 denote the premium service class for video streams.

The audio clients have an arrival rate $\lambda_1 = 1$, a typical stream duration of $\delta_1 = 180$ seconds (i.e., the typical length of a song), an average maximum subscription level of $\sigma_1 = 0.1$ Mb/s, and a service class guarantee of $\alpha_1 = \frac{1}{4}$. The distributions for audio client stream durations and maximum subscription levels are both exponentials. Thus, $F_{D_1}(d) = 1 - \exp\left(-\frac{d}{\delta_1}\right)$ and $F_{S_1}(s) = 1 - \exp\left(-\frac{s}{\sigma_1}\right)$.

The video clients have an arrival rate of $\lambda_2 = 0.01$, where the arrival rate is determined by the demand function evaluated at the price charged by the network to use the premium class. The typical video stream duration is $\delta_2 = 1800$ seconds (e.g., a half-hour television program), and the average maximum subscription level is $\sigma_2 = 1.0$ Mb/s. The video content provider offers a minimal stream encoding with an adaptivity of $\alpha_2 = \frac{1}{4}$ (just like the audio streams), but the premium service class provides a QoS guarantee of $\alpha_2 = \frac{3}{4}$. Thus, video clients with a low willingness to pay will choose class 1, and likely receive a low-quality video stream with adaptivity $\frac{1}{4}$, while video clients with a high willingness to pay will choose class 2, and likely receive a high-quality video stream with adaptivity $\frac{3}{4}$. The distributions for video client stream durations and maximum subscription levels are both (effectively unbounded) exponentials. Thus, $F_{D_2}(d) = 1 - \exp\left(-\frac{d}{\delta_2}\right)$ and $F_{S_2}(s) = 1 - \exp\left(-\frac{s}{\sigma_2}\right)$.

Note that the minimum offered load for the audio clients class is $\underline{\rho}_1 = (\lambda_1 \delta_1)(\alpha_1 \sigma_1) = (1 \times 180)(\frac{1}{4} \times \frac{1}{10}) = 4.5$ Mb/s, and the maximum offered load for the audio clients is $\bar{\rho}_1 = (\lambda_1 \delta_1)(\sigma_1) = (1 \times 180)(\frac{1}{10}) = 18$ Mb/s. The minimum offered load for the video clients when no premium service class is offered (e.g., the first link architecture with a single service class) is $\underline{\rho}_2 = (\lambda_2 \delta_2)(\alpha_2 \sigma_2) = (\frac{1}{100} \times 1800)(\frac{1}{4} \times 1) = 4.5$ Mb/s. The minimum offered load for the video clients when a premium service class is offered (e.g., the second and third link architectures) is $\underline{\rho}_2 = (\lambda_2 \delta_2)(\alpha_2 \sigma_2) = (\frac{1}{100} \times 1800)(\frac{3}{4} \times 1) = 13.5$ Mb/s. The maximum offered load for the video clients (for all three scenarios) is $\bar{\rho}_2 = (\lambda_2 \delta_2)(\sigma_2) = (\frac{1}{100} \times 1800)(1) = 18$ Mb/s. Thus the overall minimum offered load is 9 Mb/s when no premium service class is offered, and is 18 Mb/s when the premium service class is offered. The overall maximum offered load is 36 Mb/s. Note that the maximum offered load is 18 Mb/s for both the

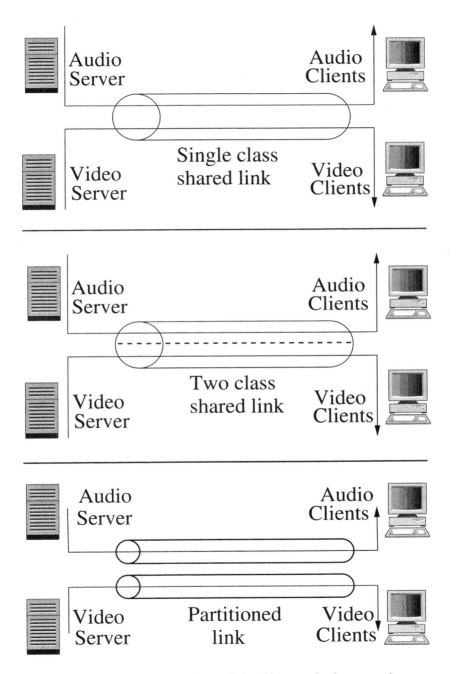

Figure 18.1. Illustration of three link architectures for the case study.

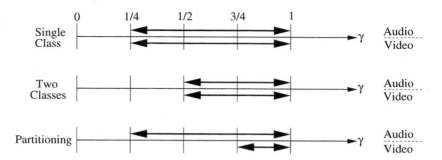

Figure 18.2. Illustration of the rate-adaptive regimes for audio and video streams under each of the three link architectures.

audio and video streams. This is the rational behind partitioning the bandwidth evenly into two channels for the third link architecture.

The different link architectures will have different scaling regimes because of the different service classes and adaptation policies. These regimes are illustrated in Figure 18.2. Consider the first link architecture where both audio and video are guaranteed a normalized subscription level of $\alpha_1 = \frac{1}{4}$, and the optimal single service class adaptation policy is used. The overall adaptivity for this link architecture is $\frac{\rho}{\bar{\rho}} = \frac{9}{36} = \frac{1}{4}$, hence the rate adaptive regime for both audio and video streams corresponds to $\frac{1}{4} \le \gamma \le 1$. Consider the second link architecture where audio streams have a guaranteed normalized subscription level of $\alpha_1 = \frac{1}{4}$ and video streams have a guaranteed normalized subscription level of $\alpha_2 = \frac{3}{4}$. The overall adaptivity for this link architecture is $\frac{\rho}{\bar{\rho}} = \frac{18}{36} = \frac{1}{2}$, hence the rate adaptive regime for both audio and video streams corresponds to $\frac{1}{2} \le \gamma \le 1$. The rate adaptive regime is smaller for this scenario than for the previous scenario because the video streams are now guaranteed a larger normalized subscription level. Consider finally the third link architecture, where audio and video streams use separate channels, audio streams are guaranteed a normalized subscription level of $\alpha_1 = \frac{1}{4}$ and video streams are guaranteed a normalized subscription level of $\alpha_2 = \frac{3}{4}$. Because they are on separate channels, the rate adaptive regime for the audio streams corresponds to $\frac{1}{4} \le \gamma \le 1$, while the rate adaptive regime for the video streams corresponds to $\frac{3}{4} \le \gamma \le 1$.

We can therefore think of the different link architectures as having different trade offs between blocking probabilities and QoS guarantees. The first link architecture, with a single service class and no premium QoS guarantee for video streams, has the smallest overloaded regime, $0 \le \gamma < \frac{1}{4}$, which corresponds to the regime with non-zero asymptotic blocking. The second link architecture, with two service classes sharing the link capacity and a premium QoS guarantee for video streams, has a common overloaded regime of $0 \le \gamma \le \frac{1}{2}$. Roughly speaking, the increased width of the overloaded regime interval, i.e., $\frac{1}{4} \leq \gamma \leq \frac{1}{2}$ is the cost of increasing the QoS guarantee of video streams from $\frac{1}{4}$ to $\frac{3}{4}$. The third link architecture, with two separate channels for audio and video streams, and a premium QoS guarantee for video streams, has different scaling regimes for the two channels. The audio channel is only overloaded for $0 \leq \gamma \leq \frac{1}{4}$, but the video channel is overloaded for $0 \leq \gamma \leq \frac{3}{4}$.

Computation results

In this section we compute the asymptotic QoS under for audio and video streams under each of the three link architectures. Consider the first link architecture where audio and video streams share the same channel and share the same normalized subscription level guarantee of $\alpha_1 = \frac{1}{4}$. This is equivalent to a multiple service class model where all service classes have the same QoS guarantee. The asymptotic normalized subscription level for the audio (class 1) and video (class 2) streams is therefore given by

$$q_1^{\gamma,1} = 1 - (1 - \alpha_1)\bar{F}_{V_1}(F_{\hat{V}_1}(v_1^*(\gamma))) \tag{18.13}$$

$$q_2^{\gamma,1} = 1 - (1 - \alpha_1)\bar{F}_{V_2}(F_{\hat{V}_2}(v_1^*(\gamma))) \tag{18.14}$$

where $v_1^*(\gamma)$ is the v that solves

$$(\bar{\rho}_1 - \underline{\rho}_1)F_{\hat{V}_1}(v) + (\bar{\rho}_2 - \underline{\rho}_2)F_{\hat{V}_2}(v) = \gamma\bar{\rho} - \rho. \tag{18.15}$$

For the first link architecture we have $\bar{\rho}_1 = 18$, $\underline{\rho}_1 = 4.5$, $\bar{\rho}_2 = 18$, $\underline{\rho}_2 = 4.5$, $\bar{\rho} = 36$ and $\rho = 9$. Substituting these values and simplifying, we obtain that $v_1^*(\gamma)$ is the $\bar{v}$ that solves

$$F_{\hat{V}_1}(v) + F_{\hat{V}_2}(v) = \frac{8}{3}\gamma - \frac{2}{3}. \tag{18.16}$$

Consider next the second link architecture where audio and video streams share the same channel, but audio streams have a QoS guarantee of $\alpha_1 = \frac{1}{4}$ and video streams have a QoS guarantee of $\alpha_2 = \frac{3}{4}$. The asymptotic normalized subscription level for the audio and video streams is now

$$q_1^{\gamma,2} = 1 - (1 - \alpha_1)\bar{F}_{V_1}(F_{\hat{V}_1}(v_2^*(\gamma))) \tag{18.17}$$

$$q_2^{\gamma,2} = 1 - (1 - \alpha_2)\bar{F}_{V_2}(F_{\hat{V}_2}(v_2^*(\gamma))) \tag{18.18}$$

where $v_2^*(\gamma)$ solves (18.15) but with $\underline{\rho}_2 = 13.5$ and $\rho = 18$. Substituting these values and simplifying, we obtain that $v_2^*(\gamma)$ is the v that solves

$$F_{\hat{V}_1}(v) + \frac{1}{3}F_{\hat{V}_2}(v) = \frac{8}{3}\gamma - \frac{4}{3}. \tag{18.19}$$

Finally, consider the third link architecture where audio and video streams share different channels, audio streams have a QoS guarantee of $\alpha_1 = \frac{1}{4}$ and video streams have a QoS guarantee of $\alpha_2 = \frac{3}{4}$. The asymptotic normalized subscription level for audio and video streams is then given by

$$q_1^{\gamma,3} = 1 - (1 - \alpha_1)\bar{F}_{V_1}(F_{\hat{V}_1}(\frac{\gamma - \alpha_1}{1 - \alpha_1})) \qquad (18.20)$$

$$q_2^{\gamma,3} = 1 - (1 - \alpha_2)\bar{F}_{V_2}(F_{\hat{V}_2}(\frac{\gamma - \alpha_2}{1 - \alpha_2})). \qquad (18.21)$$

These equations follow directly from the single service class analysis in [21]. Equivalently, these equations are obtained by applying Theorem 18.3 using a single class for each partition.

Figure 18.3 plots the asymptotic normalized subscription levels for audio and video streams respectively under each of the three link architectures. The top figure in Figure 18.3 plots the asymptotic QoS for audio streams under a single class link architecture, $q_1^{\gamma,1}$, a two class link architecture, $q_1^{\gamma,2}$, and a partitioned architecture, $q_1^{\gamma,3}$, while the bottom figure plots the asymptotic QoS for video streams under a single class link architecture, $q_2^{\gamma,1}$, a two class link architecture, $q_2^{\gamma,2}$, and a partitioned architecture, $q_2^{\gamma,3}$.

Consider the first link architecture, i.e., the single service class. Both audio and video streams receive the minimum QoS guarantee, i.e., $\frac{1}{4}$, in the overloaded regime, i.e., $0 < \gamma \leq \frac{1}{4}$. As we increase γ in the rate adaptive regime, i.e., $\frac{1}{4} \leq \gamma \leq 1$, the audio streams show a rapid increase in QoS up to the maximum normalized subscription level of 1 at around $\gamma = 0.6$, while the increase for the video streams is rather minimal. This is because under the single service class with common QoS guarantees, the optimal adaptation policy grants preferential treatment to the smaller (audio) streams and discriminates against the larger (video) streams. As we increase γ above 0.6 we see the video streams showing a faster increase in QoS. This is because the audio streams are already receiving their maximum subscription level and so the full benefit of increasing the capacity goes to the video streams.

Next consider the second link architecture, i.e., the two service classes. Both audio and video streams receive their respective minimum QoS guarantees ($\frac{1}{4}$ and $\frac{3}{4}$ respectively) in the overloaded regime, i.e., $0 < \gamma \leq \frac{1}{2}$. As we increase γ in the rate adaptive regime, i.e., $\frac{1}{2} \leq \gamma \leq 1$, we see the audio streams again show a rapid increase in QoS up to the maximum normalized subscription level of 1 at around $\gamma = 0.9$, while the increase for the video streams is again rather minimal. Again, this is because the optimal adaptation policy discriminates against the video streams. As we increase γ above 0.9 we see the video streams showing a faster increase in QoS. Note that for $\gamma > 0.7$ the single service class architecture actually gives better average QoS to video streams than does the two

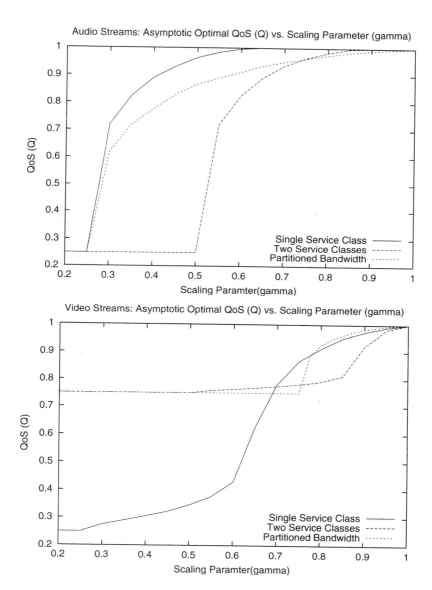

Figure 18.3. Top: Plot of the asymptotic QoS for audio clients versus the scaling parameter γ under the three scenarios. Bottom: Plot of the asymptotic QoS for video clients versus the scaling parameter γ under the three scenarios.

class architecture. This may appear somewhat counter-intuitive considering the two class architecture grants a better QoS guarantee to video streams than does the single class architecture. The explanation is that the average video QoS is higher for the single class architecture than for the two class architecture above $\gamma > 0.7$ because the single class architecture can adapt the largest video streams down to a normalized subscription level of $\frac{1}{4}$ while the two class architecture can only adapt the largest video streams down to a normalized subscription level of $\frac{3}{4}$. The two class architecture therefore must adapt *more* video streams than the one class architecture so that the *overall* average QoS for video streams is lower.

Finally consider the third link architecture, i.e., partitioned channels. We see the audio streams receive their minimum normalized subscription level of $\frac{1}{4}$ in the overloaded regime, i.e., $0 < \gamma < \frac{1}{4}$. Similarly, video streams receive their minimum subscription level of $\frac{3}{4}$ in the overloaded regime, i.e., $0 < \gamma < \frac{3}{4}$. As we increase γ in the rate adaptive regime for the audio streams, i.e., $\frac{1}{4} \leq \gamma \leq 1$, the audio streams show a rapid increase in QoS, which, for most of the rate adaptive regime, lies between the audio QoS under the single and two class architectures. The audio QoS under partitioning is strictly below the audio QoS under a single service class because, under the single service class, there are always video streams to adapt before audio streams, while there are no video streams available to adapt under the partitioned architecture. Moreover, the audio QoS under partitioning is higher than under the two class architecture for $\frac{1}{4} \leq \gamma \leq \frac{3}{4}$ because, under the partitioning architecture, we are blocking video streams in this regime. Once we are not blocking video streams under the partitioning architecture, i.e., $\frac{3}{4} \leq \gamma \leq 1$, the audio QoS is equivalent under the partitioning and two-class architecture. Next consider the video QoS under the partitioning architecture. We see that the video QoS is better under a two class architecture than under partitioning for $\frac{1}{2} < \gamma \leq \frac{3}{4}$; this is because video streams are still being blocked under partitioning in this regime, and so all video streams receive their minimum subscription level. Once video streams are not being blocked under partitioning, i.e., $\frac{3}{4} \leq \gamma \leq 1$, the video QoS is higher under partitioning than under a two class architecture. This is because video QoS under the two class architecture is still being sacrificed for higher audio QoS in this regime due to the optimal volume discrimination policy.

In summary, the link designer may use Figure 18.3 to design how to implement an adaptation policy to meet a combined target of low blocking and high normalized subscription levels. If the link designer can afford to provision the link above $\gamma > \frac{3}{4}$ then a partitioning strategy obtains the maximum QoS for both audio and video classes and has zero asymptotic blocking as well. If the link designer can only afford to provision the link in the regime $\frac{1}{2} \leq \gamma \leq \frac{3}{4}$, then the link designer might choose a two class architecture because obtains asymptotic zero blocking for both audio and video and provides a strong QoS guarantee for video streams. If low blocking is more important than offering a QoS guarantee and the link designer can only afford to provision the link in the regime $\frac{1}{4} \leq \gamma \leq \frac{1}{2}$, then the link designer might choose a single class link architecture.

References

[1] N. Argiriou and L. Georgiadis. Channel sharing by rate adaptive streaming applications. In *Proceedings of IEEE Infocom*, 2002.

[2] Alan Bain and Peter Key. Modelling the performance of in–call probing for multi–level adaptive applications. Technical Report MSR–TR–2002–06, Microsoft Research, October 2001.

[3] B.Vickers, C. Alburquerque, and T. Suda. Source-adaptive multi-layered multicast algorithms for real-time video distribution. *IEEE/ACM Transactions on Networking*, December 2000.

[4] Jiann-Jone Chen and D.W. Lin. Optimal bit allocation for coding of video signals over ATM networks. *IEEE Journal on Selected Areas in Communications*, 15(6):1002–1015, August 1997.

[5] Po-Yuen Cheng, Jin Li, and Jay Kuo. Rate control for an embedded wavelet video coder. *IEEE Transactions on Circuits and Systems for Video Technology*, 7(4):696–702, August 1997.

[6] Chun-Ting Chou and Kang Shin. Analysis of combined adaptive bandwidth allocation and admission control in wireless networks. In *Proceedings of IEEE Infocom*, 2002.

[7] Sergey Gorinsky, K. K. Ramakrishnan, and Harrick Vin. Addressing heterogeneity and scalability in layered multicast congestion control. Technical report, Department of Computer Sciences, The University of Texas at Austin, 2000.

[8] Sergey Gorinsky and Harrick Vin. The utility of feedback in layered multicast congestion control. In *Proceedings of NOSSDAV*, 2001.

[9] Zhihai He, Jianfei Cai, and Chang Wen Chen. Joint source channel rate-distortion analysis for adaptive mode selection and rate control in wireless video coding. *IEEE Transactions on Circuits and Systems for Video Technology*, 12(6):511–523, June 2002.

[10] Koushik Kar, Saswati Sarkar, and Leandros Tassiulas. Optimization based rate control for multirate multicast sessions. Technical report, Institute of Systems Research and University of Maryland, 2000.

[11] A. Ortega and K. Ramchandran. Rate-distortion methods for image and video compression. *IEEE Signal Processing Magazine*, November 1998.

[12] Serge Plotkin. Competitive routing of virtual circuits in ATM networks. *JSAC*, 13(6):1128–1136, 1995.

[13] K. Ramchandran, A. Ortega, and M. Vetterli. Bit allocation for dependent quantization with applications to multiresolution and MPEG video coders. *IEEE Transactions on Image Processing*, 3:533–545, September 1994.

[14] Reza Rejaie, Mark Handley, and Deborah Estrin. Quality adaptation for congestion controlled video playback over the internet. In *SIGCOMM*, pages 189–200, 1999.

[15] Despina Saparalla and Keith Ross. Optimal streaming of layered video. In *Proceedings of Infocom*, 2000.

[16] Guido Schuster and A. K. Katsaggelos. *Rate-Distortion Based Video Compression; Optimal Video Frame Compression and Object Boundary Encoding*. Kluwer Academic Publishers, 1997.

[17] Gary Sullivan and Thomas Wiegand. Rate-distortion optimization for video compression. *IEEE Signal Processing Magazine*, November 1998.

[18] Jean Walrand. *An introduction to queueing networks*. Prentice Hall, 1988.

[19] Steven Weber and Gustavo de Veciana. Asymptotic analysis of rate adaptive multimedia streams. In G. Anandalingam and S. Raghaven, editors, *Telecommunications Network Design and Management*. Kluwer Academic Publishers, 2003.

[20] Steven Weber and Gustavo de Veciana. Network design for rate adaptive multimedia streams. In *IEEE Infocom*, 2003.

[21] Steven Weber and Gustavo de Veciana. Rate adaptive multimedia streams: Optimization, admission control, and distributed algorithms. *submitted to IEEE Transactions on Networking*, 2004.

Appendix
Proof of Theorem 18.1.

Let $B_{i,k}$ denote the random arrival time of stream i on class k. Define the *instantaneous QoS* of stream (i, k) as

$$Q_{i,k}(t) = \begin{cases} \frac{S_{i,k}(t)}{S_{i,k}D_{i,k}}, & B_{i,k} \leq t \leq B_{i,k} + D_{i,k} \\ 0, & \text{else} \end{cases}.$$

Define the *class k aggregate instantaneous QoS* at time t as

$$Q_{agg,k}(t) = \sum_{k=1}^{N_k(t)} Q_{i,k}(t).$$

Define the *class k expected aggregate instantaneous QoS* as

$$\mathbb{E}[Q_{agg,k}(t)] = \lim_{t \to \infty} \frac{1}{t} \int_0^t Q_{agg,k}(s)ds,$$

where the t in the LHS is understood to be a typical time. Define the *class k client average QoS* as

$$\mathbb{E}^0[Q_k] = \lim_{n_k \to \infty} \frac{1}{n_k} \sum_{i=1}^{n_k} \int_{-\infty}^{\infty} Q_{i,k}(t)dt.$$

Straightforward application of Brumelle's Theorem [18] shows that

$$\mathbb{E}[Q_{agg,k}(t)] = \lambda_k^a \mathbb{E}^0[Q_k],$$

where λ_k^a is the rate at which class k clients are admitted onto the link.
Define the *overall aggregate instantaneous QoS* at time t as

$$Q_{agg}(t) = \sum_{k=1}^{K} Q_{agg,k}(t).$$

The *expected aggregate instantaneous QoS* is defined as

$$\mathbb{E}[Q_{agg}(t)] = \lim_{t \to \infty} \frac{1}{t} \int_0^t Q_{agg}(s)ds,$$

where the t in the LHS is again understood to be a typical time. Define the *overall client average QoS* as

$$\mathbb{E}^0[Q] = \sum_{k=1}^{K} \frac{\lambda_k^a}{\lambda^a} \mathbb{E}^0[Q_k],$$

where $\lambda^a = \sum_{k=1}^{K} \lambda_k^a$ denotes the overall admission rate. This implies

$$\mathbb{E}[Q_{agg}(t)] = \sum_{k=1}^{K} \mathbb{E}[Q_{agg,k}(t)] = \sum_{k=1}^{K} \lambda_k^a \mathbb{E}^0[Q_k] = \lambda^a \mathbb{E}^0[Q].$$

The conclusion is that maximizing the overall client average QoS is equivalent to maximizing the overall aggregate instantaneous QoS.

We define the filtration $\sigma(t)$ representing the information available at time t, which includes stream arrival times, stream durations, stream maximum subscription levels, and stream adaptivities. Maximizing the overall aggregate instantaneous QoS at each time t means our objective can be written

$$q_{agg}(t) = \mathbb{E}[Q_{agg}(t) \mid \sigma(t)] = \sum_{k=1}^{K} \sum_{n=1}^{n_k(t)} \frac{s_{i,k}(t)}{s_{i,k} d_{i,k}}.$$

Applying the capacity constraints and the stream constraints means that the optimal adaptation policy for multiple service classes is the solution, at each time t, of the following integer programming problem:

$$\max_{s(t)} \quad q_{agg}(t) = \sum_{k=1}^{K} \sum_{i=1}^{n_k(t)} \frac{s_{i,k}(t)}{s_{i,k} d_{i,k}}$$

$$s.t. \quad \sum_{k=1}^{K} \sum_{i=1}^{n_k(t)} s_{i,k}(t) \le c,$$

$$s_{i,k}(t) \in (\alpha_l s_{i,k}, l = k, \dots, K) \cup s_{i,k}$$

$$\forall i = 1, \dots, n_k(t), k = 1, \dots, K$$

This proves the theorem.

Proof of Corollary 18.2.

Consider a relaxation of the above problem, where we relax the assumption that the set of offered subscription levels is a discrete set. In particular, we assume $s_{i,k}(t) \in [\alpha_k s_{i,k}, s_{i,k}]$. We apply the change of variables $x_{i,k}(t) = \frac{s_{i,k}(t) - \alpha_k s_{i,k}}{1 - \alpha_k}$ and the constraint relaxation to obtain

$$
\begin{aligned}
\max_{\mathbf{x}(t)} \quad & \sum_{k=1}^{K} \sum_{i=1}^{n_k(t)} \frac{(1 - \alpha_k) x_{i,k}(t)}{s_{i,k} d_{i,k}} \\
\text{s.t.} \quad & \sum_{k=1}^{K} \sum_{i=1}^{n_k(t)} (1 - \alpha_k) x_{i,k}(t) \leq c', \\
& 0 \leq x_{i,k}(t) \leq 1, \forall i = 1, \ldots, n_k(t), k = 1, \ldots, K
\end{aligned}
$$

where $c' = c - \sum_{k=1}^{K} \sum_{i=1}^{n_k(t)} \alpha_k s_{i,k}$. This is seen to be a relaxation of a knapsack problem, where the item values are $u_{i,k} = \frac{1-\alpha_k}{s_{i,k} d_{i,k}}$ and the item weights are $w_{i,k} = 1 - \alpha_k$. The solution is to sort items by maximum value per unit weight, i.e., $\frac{u_{i,k}}{w_{i,k}} = \frac{1}{s_{i,k} d_{i,k}}$. Thus, the solution of the relaxation is to sort streams by their volume, $v_{i,k} = s_{i,k} d_{i,k}$.

As was shown in [21], the solution to the relaxed problem has the characteristic that at most one stream receives a subscription level intermediary between its minimum and maximum subscription level. A little thought shows that $\bar{n}$ in (18.7) identifies that stream. Let $G(\mathbf{s}^{\tilde{\pi}_m}(t))$ denote the value of the objective under the allocation given in (18.6). Let $G(\mathbf{s}^{\pi_m}(t))$ denote the value of the objective under the allocation solving the (non-relaxed) integer programming problem stated in the theorem. Finally, let $G(\mathbf{s}(t))$ denote the value of the objective under the allocation solving the relaxed linear programming problem stated above. Note that $G(\mathbf{s}^{\tilde{\pi}_m}(t)) < G(\mathbf{s}^{\pi_m}(t)) < G(\mathbf{s}(t))$ since $\mathbf{s}^{\tilde{\pi}_m}(t)$ is in the feasible set of both the relaxed and non-relaxed problem, and since the relaxed problem necessarily has a higher objective value than the non-relaxed problem. We can therefore bound the difference in the objective under allocations $\tilde{\pi}_m$ and π_m as

$$
G(\mathbf{s}^{\pi_m}(t)) - G(\mathbf{s}^{\tilde{\pi}_m}(t)) \leq G(\mathbf{s}(t)) - G(\mathbf{s}^{\tilde{\pi}_m}(t)) \leq \bar{s},
$$

where $\bar{s}$ is the maximum possible subscription level. Thus the difference in the objective is a constant. The relative difference is easily shown to be bounded as

$$
\frac{G(\mathbf{s}^{\pi_m}(t)) - G(\mathbf{s}^{\tilde{\pi}_m}(t))}{G(\mathbf{s}^{\pi_m}(t))} \leq \frac{\bar{d}\bar{s}}{\underline{\alpha} n(t)} = \frac{\kappa_m}{n(t)},
$$

where the maximum possible stream duration is $\bar{d}$ and the maximum α is $\underline{\alpha} = \min_{1 \le k \le K}\{\alpha_k\}$. Thus, the difference goes to zero for links servicing large numbers of streams. ■

Proof of Theorem 18.3.

Let Q_k^{m,π_m} denote the QoS of a typical class k stream in the mth scaling of the link capacity under the optimal multi-class adaptation policy π_m. Similarly, let $S_k^{m,\pi_m}(t)$ denote the instantaneous allocation to a typical class k stream at some time t after that stream's admission:

$$q_k^{\gamma,\pi_m} = \lim_{m \to \infty} \mathbb{E}^0[Q_k^{m,\pi_m}] = \lim_{m \to \infty} \mathbb{E}^0[\frac{1}{D} \int_0^D \frac{S_k^{m,\pi_m}(t)}{S} dt].$$

We can condition on $S = s$ and $D = d$ to obtain $q_k^{\gamma,\pi_m} =$

$$\lim_{m \to \infty} \int_0^\infty \int_0^\infty \mathbb{E}^0[\frac{1}{D} \int_0^D \frac{S_k^{m,\pi_m}(t)}{S} dt \mid D = d, S = s] dF_{D_k}(d) dF_{S_k}(s).$$

Note that, because the optimal multi-class adaptation policy does not depend on the time t since the stream's admission into the system, we can claim

$$\mathbb{E}^0[\frac{1}{D} \int_0^D \frac{S_k^{m,\pi_m}(t)}{S} dt \mid D = d, S = s] =$$
$$\mathbb{E}^0[\frac{S_k^{m,\pi_m}(t)}{S} \mid D = d, S = s],$$

for the t in the RHS understood to be a typical time. This allows

$$q_k^{\gamma,\pi_m} = \lim_{m \to \infty} \int_0^\infty \int_0^\infty \mathbb{E}^0[\frac{S_k^{m,\pi_m}(t)}{S} \mid D = d, S = s] dF_{D_k}(d) dF_{S_k}(s).$$

Next, note that under the optimal multi-class adaptation policy $\frac{S_k(t)}{S}$ is either 1 or α_k depending on whether or not the stream is adapted at time t. Also, note that the whether or not the stream is adapted is independent of α_k. We write $p(m, t, s, d)$ for the probability that a stream with parameters $S = s$ and $D = d$ is adapted at a typical time t in the mth link.

$$\mathbb{E}^0[\frac{S_k^{m,\pi_m}(t)}{S} \mid D = d, S = s] = 1 - (1 - \alpha_k)p(m, t, s, d).$$

Dominated convergence allows us to move the limit inside the integrals:

$$q_k^{\gamma,\pi_m} = 1 - (1 - \alpha_k) \int_0^\infty \int_0^\infty \lim_{m \to \infty} p(m, t, s, d) dF_{D_k}(d) dF_{S_k}(s).$$

We focus now on $\lim_{m\to\infty} p(m,t,s,d)$. Let $\mathbf{N}(m,t) = (N_k(m,t), k = 1,\ldots,K)$ denote the number of active streams in each class on the mth link at a typical time t. The event that a stream with volume sd is adapted at a typical time t is equivalent to the event

$$\sum_{k=1}^{K} \sum_{i=1}^{N_k(m,t)} S_{i,k}\mathbb{I}(S_{i,k}\hat{D}_{i,k} \leq sd) + s$$

$$+ \sum_{k=1}^{K} \sum_{i=1}^{N_k(m,t)} \alpha_k S_{i,k}\mathbb{I}(S_{i,k}\hat{D}_{i,k} > sd) \geq c(m),$$

where we write $\hat{D}$ to denote that the durations of the streams active at time t have stretched distributions. Thus

$$p(m,t,s,d) = \mathbb{P}(\sum_{k=1}^{K} \sum_{i=1}^{N_k(m,t)} S_{i,k}\mathbb{I}(S_{i,k}\hat{D}_{i,k} \leq sd) + s$$

$$+ \sum_{k=1}^{K} \sum_{i=1}^{N_k(m,t)} \alpha_k S_{i,k}\mathbb{I}(S_{i,k}\hat{D}_{i,k} > sd) \geq c(m))$$

We now define the random variable $Z(m,t,s,d)$ as

$$Z(m,t,s,d) = \frac{1}{\bar{\rho}(m)}\Big(\sum_{k=1}^{K} \sum_{i=1}^{N_k(m,t)} S_{i,k}\mathbb{I}(S_{i,k}\hat{D}_{i,k} \leq sd)$$

$$+ \sum_{k=1}^{K} \sum_{i=1}^{N_k(m,t)} \alpha_k S_{i,k}\mathbb{I}(S_{i,k}\hat{D}_{i,k} > sd)\Big)$$

so that

$$\lim_{m\to\infty} p(m,t,s,d) = \lim_{m\to\infty} \mathbb{P}(Z(m,t,s,d) \geq \gamma - \frac{s}{\bar{\rho}(m)}).$$

We next find the mean and variance of $Z(m,t,s,d)$.

$$\mathbb{E}[Z(m,t,s,d)] = \frac{1}{\bar{\rho}(m)}\mathbb{E}\Big[\sum_{k=1}^{K} \sum_{i=1}^{N_k(m,t)} S_{i,k}\big(\mathbb{I}(S_{i,k}\hat{D}_{i,k} \leq sd)\big]$$

$$+ \alpha_k\mathbb{I}(S_{i,k}\hat{D}_{i,k} > sd))\Big].$$

By Wald's identity,

$$\mathbb{E}[\sum_{k=1}^{K} \sum_{i=1}^{N_k(m,t)} S_{i,k}\mathbb{I}(S_{i,k}\hat{D}_{i,k} \leq sd)] = \sum_{k=1}^{K} \mathbb{E}[N_k(m,t)]\mathbb{E}[S_k\mathbb{I}(S_k\hat{D}_k \leq sd)].$$

Recall $N_k(m,t) \sim Poisson(\lambda_k(m)\delta_k)$, so that $\mathbb{E}[N_k(m,t)] = \lambda_k(m)\delta_k$. Also,

$$\mathbb{E}[S_k\mathbb{I}(S_k\hat{D}_k \le sd)] = \int_0^\infty \int_0^\infty x\mathbb{I}(xy \le sd)dF_{\hat{D}_k}(y)dF_{S_k}(x)$$

$$= \int_0^\infty x\left[\int_0^{\frac{sd}{x}} dF_{\hat{D}_k}(y)\right]dF_{S_k}(x)$$

$$= \int_0^\infty x\left[\int_0^{\frac{sd}{x}} \frac{1}{\mathbb{E}[D_k]}ydF_{D_k}(y)\right]dF_{S_k}(x).$$

Now introduce the change of variables $z = xy$:

$$\mathbb{E}[S_k\mathbb{I}(S_k\hat{D}_k \le sd)] = \frac{1}{\mathbb{E}[D_k]}\int_0^\infty \int_0^{sd} zdF_{D_k}(\frac{z}{x})\frac{1}{x}dF_{S_k}(x)$$

$$= \frac{1}{\mathbb{E}[D_k]}\int_0^{sd}\left[\int_0^\infty \frac{z}{x}f_{D_k}(\frac{z}{x})f_{S_k}(x)dx\right]dz$$

$$= \frac{1}{\mathbb{E}[D_k]}\int_0^{sd} z\left[f_{V_k}(z)\right]dz$$

$$= \frac{\mathbb{E}[V_k]}{\mathbb{E}[D_k]}\int_0^{sd} \frac{z}{\mathbb{E}[V_k]}dF_{V_k}(z)$$

$$= \sigma_k F_{\hat{V}_k}(sd).$$

A similar argument shows that $\mathbb{E}[\alpha_k S_k\mathbb{I}(S_k\hat{D}_k > sd)] = \alpha_k\sigma_k\bar{F}_{\hat{V}_k}(sd)$. We combine the above results and note that the $m's$ cancel to obtain

$$\mathbb{E}[Z(m,t,s,d)] = \frac{1}{\bar{\rho}}\sum_{k=1}^K \bar{\rho}_k(F_{\hat{V}_k}(sd) + \alpha_k\bar{F}_{\hat{V}_k}(sd)).$$

We next bound the variance of $Z(m,t,s,d)$. We can write

$$Z(m,t,s,d) = \frac{1}{\bar{\rho}(m)}\sum_{k=1}^K \sum_{i=1}^{N_k(m,t)} W_{i,k}$$

for $W_{i,k} = S_{i,k}(1 - (1 - \alpha_k)\mathbb{I}(S_{i,k}\hat{D}_{i,k} \geq sd))$. and thereby obtain

$$
\begin{aligned}
Var(Z(m,t,s,d)) &= \frac{1}{(\bar{\rho}(m))^2} Var(\sum_{k=1}^{K} \sum_{i=1}^{N_k(m,t)} W_{i,k}) \\
&= \frac{1}{(\bar{\rho}(m))^2} \sum_{k=1}^{K} Var(\sum_{i=1}^{N_k(m,t)} W_{i,k}) \\
&= \frac{1}{(\bar{\rho}(m))^2} \sum_{k=1}^{K} \Big[\mathbb{E}[N_k(m,t)]Var(W_k) \\
&+ \mathbb{E}[W_k]^2 Var(N_k(m,t))\Big] \\
&= \frac{1}{(\bar{\rho}(m))^2} \sum_{k=1}^{K} \Big[\lambda_k(m)\delta_k Var(W_k) \\
&+ \lambda_k(m)\delta_k \mathbb{E}[W_k]^2\Big] \\
&= \frac{1}{(\bar{\rho}(m))^2} \sum_{k=1}^{K} \lambda_k(m)\delta_k \mathbb{E}[W_k^2] \\
&\leq \frac{1}{(\bar{\rho}(m))^2} \sum_{k=1}^{K} \lambda_k(m)\delta_k \mathbb{E}[S_k^2] \\
&= \frac{1}{m(\bar{\rho})^2} \sum_{k=1}^{K} \lambda_k\delta_k \mathbb{E}[S_k^2].
\end{aligned}
$$

The second equality follows since the random variables $N_k(m,t)$ and $N_{k'}(m,t)$ are independent (in a low blocking regime).

We consider three cases: $i)$ $\mathbb{E}[Z(m,t,s,d)] < \gamma$, $ii)$ $\mathbb{E}[Z(m,t,s,d)] = \gamma$, $iii)$ $\mathbb{E}[Z(m,t,s,d)] > \gamma$. Consider the first case. Define $\epsilon(m) = \gamma - \frac{s}{\bar{\rho}(m)} - \mathbb{E}[Z(m,t,s,d)]$. Note that $\mathbb{E}[Z(m,t,s,d)] < \gamma$ implies there exists an m' such that $\epsilon > 0$ for all $m > m'$. A little thought shows

$$
\mathbb{P}(Z(m,t,s,d) \geq \gamma - \frac{s}{\bar{\rho}(m)}) \leq \mathbb{P}(|Z(m,t,s,d) - \mathbb{E}[Z(m,t,s,d)]| > \epsilon(m))
$$

for all $m > m'$. Chebychev's inequality yields

$$
\begin{aligned}
&\mathbb{P}(|Z(m,t,s,d) - \mathbb{E}[Z(m,t,s,d)]| > \epsilon(m)) \\
&\leq \frac{Var(Z(m,t,s,d))}{\epsilon(m)^2}, \quad \forall m > m'.
\end{aligned}
$$

Noting that $\lim_{m\to\infty} \epsilon(m)$ is a constant:

$$\lim_{m\to\infty} Var(Z(m,t,s,d)) = 0 \Rightarrow \lim_{m\to\infty} \mathbb{P}(Z(m,t,s,d) \geq \gamma - \frac{s}{\bar\rho(m)}) = 0$$

when $\mathbb{E}[Z(m,t,s,d)] < \gamma$. A similar analysis for the third case yields

$$\lim_{m\to\infty} \mathbb{P}(Z(m,t,s,d) \geq \gamma - \frac{s}{\bar\rho(m)}) = 1$$

when $\mathbb{E}[Z(m,t,s,d)] > \gamma$. Finally, the set of pairs (s,d) such that $\mathbb{E}[Z(m,t,s,d)] = \gamma$ has measure zero. Thus, we conclude

$$\lim_{m\to\infty} p(m,t,s,d) = \lim_{m\to\infty} \mathbb{P}(Z(m,t,s,d) \geq \gamma - \frac{s}{\bar\rho(m)})$$
$$= \mathbb{I}(\mathbb{E}[Z(m,t,s,d)] > \gamma).$$

Note that $\mathbb{I}(\mathbb{E}[Z(m,t,s,d)] > \gamma)$ is equivalent to

$$\mathbb{I}\Big(\sum_{k=1}^{K} \bar\rho_k(F_{\hat V_k}(sd) + \alpha_k \bar F_{\hat V_k}(sd)) > \gamma\bar\rho\Big)$$

This is easily simplified to

$$\mathbb{I}\Big(\sum_{k=1}^{K} (\bar\rho_k - \underline\rho_k)F_{\hat V_k}(sd) > \gamma\bar\rho - \underline\rho\Big).$$

Notice that for $\gamma < \alpha$, i.e., when the link is provisioned in the overloaded regime, the indicator function is satisfied for all values sd. To see this, note that $\gamma < \alpha$ implies $\gamma\bar\rho - \underline\rho < 0$, and so the indicator requires a sum of positive numbers exceed zero. Thus, $\lim_{m\to\infty} p(m,t,s,d) = 1$. Similarly, for $\gamma > 1$, i.e., when the link is provisioned in the underloaded regime, the asymptotic probability the stream is adapted is zero. To see this, note that

$$\sum_{k=1}^{K}(\bar\rho_k - \underline\rho_k)F_{\hat V_k}(sd) \leq \sum_{k=1}^{K}(\bar\rho_k - \underline\rho_k) = \bar\rho - \underline\rho.$$

Hence, the indicator function is never satisfied because it requires a sum of numbers bounded above by $\bar\rho - \underline\rho$ exceed a number $\gamma\bar\rho - \underline\rho > \bar\rho - \underline\rho$. Thus, $\lim_{m\to\infty} p(m,t,s,d) = 0$. Substituting these values into the integral yields

$$q_k^{\gamma,\pi_m} = 1 - (1-\alpha_k)\int_0^\infty \int_0^\infty (1)dF_{D_k}(d)dF_{S_k}(s) = \alpha_k,$$

for $\gamma < \alpha$, and

$$q_k^{\gamma,\pi_m} = 1 - (1-\alpha_k)\int_0^\infty \int_0^\infty (0)dF_{D_k}(d)dF_{S_k}(s) = 1,$$

for $\gamma > 1$.

Finally, consider the case when the link is provisioned in the rate adaptive regime, i.e., when $\alpha \leq \gamma \leq 1$. Substituting this into the integral yields the equation given in the theorem. ∎

Proof of Theorem 18.4. When $\gamma < \alpha$ the optimal threshold is zero, hence the asymptotic QoS for class k clients is $q_k^{\gamma,\pi_{am}} = \alpha_k = q_k^{\gamma,\pi_m}$. Similarly, for $\gamma > 1$ the optimal threshold is infinite, hence the asymptotic QoS for class k clients is $q_k^{\gamma,\pi_{am}} = 1 = q_k^{\gamma,\pi_m}$. Consider the case for the rate adaptive regime, $\alpha \leq \gamma \leq 1$. The asymptotic QoS for class k clients is 1 for clients with volumes less than $v^{\gamma,\pi_{am}}$ and α_k for clients with volumes exceeding $v^{\gamma,\pi_{am}}$. We can therefore write the asymptotic QoS as

$$q^{\gamma,\pi_{am}} = F_{V_k}(v^{\gamma,\pi_{am}}) + \alpha_k \bar{F}_{V_k}(v^{\gamma,\pi_{am}}).$$

Simple rearranging yields

$$q^{\gamma,\pi_{am}} = 1 - (1 - \alpha_k)\bar{F}_{V_k}(v^{\gamma,\pi_{am}}).$$

This is the same expression for the asymptotic QoS under the optimal multi-class adaptation policy, q^{γ,π_m}. This proves the theorem. ∎